JOURNAL FOR THE STUDY OF THE OLD TESTAMENT SUPPLEMENT SERIES
207

Sheffield Academic Press

The Bible in Ethics

The Second Sheffield Colloquium

edited by
John W. Rogerson,
Margaret Davies &
M. Daniel Carroll R.

Journal for the Study of the Old Testament
Supplement Series 207

Copyright © 1995 Sheffield Academic Press

Published by Sheffield Academic Press Ltd
Mansion House
19 Kingfield Road
Sheffield, S11 9AS
England

Printed on acid-free paper in Great Britain
by Bookcraft Ltd
Midsomer Norton, Bath

British Library Cataloguing in Publication Data

A catalogue record for this book is available
from the British Library

ISBN 1-85075-573-6

CONTENTS

ACKNOWLEDGMENTS

Those who took part in the symposium owe an enormous debt of gratitude to Meg Davies, for putting into operation an idea that came originally from Danny Carroll. She invited the speakers, made the physical arrangements for the conference and obtained grants to support it. Particular thanks are due to the British Academy for a grant supporting the expenses of two of the guests from abroad, and to the University of Sheffield for a grant from its research fund in support of the symposium. Further assistance was provided by Becca Doyle, and by the Secretaries in the Department of Biblical Studies, Gill Fogg and Alison Bygrave. Eric Christianson at Sheffield Academic Press facilitated the editing of the volume by his careful and patient help.

The Editors
Sheffield, October 1995

ABBREVIATIONS

AASR	Australian Association for the Study of Religion
AB	Anchor Bible
ABD	*Anchor Bible Dictionary*
AJT	*American Journal of Theology*
BBB	Bonner biblische Beiträge
BDB	F. Brown, S.R. Driver and C.A. Briggs, *Hebrew and English Lexicon of the Old Testament*
BKAT	Biblischer Kommentar: Altes Testament
BNTC	Black's New Testament Commentaries
BTB	*Biblical Theology Bulletin*
BWANT	Beiträge zur Wissenschaft vom Alten und Neuen Testament
CBQ	*Catholic Biblical Quarterly*
GKC	*Gesenius' Hebrew Grammar*, ed. E. Kautzsch, trans. A.E. Cowley
HSM	Harvard Semitic Monographs
HTR	*Harvard Theological Review*
ICC	International Critical Commentary
JBL	*Journal of Biblical Literature*
JSNT	*Journal for the Study of the New Testament*
JSNTSup	*Journal for the Study of the New Testament*, Supplement Series
JSOT	*Journal for the Study of the Old Testament*
JSOTSup	*Journal for the Study of the Old Testament*, Supplement Series
JTS	*Journal of Theological Studies*
NCB	New Century Bible
NICOT	New International Commentary on the Old Testament
NRSV	New Revised Standard Version
NTS	*New Testament Studies*
OBT	Overtures to Biblical Theology
OTL	Old Testament Library
REB	Revised English Bible
RSV	Revised Standard Version
SBL	Society of Biblical Literature
SBLDS	SBL Dissertation Series
SBLMS	SBL Monograph Series
SJT	*Scottish Journal of Theology*
SNTSMS	Society for New Testament Studies Monograph Series
SOTSMS	Society for Old Testament Study Monograph Series
TDNT	G. Kittel and G. Friedrich (eds.), *Theological Dictionary of the New Testament*

TS	*Theological Studies*
VT	*Vetus Testamentum*
VTSup	*Vetus Testamentum*, Supplements
WBC	Word Biblical Commentary
ZNW	*Zeitschrift für die neutestamentliche Wissenschaft*

LIST OF CONTRIBUTORS

Professor John Rogerson, Department of Biblical Studies, University of Sheffield

Professor John Haldane, Department of Moral Philosophy, St Andrews University

Dr Mark D. Chapman, Ripon College, Cuddesdon

Professor John Barton, Faculty of Theology, Oxford University

Professor David Clines, Department of Biblical Studies, University of Sheffield

Professor Norman Gottwald, formerly Professor of Hebrew Bible, New York Theological Seminary

Professor Bruce C. Birch, Wesley Theological Seminary, Washington DC

Dr Mark G. Brett, Whitley College, University of Melbourne

Professor Philip Davies, Department of Biblical Studies, University of Sheffield

Dr Gerald West, School of Theology, University of Natal

Dr M. Daniel Carroll R. (Rodas), Seminario Teologico Centroamericano, Guatemala

Professor Christopher Rowland, Faculty of Theology, Oxford University

Professor Sharon H. Ringe, Wesley Theological Seminary, Washington DC

Professor J. Cheryl Exum, Department of Biblical Studies, University of Sheffield

Professor Lisa Sowle Cahill, Department of Theology, Boston College, Massachusetts

Dr Walter Houston, Department of Biblical Studies, University of Sheffield

Dr Margaret Davies, Department of Biblical Studies, University of Sheffield

Dr Stephen Fowl, Loyola College, Maryland

INTRODUCTION

In a classic article entitled 'The Meaning of "Biblical Theology"',
Gerhard Ebeling distinguished between two possible meanings of the
phrase 'biblical theology': theology that is contained in the Bible, and
theology that is in accordance with the Bible.[1] As he indicated, the distinction is not without its problems, one of which is that of the identity
and interests of the individual or community that decides what the
teaching of the Bible is, which is to serve as a yardstick for theology. In
spite of its problems, the distinction serves the useful purpose of indicating that phrases such as 'biblical theology' or 'biblical ethics' have a
number of connotations that need to be unravelled.

The volume of essays here presented is not strictly about biblical
ethics, but about ethics and the Bible; yet Ebeling's distinction, applied
to the essays, yields an interesting result. Some of the essays describe
what the Bible contains on matters ethical, while others imply that ethics
can or should be in accordance with the teaching of the Bible. Most contributors appear to accept that the Bible's ethics can or should be in
some way normative for religious, and specifically, Christian communities.
Given that a majority of contributors work at institutions such as
seminaries, where there is an unwritten, if not written, commitment to
the Bible as a foundation for faith, it should not be a surprise that so
many of the essays take the Bible to be normative. But this volume also
contains contributions presenting formidable arguments against the possibility of using the Bible in ethics, arguments in addition to the well-known
problem that the Bible contains ethical material that can be offensive to
modern sensitivities, and that it appears to have little or nothing to say
about modern problems such as the morality of manufacturing or
possessing nuclear weapons. The basic problem raised by this difference

1.   G. Ebeling, 'The Meaning of "Biblical Theology"', in *Word and Faith*
(London: SCM Press, 1963), pp. 78-97 (translated from *Wort und Glaube* [Tübingen:
J.C.B. Mohr, 1960]). See p. 78: 'it [biblical theology] can mean either "the theology
contained in the Bible, the theology of the Bible itself", or "the theology that accords
with the Bible, scriptural theology". Both possible meanings bristle with a host of
problems'.

of stance (that of the normativeness of the Bible in ethical matters) was
not the especial concern of the Colloquium. Its purpose, rather, was to
explore the range of claims that can be made about the role of the Bible
in ethics.

The intention of this introduction will be to sketch that range as it has
come to expression in the essays, and it will deliberately not follow the
order in which the essays appear.

It will be convenient to begin with the essays questioning the applicability of the Bible to the ethical questions of today. Philip Davies argues
strongly that the Hebrew Bible contains several, at times conflicting,
strands of material with ethical content, which, in any case, are often not
ethical by modern standards. He takes particular exception to those passages that require obedience to divine commands. Such a requirement, he
argues, is not ethical in a world where 'I was only obeying orders' has
ceased to be a convincing ethical stance. There can only be responsible
behaviour where individuals (and presumably societies, if they can be
said to make choices) are allowed to choose a course of action. He illustrates this point with the Garden of Eden narrative in Genesis 3, in
which the woman has to choose whether or not to obey the divine
command not to eat the fruit of the tree of knowledge. Thus Davies calls
into question whether the Bible can be normative for ethics while it
seems to contain requirements that must be obeyed simply because they
are in the Bible.

Cheryl Exum's approach is more indirect. She alerts readers to the
ethical problem of the prophetic images in which faithless Israel is portrayed as a faithless wife or as a prostitute, while faithful God is presented as a faithful husband. She argues that such language betrays a
male view of what it means to be a husband or a wife. Further, this
viewpoint has been perpetuated in the almost exclusively male-authored
standard commentaries on prophetic books. By criticizing the prophets
in this way, Exum attacks precisely that part of the Hebrew Bible that
has traditionally been thought to express the most important ethical
insights of ancient Israel: social justice and concern for the poor. Of
course, these concerns are not found only in the prophets, nor does
Exum's approach necessarily declare them to be worthless; but her essay
is certainly a warning against the uncritical use of prophetic material.

Whereas traditionally, the New Testament has been regarded as more
important for (Christian) ethics and theology, Philip Davies and Cheryl
Exum write as scholars concerned with the Hebrew Bible. However,

more than one paper highlights the problematic character of the New Testament in the ethical field. Meg Davies, for example, contrasts the New Testament unfavourably with the Hebrew Bible on the question of slavery. Given that the latter has laws that allow slaves to become free after six years, as well as a law prohibiting the return of a runaway slave to its master,[2] the attitude of Paul as recorded in the New Testament seems ethically inferior. In all his pronouncements about slaves he never once hints that they can or should be freed after six years, and he actually returns a runaway slave, Onesimus, to his master! The attempt to justify Paul's action by saying, for example, that he believed that the parousia was imminent and that the release of slaves was therefore irrelevant, or that the Hebrew laws did not apply to non-Jews, relativizes the value of Paul's ethical imperatives for many modern readers. Sharon Ringe, while taking a generally positive view of the value of the Bible for ethics, also points to one apparent decline in ethical standards in the New Testament; that is, that the commitment of Jesus to the poor and marginalized is modified and obscured in later texts such as Ephesians and Luke's Gospel.

Two other essays that put question marks against the way that the Bible has traditionally been used in ethics are those by John Rogerson and David Clines. Writing from a commitment to the discourse ethics of Jürgen Habermas, Rogerson comments on the inadequacy of categorical statements, such as those in the Decalogue, that have been seen as the foundation of biblical ethics. As long as such statements express abstract or ideal principles they seem to be important. However, as soon as they have to be applied to specific cases they become problematic, as is most famously illustrated by the dilemma faced by the Maccabees. Should they observe the Sabbath and thus let themselves be killed by their enemies, or should they break the Sabbath commandment and defend themselves?[3] Clines also, taking a deconstructive approach, argues that at least some of the ethical statements of both the Old and New Testaments deconstruct themselves and are therefore problematic for use in an ethical system. The command, for example, about not returning a runaway slave to its master seems to invite slaves to become free

2.   See Exod. 21.1-11 and Deut. 15.12-18 for laws of releasing slaves. The law about not returning a runaway slave is at Deut. 23.15-16.

3.   See 1 Macc. 2.32-41. Rogerson does not discuss this specific example, but shows that there is a good deal of discourse actually in the Hebrew Bible about the application of categorical requirements to particular situations.

simply by running away, thus undermining the whole institution of slavery and its attendant laws. These essays focus on some of the difficulties involved in using the Bible in ethics.

Other essays in this volume draw attention to ethical values inherent in the Bible. Norman Gottwald is concerned about the violence against the Canaanites commanded by God in the book of Joshua. The text runs contrary to the idea of the moral integrity of God. To address the problem, Gottwald proposes that Joshua should be read in three different ways: from the standpoint of tribal Israel, from the monarchic perspective and from the colonial viewpoint, each 'horizon' representing a stage in the formation of the book of Joshua. Thus, at the tribal level, Israel was engaged in self-preservation and did not believe that God had commanded violence against the Canaanites. This idea was introduced as the book developed into its final form.

Bruce Birch finds a link between the canonical shaping of the Hebrew Bible and the formation of Israel as a moral community shaped by allegiance to a normative story. Birch appeals particularly to the story of the exodus, which gives Israel a new identity in relation to God, and he defines ethics as an entering into the life of God rather than as obedience to a code. Interestingly, a focus on the final canonical shape seems more favoured by Birch than by Gottwald, for it is precisely the canonical version of Joshua that Gottwald wishes to avoid, on account of its divinely commanded violence.

Walter Houston's essay analyses an account of Deuteronomy's attitude to the treatment of the poor; Israel is addressed as a family of brothers and sisters, each of whom has a responsibility for helping the poor. No doubt, there is a certain idealization of Israel in Deuteronomy as a family, and families are not always portrayed positively in the Hebrew Bible;[4] moreover, the family as an institution is not perhaps unproblematic itself (some modern readers may have personal experience of families that they would not wish others to have). Nonetheless, the ethical importance of constructing society at large as a family, with the obligations and commonality that implies, cannot be gainsaid.

Other biblical themes in ethics are explored in the essays by Ringe, Cahill and Rowland. Sharon Ringe wants to stress Jesus' commitment to

---

4.   For example, there is fratricide in two families (Gen. 4.1-16 and 2 Sam. 13) and jealousy, rivalry and lack of trust in others (Gen. chs. 27, 29 and 31; 1 Sam. 1.1-8). Whether or not these narratives are historical, they represent a perception of family life that is not always reassuring.

the poor and marginalized. Lisa Cahill wishes to replicate the radical social challenge of early Christianity, and Christopher Rowland's study of attitudes to the poor and poverty in the churches is undergirded by the assumption that the Bible contains an option for the poor. Collectively, these essays argue strongly that responsible application in today's world of the significance of the mission and message of Jesus will commit Christians to the side of the poor.

All the essays in this volume point to the complexity of the issue of the Bible and ethics. Those that remain to be mentioned, however, bring forcefully before the reader the enormous range of considerations that may be relevant. Today's world is one in which various types of fundamentalism advocate a clear-cut approach to morality. Traditionally, Christianity has been expected to give a clear lead, and the Bible has been seen as a basis for Christian morality, especially in providing categorical imperatives such as the Ten Commandments. 'Liberal' Christians are accused of undermining morality by their alleged disregard for the teaching of the Bible. The traditional view is an example of closure; of the view that morality is a system of basic and invariable principles, even if they have to be applied to particular situations in today's world. The essay by John Haldane, while not necessarily advocating closure, seeks to show that Pope John Paul II's defence of traditional Catholic moral teaching in *Veritatis Splendor* is a compelling account of morality from a Thomist-Aristotelian standpoint as enriched by encounter with the example of the life of Christ.

Gerald West's paper, with its exposition of J.C. Scott's *Domination and the Arts of Resistance*, warns against any simplistic understanding of a society or reading of the Bible that assumes the complete powerlessness of the under-classes.[5] Such classes have their own strategies for coping with a lack of power, strategies that can easily be overlooked by observers. Danny Carroll's paper explores the problems of a non–indigenous observer trying to understand a culture; in this case, the Maya of Guatemala. He shows that the religious self-understanding, vis à vis the Bible, of various groups within the Maya is very complex, and dependent on a variety of historical and cultural factors. Mark Brett's essay shows how difficult it is to define how nationalism and universalism are understood in the Bible. The story of Israel, argues Brett, is

5.   J.C. Scott, *Domination and the Arts of Resistance: Hidden Transcripts* (New Haven: Yale University Press, 1990).

not so much the history of a race, but a series of counter-assertions of dignity.

The essays of West, Carroll and Brett lead us to ask whether any description of the social life of ancient Israel or any generalisation about its poor can be any more than simplistic at best and hopelessly misleading at worst. If observers of contemporary societies (or of the strategies used by the powerless) perceive the task of understanding to be so complex, what hope is there that contemporary students of the fragmentary information about ancient Israel or the early Church (including that contained in the Bible) will arrive at an interpretation that in any way reflects the complexities of those situations? And if these interpretations are seriously deficient, of what value will they be for using the Bible in ethics? Will they be any more than a cracked or distorting mirror in which viewers see versions of their own society—assuming, that is, that they understand adequately how their own society works? Nevertheless, the complexity of the issues should not inhibit use of the Bible in ethics; it is, rather, a challenge that has to be met.

The essays in this volume show how important pre-understanding is when a topic such as the Bible and ethics is tackled. The contributors here include atheists, Catholics and Protestants, variously located in British universities, North American seminaries, South African townships and Guatemalan rural settings, to name only some. *The Bible in Ethics* is thus not a simple exercise in biblical interpretation, but is carried out in the context of widely differing commitments and locations, all of which in some way affect the outcome. This is, perhaps, the most important contribution of these essays to the larger debate; but they will also have fulfilled their purpose if they indicate to readers some of the main problems involved in using the Bible in ethics, and provide some pointers for further research and discussion.

The Editors
Sheffield, October 1995

DISCOURSE ETHICS AND BIBLICAL ETHICS

John Rogerson

The discourse ethics to be employed in this paper is that outlined and defended by Jürgen Habermas;[1] the biblical material will be taken from the Old Testament.

Discourse ethics arises from Habermas's movement away from an (individualistic) philosophy of consciousness to a (collective) philosophy of communicative action; from practical reason to the logic implicit in communicative action.[2] Discourse ethics enables Habermas to propound a type of ethics that is universalistic, collective and cognitive, in opposition to approaches that are relativistic, individualistic and emotive. His starting-point is the fact of language and communication, and that in everyday life we take for granted a whole series of conventions without which inter-personal communication would be impossible. Fundamental to such conventions is the notion of truth, in the sense that in dealings

---

1. Inconsistently, I shall refer to discourse ethics as singular and biblical ethics as plural. For Habermas's expositions and elaborations see 'Diskursethik–Notizen zu einem Begründungsprogramm', in J. Habermas, *Moralbewußtsein und kommunikatives Handeln* (Frankfurt am Main: Suhrkamp, 1983; 3rd edn, 1988), pp. 53-125; 'Moralbewußtsein und kommunikatives Handeln' in *Moralbewußtsein*, pp. 127-206; *Erläuterungen zur Diskursethik* (Frankfurt am Main: Suhrkamp, 1991; 2nd edn, 1992). Discussions in English include D.M. Rasmussen, *Reading Habermas* (Oxford: Basil Blackwell, 1990), pp. 56-74; S.K. White, *The Recent Work of Jürgen Habermas* (Cambridge: Cambridge University Press, 1988), pp 69-89. German discussions include F.S. Fiorenza, 'Die Kirche als Interpretationsgemeinschaft. Politische Theologie zwischen Diskursethik und hermeneutischer Rekonstruktion', in E. Arens (ed.), *Habermas und die Theologie* (Düsseldorf: Patmos Verlag, 1989), pp. 115-44; W. Lesch, 'Theologische Ethik als Handlungstheorie', in E. Arens (ed.), *Gottesrede-Glaubenspraxis. Perspektiven theologischer Handlungstheorie* (Darmstadt: Wissenschaftliche Buchgesellschaft, 1994), pp. 89-109.

2. The major work that marks the shift is Habermas's *Theorie des kommunikativen Handelns* (2 vols.; Frankfurt am Main: Suhrkamp, 1981).

with each other we take it for granted that we can by argument persuade others or be ourselves persuaded that something is right. This activity is collective in the sense that it involves at least two people, universalistic in the sense that we believe that we can persuade or be persuaded by people from different cultures or backgrounds from our own, and cognitive in the sense that the outcome of such discussions is knowledge. Habermas believes that relativists are guilty of a performative contradiction. In order to maintain their view that truth or ethics are relative to a given group or culture, relativists depend upon the universalistic possibility of convincing others of the truth of their position by argument; but if the relativism that they advocate is true, there are no such universal grounds on which they could base their assertions.[3]

As applied to ethics, Habermas's approach distinguishes between the structure of ethics and its content, and is concerned mainly with the former. Discourse ethics provides in the first instance an enabling framework called by Habermas the *Universalisierungsgrundsatz* (U) which states that

> every valid norm must fulfil the condition that the foreseeable consequences and side-effects which foreseeably result from its general application in order to satisfy the interests of all, can be accepted by all those concerned without compulsion, and can be preferred to the consequences of all known possible alternative arrangements.[4]

This is supplemented by the *diskursethiker Grundsatz* (D) which states that

> only those norms can be considered valid that receive the acceptance of all involved as people who do or can take part in practical discourse.[5]

3.   See, for example, Habermas's criticism along these lines of A. MacIntyre in *Erläuterungen*, pp. 209-218.

4.   *Erläuterungen*, p. 134: 'jede gültige Norm muß der Bedingung genügen, daß die voraussichtlichen Folgen und Nebenwirkungen, die sich aus ihrer *allgemeinen* Befolgung für die Befriedigung der Interessen *eines jeden* voraussichtlich ergeben, *von allen* Betroffenen zwangslos akzeptiert (und den Auswirkungen der bekannten alternativen Regelungsmöglichkeiten vorgezogen) werden könnten' (my translation above, omitting Habermas's emphases which are given in the German). There are several versions of U (cp. *Moralbewußtsein*, p. 131), but what is given here is the fullest version that I have found. See also the further discussion in *Erläuterungen*, pp. 137-39, where further possible refinements that have been proposed are considered.

5.   *Moralbewußtsein*, p. 103: 'nur die Normen Geltung beanspruchen dürfen, die die Zustimmung aller Betroffenen als Teilnehmer eines praktischen Diskurses finden (oder finden könnten)'.

Several comments need to be made on these *Grundsätze*.

First, it is clear that discourse ethics does not provide norms and principles for applying these norms; it rather states the ideal conditions under which norms can be discovered and applied. Second, while aiming to provide a universalistic framework for ethics, discourse ethics allows that in a particular period or culture the agreed norms will be relative to those situations. This entails; third, what Habermas calls the in-built fallibility of discourse ethics; that is, the admission that inability to know or foresee all the consequences of applying a norm may lead to mistakes.[6] Fourth, discourse ethics is participatory in that it does not allow norms to be discovered or applied by individuals detached from the situations and people involved. Fifth, discourse ethics avoids the charge that can be brought against the Kantian categorical imperative, that it is egoistic and represents particular class or gender interests. Finally, although the word 'argument' does not appear in either 'U' or 'D' the norms are to be mutually established by argument, and it is important to know that Habermas includes under this term the exchange and evaluation of information, principles, terminology (including the revision of vocabulary or descriptions) and expert opinion.[7]

Discourse ethics is a determinedly post-metaphysical exercise, and Habermas is ever-ready to criticise 'platonic' or Kantian-type transcendental notions which lie behind ethical theories. At first sight, this is not a good starting-point for discussing biblical ethics, with their metaphysical commitment to God as the ultimate author and upholder of justice. But it has to be acknowledged that any modern reading of the Bible, including that by believers, inevitably criticises biblical ethics from a modern ethical position, whether the reader is consciously aware of commitment to a particular ethical stance or not. This is true for the most obviously unacceptable statements in the Bible such as, 'Whoever curses father or mother shall be put to death' (Exod. 21.17).

But it is also true for what we might call biblical ethics as a whole; for biblical ethics presupposes a world view that is not our own, and the history of Christian ethics is a series of attempts to harmonise biblical and Christian viewpoints with successive philosophical positions.[8] In examining biblical ethics from the standpoint of discourse ethics I shall

6.   *Erläuterungen*, pp. 165-66.
7.   *Erläuterungen*, p. 164.
8.   Cp. N.H.G. Robinson, *The Groundwork of Christian Ethics* (London: Collins, 1971).

discuss (1) categorical statements such as those in the Decalogue, (2) the discourse ethical implications of passages such as Gen. 18.22-33, (3) the problem of those unable to discuss, (4) the relation between ethics and law and (5) sacrifice.

1. In his recent *Erläuterungen zur Diskursethik* Habermas devotes a section to B. Gert's modern statement of the Ten Commandments, most of which have the form 'you shall not...'.[9] Habermas acknowledges that such statements seem to be at the heart of attempts to state moral obligations in a categorical way, and to support the deontological separation of the right from the good, and the deontological insistence that the primacy of such obligations is undermined if attempts are made to relate them to specific goods or goals. However, he criticises this position as exhibiting what he calls an individualistically diminished moral category (*ein individualistisch verkürtzter Moralbegriff*) which results in a monological negative command addressed to an anonymous community.

From the point of view of discourse ethics, obligations cannot be imposed; they must be seen to be justified and must be capable of being willingly accepted. For example, the assertion, 'You shall not deceive anyone', does not take account of instances such as those where to deceive someone about the nature of an illness can arguably be justified if the deception is intended to aid a person's recovery. Habermas wants duties to be discussed and agreed, with the result that, in terms of discourse ethics, they will be stated positively not negatively. Thus the assertion, 'You shall not lie', should be positively formulated as,

> act in a manner directed towards understanding, and allow each person the communicative freedom to adopt a position with regard to claims of validity.[10]

As applied to biblical ethics this approach has two implications. First, we can see within the biblical tradition a tension between (usually) negative categorical statements and positive situated statements that rely on consent rather than imposition. Thus, as well as the negative categorical statement, 'You shall not murder' (Exod. 20.13), there is the more situated statement, following a categorical positive statement prescribing the death penalty for anyone who kills another:

9. *Erläuterungen*, pp. 171-76.
10. *Erläuterungen*, p. 173: 'Handle verständigungsorientiert und lasse jedem die kommunikative Freiheit, zu Geltungsansprüchen Stellung zu nehmen'.

if it [the act of killing] was not premeditated, but came about by an act of God, then I will appoint for you a place to which the killer may flee (Exod. 21.13).

As well as the categorical statements there is a statement that implies discussion, or recognition of the injustice of putting to death someone guilty of accidental as opposed to deliberate killing. These two types of law are usually described as apodictic and casuistic, and attempts have been made to relate them to different form-critical or liturgical backgrounds. Whatever the truth of these attempts, from an ethical point of view most readers, I would maintain, would find the passage in Exod. 21.13 preferable to the categorical statements, because it is more humane and implies agreement about how ethical principles are to be put into practice.

The second implication is that if we agree with Habermas that obligations should be established by agreement and not imposition (and we also see this in some cases exemplified in the Bible), then we shall have a useful procedure for trying to apply biblical ethics in modern society. The debates about abortion and euthanasia which are based upon Exod. 20.13 might be more constructive if opponents were required to consider the nature of the categorical statements to which they appeal. The same would be true of the categorical statements about homosexual actions in Leviticus 18 and 20. Further, an attempt to get agreement about whether, and if so why, adultery is wrong (cp. Exod. 20.14) would be preferable to attempts to impose the view that it is wrong upon a society that is encouraged by literature, films and the media to believe that adultery is trivial. Discourse ethics would require that the interests of all parties affected by adultery were considered, and its rightness or wrongness would be an agreed decision that was in the interests of all parties.

2. Discourse ethics is set in the framework of a discussion of norms by all affected parties. The Bible records no such discussions, although the book of Job contains a series of dialogues on the question of suffering. However, an interesting feature of the Bible is the extent to which individuals engage in dialogue with God, often about matters which impinge on justice.

An elaborate instance is found in Malachi, where God, speaking through the prophet, answers a series of statements or objections voiced by 'the people'. The climax of these questions comes in Mal. 2.17:

> You have wearied the LORD with your words. Yet you say, 'How have we
> wearied him?' By saying, 'All who do evil are good in the sight of the
> LORD, and he delights in them'. Or by asking, 'Where is the God of
> justice?'

This is a kind of dialogue where the shared assumption is that justice can
be recognised independently of God, and that God has a duty to uphold
it. God is, in effect, accused of acting unjustly, a charge to which he
responds robustly in ch. 3, where he warns that he will send his
messenger who will visibly enforce what is just.

Another instance of dialogue is in Gen. 18.22-33, where Abraham
intercedes with God to spare the city of Sodom. The basis of Abraham's
argument is that it would be unjust to destroy righteous people along
with the wicked, and he bargains God down to agreeing that the city
could be spared if there were ten righteous people in it. He asks, 'shall
not the Judge of all the earth do what is just?' (Gen. 18.25). Here again
the implication seems to be that what is just can be established independently of God, and that God as supreme judge must act justly. Further,
in this passage justice is not simply an abstract notion. It is applied to
particular circumstances, and it is argument that establishes what, in this
case, it would mean to act justly, and in the interests of at least ten
righteous people in Sodom (if they existed).

Passages such as Gen. 18.22-33 show that within the Old Testament
there are conflicting ethical strands, some of which assert moral obligations or find no difficulty in the notion of corporate responsibility,[11]
others of which imply that what is just in a given situation is to be established by dialogue, taking into account the interests of individuals. An
approach via discourse ethics will identify with the latter strand, and will
include among passages that accord with this approach texts not
normally regarded as ethical, such as psalms and intercessory dialogues
in which the speakers engage with God on the question of what is right
and just.[12]

3. Habermas's *diskursethiker Grundsatz* assumes that norms are to be
established by those who can or do participate in practical discourse.

---

11. I have in mind passages such as Exod. 20.5 which speak of God visiting the
sins of the fathers upon the children to the third or fourth generation.

12. Examples would include Psalms 9 and 10 and similar complaints against the
wicked, and the passages in Exodus and Numbers where Moses intercedes with God
about the plight of the people.

What about those who cannot?[13] At the end of the *Erläuterungen* Habermas discusses the moral status of animals.[14] He rejects the view that our respect for animals can be grounded in an obligation not to make them suffer. He regards it as a paradox that, on the one hand, our conviction that they should not suffer is based upon a human understanding of suffering which is then applied to animals, while on the other hand, most humans have no qualms about killing animals in order to eat them; that is, the analogy with humans breaks down at this point. Discourse ethics understands the process of becoming an individual human as the discovery of the self as one becomes ever more integrated into a network of social reciprocities, in which the claims and needs of others are fully recognised.[15] Animals belong to the networks into which we integrate, and although our relationships with animals are always asymmetrical (we talk to them not vice versa) they become part of our social world in such a way that we accept that we have moral obligations to them (in discourse ethical terms) as we do to other humans. Habermas evidently has some sympathy with vegetarians and does not exclude the possibility that their view expresses a correct moral intuition.

The point that I wish to take from this is that discourse ethics can envisage a role for those who engage in practical discourse as speaking for, or protecting those, who are excluded from the process. In certain types of society the disadvantaged will not only include animals, but the poor and oppressed; and this brings us to the heart of biblical ethics. The obligation of the king to uphold the rights of the poor and oppressed is well known in the Old Testament, as well as prophetic denunciations of the failure of kings to do this, and the belief that ultimately God will defend the defenceless in default of humans meeting their obligations.[16] Within the context of the Old Testament this complex of ideas is grounded in the exodus event, when God freed the Israelites from slavery in Egypt and formed a nation whose social arrangements were meant to embody the principle of freedom from oppression which found practical expression in the exodus.[17] From the perspective of discourse

---

13. This question is raised by F.S. Fiorenza in his article cited in footnote 1 above. Habermas has since addressed the question, as my discussion here shows.

14. *Erläuterungen*, pp. 219-26.

15. See further Habermas, 'Individuierung durch Vergesellschaftung', in his *Nachmetaphysisches Denken* (Frankfurt am Main: Suhrkamp, 1988), pp. 187ff.

16. Passages that can be cited include Psalm 72 and Ezekiel 34.

17. The issue is not whether, and if so in what way, the exodus happened, but how

ethics (and this probably reflects what happened in ancient Israel) the story of the exodus became a powerful explanatory symbol for an Israelite conception of justice which transcended class interests and affirmed the interests of all who would be potentially affected by decisions taken in the name of the nation or sections of it. The *diskursethiker Grundsatz* (that every valid norm must have the agreement of all those involved as regards their interests) is in effect invoked by biblical authors who represent the prophets in particular as denouncing situations in which the agreement of those potentially affected by the behaviour of the rulers is certainly not present.

4. This latter point leads to the question of the relation between ethics and law in the perspective of discourse ethics. This is a subject that Habermas has addressed in his most recent major book of over 700 pages, *Faktizität und Geltung*, and which, at the time of writing this paper, I have not studied sufficiently closely.[18] However, at various points in earlier writings Habermas speaks of the role of institutions in safeguarding and mediating ethical principles, and in enabling individuals to discover these in the process of socialisation. This suggests the following thoughts.

In the Old Testament there are collections of laws that can be described as utopian. These include sections of Deuteronomy and the Jubilee law in Leviticus 25. These collections require communicative action that places a high premium on the rectification of inequalities and disadvantages that result in some people becoming poor, homeless, debt-ridden and enslaved. Whether or not these laws were, or could have been, enforced, is a topic that has been much discussed; and it is easy to dismiss them as impracticable. However, these collections can be seen as an ideal statement of principles of social justice that would have been agreed to be in the interests of all had such a discussion been able to take place. Their function is to encourage people to regard seriously the interests of all classes, to warn those who disregard the interests of

the exodus story was used to enjoin upon the Israelites the 'imitation of God' who had acted according to the story to free the people from oppression. In Exodus and Deuteronomy we repeatedly meet the motive clause which states that the Israelites must act in a certain way because they were once slaves in Egypt, and God redeemed them from there.

18. Habermas, *Faktizität und Geltung. Beiträge zur Diskurstheorie des Rechts und des demokratischen Rechtsstaats* (Frankfurt am Main: Suhrkamp, 1992, rev. edn, 1994).

others and to give hope to those whose interests are disregarded. They add what might be called a prophetic dimension to discourse ethics.

5. Is a prophetic dimension appropriate to discourse ethics? In a remarkable passage in the *Erläuterungen*, Habermas writes as follows:

> The validity of moral commands is linked to the condition that they will be generally obeyed as the basis for common behaviour. Only when this condition of general acceptance is fulfilled do the commandments express what everyone could wish. Only then do the moral commands lie in the common interest and make no claims on deeds of supererogation, because they are equally good for all. In this way the morals of reason set their seal on the abolition of sacrifice. Nevertheless those people deserve our admiration who follow, for example, the Christian commandment of love and make sacrifices in the interests of their neighbours that go beyond the equitable demands of morality; for deeds of supererogation can be understood as ventures in cases of a tragic situation or under barbaric living conditions, which call upon our moral indignation to combat fateful unjust suffering.[19]

If one were unfamiliar with Habermas's writings it could easily be concluded that he had seriously underestimated the amount of evil in the world, and was writing as though tragic situations or barbaric living conditions were the exception in today's world. In fact, inhumanity predominates in today's world just as it did in the world of ancient Israel. Wonderful as it would be if the ideal situation envisaged by discourse ethics were to exist so that there was indeed no need for sacrifices in pursuit of loving one's neighbour, we are far from this ideal and will probably never attain it. This counter-factuality does not invalidate discourse ethics, but rather points to what I call a prophetic factor.

The prophetic witness in the Old Testament (including parts of

---

19. *Erläuterungen*, pp. 136-37: 'Die Gültigkeit moralischer Gebote ist an die Bedingung geknüpft, daß diese als Grundlage einer allgemeinen Praxis *generell* befolgt weden. Nur wenn diese Zumutbarkeitsbedingung erfüllt ist, bringen sie das zum Ausdruck, was alle wollen könnten. Nur dann liegen moralische Gebote im gemeinsamen Interesse und stellen—eben weil sie gleichermaßen gut für alle sind—keine supererogatorischen Ansprüche. Insofern beseigelt die Vernunftmoral die Abschaffung des Opfers. Gleichwohl verdient derjenige, der beispielsweise dem christlichen Liebesgebot folgt und im Interesse des Nächsten moralische unzumutbare Opfer bringt, unsere moralische Bewunderung; denn supererogatorische Taten lassen sich als Versuche verstehen, in Fällen tragischer Verwicklung oder unter barbarischen Lebensbedingungen, die unsere moralische Empörung hervorrufen, gegen das schicksalhaft ungerechte Leiden anzugehen.'

Leviticus and Deuteronomy) is uncompromising in its advocacy of social and ethical arrangements that are in the interests of all members of society, including the poor and the powerless. It is also often the case that the very survival of the nation is put into question because the people have acted unjustly;[20] and there are visions of a future just world in which the Israelite national interest is transcended to embrace the interests of all the nations and the interests of the natural order.[21] This witness runs far ahead of what rulers and people could either comprehend or were prepared to consider. The prophets often suffered persecution for their stand, and in the concept of a righteous remnant we have a glimpse of a small minority who were prepared to stand against the inhumanity of the larger society.

Thus within the Bible we not only see discussion taking place about what it would mean to act justly in a given situation (cp. Gen. 18.22-33), we see groups prepared to suffer for their commitment to justice and who believe that their suffering will be a powerful means of helping others willingly to embrace the same vision.[22] Discourse ethics throws this factor into sharp relief and helps the Bible to add a new dimension to what Habermas includes under the category of the argumentation designed to bring universal agreement.

20. Cp. Amos 3.1-15; 7.19; 8.1–9.10.
21. Cp. Mic. 4.1-4; Ps. 96.
22. Cp. Isa. 53.1-12.

FROM LAW TO VIRTUE AND BACK AGAIN: ON *VERITATIS SPLENDOR*

John Haldane

> *The dialogue of Jesus with the rich young man*, related in the nineteenth chapter of Saint Matthew's Gospel, can serve as a useful guide *for listening once more* in a lively and direct way to his moral teaching: 'then someone came to him and said "Teacher, what good must I do to have eternal life?" And he said to him, "Why do you ask me about what is good? There is only one who is good. If you wish to enter into life, keep the commandments". He said to him, "Which ones?" And Jesus said, "You shall not murder; You shall not commit adultery; You shall not steal; You shall not bear false witness; Honour your father and your mother; also, You shall love your neighbour as yourself." The young man said to him, "I have kept all these; what do I still lack?" Jesus said to him, "If you wish to be perfect, go, sell your possessions and give the money to the poor, and you will have treasure in heaven; then come, follow me"' (Mt. 19.16-21) (*Veritatis Splendor*, pp. 12-13).

I

The invitation to reflect upon the use of the Bible in ethics is a welcome challenge. For a philosopher working within the analytical tradition, who thinks of ethics principally as moral philosophy, it is rather like being asked to consider the role of woodcarving in the decoration of supermarkets—generally speaking it is not to be found there. But, as in that case also, one cannot help wondering whether the omission is not to be regretted.

Certainly some philosophical authors make reference to the idea of divine commands and occasionally even go so far as to specify one; but that is usually in the context of setting up the Euthyphro dilemma in order to show the purported irrelevance of religion to morality.[1] The dilemma (deriving from one posed by Socrates in the dialogue from

1. See, for example, Jonathan Berg, 'How Could Ethics Depend on Religion?', in P. Singer (ed.), *A Companion to Ethics* (Oxford: Basil Blackwell, 1990), pp. 525-33.

which it takes its name) involves the question of whether God commands what is good because it is good, or whether what is good is so because God commands it. The apparent problem for the believer in divine commands is that the first option accords antecedent (pre-legislated) standing to values and so seems to render God's prescriptions irrelevant or, at best, instrumentally useful after the manner of advice; while the second preserves the ontological priority of God's commands but at the price of rendering them ungrounded or arbitrary, with God being like a whimsical sovereign simply willing that this or that be done.

This is an old problem but discussions of it rarely engage with the form and content of Judaeo-Christian Scripture. An interesting and little known exception to this neglect, however, is the debate between Christian philosopher-theologians of the medieval and reformation periods. These divided on 'realist' and 'voluntarist' lines—taking the first and second horns respectively—and often cited Scripture in challenge and defence. The two most often quoted and debated episodes are the command to Abraham to sacrifice Isaac (Gen. 22) and the order to the Israelites to despoil the Egyptians (Exod. 11). Much theological and philosophical ingenuity went into the reading of these cases. Aquinas, for example, introduces the idea of *mutatio materiae* (change of matter) to argue that God was able to prescribe the taking of goods from the Egyptians without revoking or violating the prohibition against theft because he had changed the underlying material facts by transferring property—which in truth is his—from the Egyptians to the Israelites. In short, the Jews were taking what, by virtue of divine re-assignment, was already rightly theirs.[2]

This sort of serious and respectful attention to the content of a biblical text is hard to find in present day philosophical writings. Occasionally, however, a philosopher will cite an episode recounted in Scripture in order to make some general point about the nature of evil, or about a form of moral thought. Peter Winch's fine essay 'Who is my Neighbour?' is an interesting instance of the latter. He begins as follows: 'Philosophical discussion needs well-formulated examples; and I want to introduce my subject with a very well known example from the New Testament: the parable of the Good Samaritan'.[3] There then follow

---

2. For further discussion see J. Haldane, 'Voluntarism and Realism in Medieval Ethics', *Journal of Medical Ethics* 15 (1989), pp. 39-44.

3. Peter Winch, 'Who is my Neighbour?', in *idem* (ed.), *Trying To Make Sense* (Oxford: Basil Blackwell, 1987), p. 154.

some sensitive reflections on the meaning of Christ's words, but by the end of the essay it is clear that the aim has been to argue for certain ideas about the character of moral psychology which could as easily have been developed (as in others of Winch's essays) by considering a passage from some work of modern literature. Winch concludes: 'My central point is that in questions concerning our understanding of each other our moral sensibility is indeed an aspect of our sensibility, of the way we see things, of what we make of the world we are living in'.[4]

So the use of Scripture as a foil, or as a source of examples, is not unknown in analytical writings. What is very much rarer—indeed probably rarer than woodcarving in supermarkets—is any consideration of the general relationship between Judaeo-Christian sacred writings and the form and content of philosophical ethics. This, however, is my theme; and to explore it, if only very briefly (and certainly inadequately), I have chosen the method of case study. I shall be discussing a specific use of Scripture: Pope John Paul II's reflections on Mt. 19.16-21, in the encyclical letter *Veritatis Splendor* addressed to the Catholic Bishops 'regarding certain fundamental questions of the Church's moral teaching'.[5] While I am concerned with a single case, what I hope to show is that this instance of an appeal to Scripture is of entirely general significance; for in one sense what is at issue in the encyclical is the whole of ethics—biblical and philosophical.

Veritatis Splendor is divided into three chapters concerning 'Christ and the answer to the question about morality', 'The Church and the discernment of certain tendencies in present-day moral theology' and 'Moral good for the life of the Church and of the world' respectively. For present purposes the first and the second chapters are of most relevance. I shall not say anything about their detail as my interest is in certain framework issues, but I will give an idea of what they contain. In the following sections, then, I begin with preliminary scene-setting before sketching some of the contents of the encyclical. Following that I take up a series of general questions about the relations between the old law of Moses and the new law of Christ; and between rule and virtue, nature and function; and between Scripture and philosophy.

4. Winch, 'Who is My Neighbour', p. 166.
5. *Veritatis Splendor* (London: Catholic Truth Society, 1993).

II

Among the conciliar documents of Vatican II is the *Decree on Priestly Formation* (*Optatam Totius*). This sets out a series of directives and counsels including several concerning the revision of ecclesiastical studies. There we read that 'the first object in view must be a better integration of philosophy and theology' and later, in the sections on theology, that 'special attention needs to be given to the development of moral theology. Its scientific [systematic and theoretical] exposition should be more thoroughly nourished by scriptural reading.'[6]

Vatican II induced something of a renaissance in Catholic scriptural studies; and certainly it became increasingly common in catechetics and homiletics to focus on the life and teachings of Christ and then on the activities of the apostles in forming the first Christian communities. This attention to what is given in Scripture contrasts with earlier approaches which emphasised the doctrines and laws of the Catholic Church, presenting them with a determination and confidence borne of counter-reformation thought and subsequent affirmations of the magisterium. So far as concerns moral theology, the tradition of the inter-Council years was of the systematic elaboration of prohibitions, requirements, permissions and exceptions deriving from the Decalogue; the Ten Commandments being conceived of as a set of absolute (non-relative and exceptionless) prescriptions.

This somewhat abstract and formal approach then gave way to styles of ethical reflection in which contexts and particularities were emphasised in the service of the idea that few if any general 'for always and everywhere' judgements are possible. In place of the idea that certain types of action are forbidden or morally impossible, there developed notions of 'contextuality' or 'situationality' and of a 'fundamental option' (or in Karl Rahner's terminology, 'the human person's disposition of his self as a whole') in terms of which it was argued that right action is that which issues from a personality imbued with Christ-like charity and is sensitive to the special circumstances of each occasion. Instead of asking what God has commanded it became common to wonder what Christ would do, and in answering the latter question to suppose that he would seek to bring about the best outcome for those

---

6.   'Decree on Priestly Formation', in W.M. Abbot, SJ and J. Gallagher (eds.), *The Documents of Vatican II* (New York: Guild Press, 1966), pp. 450, 452.

involved. Thus was effected the transition from a legalistic ethic of strict and largely negative duty to one of positive virtue, with beneficence being the principal disposition in the latter orientation.

III

Pope John Paul II is noted for his theological orthodoxy and for his willingness to censure Catholic theologians whom he judges to have moved outside the sphere of legitimate interpretation. It is unsurprising, therefore, that he should have chosen to address an encyclical to the issue of the moral teaching of the Catholic Church.[7] It was also to be expected that in doing so he would take issue with certain views developed within recent moral theology.[8] Equally predictable were the responses that followed it. Since the publication of *Veritatis Splendor* in August 1993 at least three sets of commentaries and many journal articles have appeared. For the most part the authors of these have been critical of John Paul's theological and philosophical conservatism, and defensive of the revisionist tendencies which he challenges[9]—though there are some distinguished exceptions, including Alasdair MacIntyre. McIntyre examines the ways in which the encyclical manages to be both a teaching document and a philosophical text and relates its critical moments to a synthesis of these two functions. He writes:

7.   More recently he has returned to the theme of moral absolutes in discussing the ethics of life an death—see *Evangelium Vitae* (London: Catholic Truth Society, 1995).

8.   He writes: 'The specific purpose of the present Encyclical is this: to set forth, with regard to the problems being discussed, the principles of a moral teaching based upon Sacred Scripture and the living Apostolic Tradition, and at the same time to shed light on the presuppositions and consequences of the dissent with which that teaching has met', *Veritatis Splendor* (London: Catholic Truth Society, 1993), p. 11.

9.   See the various contributions in J. Wilkins (ed.), *Understanding Veritatis Splendor* (London: SPCK, 1994); these were originally published in the *Tablet*. Another cluster of responses is to be found in *Studies in Christian Ethics*, 7 (1994); and a third in J.A. Selling and J. Jans (eds.), *The Splendor of Accuracy* (Grand Rapids, MI: Eerdmans, 1994). See, also the following: J. Berkman, 'Truth and Martyrdom: The Structure of Discipleship in *Veritatis Splendor*', *New Blackfriars* 75 (1994), pp. 533-41; F. Kerr, 'The Quarrel over Morals in the Catholic Church', *New Blackfriars* 75 (1994), pp. 500-11; R. McCormick, 'Some Early Reactions to *Veritatis Splendor*', *TS* 55 (1994), pp. 481-506; and S. Pinckaers, OP, 'The Use of Scripture and the Renewal of Moral Theology: The *Catechism* and *Veritatis Splendor*', *The Thomist* 59 (1995), pp. 1-19.

Veritatis Splendor is and will remain a striking Christian intervention in moral debate, at once authoritative teaching and a voice in that continuing philosophical conversation between Christianity and modernity to which Pascal and Kierkegaard, Newman and Barth and von Balthasar, have all been contributors. *Veritatis Splendor* continues the same evangelical and philosophical conversation with secular modernity, and the appropriate initial response of each of us to it should concern our own past and present defects and errors rather than those of others. There is much work to be done.[10]

The nominal targets of the Pope's criticisms are moral philosophical-cum-theological positions (e.g. 'consequentialism' and 'proportionalism') and not the individuals who occupy them. However, it is easy enough to identify some of those who might be in the line of fire: Charles Curran, Bernhard Häring, Joseph Fuchs and Richard McCormick. (It is also interesting to speculate, on stylistic grounds, on the identity of the Pope's philosophical and theological consultants—Fr. Andrzej Szostek of Lublin and John Finnis of Oxford[11] have been mentioned in this connection, especially with regard to ch. 2). What the Pope objects to as much as anything else in the 'new' moral theologies is the suggestion that reflection on the words and deeds of Christ, as given in Scripture, permits or requires a departure from familiar moral teaching, including most especially its exceptionless prohibitions. His aim, therefore, is to uphold that teaching by the ancient method developed by Anselm, Aquinas and others, of showing it to be warranted by Holy Scripture, Church tradition and philosophical argument. [12]

10. A. MacIntyre, 'How Can we Learn what *Veritatis Splendor* Has to Teach?', *The Thomist* 58 (1994), pp. 171-95 (195).

11. Compare ch. 2 of the encyclical with J. Finnis, *Moral Absolutes: Tradition, Revision, and Truth* (Washington, DC: Catholic University of America Press, 1991).

12. It is interesting in this connection to note what M. Daniel Carroll R. writes in his contribution to this volume when discussing the work of the Dominican Bartolomé de Las Casas (1474–1564). Carroll observes that 'His use of the Bible is best exemplified in H.R. Parish (ed.), *The Only Way to Draw All People to a Living Faith* [trans. F.S. Sullivan; New York: Paulist Press, 1992]. In this work Las Casas presents arguments based on papal pronouncements, tomes of ancient philosophers, and Church tradition for evangelising in a peaceable manner so as to win the willing consent of the indigenous to the Catholic Faith. *The Only Way* is also heavily sprinkled with biblical references [including Mt. 19]'. See 'The Bible and the Religious Identity of the Maya of Guatemala at the Conquest and Today: Considerations and Challenges for the Nonindigenous', below, p. 196.

Although the last of these is broadly in line with scholastic Aristotelianism as represented by Aquinas, the Pope adds a distinctive note by adopting a 'personalist' perspective. In the form associated with the University of Lublin (where he had previously taught philosophy and theology), personalism is a blend of Thomist metaphysics and anthropology, with phenomenological epistemology and ethics. That is to say it assumes that persons are unified substances possessed of rational powers and that we come to understand (and change) ourselves by reflection upon the meaning of our agency as this is implicit within deliberative consciousness.

One of the central elements of Thomist personalism is the denial of Cartesian and Kantian dualisms according to which the true subject of deliberation—and thus the true moral agent—is an entity (a *res cogitans* or *noumenal self*, respectively) distinct from and transcendent of its contingent embodiment in nature. Arguing on anti-dualist lines that human beings are rational animals whose bodies are already in the domain of meaning, an interesting connection between personalist philosophy of mind and sexual ethics is suggested in ch. 2:

> ...one has to consider carefully the correct relationship between freedom and human nature, and in particular *the place of the human body in questions of natural law.*
>
> A freedom which claims to be absolute ends up treating the human body as a raw datum, devoid of any meaning and moral values until freedom has shaped it in accordance with its design. Consequently, human nature and the body appear as presuppositions or preambles, materially necessary for freedom to make its choice, yet extrinsic to the person, the subject and the human act...
>
> This moral theory does not correspond to the truth about man and his freedom. It contradicts the *Church's teachings on the unity of the human person*, whose rational soul is *per se et essentialiter* the form of his body...
>
> A doctrine which dissociates *the moral act from the bodily dimensions of its exercise is contrary to the teaching of Scripture and Tradition* (*Veritatis Splendor*, pp. 75-77).

IV

Veritatis Splendor is an ambitious attempt to reaffirm orthodoxy on the eve of the third millennium, and in the face of challenges to the effect that what it teaches is no longer tenable. If I am broadly right in my interpretation and in the argument of the following section, then this re-affirmation can be seen to be an interesting and, to some extent, effective deployment of the same range of resources that dissenters have sought to use on behalf of their own reformed moral theology. This may be in part an *ad hominem* response but it is much more an application of methods long-established within Catholic thought—a pre-modern challenge to modernist and post-modernist errors.

Chapter 1 is an extended reflection on the meaning of the exchange between the wealthy questioner and Christ. In asking 'what good must I do?' the young man represents the general human search for a source of meaning; and in replying '...come, follow me', Christ shows that the question is in essence a religious one to which God himself is the answer. Later, John Paul links this idea with natural and revealed law by arguing that both the exercise of reason and the commandments 'show man the path of life' (p. 20). What the encounter with Christ adds is a model of perfected virtue: 'Jesus' way of acting and his words, his deeds and his precepts constitute the moral rule of Christian life' (p. 34).

In ch. 2, the tone is less inspirational, more systematically philosophical and in parts unmistakably critical. The main concern throughout is to show that a proper understanding of human agency implies that certain kinds of actions are intrinsically bad (*intrinsece malum*) and not such as can be justified by a pre-established fundamental option, good motives (*causis bonis*) or by a specific intention to produce beneficial outcomes. As before, appeals to Scripture and reason are interwoven:

> Reason attests that there are objects of the human act which are by their nature 'incapable of being ordered' to God, because they radically contradict the good of the person made in his image...
>
> In teaching the existence of intrinsically evil acts, the Church accepts the teaching of Sacred Scripture [cf. 1 Cor. 6.9-10]...
>
> Consequently, circumstances or intentions can never transform an act intrinsically evil by virtue of its object into an act 'subjectively' good or defensible as a choice (*Veritatis Splendor*, p. 125).

The concluding chapter then addresses various implications for the Church's prophetic function of Christ's call to perfection and the rational defence of moral absolutes—in one guise the dictates of right reason attuned to the proper goal of human life, and in another the revealed will of God. Against the background of rampant secularism and moral relativism, the task of instruction is taken to be urgent and the duty to bear witness inescapable.

V

John Finnis has written that the theme of *Veritatis Splendor* is faith not sex.[13] There is in fact very little said about specific kinds of behaviour, though contraception is mentioned along with other offences against chastity and justice.[14] Unsurprisingly, though, it was sexual issues that caught the interest of the press and other media. Here I am not concerned to challenge or defend Papal teaching on these or any other any specifics;[15] for my interest is in the way in which the encyclical brings together Scripture and reason, and law and virtue. If some interpretation of this constructive enterprise provides a correct and adequate *form* of moral-cum-religious thinking, then one may adopt it in advance of agreeing to particular norms and requirements. Let me offer, then, an outline of what I believe to be such an interpretation.

It is often claimed that there is an ethical contrast between Hebrew and Christian Scriptures inasmuch as the former emphasise the regal dominion of God over his people and the promulgation of his commandments, while the latter advance the idea of divine concern and the restoration of a fallen order of nature through the perfection of Christ.

13. John Finnis, 'Beyond the Encyclical', in Wilkins (ed.), *Understanding Veritatis Splendor*.

14. See *Veritatis Splendor*, sections 49, 80 and 81 (pp. 77-78 and 122-25).

15. Given the interest in the issue, perhaps I might note in passing that even educated commentators seem to misunderstand the logic of the teaching on contraception. In his introduction to *Understanding Veritatis Splendor*, John Wilkins recognises the unambiguous nature of the condemnation of 'contraceptive practices' as *intrinsece malum*, but observes that many Catholics do not regard contraception as intrinsically wrong. He then adds: 'They observe, for example, that in Paul VI's encyclical *Humanae Vitae* it is stated that contraception is admissible for therapeutic purposes. So intention counts' (p. xiii). No one could seriously suppose that John Paul II denies that intention counts; the point is that it is not sufficient to determine the morality of an act: 'Activity is morally good when it attests to and expresses the voluntary ordering of the person to his ultimate end and the conformity of a concrete action with the human good as it is acknowledged in its truth by reason' (*Veritatis Splendor*, p. 110). As regards permissible uses of contraceptives, the point is that while it is always forbidden intentionally to render a sexual act infertile (to *practice* contraceptive sex) it is not necessarily forbidden to provide or receive a therapy the foreseen but unintended consequence of which is infertility. The distinction is between using something which is contraceptive in effect, and intentionally acting contraceptively. The conditional permissibility of the former is an instance of a principle of double effect.

Allied to this contrast is a somewhat less familiar distinction between deontological and virtue-ethics; that is to say, between an account of right action that ties it to the observance of various categorical duties, and a view which sees it as the expression of a certain kind of valuable character. It is natural, then, to see Christ as the perfect embodiment of virtue and to read into the encounter with the rich man the superiority of good character over obedience to law. After all, we read that the rich man observed the latter but was not on that account morally perfect.

With these sorts of contrasts in mind, and recalling what was said earlier about the styles of moral theology pre- and post-Vatican II, it is perhaps tempting to regard John Paul's emphasis on moral absolutes as an effort to return to a narrowly deontological and decalogical interpretation of morality and to downplay the role of character and circumstance in the determination of right action. However, this is difficult to square with the choice of Matthew's text; and it neglects the Pope's Thomistic-cum-phenomenological philosophy. Of course, one might take the view of some of its critics that *Veritatis Splendor* is a mishmash of disparate elements; but I think a more plausible reading of it as a fairly systematically ordered and largely unified thesis is available. There are irregularities in its style, and its general character is somewhat scholastic. These are, however, recurrent features of Vatican documents and should be set aside when considering the overall form of its argument.

The basic philosophical-cum-theological framework is that provided by St Thomas in the *Summa Theologiae*. We are part of a created and beneficial order, an interlocking system of substances possessed of defining powers and characteristics. What it is to be a such and such— an oak tree, a cat, or a human being—is to be so much matter organised to function in various ways so as to attain certain (species-specific and species-transcendent) ends. Matter is taken up by the form of the tree and is maintained in a dynamic organisation involving nutrition, growth and replication. Likewise a human being is an organised substance in which various vital processes are subordinated to the service of rational action. All being well, the end-related functions and activities contribute to the movement of life towards some enduring state of well-being (for Aristotle *eudaimonia*, for Aquinas *beatitudo*). But Judaeo-Christian Scripture tells us that all is now not well, that creation is 'fallen', not irredeemably impaired but liable to go dangerously wrong; and as cancer is to healthy tissue so wrongdoing is to the moral self—that is, progressively destructive.

It may be useful to think of this in terms of an object, a sphere say, that is perfectly fashioned and provided with a principle of self-directed movement. Imagine further that the terrain across which it moves is likewise well-formed and free of threats and dangers. Under these conditions it makes its way easily, rolling onwards towards its destination. Suppose, however, that something happens to damage the sphere and its environment. Its surface becomes deformed, its guidance system is rendered less reliable, and the terrain is now strewn with obstacles and pitted with craters. In these changed circumstances the object is unlikely to reach its destination unless some external influence is applied, say by the introduction of a system of barriers and tracks and by the periodic application of pressure in the direction of its goal.

This serves as an image of the human condition before and after the Fall and makes sense of the Decalogue as a device for trying to keep us away from deathly dangers, and of the prophets as (themselves flawed) pilots attempting to re-orient us towards our eternal destiny. It also suggests the form of a better solution: the restoration of the pre-lapsarian order starting with the reformation of human beings. This is the condition and role of Christ in whom human nature is made perfect. The specialness of Jesus in this regard is not the example offered by his divine nature—after all, what do we, or most, if not all, of those who encountered him know of that?—it is the example presented by his humanity.[16] To adapt Paul, 'as in Adam humankind fell, so in Christ it is raised up again'. Whereas before a series of instructions was required to try and help to reach our destination, now an example of proper functioning is available, as is the promise that if it is followed we will ourselves become perfect.

On this account the transition from an ethics of law to one of virtue is not a matter of changing direction, but that of acquiring an adequate principle of movement from within (*ab intrinseco*, as the scholastics had it) whereby one is better able to reach the same destination as one was previously directed towards. Grace perfects and does not repeal nature; and Christ comes to fulfil and not to annul the law. So the difference between the Hebrew and Christian Testaments and between duty and

---

16. In other words, I am claiming that Christ-qua-human (not qua-Second Person of the Trinity) was a perfect human agent. For some discussion of a proposed logic of Christological predications, see J. Haldane, 'Incarnational Anthropology', in D. Cockburn (ed.), *Human Beings* (Cambridge: Cambridge University Press, 1990), pp. 191-211.

virtue lies not in what each prescribes but in how they achieve one and the same end. What is sought under the species of the virtuous and aimed at under the guise of the obligated are one and the same thing, that is, realisation of one's nature in union with God. The rich man asked 'what must I do to have eternal life?' and Christ replied 'If you wish to enter into life, keep the commandments'. The young man said 'I have kept these what do I still lack?' Christ's second answer does not revoke the commandments; indeed, it does not obviously add to them, for giving to the poor might reasonably be thought to be an instance of loving your neighbour as yourself. The significance lies in what follows the instruction to act charitably, in the words 'then come, follow me'.

Notice that in effecting this reconciliation between moral law and moral virtue it was necessary to draw upon certain metaphysical resources—the Thomistic account of nature as a system of teleologically ordered substances. This philosophical understanding gives rise to a further sense in which morality pertains to law, for it has long been the practice in Catholic moral theology to speak of human goods and of patterns of action directed towards them in terms of 'natural law'. Again, this is not something to be contrasted with scriptural ethics, whether in decalogical or Christological forms; rather it is the same reality towards which both direct us but it is now regarded from the point of view of reason rather than of revelation.[17] And just as the requirements and prohibitions of the Decalogue are not rescinded or relaxed by Christ's injunction to charity, so the conclusions of practical reasoning about how to attain the end of human life must include absolute prohibitions, inasmuch as a course of action that is at odds with this goal is thereby excluded, both as an end and as a means. The evil of torture does not lie solely nor for the most part in its effects, as if these might in some cases be outweighed by beneficial consequences. In the first instance torture is evil and thus morally prohibited because of what it *is* and not simply because of what it produces. To act in that way is to attack a basic human good; and it is a teaching of both Aristotelian ethics and of Christian Scripture that some actions are such that they may never be performed and that those who violate these prohibitions thereby show themselves to be of vic[e]ious character. First Aristotle and then St Paul:

17. For a short account of the history of this tradition in Christian ethics see J. Haldane, 'Medieval and Renaissance Ethics', in P. Singer (ed.), *A Companion to Ethics* (Oxford: Basil Blackwell, 1990), pp. 133-46.

Some [actions and passions] have names that already imply badness, e.g. spite, shamelessness, envy, and in the case of actions adultery, theft, murder...It is not possible then ever to be right with regard to them; one must always be wrong. Nor does goodness or badness with regard to such things depend on committing adultery with the right woman, at the right time, and in the right way, but simply to do any of them is to go wrong.[18]

Do you not know that the unrighteous will not inherit the kingdom of God? Do not be deceived: neither the immoral, nor idolaters, nor adulterers, nor sexual perverts, nor thieves, nor the greedy, nor drunkards, nor revilers, nor robbers will inherit the Kingdom of God.[19]

VI

Here I have been concerned to argue that the use made of the opening Gospel passage in *Veritatis Splendor* is not at odds with the appeal to revealed and natural law, and that it is not incompatible with the teleological virtue-theory elaborated in ch. 2, or with the moral absolutism upon which the Pope insists at every turn. On the contrary, the elements of philosophy and Scripture are effectively integrated and pose a significant challenge to those contemporary moral theologians who favour weaker and often relativistic interpretations of Christ's invitation to be perfect.

Let me end by indicating why in these matters Scripture, and in particular the New Testament, is not merely an interesting route to a conclusion which can be reached by other means. Thomistic-Aristotelianism provides a compelling account of the *form* of morality as a set of rational dispositions to act and to refrain from acting—dispositions that are in part instruments to our flourishing and in part constituents of it. But, thus far, this is only a formal characterisation without any specification of the human *telos* or of the virtues that lead to and form part of it. Experience and reason can help inform us of how we should live; but given the wounded condition of human nature their deliverances are at best partial and underdetermine the content of morality. Thus the encounter with Christ, the Son of Man and the perfect human being, offers a unique possibility of answering fully the principal questions of ethics: *what should we be?* and *what should we do in*

---

18. Aristotle, *Nicomachean Ethics*, in R. McKeon (ed.), *The Basic Works of Aristotle* (trans. W.D. Ross; New York: Random House, 1941), 1107a.9-17.

19. 1 Cor. 6.9-10, as quoted in *Veritatis Splendor*, p. 124.

order to be it? That is why, I believe, Pope John Paul begins with and returns to the young man's encounter, and also why he uses a good deal of philosophy and theology to integrate the general meaning of this resonant episode within a rational and affective moral psychology. Rather than being a reactionary and retrograde tract, as the revisionists assume, *Veritatis Splendor* presents a challenge and offers a model for a new phase of religious ethics; one in which Scripture, reason and tradition are worked together to produce an authoritative theology of the right and the good.[20]

20. A further aspect of the interest of *Veritatis Splendor* is its potential to expose inadequacies, or at least controversial elements, in secular accounts of moral and social thought. One implicit thesis of *Veritatis Splendor* is the indivisibility of practical reasoning. So put this may sound like a characteristically scholastic doctrine but it has important implications for political philosophy. Contemporary deontological liberalism of the sort advocated by John Rawls and others distinguishes between the right and the good and then argues that different principles of each are appropriate for conduct within the ethical and the political spheres. On this basis it is argued by Rawls that any view that excludes or greatly restricts a woman's right to abortion in the first trimester is thereby 'unreasonable' (*Political Liberalism* [New York: Columbia University Press, 1993], p. 243). This argument derives from assumptions—about what may legitimately count as a political consideration—which are challenged by the unified notions of right and wrong articulated in *Veritatis Splendor* and in its sequel *Evangelium Vitae*. For further discussion, see J. Haldane, 'The Individual, the State and the Common Good', *Social Philosophy and Policy* 13 (1996), pp. 59-79.

IDEOLOGY, THEOLOGY AND SOCIOLOGY: FROM KAUTSKY TO MEEKS

Mark D. Chapman

1. *Sociological Method and the Liberation from Theology*

For some interpreters of the New Testament the speedy growth of sociological interpretation in the last couple of decades or so has come as something of a liberation from what have often been seen as narrowly spiritual or (as they are sometimes called) 'theological' interpretations. In this essay I want to investigate some theological implications of the use of sociological theory in biblical interpretation and, more generally, in theology. First, I will suggest that sociology has always claimed a theological dimension and, by extension, the application of sociological method to Scripture has, throughout its long history, been motivated by a desire to move beyond and even criticize 'theological' readings. Secondly, I hope to show historical similarities, at least in motive, between the socio-historical method of Chicago and the relatively unsophisticated Marxism of Kautsky, and to point out some affinities between these approaches and the method adopted in some contemporary biblical studies. Thirdly, however, while wishing neither to belittle the significance of this emphasis on the social embodiment of any religious text, nor to deny its heuristic importance, I will suggest that sociological interpretations carry with them (normally implicit) assumptions about theology, ethics and the nature of religion, and that such assumptions can have a profound impact on theological hermeneutics and on the critical dimension of theology. While it is not my intention to comment on the actual interpretations of those adopting a sociological approach, I hope nevertheless to show, by a fairly arbitrary selection of interpreters past and present, that some methods of the sociological analysis of religion can all too easily exercise a subtle and authoritarian control on the pursuit of a critical theology.[1] In the final section, I will

1. There are some useful discussions of the ideological and theological dimension in sociology in J. Milbank, *Theology and Social Theory* (Oxford: Basil

suggest that some other models of sociological analysis, even those which at first sight appear to deny the very possibility of religion, can nevertheless be of great value for a critical theology.

a. *Sociology, Theology and Ethics*
The very origins of the discipline of sociology reveal extremely close connections between sociology, theology and ethics; at least to the extent that sociological method was frequently seen as an escape from the supernatural theological edifice of the pre-modern world. For example, the French positivists, following in the line of Saint-Simon and Comte, were clear that in organising a religion of humanity a science of society should act as a substitute for what they regarded as an outmoded theology which, according to Saint-Simon, 'should not be of great importance for a truly Christian clergy' since it detracts from true religion, which is morality.[2] Similarly, for Comte and later for Durkheim, even though both believed that the theological stage of thought had been surpassed by science, religion itself was not to be overcome but was functionally necessary for society. However, only sociology in the place of theology could provide its new scientific foundation.

Thus Durkheim, in his *Division of Labour in Society*,[3] asks a question which Comte had addressed before him: 'If pre-industrial societies were held together by common ideas and sentiments, by shared norms and values, what holds an industrial society together?'[4] Durkheim was here echoing Tönnies's call for a strong central authority which would recreate the historical-organic virtues of community (*Gemeinschaft*) in modern industrial society (*Gesellschaft*) founded on contract and strong organisation.[5] Unlike Tönnies, however, Durkheim did not see the need for a powerful centralised authority to create a harmonisation or solidarity between the social whole and the individual, but instead saw society as capable of developing *organically*, even if the precise

Blackwell, 1990), esp. pt. 2. Biblical sociology is discussed and criticized on pp. 111-21, though from a different perspective from that offered here.

2.   H. Saint-Simon, *Selected Writings on Science, Industry and Social Organisation* (trans. and ed. K. Taylor; London: Croom Helm, 1975), p. 292.

3.   *The Division of Labour in Society* (1893) (trans. G. Simpson; New York: Macmillan, 1933).

4.   S. Lukes, *Emile Durkheim* (Harmondsworth: Penguin, 1973), p. 141.

5.   F. Tönnies, *Gemeinschaft und Gesellschaft* (1881). English translation: *Community and Society* (East Lansing: Michigan State University Press, 1957).

mechanics of the creation of a harmony of interests between individuals was left open to question:

> What we must do to relieve *anomie* is to discover the means for making the organs, which are still wasting themselves in discordant movements, harmoniously concur, by introducing into their relations more justice by more and more extenuating the external inequalities which are the source of the evil...In short, our first duty is to make a moral code for ourselves.[6]

Whatever the specific inadequacies of Durkheim's analysis, however, the moral and even religious impetus behind his work is beyond dispute. Thus, for Durkheim, religion (or at least a functional equivalent compatible with the evolutionary level of modern society) was charged with the cultic and social affirmation of true community, expressive of its *conscience collective*. Indeed, despite all assertions to the contrary, not least by the sociologists themselves who frequently claimed a so-called value-neutrality, the profoundly normative and even religious character of early sociology, which at the same time involved a critique of theology, cannot be underestimated.[7]

b. *Chicago*
An even more telling example of the close interaction between sociology, ethics and theology, comes from the early history of the University of Chicago,[8] which bears witness to the radically ethical character of sociology. It was a discipline which, as Albion Small,[9] the first Professor of

6. *Division of Labour in Society*, p. 409. In time, Durkheim claimed, the division of labour would 'give rise to rules which ensure the peaceful and regular co-operation of divided functions' (p. 406).

7. On this, see also R.A. Nisbet, *The Sociological Tradition* (London: Heinemann, 1967), pp. 47-106; and R. Martin, 'Sociology and Theology', in D.E.H. Whiteley and R. Martin (eds.), *Sociology, Theology and Conflict* (Oxford: Basil Blackwell, 1969), pp. 14-37.

8. On the foundation of the University of Chicago, see esp. T.W. Goodspeed, *A History of the University of Chicago: The First Quarter Century* (Chicago: Chicago University Press, 1916); and R.J. Storr, *Harper's University* (Chicago: Chicago University Press, 1966). On the rise of Chicago sociology, see A.W. Small, 'Fifty Years of Sociology in the United States', *American Journal of Sociology* 21 (1916), pp. 721-864 (788). For brief accounts of the history of American sociology, see L.A. Coser, 'American Trends', in T. Bottomore and R. Nisbet (eds.), *A History of Sociological Analysis* (London: Heinemann, 1979), pp. 287-320; and G. Hawthorn, *Enlightenment and Despair* (Cambridge: Cambridge University Press, 1976), ch. 9.

9. On Small, see H.E. Barnes, 'Albion Woodbury Small', in *idem* (ed.), *An*

Sociology, remarked, was to act 'as all men's proxy in finding out all that can be known about what sort of world this is, and what we can do in it to make life worth living'.[10] Sociology was no mere statistical and empirical analysis, but was defined as a practical discipline guided by the desire for amelioration of social deprivation and inequality.[11] This becomes clear in Small's book-length account of the development of American sociology from 1865–1915 where he summarised the points of agreement between American sociologists under two headings: first, 'an impulse to improve ways of improving the world' and second, 'an impulse to improve ways of interpreting the world'.[12] Sociology was thus practised with two parallel ends in sight: better statistics and more scientific methods for the description of society, and alongside this, the use of such knowledge to improve social conditions.[13] Thus, Small claimed, 'social science is at its highest power when it has arrived at ethical expression'.[14]

This ethical and almost religious aspect of sociology which dominated the Chicago Department in its early days served to distinguish it from more utilitarian sociological methods. Indeed, much of the work of the Department reveals a strongly Christian influence.[15] Small himself, like most of the other early members of the Chicago Sociology Department, was a practising Christian who found more hope in the new science of sociology for the practical expression of Christianity than in what he considered the rather more sterile and aloof discipline of theology. Indeed, he felt social science to be nothing less than 'the holiest sacrament open to men'. Similarly, Lester Ward, another of America's sociological pioneers, felt sociology had replaced theology as the 'last and the highest

Introduction to the History of Sociology (Chicago: Chicago University Press, 1948), p. 791; and V. Dibble, *The Legacy of Albion Small* (Chicago: Chicago University Press), 1975.

10. A.W. Small, *The Meaning of Social Science* (Chicago: Chicago University Press, 1910), p. 260.

11. R.C. Hinkle Jr and G.J. Hinkle, *The Development of Modern Sociology: its Nature and Growth in the United States* (Garden City, NY: Doubleday, New York, 1954), p. 16.

12. 'Fifty Years of Sociology', p. 828. Cf. A.W. Small, 'Points of Agreement among Sociologists', *Publications of the American Sociological Society* I (1907), pp. 55-71.

13. 'Fifty Years of Sociology', p. 864.

14. 'Fifty Years of Sociology', p. 854.

15. Cf. A.W. Small, *Adam Smith and Modern Sociology* (Chicago: Chicago University Press), 1907.

of the sciences...the cap sheaf and crown of any true system of classification of the sciences, and it is also the last and highest landing on the great staircase of education'.[16] In some ways these early American sociologists saw themselves functioning as secular equivalents of the clergy, and sociology, rather than theology, became the new science of religion.

This is clear in the career of the University Chaplain and sociologist, Charles Henderson, who though adopting a thoroughgoing empirical and statistical approach to sociology, could nevertheless write that 'to assist us in the difficult task of adjustment to new situations God has providentially wrought for us the social sciences and placed them at our disposal'.[17] Guiding sociological investigation from the outset, then, was a powerful moral and religious impulse which was shared by John D. Rockefeller Sr, Chicago's leading benefactor (who eventually parted with over $30,000,000), and which was reflected in the very ethos of the Chicago foundation. This placed particular stress on the interaction between pure research and its practical expression, or what became known as Harper's 'dialectic'[18] of theory and practice, after the first University President.[19]

This ethical and ameliorative approach to sociology similarly set the agenda for the Chicago Divinity School. Theology could no longer rely on its own peculiar method but had, to some extent, to adopt the method of the social scientists.[20] As Edward Scribner Ames later put it, President Harper 'hoped to create a central scientific school of religion in place of a traditional seminary'.[21] However, beyond this

16. L. Ward, 'The Place of Sociology among the Sciences', *American Journal of Sociology* I (1895), pp. 21, 27.

17. C.R. Henderson, 'The Ministry of Today—Its New Equipment', *University of Chicago Record* (20 Jan 1899), p. 281. Cited in M. Bulmer, *The Chicago School of Sociology: Institutionalization, Diversity and the Rise of Sociological Research* (Chicago: Chicago University Press, 1984), p. 35.

18. On this, see W.J. Hynes, *Shirley Jackson Case and the Chicago School: The Socio-Historical Method* (Chico, CA: Scholars Press, 1981), ch. 1.

19. Cf. S.J. Diner, 'Department and Discipline: The Department of Sociology at the University of Chicago, 1892–1920', *Minerva* 13 (1975), p. 550. Cited in Bulmer, *The Chicago School of Sociology*, p. 24.

20. Cf. Mathews, 'A Positive Method for an Evangelical Theology', *AJT* 13 (1909), pp. 21-46.

21. V.M. Ames (ed.), *Beyond Theology: The Autobiography of Edward Scribner Ames* (Chicago: Chicago University Press, 1959), p. 172. The title of this work betrays something of the move to sociology.

strictly scientific concern, the Divinity School was also encouraged to develop 'a policy of maintaining a relationship with organised church life'.[22] It was thus to be at once both a detached school of religion as well as a potent force in the religious movement for social change, and would thereby reflect Harper's dialectic. Thus, instead of merely reproducing the traditional theological seminary, the new Divinity School was to be guided by the study of sociology as the discipline best suited for equipping ministers for their tasks.[23]

Sociology, with its emphasis on the practical, provided a possible escape from the apparent impotence of the churches which so often seemed little more than safe havens for individual salvation and which were increasingly distant from involvement in social reform. Shailer Mathews,[24] Dean of the Divinity School from 1908–1933, recalled of his conservative evangelical upbringing in his autobiography that social life was practically ignored in teaching and preaching. Instead, the 'business of the ministry was to save souls and produce lives that would not yield to the temptations of the world'.[25] This form of what Martin Marty has called 'private Protestantism'[26] tended to relegate religion to the sphere of 'personal salvation' and neglected the social expression of Christianity. In such a form of religion, clergymen, who had so often been at the forefront of social reform in the past, were forced 'to defer meekly to far more affluent vestrymen'.[27] The reaction away from theology to sociology can in turn be plausibly understood as 'an attempt to restore through secular leadership some of the spiritual influence and authority and social prestige that clergymen had lost through the upheaval in the system of status and the secularization of society'.[28] Thus sociology,

---

22. *New Faith for Old* (New York: Macmillan, 1936), p. 58.

23. See esp. William Rainey Harper, 'Shall the Theological Curriculum be Modified, and How?' *AJT* 3 (1899), p. 53.

24. On Mathews, see my essay, 'Sociology, Theology and Ethics: The Principle of Fraternity in Shailer Mathews and Max Weber', in J. Davies and I. Wollaston (eds.), *The Sociology of Sacred Texts* (Sheffield: JSOT Press, 1993), pp. 111-26. It is significant that Mathews published his 'Christian Sociology' (later published in book form as *The Social Teachings Of Jesus* [New York: Macmillan, 1897]) in the first two volumes of the *American Journal of Sociology*.

25. *New Faith for Old*, p. 29.

26. M.E. Marty, *Righteous Empire: The Protestant Experience in America* (New York: The Dial Press, 1970), pp. 177-87.

27. R. Hofstadter, *The Age of Reform* (New York: Vintage Books, 1960), p. 151.

28. *The Age of Reform*, p. 152.

according to Mathews, might serve to overcome the social failings of orthodox Christianity:

> The world needs new control of nature and is told that the Bible is verbally inerrant...It needs a spirit of love and is told that love without Orthodoxy will not save from hell...It needs hope for a better world and is told to await the speedy return of Christ from heaven to destroy sinners, cleanse the world by fire, and establish an ideal society composed of those whose bodies have been raised from the sea and earth.[29]

The zeal for social improvement and the understanding of sociology as, in part, a liberation from theology, were reflected in the academic studies of the Divinity School. Most importantly, the socio-historical method, which developed in Chicago in the early part of the present century, sought to carry out sociological investigations into the biblical texts by viewing them chiefly as products of their environment; in this way it was hoped that biblical studies would be freed from their imprisonment in lower criticism. As Shirley Jackson Case, who joined the Chicago Department in 1908 and who later became its leading representative, put it, we 'began to wonder whether, after all, the eternal welfare of human souls depended upon knowing the exact meaning of a Greek preposition in one of the Pauline epistles or the shade of distinction between *hiphil* and *hophal* of a Hebrew verb'.[30] In short, despite the many problems and many failings of the socio-historical method of the Chicago School, not least its over-rigid functionalism,[31] sociology seemed to provide an escape from theology.

c. *Kautsky's Materialist Critique of Theology*

This emphasis on sociological liberation and explanation in Chicago can be seen as, in many ways, a parallel development to the rather more hostile materialist critique of religion which occupied some European thinkers in the early years of this century.[32] What unites the approaches

29. S. Mathews, *The Faith of Modernism* (Chicago: Chicago University Press, 1924), p. 10.

30. S.J. Case, 'Education in Liberalism', in V. Ferm (ed.), *Contemporary American Theology*, I (Plainview, NY: Books for Libraries, 1933), pp. 107-22 (109).

31. On this, see Hynes, *Shirley Jackson Case*, ch. 3.

32. On this, see J. Bentley, 'Three German Marxists Look at Christianity: 1900–1930', *Journal of Church and State* 22 (1980), pp. 505-17; and G. Hübinger, *Kulturprotestantismus und Politik. Zum Verhältnis Liberalismus und Protestantismus im wilhelminischen Deutschland* (Tübingen: J.C.B. Mohr [Paul Siebeck], 1994).

was a faith that social analysis could provide a critique of theology. This can be seen in one of the first, and certainly one of the most straightforward anti-theological interpretations of the New Testament: Karl Kautsky's (1854–1938) *Foundations of Christianity* of 1908.[33] Here again the theological context is provided by a spiritualised (though somewhat more intellectually sophisticated) understanding of religion as displayed, for example, by Harnack's understanding of the gospel as (essentially) 'above the world and politics'.[34] Similarly, most of the members of the so-called *Religionsgeschichtliche Schule* adopted an understanding of religion which was concerned with a separate realm of the Spirit somewhat removed from the concrete social and political realm.[35] In a manner which was dismissive of such interpreters, Kautsky sought to locate the origins of Christianity in the class struggles of the proletariat which would, he claimed, offer him a particular insight that theologians could not possibly share:

> Nor can I venture to compare myself in learning, as to matters of religious history, with the theologians who have made this study their life task...But possibly my intensive share in the class struggles of the proletariat has afforded me precisely such glimpses of the essence of primitive Christianity as may remain inaccessible to the professors of Theology and Religious History.[36]

While not claiming expertise in biblical studies (though for a journalist and political activist his learning was undoubtedly impressive),[37] Kautsky maintained the perhaps naïve view that engagement in the class struggle gave him a privileged access to the meaning of history. Thus only by historical investigation which took serious account of the relationship to the economic means of production was it possible to 'provide the clue

33. *Foundations of Christianity* (London: Orbach and Chambers, 1925). The importance of this work 'as the first book in the field of the study of Jesus to be based on a strict determinism' has been emphasised by the recent materialist critic, M. Machovec, *A Marxist Looks at Jesus* (London: Darton, Longman and Todd, 1976), pp. 216-17.

34. 'Das doppelte Evangelium in dem neuen Testament', in *Aus Wissenschaft und Leben*, II (Giessen: A. Töpelmann, 1911), p. 215.

35. On this, see my essay, 'Religion, Ethics and the History of Religion School', *SJT* 46 (1993), pp. 43-78.

36. *Foundations*, p. 8.

37. On this, see Machovec, *A Marxist Looks at Jesus*, p. 8. For an overview of Kautsky's political theory and involvement in working class politics, see D. Geary, *Karl Kautsky* (Manchester: Manchester University Press, 1987).

by means of which we can find our bearings in the labyrinth of reality'.[38]

A materialist view of history was thus able, according to Kautsky, to 'oppose [the] tendency towards spiritual stagnation and stupidity, and to direct the attention of proletarians to great points of view, to large prospects, to worthy goals'.[39] In this way the study of the past moved from being an 'antiquarian hobby' and became instead 'a mighty weapon in the struggle of the present, with the purpose of achieving a better future'.[40] Kautsky's motives seem to lie in the critical power of 'lay science', rather than theology,[41] to overcome the oppressive ideology of the church, which almost from its outset merely served to legitimate class domination, 'either in the interest of its own dignitaries, or the dignitaries of another organisation, the state'.[42] Thus issues between what Kautsky called the sects of early Christianity, which manifested themselves in the reported sayings of Christ, developed out of the 'realistic [i.e. material] interests' of the groups themselves.[43] Following Kalthoff and Arthur Drews, but in a manner consistent with his historical materialism, Kautsky was thus able to see the historical figure of Jesus as of little significance. Instead, far more important were the very real economic struggles which led to Christianity, a religion which Kautsky characterized as a primitive form of communism, which only later degenerated into a form of class oppression.

Furthermore, in the same way that the Chicago School was inspired by a strong moral impetus towards social improvement, so Kautsky was concerned with improving the lot of the contemporary proletariat by means of sociological investigation and practical activity. Thus a knowledge of the failures and degeneration of primitive Christianity, of how it had failed to maintain its initial anti-establishment thrust, could help in the task of furthering the lot of the working class. Kautsky's basic point is that the early Christians, as urban proletarians, were forced to compromise with, and to gain the favour of, the rich who were then able to dominate the ecclesiastical bureaucracy. Because the proletariat in the Roman Empire was unaware (due to the institution of slavery) and to some extent deprived of its productive power (by moral degeneracy and

38. *Foundations*, p. 12.
39. *Foundations*, p. 17.
40. *Foundations*, p. 17.
41. *Foundations*, p. 22.
42. *Foundations*, p. 21.
43. *Foundations*, p. 40.

slothfulness), so it fell victim to supernatural illusions, which themselves were easily prey to 'any clever impostor'.[44]

The modern proletariat, however, was different: it knew that society depended on its labouring power, and increase in democracy depended on the assertion of this power. However, there was another lesson to be learned from the past: although the early Christians were democratic, they were unaware of the sources of democratic power in their control of productive labour, because their society had not yet reached the necessary level of economic development or awareness of the relationship between surplus and production. Similarly, because they did not demand wholesale rejection of the hitherto dominant relationships between the classes of society and sought to exist merely *alongside* the wider society, they were unable to prevent the usurpation of the powers of the initial revolutionary movement by the dominant forces of society. The reason for this, according to Kautsky, was clear: 'Communism may not be produced by the formation of little organizations within capitalist society, which would gradually absorb the society as they expand, but only by the attainment of a power sufficient to control and transform the whole of social life'.[45]

Kautsky's extremely materialist and unphilosophical[46] Marxism has provoked an enormous and hostile literature, which is particularly critical of his failure both to appreciate the power of bourgeois ideology and to see the strength of the social determination of liberal social processes.[47] However, there are three points which his method, and to some extent his conclusions, can alert us to. First, he shared with other interpreters of the New Testament a belief that sociology (or at least his materialist social analysis) was capable of criticising what he regarded as narrowly theological viewpoints. Secondly, and more importantly, however, the rigidities of his Marxist approach can perhaps arouse a suspicion that other sociological theories, while less overtly anti-Christian and less obviously materialist, are nevertheless equally loaded with presuppositions and laden with assumptions about the future workings of economics and society. Thirdly, as a comparison between Kautsky and Lindbeck and Meeks may even suggest, there may be some theological

44. *Foundations*, p. 465.
45. *Foundations*, p. 468.
46. See especially L. Kolakowski, *Main Currents of Marxism* (Oxford: Clarendon Press, 1978), pp. 31-60.
47. Cf. Geary, *Karl Kautsky*, p. 126.

relevance in a materialist approach to interpretation. However, before looking in more detail both at Meeks and some of the more recent materialist interpretations of the Bible, I want to look briefly at some contemporary sociological investigations of the Bible, which in their sociological critiques of theological readings in some ways parallel the sort of interests that developed both in Chicago and, to some extent, in Kautsky's work.

d. *Some Contemporary Sociological Critiques of Theological Interpretation*
Robin Scroggs, for instance, recognises that

> [i]nterest in the sociology of early Christianity is no attempt to limit reductionistically the reality of Christianity to social dynamic; rather it should be seen as an effort to guard against a reductionism from the other extreme, a limitation of the reality of Christianity to an inner-spiritual, or objective-cognitive system. In short, sociology of early Christianity wants to put body and soul back together again.[48]

It is quite clear that such a view is concerned with overcoming a perceived tendency of some theological interpretations towards what Bengt Holmberg has dubbed the 'fallacy of idealism',[49] which overlooks, or at least undervalues, the social, political and economic background of the New Testament texts. The pursuit of sociology, at least for such interpreters, thus appears inspired in part by a critique of a disembodied religion.[50]

In such a guise, sociological hermeneutics fulfils something of the critical role hitherto reserved for theology, but far more engaged with concrete political and social reality. Sociology thereby becomes a critique of a type of theology which fails to act as a world transforming power. This understanding is most obvious in Scroggs who believes the sociological analysis of the early church will reveal a group of people who have 'experienced the hurt of the world and the healing of communal

---

48. R. Scroggs, 'The Sociological Interpretation of the New Testament: The Present State of Research', *NTS* 26 (1980), pp. 165-66.

49. *Sociology and the New Testament: An Appraisal* (Minneapolis: Augsburg–Fortress Press, 1990), p. 2.

50. This is equally true for Wayne A. Meeks, though with different implications for theology. See especially 'A Hermeneutics of Social Embodiment', *HTR* 79 (1986), pp. 176-86; also, *Christians Among Jews and Gentiles* (Philadelphia: Fortress Press, 1986).

acceptance' instead of the traditional picture of the church as 'theological seminary'.[51] On this account, sociology, in a manner reminiscent of the Chicago school, can correct theology (or at least bad theologies).

There are obviously many more examples which could be cited where sociology has been claimed to have a liberating effect on earlier purely religious interpretation. One such is Norman Gottwald's *The Tribes of Yahweh*.[52] Against so much interpretation of the Hebrew Bible which looked at religion divorced from its social, political and ethical setting, Gottwald has sought to relocate religion within its wider environment. Belief in Yahweh thus implied a just and fraternal way of life:

> 'Yahweh' is the historically concretized, primordial power to establish and sustain social equality in the face of counter-oppression from without and against provincial and nonegalitarian tendencies from within the society.[53]

Without wishing to comment on the possibilities of a historical sociology of the Old Testament, objections to which have been raised by Cyril Rodd among others,[54] what is important is that a 'sociological' reading has been used as a perceived corrective to over-spiritualized and theological readings (the Yahwistic cult, for instance, is rooted in the socio-economic practice of the Tribes of Yahweh). Such readings, although problematic, are important reminders of the ethical, political and economic implications of, and interactions with, religious belief. What I hope to show in the next section, however, is that not all sociology is so benign. Indeed, a sociology which at first sight appears more favourable to the Christian religion than the materialist readings discussed can in fact exert a highly conservative theological influence.

2. Meeks and Lindbeck: the Ethical and Theological Implications of Cultural-Linguistic Models of Religion

In something of an aside in his *The First Urban Christians*, Wayne Meeks argues for an understanding of sociological method as somehow capable of criticising theology:

51. R. Scroggs, 'The Earliest Christian Communities as Sectarian Movement', in J. Neusner (ed.), *Christianity, Judaism and Other Greco-Roman Cults* (Leiden: Brill, 1975), pp. 1-23 (21).
52. *The Tribes of Yahweh* (London: SCM Press, 1981); esp. p. 17.
53. *The Tribes of Yahweh*, p. 692.
54. 'On Applying a Sociological Theory to Biblical Studies', *JSOT* 19 (1981), pp. 95-106.

> I hope [this book] will not be…viewed as antitheological. Yet it will be, so
> long as the prevailing models of religion implicit in theological discourse
> are, as George Lindbeck has recently observed, either 'cognitive-
> propositional' or 'experiential-expressive'. Lindbeck himself, however,
> urges theologians to adopt a 'cultural-linguistic' model rather like that
> employed here. If they did so, theologians might find raw material in these
> explorations of Pauline Christianity.[55]

By sleight of hand, Meeks is claiming that the model of religion that he is using to explain the New Testament ('rather like' the cultural-linguistic model developed by George Lindbeck for polemical purposes) is in fact the only model appropriate for theological discourse. Though Meeks is not patently anti-theological in the same sense as Marxist historians of Christian origins like Kautsky, it is nevertheless not clear that he 'suffers from no anti-theological animus', as Robert Morgan maintains.[56] Indeed, *The First Urban Christians* can be considered as not anti-theological, only if one first accepts that religion and its theological system are themselves to be defined primarily in terms of a particular sociology.

As Meeks makes clear in a recent article, the sort of project he undertook was a

> 'thick description' of the ways in which the early Christian groups worked
> as religious communities, within the cultural and subcultural contexts
> peculiar to themselves…In order to determine what a text meant, therefore,
> we must uncover the web of meaningful signs, within which the text did its
> work.[57]

Meaning is thus dependent on a web of signs; it does not stand outside or beyond the community and its system, but rather depends on the 'formation of a community whose forms of life correspond to the symbolic universe rendered or signalled by the text'.[58] There is thus no extra-systematic control on meaning, no 'objectively true propositions' beyond the text; instead, religion as a form of life is the practical embodiment of a text. This model of religion presupposes a form of life shaped by a cultural narrative which contains all meaning and truth and which therefore stands beyond any criticism from beyond the system.

On Lindbeck's view of doctrine, the believer is the one who is most

---

55. *The First Urban Christians* (New Haven: Yale University Press, 1983), p. 7.
56. R. Morgan (with J. Barton), *Biblical Interpretation* (Oxford: Oxford University Press, 1988), p. 148.
57. 'A Hermeneutics of Social Embodiment', p. 179.
58. 'A Hermeneutics of Social Embodiment', pp. 184-85.

schooled in the language and the cultural symbols of the community established by cultural, anthropological and sociological methods. Indeed, the raw material of theology (either in the past or the present) is constructed from sociological analysis in so far as theology involves the rational reflection on the inter-relationships between the different aspects of the system. Though Meeks is highly critical of Lindbeck's understanding of intratextuality in relation to the New Testament (where Lindbeck is included, somewhat ironically, in the symbolic-expressivist camp) Meeks nevertheless tries to apply a cultural-linguistic model to historical criticism of the New Testament. Just as for Lindbeck '[the] function of church doctrines that becomes most prominent...is their use, not as expressive symbols or as truth claims, but as communally authoritative rules of discourse, attitude and action',[59] so for Meeks sociology tries to understand 'the meaning of what the actors and writers did within their culture and their peculiar subculture'.[60]

It is difficult to see how Lindbeck's model of theology (which reduces theology to an expression of a cultural system) is able to offer any significant critique of the system. Instead, it explains and works out the rules of a particular subculture or 'form of life'; rules which 'regulate truth claims by including some and ruling out others'.[61] Consequently, Lindbeck offers a functionalist understanding of church doctrines, as 'communally authoritative teachings regarding beliefs and practices that are considered essential to the identity or welfare of the group in question'.[62] Theology in turn must therefore be viewed as a descriptive analysis of the linguistic and cultural system by which a religious group lives: the cultural-linguistic system (which to all intents and purposes can be called the tradition) is consequently the 'permanently authoritative' paradigm.[63]

Whereas Scrogg's (and the Chicago School's) more straightforward sociological interpretation of the New Testament worked as a critique of a particular type of spiritualised theology, Meeks and Lindbeck's so-called 'post-liberal' system seems somewhat different and perhaps little more than a plea for community against a perceived lack of communal identity, particularly within Christian churches where '[t]he modern

59. *The Nature of Doctrine* (London: SPCK, 1984), p. 18.
60. 'A Hermeneutics of Social Embodiment', p. 181.
61. *The Nature of Doctrine*, p. 19.
62. *The Nature of Doctrine*, p. 74.
63. *The Nature of Doctrine*, p. 96.

mood is antipathetic to the very notion of communal norms'.[64] In turn, it comes as no surprise to learn that Lindbeck makes a great diatribe against privatised religion and a plea for true churches within churches, for what he calls a 'sociological sectarianism'. Thus 'cultural-linguistic' theology turns out to lead to a particular type of sectarian ecclesiology. What attracts Lindbeck to such a theology seems to be a vision of a small Christian community, whose members for their very survival must 'strive without traditionalist rigidity to cultivate their native tongue and learn to act accordingly'.[65] With this call for sociological sectarianism, it should come as little surprise that the doctrine of election ('the people-of-God') and what he calls the 'historically embedded functionalism' of authoritative episcopal structures figure highly in Lindbeck's writings in ecclesiology.[66]

Lindbeck seems to be using *sociological* criteria for theological purposes. Indeed, in an article on ecclesiology this is made explicit:

> The Church consists of those...who are stamped with the marks of membership in elect communities...To put this point in the terminology of the social sciences, the people of God consists of cultural-linguistic groupings that can be meaningfully identified by ordinary sociological and historical criteria as Christian or Jewish.[67]

With such an understanding the possibility of mission and service (*diakonia*) is severely weakened, since the primary focus of any such cultural-linguistic community (sect) must be to build itself up and to learn to speak its own language better. The goal of the church is thus not primarily that of liberation but to 'build up sisters and brothers in the faith' from which, apparently, the wider community can only benefit. This leads by means of a kind of 'trickle down' effect to a concern for the wider world.

It is not difficult to locate the subtext of Lindbeck's book in a thinly veiled attack on modernity and its theological counterpart, a somewhat caricatured and misrepresented liberal theology. His less than eirenic thrust is clear in his rather eccentric piece of rhetoric that 'Christian fellow travellers of both Nazism and Stalinism generally used liberal

---

64. *The Nature of Doctrine*, p. 77.
65. *The Nature of Doctrine*, pp. 133-34.
66. 'The Church', in G. Wainwright (ed.), *Keeping the Faith* (London: SPCK, 1989), p. 196. See also, 'The Sectarian Future of the Church', in J.P. Whelan (ed.), *The God Experience* (Westminster, MD: Newman, 1971), pp. 226-43.
67. 'The Church', p. 193.

methodology to justify their positions'.[68] Against such an identification of Christian truth with secular ideology, true religion, according to Lindbeck, is concerned less with propositional truth than with the purity of its own authoritative system, to which all truth is relative, over and against a hostile world.[69]

Whatever the impact of Meeks's *The First Urban Christians* on the study of the New Testament, it is impossible to escape the conclusion that the theory of religion he has adopted (which defines early Christianity as a bounded 'subculture'), though undoubtedly heuristically impressive as a historical tool, can at the same time become highly conservative if it is assumed to have theological implications. If one follows the logic of cultural-linguistic theology then sociological or at least anthropological description becomes the very foundation of theology which is nothing more than the (descriptive) language of a fairly rigidly bounded cultural-linguistic system.

Looking more closely at Meeks's New Testament interpretation, it is clear that Lindbeck's theological edifice, with its dismissal of apologetics as 'increasingly a nineteenth century enclave in a twentieth century milieu',[70] bears comparison with Meeks's seminal essay on John, in which a Christian 'sect' adopted a particular and highly distinctive 'symbolic universe' which made sense of the group's history in relation to its environment.[71] 'Faith in Jesus', Meeks claims, 'means a removal from "the world", because it means transfer to a community which has totalistic and exclusive claims'.[72] He bases this on the 'sociology of knowledge' which sees the world 'as the symbolic universe within which one functions, which has "objectivity" because it is constantly reinforced by the structures of the society to which it is specific'.[73] Truth, for the Johannine 'sect', is thus intrasystematic, and stems from 'a case of continual, harmonic reinforcement between social experience and ideology'.[74] Meeks's understanding of Johannine soteriology with its 'closed metaphorical system' (which is literally understood to require a

68. *The Nature of Doctrine*, p. 126.
69. Cf. *The Nature of Doctrine*, p. 126.
70. *The Nature of Doctrine*, p. 130.
71. 'The Man from Heaven in Johannine Sectarianism', in J. Ashton (ed.), *The Interpretation of John* (London: SPCK, 1986), p. 145.
72. Meeks, 'The Man from Heaven', p. 163.
73. 'The Man from Heaven', p. 163.
74. 'The Man from Heaven', p. 164.

removal from the world) has evident similarities to Lindbeck's advocacy of a sectarian ecclesiology and his dismissal of apologetics. As Stephen Barton has pointed out: 'it is a wonder that anyone made it into the Johannine community at all!'[75]

Though there is nothing necessarily wrong with Meeks's characterisation of the early church communities as sectarian, problems arise once *theological* and *ethical* consequences are drawn from what is, at least ostensibly, a descriptive analysis.[76] The characterisation of theology as a descriptive 'cultural-linguistic system', which at first sight seems harmless enough, might, on further analysis, lead to what can easily become a highly sectarian and even authoritarian understanding of the community since 'the interpreter may be obliged to find or to try to create a community competent to understand, and that means a community whose ethos, world view, and sacred symbols...can be tuned to the way in which that text worked in the past'.[77] In this context, Meeks cites the work of Clifford Geertz who defines religion in terms of a symbolic formulation of a 'basic congruence between a particular style of life and a specific metaphysic, and in so doing sustains each with the borrowed authority of the other'.[78] For Geertz, the system itself takes on a realistic life of its own as an authoritative answer to the problems of bafflement, suffering and evil. The system is defined primarily by attempting to establish its ideas as true beyond doubt as they are accepted as authoritative and constantly reaffirmed in religious ritual and structures. According to Geertz, religious perspectives gain their power to influence society chiefly on account of their imperviousness to doubt. What this seems to imply is a rigid symbolic authoritarianism: performing the ritual just is an acceptance of its authority and power, and once one is in the system, critique becomes impossible without denying the basis of religion

75. 'Early Christianity and the Sociology of the Sect', in F. Watson (ed.), *The Open Text* (London: SCM Press, 1993), p. 148.

76. Cf. 'A Hermeneutics of Social Embodiment', p. 185: 'It is time that we took seriously [in a conversation between Christian ethicists and social historians] the well-known fact that most of the New Testament documents, including the Pauline Epistles that have provided the central motifs of Protestant theology, were immediately addressed to problems of behaviour within the communities, of moral formation and what a sociologist could only call the institutionalization of the new sect'.

77. 'A Hermeneutics of Social Embodiment', p. 184.

78. 'Religion as a Cultural System', in M. Banton (ed.), *Anthropological Approaches to the Study of Religion* (London: Tavistock, 1966), p. 4.

itself, since the nature of religion lies in its categorical certainty. Similarly, the more one performs the ritual, the more authoritative it becomes and the more the status quo is sacralized.

3. *Sociology and Critical Theology*

The application of a particular type of sociology to theology by Lindbeck, and to a lesser extent by Meeks, thus has obvious implications for an understanding of the tasks of theology. Most importantly, it can have disastrous effects if the task of theology is regarded as that of exercising a self-critical function over the very socio-linguistic community which it is claimed to regulate. The question which I will discuss in this section concerns the very nature of theology itself: the question of whether theology merely exercises a descriptive function within a pre-existing and culturally rigid community, or whether it should function as a normative critique of a socio-cultural tradition. Indeed, it might be claimed that such a critical function bears an affinity with the sociological and materialist critiques of spiritualised theology practised in Chicago, and by Kautsky. However, if theology is merely a descriptive regulation and reinforcement of a system, which seems to me to be a possible implication of a cultural-linguistic understanding of theology and religious language, then it cannot pass any judgment on that system. This implies that theology is likely to become a prisoner of the guardians of the tradition. And, if that is the case, this should perhaps arouse a certain suspicion of the ideological agenda of cultural-linguistic theology. As John Webster writes: 'The fact that the community's symbolic life is not immune from the political processes of the construction of meaning ought to alert us to the ideological potential of what is taking place here.'[79]

79. J. Webster, 'The Church as Theological Community', *Anglican Theological Review* 75 (1993), pp. 102-15 (107-108). Indeed, it is possible to detect a similarity between the cultural-linguistic understanding of religion and the defence of the conservative politicisation of the state Church offered by Roger Scruton (in *The Meaning of Conservatism* [Harmondsworth: Penguin Books, 1980], p. 169; cited in D.B. Forrester, *Theology and Politics* [Oxford: Basil Blackwell, 1988], p. 52): 'All ceremony requires a symbolic depth...a sense that it reaches below the surface of things, and touches upon realities which cannot be translated into words...The emotions which attach themselves to the ceremonies of the state constantly outrun the objects which occasion them. Participant and observer find themselves taken up into something greater, of which the reality of military or political power is no more than a pale reflection. Thus there emerges the myth of the "glory" of the nation, the myth of its unqualified *right* to allegiance'.

In such a system it is all too easy for religious myth and ritual to function primarily to bolster the power of an inherited tradition from which there is no escape except by wholesale rejection of the tradition itself. There is no dissent (or what Habermas calls 'internal foreign territory') possible within the tradition. Instead the only level of disagreement allowed by Lindbeck is that offered to theology in its task of assisting a community in speaking its language better. Although this may indeed count as criticism, it may equally serve merely to reinforce a dominant ideology. What seems to be impossible in a cultural-linguistic understanding of religion and theology is any theological method for uncovering what F.J.A. Hort referred to as the 'thick air' of 'bastard traditions which carry us unawares while we seem to be exercising our freedom and our instinct for truth'.[80]

If theological appropriation of sociological method is not forced by that very method to lose its critical edge, then what becomes important is that some extra-sociological criteria are retained, whereby 'bastard' traditions can be unearthed and exorcized. If, as I hope I have shown, a theology which is given a purely descriptive function can never fulfil such a task and is literally 'post-critical'[81] and unable to pass judgment, then, in contrast, a critical theology has to exercise something of a normative function in appropriating and describing the socio-linguistic tradition. Where a critical theology seems required to intervene is in the task of unearthing linguistic distortions within the socio-linguistic system itself, thereby preventing the reduction of theology to this social system.

Such an unmasking of ideological distortion within social systems evidently requires a method which is able to see religious language as rooted in and vitally related to its social conditions and expressive of the distortions and oppression within such conditions. What sociological interpretation has helped to emphasize, particularly against more existentialist and individualist readings of the Bible, is that the textual and ecclesial tradition is necessarily related to the social, political and economic conditions of the wider society. What a critical theology adds is a theological appraisal of these conditions and the texts they, at least in

---

80. F.J.A. Hort, *The Way, The Truth, The Life* (Hulsean Lectures of 1871) (London: Macmillan, 2nd edn, 1897), pp. 91-92.

81. This is Avery Dulles's term. See especially 'Toward a Post-critical Theology', in *idem* (ed.), *The Craft of Theology* (Dublin: Gill and Macmillan, 1992), pp. 3-15. Dulles relies, as a fundamental premise, on a 'hermeneutics of trust, not of suspicion. [Theology's] purpose is constructive, not destructive' (p. 7).

part, engender. The critique of spiritualized readings of Scripture made both by the Chicago School and Kautsky has been re-emphasized by many of the liberation theologians and has often been accompanied by a critical theological appraisal of the social context itself.

This approach can be seen in the many attacks made by liberation theologians on what is often perceived as Bultmann's radically individualist interpretation in which meaning is conferred purely in the sphere of human inwardness. Dorothee Sölle, for instance, is critical of what she calls 'bourgeois theology' which, she claims, 'will inevitably seek to reverse the incarnation. Its tendency is to exalt God more, to set him at a distance, to make the experience of God independent of the material, to separate it from popular piety and to spiritualize it'.[82] Similar statements about the importance of the social rootedness of all theology are made by a host of liberation theologians from Latin America.

However, there is a further point which goes beyond the mere rooting of religion in social context and which is of fundamental importance for theology. It involves the theological and ideological critique of the social context. Theology is given the task of pointing to iniquity and injustice and overcoming it in the praxis of liberation. This means that theology exercises a critical function, thus developing what Miranda referred to as the 'prophetic' enterprise of Marx.[83] In this light, Leonardo Boff remarks that '[after] Marx, theology could no longer put into parenthesis the material conditions of life without the charge of mystifying the reality of iniquitous conditions'.[84]

Here it is illuminating to look once again at Kautsky. Though it is hard to take his rigidly orthodox materialism particularly seriously, his method is nevertheless of value in that it requires so-called religious language to be interpreted as a historically necessary product of social, economic and political relationships which arises in the very process of

82. D. Sölle, 'Between Matter and Spirit: Why and in What Sense Must Theology be Materialist?', in W. Schottroff and W. Stegemann (eds.), *God of the Lowly: Socio-historical Interpretations of the Bible* (Maryknoll, NY: Orbis Books, 1984), pp. 86-102 [92]. See also my essay, 'The Kingdom of God and Ethics: From Ritschl to Liberation Theology', in R.S. Barbour (ed.), *The Kingdom of God and Human Society* (Edinburgh: T. & T. Clark, 1993), pp. 140-63, esp. pp. 157-62.

83. J.P. Miranda, *Marx and the Bible: A Critique of the Philosophy of Oppression* (London: SCM Press, 1977), p. xvii.

84. *Do Lugar do Pobre* (Petropolis 1984), p. 42; cited in J. O'Brien, *Theology and the Option for the Poor* (Theology and Life Series, 22; Collegeville: Michael Glazier, 1992), p. 27.

criticizing and transforming these relationships. Whereas Lindbeck and Meeks have sought to *identify* religion with these social relationships, as both ritualized response and re-affirmation, Kautsky (perhaps ironically) retained an independent (though limited) sphere for the Christian religion as a primitive critical response to the oppression deriving from inequalities of power in control over material conditions. The Christian religion, for Kautsky, is thus at once both a product of material conditions and also a primitive communist (although ultimately doomed) critique of these conditions. Thus even in Kautsky, Christianity functions as a critique of and reaction to the oppression prevalent in society.

It is possible to detect a similar critical thrust, but more clearly directed against traditional religion as an expression of social oppression, in some more recent materialist interpretation. Thus Fernando Belo, a Portuguese Marxist Civil Engineer exiled in France, in his important 1974 study,[85] attempted what might be called a political demythologization of Mark's Gospel. Although it is couched in impenetrable structuralist jargon, the outline of his interpretation is clear. The narrative of the Gospel is treated as expressive of the conflict between Jesus and the Temple which is regarded as the sustainer of the ideological viewpoint of the priestly elite. Jesus makes use of an alternative strand of the Old Testament tradition which subverts this Priestly tradition (namely the egalitarian deuteronomic laws) which results in a radical questioning of the prevailing religious and political norms. For Belo, Jesus' actions are far more powerful a manifestation of his messianic *praxis* or activity than his words, and cannot be explained away in a bourgeois spiritualisation of the Gospel.

Thus Jesus' body, his geographical location, as well as his use of specific symbols, become vital in expressing his subversion of the Temple tradition. In the end he is killed because he wishes to tear down the Temple and build a new one outside the Holy City. Jesus thus becomes not a revolutionary nationalist but a communist internationalist aiming to restore the purity of the Deuteronomic code. For Belo, the cross, which is usually seen as the focal point of Mark's Gospel, is nothing more than a theological attempt to explain the failure of Jesus, but in so doing it removes the emphasis on the messianic activity of Jesus: the Deuteronomic code, which is summarized by Belo as 'charity as practice', soon becomes subordinate to doctrinal orthodoxy. The cross is thus to be regarded as an ideological device inserted by Mark to warn against all

---

85. *A Materialist Reading of the Gospel of Mark* (Maryknoll, NY: Orbis Books, 1981).

naïve idealism; an other-worldly myth far removed from the subversion
of the messianic claimant.

Belo's interpretation of Mark, which seeks to show that the cross was
the original bourgeois accretion, has been questioned by Ched Myers in
Binding the Strong Man.[86] Myers develops an alternative political
reading of Mark which does not explain away the cross but which does
justice to the whole text. For Myers, Jesus dies on the cross for God's
justice. Even the ultimate sanction of the hegemonic ideology of the
ruling classes—the threat of death itself—cannot overcome the willingness of the disciple to die in non-violent resistance for the justice of God.
Belo's populariser, Clévenot, offered a similar criticism: 'It is because we
struggle to overcome the society of classes and the exploitation of
human beings that we want to reread the texts in which a desire is born
that was strong enough to face death.'[87]

Despite such criticisms, however, Belo succeeded in pointing the
interpreter to the material character of the text. He is thus deeply critical
of any failure to emphasise the 'narrative of power' or the 'messianic
narrative' in favour of a spiritualisation of the text. Instead, Belo points
to Jesus's activity of subversion. Exegetes like Bultmann, Belo writes,
'may talk about "the history of salvation" but in fact history has been
dissolved into the timelessness of consciousness and interiority and its
relationship to the "eternity" of God'.[88] A materialist interpretation, on
the other hand, forces a reincorporation of the Gospel into its physical
environment, into time and history, and, at the same time, a relocation of
the interpreter within her or his social and political context. Once this
relocation has been achieved, the real business of criticism can begin,
and, as Belo makes clear, this can be seen to involve an *inner-religious*
critique of the tradition. Materialist criticism once again seems to provide
resources for understanding the dynamic thrust of religious language to
be capable of criticising and transforming the inherited tradition, and not
merely of *describing* the tradition. Moreover, it appears to be less
reductionist than cultural-symbolic models: Christ is at least free to
question and transform his tradition.

In what I have so far discussed, I hope that at least some case has
been made for the importance of materialist interpretation as a potential

---

86. *Binding the Strong Man* (Maryknoll, NY: Orbis Books), 1988.

87. *Materialist Approaches to the Bible* (Maryknoll, NY: Orbis Books, 1985),
p. 121.

88. *A Materialist Reading of the Gospel of Mark*, p. 284.

partner in the task of theological hermeneutics, and one which is both less reductionist and certainly less conservative than a cultural-linguistic model. Indeed, there is every reason to suppose that in the process of unearthing expressions of economic and political power and oppression within religious language, as well as of attempting to expose his or her own unvoiced ideological presuppositions, the theologian might perhaps reach further into the message of God both within Scripture and the language of the Church's tradition. Materialist critique seems to allow and offer resources for a critique of the 'narrative of power', which Ched Myers sees as the heart of the theological task:

> the proper vocation of theology is the practice of 'ideological literacy', the critical discipline of political hermeneutics. It calls for discernment when liberating ideologies, including Christian theologies, become oppressively hegemonic.[89]

If theological hermeneutics is, at least in part, the attempt to discern the activity and words of God in Scripture and tradition, then it cannot simply identify truth with living in that tradition, and requires some awareness of the ideological distortions of that very tradition; or what Comblin has called 'false theologies'.[90] This critical understanding of theology[91] requires a concept of tradition, not as a closed system or 'semantic universe' on Lindbeck's model, but one which is open to criticism and to the future.

Finally, I want to point to some obvious parallels between what I have been discussing and the celebrated dispute between Gadamer and Habermas.[92] In arguing against Gadamer, Habermas claims that

89. Myers, *Binding The Strong Man*, p. 21. See also, John Webster's understanding of the task of theology as that of alerting 'the church to the dangers of social immanence, of reducing the transcendent to a function of one and only one locale, and so of countering the drift to ideology and idolatry which is the constant temptation of all positive religion' ('Locality and Catholicity: Reflections on Theology and the Church', *SJT* 45 [1992], pp. 1-17 [6]).

90. In *Frontiers of Theology in Latin America* (Maryknoll, NY: Orbis Books, 1979), p. 63.

91. On critical theology see C. Davis, *Theology and Political Society* (Cambridge: Cambridge University Press, 1980), ch. 5. A less overtly materialist understanding of critical theology which focuses on rhetorical criticism has been recently developed by G. Jones in his *Critical Theology* (Oxford: Polity Press, 1995).

92. The relevant documents are translated in K. Mueller-Vollmer (ed.), *The Hermeneutics Reader* (Oxford: Basil Blackwell, 1986), pp. 256-319. For a perceptive analysis, see W. Jeanrond, *Theological Hermeneutics* (London: Macmillan, 1991),

reflection does not leave its subject unchanged. Instead, '[reflection] recalls that path of authority along which grammars of language games were dogmatically inculcated as rules for interpreting the world and for action. In this process, the element of authority that was simply domination can be stripped away'. The attempt to describe is at once a critique of authority and of domination which expresses itself in 'social power'.[93] The problem with linguistic analogies, which are used extensively by both Gadamer and Lindbeck, is that they seem to lack a criterion to distinguish what Habermas calls 'pseudo-communication', in which the inherited tradition itself might be shown to be a distorted form of communication.[94] Linguistic analogies appear to lead inexorably to a 'hypostatisation of the traditional context',[95] and thus it is all too easy to see the cultural-linguistic model as 'a consciousness forged of compulsion'.[96]

Theological hermeneutics (if it is to adopt the kind of ideological critique of tradition espoused by Habermas whereby it can unearth oppressive power relationships and inequalities in dialogue) requires an understanding of tradition in which it 'loses the appearance of an absolute that a self-sufficient hermeneutics falsely lends to it'.[97] In a theory of truth like Lindbeck's, that is wholly 'intra-systematic',[98] on the other hand, there can be no room for criticism, no recognition that the system itself is in dialogue with other systems, and consequently open to all manner of ideological distortion. In such a closed system, theology is impossible except as the passive appropriation of the historical structures, symbols and practices of an ecclesial community complete with

pp. 64-70. For theological appropriations of Habermas, see especially C. Davis, *Religion and the Making of Society: Essays in Social Theology* (Cambridge: Cambridge University Press), 1994, and his earlier work, *Theology and Political Society*.

93. Habermas, 'Review of Gadamer's *Truth and Method*', in T. McCarthy and F. Allmayr (eds.), *Understanding and Social Enquiry* (South Bend, IN: Notre Dame, 1977), pp. 358, 360.

94. Cf. J. Habermas, 'On Hermeneutics' Claim to Universality', in *The Hermeneutics Reader*, pp. 294-319: 'Pseudocommunication produces a system of misunderstandings which remain opaque because they are seen in the light of a false consensus' (p. 302). See also Jeanrond, *Theological Hermeneutics*, p. 67.

95. Habermas, 'On Hermeneutics' Claim to Universality', p. 314.

96. 'On Hermeneutics' Claim to Universality', p. 317.

97. Habermas, 'Review', p. 361.

98. Lindbeck, *The Nature of Doctrine*, pp. 63-69.

their distortions and 'narratives of power', however idolatrous. Such a view, however, also makes religious change and reformation impossible; and that brings into question the creative and critical power of Christ. A great deal is therefore at stake in the cultural-linguistic understanding of theology: nothing less than the religious genius of Christ himself.[99]

99. Cf. J.K. Riches, *A Century of New Testament Study* (Cambridge: The Lutterworth Press, 1993), esp. p. 100: 'in what sense is it possible to say something new? How far are our beliefs determined by the beliefs we inherit?'

READING FOR LIFE:
THE USE OF THE BIBLE IN ETHICS AND THE WORK OF
MARTHA C. NUSSBAUM

John Barton

One of the central tenets of the Biblical Theology Movement was the idea of an enormous gulf between biblical thinking and philosophical thought—between Hebrew and classical culture. This applied as much to ethical as to metaphysical questions. It was regarded as simply obvious that the two cultures were utterly different in their approach to morality. One reason why this was superficially so plausible is that it worked by comparing two unlike things. In essence, it said that the narrative material in the Hebrew Bible was not much like Greek philosophy; put like that, the contrast is true but unsurprising. The difference is a generic one, and to make it the basis of a contrast between the whole of the two cultures involved is a category-mistake.

Nevertheless, the contrast is not completely empty. For we could ask *why* there is so much narrative in the Hebrew Bible, and so little reflective or speculative writing. Such quasi-philosophical literature as ancient Israelite culture produced is to be found, not in narrative, but in the wisdom literature; but that in many ways supports the idea of a Greek-Hebrew contrast. With the exception of Ecclesiastes, a book from the Hellenistic age which may well show the influence of the Sceptics, the biblical wisdom literature belongs generically not with philosophy but with a work such as Hesiod's *Works and Days*: aphoristic wisdom, practical advice on living, with an absence of metaphysical speculation and of any attempt to systematize knowledge or to challenge received wisdom. Though it was unreasonable to contrast Greek philosophy with Hebrew narrative, it was entirely sensible to note the relative importance of speculative literature and of narrative writing within the corpus of Greek and Hebrew literature respectively. The 'biblical theologians' had some sense that one or the other type of writing was somehow characteristic of the peculiar genius of the two cultures—and this was reasonable in itself—though they overplayed their hand. Though Greek literature is certainly not characterized by an absence of narrative, the biblical writings just as certainly lack any real philosophy, and any reader of the Old Testament sees at once that there are types of questions this literature simply is not equipped to tackle—precisely those we now normally call philosophical. Despite the fact that it changes much in what it receives, rabbinic literature is a real continuation of the Old Testament's distinctive style of thinking. If you ask an abstract question about a piece of biblical narrative, the rabbis are likely to reward you with another narrative. This is not the way we do philosophy, nor the way Greeks in the classical period did it.

Thus the sense of a difference between Israel and Greece is well enough grounded in the literature, even if it was crudely expressed in Biblical Theology. Nevertheless, it ought somehow to be possible to discuss both cultures without falling into category-mistakes at every turn. Greek tragedy may offer a bridge. Tragedy is no more philosophy than narrative or historiography is, yet through it many profound questions are addressed. And some of the narrative texts in the Old Testament have this same kind of profundity, which cannot be called philosophy, yet deal, in their own way, with some of the issues that concern, or have concerned, philosophers. But the problem of genre does still raise its head: how can one extract philosophical or ethical truth from texts that work with narrative, drama and poetry, rather than constructing that analysis in plain prose, which is what we have come to think of as philosophy?

This question is the central concern of Martha C. Nussbaum, Professor of Philosophy, Classics and Comparative Literature at Brown University. Her first book, *The Fragility of Goodness: Luck and Ethics in Greek Tragedy and Philosophy*,[1] engages profoundly with Greek tragedy from this distinctive point of view. My purpose in this paper is to consider how her work might help the student of the Old Testament—which, like Greek tragedy, is unphilosophical yet profound—to show the fruitfulness of the Bible in the human ethical enterprise. But since I have not progressed very far towards making her classical key turn in the biblical lock, I shall spend most of the paper presenting her ideas on their own terms, in the hope that others may also find them a stimulus to their work on biblical ethics.

1. Cambridge: Cambridge University Press, 1986

Nussbaum's study begins from an observation lacking in the work of most biblical theologians: it is not only that Greek culture differs from Hebrew in having philosophical writings as well as historiography, poetry, and so on, but also that Greek culture has great variations within itself and ought not to be treated as a monolith. One major distinction is that between Plato and Aristotle. To put the contrast crudely: Plato works on ethical questions from first principles, where Aristotle's method is empirical, based on the minute observation of particular cases and of what commends itself to the average person (the average person, at least, of Aristotle's own sex and class). Aristotle attends to the concrete and particular, rather than to the general and abstract. At the very beginning of the *Nicomachean Ethics* (1.3) the principle is enunciated that in every intellectual pursuit the kind and degree of certainty that can be achieved is that appropriate to the subject matter being studied. Where ethics is concerned, we do not attain to *episteme*—a theoretical body of certain knowledge—but rather to practical wisdom. To put it in modern terms, ethics is not a science but an art. Here is Nussbaum's account of Aristotle:

> First, Aristotle says two things about the ultimate criterion of correctness in ethical choice that tell strongly in favor of the non-scientific picture. He says that the standard of excellence is determined with reference to the decisions of the person of practical wisdom: what is appropriate in each case is what such a judge would select. And he says that the 'judgment' or 'discrimination' in ethical matters rests with, or is 'in', something which he calls perception (*aisthēsis*), a faculty of discrimination that is concerned with the apprehending of concrete particulars, rather than universals. The context of this claim makes it clear that he wishes to express grave reservations about universal principles as arbiters of ethical correctness: 'The person who diverges only slightly from the correct is not blameworthy, whether he errs in the direction of the more or the less; but the person who diverges *more* is blamed: for this is evident. But to say to what point and how much someone is blameworthy is not easy to determine by a principle (*tōi logōi aphorisai*): nor in fact is this the case with any other perceptible item. For things of this sort are among the concrete particulars, and the discrimination lies in perception. (*NE* 1109b.18-23) Principles, then, fail to capture the fine detail of the concrete particular, which is the subject matter of ethical choice. This must be seized in a confrontation with the situation itself, by a faculty that is suited to confront it as a complex whole. General rules are being criticized here both for lack of

concreteness and for lack of flexibility. 'Perception' can respond to nuance and fine shading, adapting its judgment to the matter at hand in a way that principles set up in advance have a hard time doing.

These two principles are pressed repeatedly by Aristotle in order to show that universal statements are posterior in ethical value to concrete descriptions, universal rules to particular judgments. 'Among statements (*logoi*) about conduct', he writes in a nearby passage, 'those that are universal (*katholou*) are more general (*koinoteroi*), but the particular are more true—for action is concerned with particulars (*ta kath' hekasta*), and statements must harmonize with these' (*NE* 1107a.29-32). Rules are authoritative only insofar as they are correct; but they are correct only insofar as they do not err with regard to the particulars. And it is not possible for a simple universal formulation, intended to cover many different particulars, to achieve a high degree of correctness. Therefore, in his discussion of justice Aristotle insists that the wise judgment of the agent must both correct and supplement the universal formulations of law:

> All law is universal; but about some things it is not possible for a universal statement to be correct. Then in those matters in which it is necessary to speak universally, but not possible to do so correctly, the law takes the usual case, though without ignoring the possibility of missing the mark... When, then, the law speaks universally, and something comes up that is not covered by the universal, then it is correct, insofar as the legislator has been deficient or gone wrong in speaking simply, to correct his omission, saying what he would have said himself had he been present and would have legislated if he had known (*NE* 1137b13ff.).

The law is here regarded as a summary of wise decisions. It is therefore appropriate to supplement it with new wise decisions made on the spot; and it is also appropriate to correct it where it does not correctly summarize what a good judge would do. Good judgment, once again, supplies both a superior concreteness and a superior responsiveness or flexibility.[2]

Now a method of ethical enquiry which places so much emphasis on particulars, and is so suspicious of universal rules, is well-adapted to take account of fictional narrative, historiography and drama. You could hardly read Greek tragedy in order to feed a Platonic understanding of ethics. For one thing, Plato was famously opposed to tragedy anyway; so that would go against the grain. But for another, the constant examination of particular people in their ethical life would be at best superfluous, at worst intolerable, for a theory that is looking always to generalize as much as possible. Whereas for an Aristotelian approach these kinds of literature are eminently suitable for ethical investigation, alongside the lives of real people in all their particularity and

2.   Nussbaum, *The Fragility of Goodness*, pp. 300-301

concreteness. For Aristotle, the plots and characters of the tragedians are ideal material for the ethicist—rather as the particularities of biblical narrative function in this way for traditional Jewish ethics.

Having established that reading tragedy may be as fruitful for the ethicist as reading moral philosophy, Nussbaum moves to a second stage, in which she tries to show what picture of ethics in fact emerges from this kind of investigation. For the tragedians, the moral life is not a matter of the human will alone, as on a Kantian model, but is made up of the interplay between the will and the actions it causes, on the one hand, and on the other the effects of chance, fortune, luck—*tyche*. The poet's task is not simply to judge people by a standard of conduct to which they ought to adhere, but to register and reflect non-judgmentally on their life as a whole: on the aspects resulting from birth and accident, as well as on those for which they can be held accountable. Using a quotation from Pindar, she argues that, for the poets and tragedians, a human life was not simply an artefact—what a person has made of him- or herself—but a plant:

> Human excellence
> grows like a vine tree
> fed by the green dew...[3]

One might recall the righteous man of Psalm 1, who is 'like a tree, planted by streams of water'—planted by someone else, that is, not by himself. Too much is *given* in our lives for us to think of them as something we ourselves have made. And these non-voluntary elements—constitution, psychological make-up, social background—are relevant ethically; they are not elements that the moralist ought to disregard because they do not proceed from the person's will.

The detachment from harsh judgment, and the compassion towards frail human beings that the poet should exercise, is well-captured when in another book she quotes Walt Whitman:

> Of these States the poet is the equable man...
> He bestows on every object its fit proportion, neither more nor less...
> He judges not as the judge judges, but as the sun falling round a helpless thing...
> He sees eternity in men and women, he does not see men and women as dreams or dots.[4]

---

3. Pindar, *Nemean* viii; cited in Nussbaum, *Fragility*, p. vi.

4. *By Blue Ontario's Shore*; cited in *Love's Knowledge: Essays on Philosophy and Literature* (Oxford: Oxford University Press, 1990), p. 54.

From this humane point of view, the poets and tragedians made it their task, above all, to *observe*—to observe the particularity of individual lives and to rehearse them for readers and audiences so as to evoke, not praise or blame, but those two great Aristotelian reactions: terror and pity. These are supremely ethical qualities, since they rest on recognizing our human affinities with those represented in tragedies or poems, and hence our vulnerability to the same mixture of wrong intention and bad luck which brings them low.

For us to learn about ethics from Greek tragedy it is necessary, above all, to be open to the uniqueness and complexity of each character we meet there. Even if we want eventually to extract general principles from the actions and fate of those characters, we should delay this until we have them sharply in focus. As Nussbaum says, this goes well beyond the standard ethical or philosophical device of using a model or example of a particular moral issue. Valid though that may be, it is very different from the tragedian's characters, who are not devised to illustrate a principle, but conceived as complete human beings woven out of many elements. They cannot be measured, says Nussbaum, with a straight and rigid ruler, but only with what Aristotle refers to as 'the Lesbian rule'. This is a flexible metal ruler, invented on Lesbos, with which it is possible to measure the curved bits of buildings. The rule has a certain objectivity—its calibration, for example—but it adapts to what it is measuring; and that is how philosophers must be if they go, for ethical teaching, not to fellow philosophers but to the dramatists.

Nussbaum provides a worked example of how an Aristotelian ethicist might read a tragedy. It is in the form of a commentary on a long speech of Hecuba in Euripides' *Trojan Women* (1158–1207). The speech is Hecuba's response to her grandson's death at the hand of the Greeks who have sacked the city:

> As a person of practical wisdom, Hecuba brings to the concrete situation of choice a disparate plurality of attachments and commitments, many of which have been nourished by early moral training, long before reflective adulthood. She also brings her *prima facie* reflections about what, for her, will count as a good life for a human being. She brings her love of her son, of her grandson; her love of Troy; her attachment to religious duties and duties to the family; a conception of proper courage, both in battle and in politics; a conception of proper reasonableness. She brings her view that a good life for a human being involves growing up in a family and a city and serving both the city's good and that of one's loved ones in it; that it involves going on to the end of life performing these excellent activities

and receiving, at the end of life, a pious burial; that it is a better thing, nonetheless, to die prematurely for these values than to make cowardly compromises. Training in these values has evidently made her well acquainted with her 'target', so that in this new situation she knows what to look for; the intentionality of her desires has a focus. As a result she is adept at sorting out the new situation before her, singling out without hesitation the features of ethical relevance.

Each of the features in the situation is seen by Hecuba as a distinct item with its own separate nature, generating its own separate claims. She does not offer definitions of the values she prizes; but this does not meant that she does not implicitly conceive of each of them as having a distinctive nature. She has a pretty good idea of what piety is, what courage and cowardice are; and it is clear from what she says about them that she takes them to be distinct and incommensurable items. There is not the slightest sign of a measuring scale, or any other reductive device.[5]

To draw any parallels here with the Bible may seem odd. It is generally assumed that the Bible does not concern itself with how to live a human life within human limits, so much as with how to be obedient to the commands which God has laid on human beings. I have myself argued that, at the level of what may be called the Bible's ethical theory, this is not a wholly fair account.[6] But Martha Nussbaum's work suggests the thought that even the actual narratives in the Bible, in which people are presented as ethical agents yet also as victims of circumstance, do not really support such a view either. Old Testament narrative clearly has little in common with Plato, and hence with Greek philosophy, *if*, that is, we take Plato as somehow the Greek philosophical norm: this was correctly seen by the Biblical Theology Movement. But it does, on the other hand, have a good deal in common with Aristotle, and with the tragedians who, before Aristotle, had already expressed their ethical thought through that minute attention to the particulars of given human lives which would later come to be thought of as Aristotelian. There are little cameos in the Old Testament of characters who would not be at all out of place in a Greek tragedy, and with whom the question of whether or not they obeyed the law of God seems to be outside the centre of interest. Some of them have been studied in Jonathan Magonet's book,

---

5. *Fragility*, pp. 314-15.
6. See J. Barton, 'Understanding Old Testament Ethics', *JSOT* 9 (1978), pp. 44-64; 'Natural Law and Poetic Justice in the Old Testament', *JTS* 30 (1979), pp. 1-14; 'Ethics in Isaiah of Jerusalem', *JTS* 32 (1981), p. 1-18.

Bible Lives.[7] Jephthah and his daughter form such an example, as does Paltiel son of Laish, in a masterpiece of laconic narration:

> David sent messengers to Ish-bosheth, Saul's son, saying, 'Give me my wife Michal, whom I betrothed at the price of a hundred foreskins of the Philistines'. And Ish-bosheth sent, and took her from her husband Paltiel, the son of Laish. But her husband went with her, weeping after her all the way to Bahurim. Then Abner said to him, 'Go, return'; and he returned (2 Sam. 3.14-16).

Indeed, most of the narrative in the books of Samuel could be read with an eye to the complexity of human ethical dilemmas, and to the need for ethical conduct even in the midst of far too many constraints on human freedom. Commentators have sometimes noted that much of 1 and 2 Samuel seems rather 'secular' in tone: God does not keep intervening here as he does in Judges or Chronicles. But after noting this as an apparent problem, biblical scholars usually go on to deny it, saying that the stories are not as secular as they look, or to excuse them on the grounds that they are ancient and understandably rather primitive. Surely neither response is correct. It would be better to see that ethical concerns are represented in the plurality of characters in these narratives, and that, if God is indeed in them, it is in the pity and terror they inspire in the readers, not in general principles which they illustrate, as if they were medieval (or modern) sermon-illustrations.

II

Five years ago, Martha Nussbaum published a further work, a collection of essays entitled *Love's Knowledge: Essays on Philosophy and Literature.*[8] Her enterprise here is the same, but the literature studied is modern, with the novels of Henry James as her primary subject. It is from this collection that I have taken the phrase 'Reading for Life', which Nussbaum in turn gets from David Copperfield, who says that he spent his childhood with his father's books as his only companions, sitting in his room and 'reading as if for life'. I take it this means 'reading for dear life'—'reading as if life depended on it'—but Nussbaum uses the expression to sum up an attitude to literature already clear in *The Fragility of Goodness*, but taken further in this more recent book. This

7.   London: SCM Press, 1992

8.   I am greatly indebted to Tal Goldfajn for introducing me to *Love's Knowledge*, and for helping me to see the fruitfulness of Nussbaum's approach.

attitude is that books, especially imaginative fiction, provide us with companions who will prepare our minds and hearts to cope with life. Against the formalism of, say, the New Criticism or early structuralism, this sounds extraordinarily naïve, far too lacking in suspicion about literature, prone to the Pathetic Fallacy, and somewhat Leavisite. But Nussbaum's programme is not concerned with great and edifying works portraying noble models for us to imitate; it is concerned with literature that offers us sharply delineated characters whose complexity and fragility are properly realized—modern literature, in fact, that has many of the characteristics of Greek tragedy. Again, her interest is in how ethics can be presented through fiction, in a way that avoids what she thinks is the reductionism and thinness of cool philosophical prose.

The key value is perception: 'the discrimination lies in perception'. Fiction can train us in such perception, and the fact that fictional characters are not real is not a problem; for, as she perceptively observes, all human love is love of fictional characters anyway—men and women that we can only love by understanding them as something like ourselves, which is already in some measure to fictionalize them, to make them in our own image:

> The love of a fictional character can be love because it is an active and inter-active relationship that sustains the reader for many hours of imagining, of fiction-making, beyond the time spent with the page itself; and because, in this relation, the mysterious and ineffable charm of interaction with a powerful presence can be experienced in much the way it is in life; because, too, the reader is at the same time a reader of his or her own life, bringing to the imagining the hopes and loves of real life. Of course this interaction takes place in fantasy. But David (Copperfield) insists upon the closeness of its links to love in life: its activation of the same generous, outgoing and erotic impulses, its power to transform the texture of the world. And he also indicates that the loves we find in life owe, themselves, a great deal to the storytelling imagination and to romantic projection. This does not mean that they are based upon *illusion* in any pejorative sense... the way one thing is associated with another, the richness of the inter-section of one image with many others, all this is not mere deception, but part of the texture of life, and a part of life's excitement. Part, too, of our ability to endow a perceived form with a human life: in that sense, all sympathy, all morality, is based on a generous fantasy.[9]

Again Nussbaum illustrates her contention that narrative prose can be the ideal vehicle for moral reflection in extended examples from Henry

---

9.   *Love's Knowledge*, pp. 354-55.

James and Dickens, too long even to summarize here. It might be fair to say that the best ethical reflection is not just narrative, but narrative plus sensitive commentary, written in a style which is itself not a matter of abstracting from the particularities of fiction, but rather of respecting them and drawing the reader's attention to them. Fiction requires rational analysis if it is to yield its powerful capacity for ethical insight; but analysis must not mean dissection, nor reduction to generalities and rules of thumb. One of the things we owe to the various formalisms of the twentieth century is the insight that literature is irreducible; that it is not merely a 'way of saying' something other than what it does, in fact, say. Narrative texts are not 'all about' some abstract virtue or vice, and they are not there to teach us this or that lesson. This is precisely Nussbaum's point. Literature is important for ethics because literature is as complicated as life itself, and cannot be decoded or boiled-down. Ethical insight comes from reading it—first sequentially and then reflectively—*not* from trying to extract a 'message' from it. A sensitive commentary will unpack the complexity in a helpful way, and that is what literary criticism has to offer to the ethical enterprise.

It seems to me that some biblical narrative texts could well be analysed or commentated in the style Nussbaum proposes. In the Old Testament, such accounts as the story of David's adultery with Bathsheba, and the ensuing disasters in his family as one of his sons rapes his daughter and another son exacts revenge, are so told that, much as with a Greek tragedy, they uncover universal human tendencies through the presentation of very particular people and situations. The resemblances between Old Testament narrative and Greek tragedy have most recently been explored by Cheryl Exum;[10] without going into detail, it seems to me that her analyses would form a possible basis for a Nussbaum-type discussion.

In conclusion, though, I should like to suggest that such an enterprise would have the effect of redrawing, in a useful way, some of the lines of demarcation between the various things biblical scholars do. At the moment, battle-lines are drawn up between those who continue to practise what is commonly called historical criticism and those who study the biblical text as a literary artefact. It is generally assumed that the first group are interested wholly in historical and not at all in aesthetic questions, and vice-versa. The second approach, a holistic, synchronic,

---

10. J. Cheryl Exum, *Tragedy and Biblical Narrative: Arrows of the Almighty* (Cambridge: Cambridge University Press, 1992).

literary reading, detaches the text wholly from its ancient moorings, and reads it as *our* text; furthermore it sometimes does this in the context of an avowedly theological agenda, reading the biblical text as part of the Holy Scripture of Christians or Jews. Nussbaum's readings seem to me hard to place on the 'historical-critical versus literary criticism' map. She is, of course, saying that the text—whether of Euripides or of Henry James—is a literary one, susceptible to literary-critical analysis. At the same time, however, she is not making any attempt to detach it from its ancient setting. The commentary on Hecuba's speech quoted above, for example, is far from trying to modernize Hecuba, and is, on the contrary, determined to 'read' her as a character in a historical context very distant from our own. What unites us with the text is not a decision to read it as if it had just been written, but the conviction that it and we are both exercised by certain fundamental questions about human beings and the world they inhabit; chief among which is 'How ought we to live?' In the terms used by biblical scholars, Nussbaum is both a historical-critical and a literary critic: the two are held together without effort, because she is, above all, concerned to seek in the texts the answer to that question—for then *and* now. One gets from her writing a sense that great texts matter, because they ask what is good for humankind, and never rest till they have found an answer.

ETHICS AS DECONSTRUCTION,
AND, THE ETHICS OF DECONSTRUCTION

David J.A. Clines

There are two parts to this paper, an exegetical part, Ethics as Deconstruction, and a more theoretical part, The Ethics of Deconstruction. What I hope they have in common is to show that literary and philosophical deconstruction has more ethical effect than is commonly supposed.

1. *Ethics as Deconstruction*

In this part of the paper, I shall look at some biblical texts where an ethical idea or prescription or hint seems to be founded on a deconstruction. Rather than attempt to explain what I mean by that in abstract terms, I shall take up my first example.

a. *Deuteronomy 23.15-16*

> You shall not give up to his master a slave who has escaped from his master to you; he shall dwell with you, in your midst, in the place which he shall choose within one of your towns, where it pleases him best; you shall not oppress him.

In Hebrew society, there was a clear distinction, most will allow, between slave and free. A person could become a slave as a captive in war, through being kidnapped, carried off and sold, through being sold as a child by parents, through selling oneself voluntarily into slavery, through hunger or debt, or, involuntarily, through defaulting on a debt. No matter how the individual had become a slave, the same basic rules seem to have applied.

The slave was a chattel of the master, and had no rights of his or her own. A slave was 'a commodity that could be sold, bought, leased, exchanged, or inherited'.[1] In the ancient Near East generally, and presumably also in Israel, any injury done to a slave required compensation to the master. There is only one case in the Bible that illustrates this principle, but there is no reason to doubt that it was at the foundation of the institution of slavery: if a slave is killed by a goring ox, the owner of the ox must compensate the master by a payment of thirty shekels of silver (Exod. 21.32)—just as a father must also be compensated for the death of a son or daughter.[2]

Various kinds of manumission were available to a slave. I. Mendelsohn has enumerated them as follows: 1. A Hebrew slave is to be released after six years of service (Exod. 21.2-4; Deut. 15.12); 2. a Hebrew who has made himself a voluntary slave is to be freed in the year of jubilee (Lev. 25.39-43, 47-55); 3. a Hebrew girl sold by her father with a view to marriage is to be released if the master does not wish to marry her when she is of age (Exod. 21.7-11); 4. a slave permanently maimed by his master is to be freed (Exod. 21.26-27).[3]

What is amazing about the law of the fugitive slave is that it enables a slave to acquire his or her own freedom—by the relatively simple expedient of running away. A slave can choose not to be a slave.

And that leaves us in a classic deconstructive situation. Classically, a deconstruction takes hold of a pair of binary oppositions that have been passing as valid currency, exposes the faults in the distinctions that are drawn between them, the definitions that claim to separate them, and shows how, to some extent, each is implied in the other. For practical purposes it may well serve to continue employing the concept of an oppositional pair, but the deconstructive enterprise has pointed out the fragility, and perhaps the ultimate futility, of the distinction.

In this case, the opposition slave–free is deconstructed if it can be shown that 'slave' includes 'free' (it would be a different move to show how the concept 'free' in ancient Israel implied 'slave'—in an economic sense, perhaps). The point here is that if a slave can choose not to be a

---

1. I. Mendelsohn, 'Slavery in the OT', in George Arthur Buttrick (ed.), *The Interpreter's Dictionary of the Bible*, IV (Nashville: Abingdon Press, 1962), pp. 383-91 (Mendelsohn is sometimes speaking of slavery in the ancient Near East as a whole, so one cannot be sure that there is Israelite evidence for all the practices mentioned above).

2. Another case in which injury to a slave must be compensated for is not strictly analogous, since the payment must be made to the sanctuary and not to the master. It is the case of a man having intercourse with a betrothed slave woman (Lev. 19.20-22).

3. Mendelsohn, 'Slavery in the OT', pp. 387-88.

slave, the concept slavery does not exist as it once was thought to exist, and the simple, commonsensical distinction between slave and free collapses.

This deconstructive collapse has of course not only linguistic and conceptual significance, but also social and ethical significance—and that is what makes it so interesting. What kind of a society can it be in which it is possible for prisoners to become free by a mere act of will? It is as strange as a society in which poor could become rich—by a mere act of will. That is the measure of the social significance of the deconstruction. But it is also an ethical issue, for—by our standards at least—there is an ethical issue involved in the institution of slavery. To our mind at least, slavery is a bad thing, and its abolition is to be desired and celebrated.[4] The Hebrew Bible does not report the abolition of slavery as a real social phenomenon, but it does announce a conceptuality according to which traditional slavery is, strictly speaking, inconceivable. If slavery is no more than a matter of a choice that slaves make, the ethical problem of slavery has well-nigh disappeared.

Not surprisingly, the deconstructive force of Deuteronomy 23 has been resisted. It has been urged, in a commonsensical way, that the law is unrealistic and not serious: 'If this law literally applied to any slave who had run away from his master, it certainly was unrealistic, for if put to practical use, it would have resulted in the immediate abolition of slavery'.[5] It is often pointed out that other ancient Near Eastern societies had no such law. The Laws of Eshnunna, for example, explicitly impose a fine for harbouring a runaway slave (§§12-13), while the Code of Hammurabi makes it a capital offence (§§15-16). In the Alalakh tablets from Syria we have evidence of a reward being paid to a person for apprehending a runaway slave.[6] On these grounds it is urged that the biblical law cannot refer to any slave who escapes from his or her master, but to 'a fugitive slave from a foreign country seeking asylum in

---

4. It is not the only evil, though I would hesitate to say as roundly as Timothy John Turnham, 'Male and Female Slaves in the Sabbath Year Laws of Exodus 21:1-11', in Ken Harold Richards (ed.), *Society of Biblical Literature 1987 Seminar Papers* (Atlanta: Scholars Press, 1987), pp. 545-49 (549), that in Israel 'slavery, while an undesirable state, is preferable to poverty'.

5. Mendelsohn, 'Slavery in the OT', p. 389.

6. See D.J. Wiseman, *The Alalakh Tablets* (London: British Institute of Archaeology at Aukara, 1953), no. 3; cf. also the Hittite Code, §§22-23 (ANET, 3rd edn), p. 188.

Palestine'.[7] Needless to say, there is not the faintest evidence in the text for such an interpretation, and the speculation witnesses only to the embarrassment of the scholar with the text.

I am, of course, not arguing that the abolition of slavery was the intention of the framers of this law; but simply that the wording itself stealthily undermines (which is to say, deconstructs) the concept of slavery—which is as good a way as any of abolishing it. Even if it does not lead immediately to a change in the social institution—and we have no evidence that it did—it remains on the statute book as an ethical principle whose time is yet to come.

There is another biblical text that points in the same direction, and here there can be no question of the slave being a foreigner. For in Exod. 21.2-6, we find:

> When you buy a Hebrew slave, he shall serve six years, and in the seventh he shall go out free, for nothing. If he comes in single, he shall go out single; if he comes in married, then his wife shall go out with him. If his master gives him a wife and she bears him sons or daughters, the wife and her children shall be her master's and he shall go out alone. But if the slave plainly says, 'I love my master, my wife, and my children; I will not go out free', then his master shall bring him to God, and he shall bring him to the door or the doorpost; and his master shall bore his ear through with an awl; and he shall serve him for life.

Here there is a concept of voluntary slavery, which is deconstructive in the alternate mode. For if Deuteronomy 23 showed that 'slave' could include 'free', Exodus 21 shows that 'free' can include 'slave'. For in this case the Hebrew slave has served his time, and is a free man. But— unlike the commonality of slaves—he chooses to be a slave. There is,

---

7. Mendelsohn, 'Slavery in the OT', p. 389; similarly A.D.H. Mayes, *Deuteronomy* (NCB; London: Oliphants, 1979), p. 319 (it is a 'fugitive slave who escapes to the land of Israel'); Peter C. Craigie, *The Book of Deuteronomy* (NICOT; Grand Rapids, Eerdmans, 1976), p. 300, who argues that to extradite a runaway slave from another country would imply a pre-existing treaty with a foreign country, 'undermining thereby the total commitment required of Israel by the covenant with the Lord'; Eduard König, *Das Deuteronomium* (KAT, 3; Leipzig: A. Deichert, 1917), p. 162, arguing that since all Israel is addressed it must be a foreign slave (!); H. Wheeler Robinson, *Deuteronomy and Joshua* (Century Bible; Edinburgh: T.C. & E.C. Jack, n.d., c. 1901), p. 174, claiming that 'within one of thy gates' implies that he is a foreign slave. M. Weinfeld, *Deuteronomy and the Deuteronomic School* (Oxford: Clarendon Press, 1972), p. 272 n. 5, on the other hand, has no recourse to that explanation; he simply thinks that 'slaves who were well treated did not flee from the[ir] masters'.

indeed, a kind of necessity upon him to become (remain) a slave, for he does not want to abandon his master or his family. But it is not the same kind of necessity that we have considered earlier, which makes a debtor voluntarily sell himself into slavery. There is a real choice here (however constrained), and the man who makes the choice to submit himself to slavery is a free man when he makes it.[8] And that action redefines slavery, and therewith also the relation between slave and free. Slavery is in a sense abolished when it ceases to be a state that a person is forced into against their will. It still survives as a social institution, indeed, but in that the line of distinction between slave and free has been blurred, it has lost its conceptual force.

You cannot found a social institution on a deconstructible conceptualization. But what I am principally arguing here is that the deconstructive uncertainty opens a space for an ethical decision.

b. *Genesis 9.5-6*

> For your lifeblood I will surely require a reckoning; of every beast I will require it and of man; of every man's brother I will require the life of man. Whoever sheds the blood of man, by man shall his blood be shed; for God made man in his own image.

This text is ostensibly a prohibition of murder.[9] It threatens the would-be murderer that his life is in danger: if he sheds the blood of a human being, his blood also will be shed.[10] It is a gnomic text, especially its core: שֹׁפֵךְ דַּם הָאָדָם בָּאָדָם דָּמוֹ יִשָּׁפֵךְ 'who sheds human blood shall have his blood shed by a human'. It is a divine sentence, and it gives all the appearance of comprehensive law.[11]

The prohibition is expressed as a prediction: if X happens, then Y will happen. Or perhaps it is not a simple prediction, for the Hebrew 'imperfect' can be used in modal senses. It could mean, 'by a human his blood *must* be shed', or, 'by a human his blood *should* be shed', or 'by a human his blood *may* be shed'.[12] That is an unsettling situation of

---

8. The delicate balance between freedom and slavehood has been well brought out by Turnham, 'Male and Female Slaves ', p. 547.

9. Claus Westermann, for one, calls it a 'prohibition of homicide' (*Genesis 1–11: A Commentary* [trans. John J. Scullion; Minneapolis: Augsburg, 1984 (1974)], p. 466).

10. I am assuming, rightly or wrongly, that the murderer envisaged is a male.

11. I do not mean this term form-critically, for there has been a discussion whether the phrase is formally a judicial formula (of an apodeictic type), a proverb or a prophetic admonition (see Westermann, *Genesis 1–11*, p. 467).

12. On the modal uses of the 'imperfect', see Paul Joüon, *A Grammar of Biblical*

indeterminacy. Perhaps the sentence is not a warning directed toward the would-be murderer, but an authorization to the community that capital punishment for murder is required. Or perhaps it means that capital punishment is not required but desirable? Or not desirable but permissible?

At this point the usual exegetical move is to ask, Which of these various possibilities is the *correct* one? Which makes best sense of the rationale given in v. 6b, which is best supported by the context, which would best cohere with the realities of legal and social life in ancient Israel, which can we parallel in other Israelite laws? Perhaps there is an answer to these questions, and one exegesis may be demonstrated to be the *best*, though it will always be a matter of probabilities.[13] But even if there is a *best* exegesis, that does not make it the *correct* one. Perhaps there is no *correct* exegesis, and *all* the meanings have to be kept open. They may well not be all *equally 'good'* exegeses. So long as they fall within the bounds of possibility (whatever *they* are), the text *means* whatever they all, severally or collectively, mean.

Now, this is a text about ethics. It professes to dissuade people from murder or else to authorize communities to carry out capital punishment of murderers—or something like that. So it claims to give authoritative guidance on an ethical issue.[14] But it deconstructs itself in that—in what it says—it does not do any such thing. For from the text itself we cannot tell if (a) it is saying to would-be murderers, You don't want to do that,

Hebrew, II (trans. and rev. T. Muraoka; Subsidia Biblica, 14/2; Rome: Pontifical Biblical Institute Press, 1991), pp. 370-72 (§113 l-n). The modal sense of 'want' is inapplicable here, as it would generally be with a passive verb. By the way, this knowledge about modal uses of the verb is not new; it is to be found, e.g., in E. Kautzsch (ed.), *Gesenius' Hebrew Grammar* (rev. A.E. Cowley; Oxford: Clarendon Press, 2nd edn, 1910), pp. 316-19 (§107 m–w). But, judging by the commentaries and translations, the possibility of invoking it in the present connection has been suppressed—because (I guess) it would be too uncomfortably indeterminate to bring it to consciousness.

13. Our versions uniformly translate יִשָּׁפֵךְ by the simple future, 'shall be shed'.

14. That, at any rate, is how all the commentaries read it. For example, '[T]he demand for life taken is a demand made by God' (Westermann, *Genesis 1–11*, p. 468).

The theological underpinning of the text—'for in the image of God he made humanity' (v. 6b)—is often taken as a reason why God *must* be demanding a death penalty for murder: that is, if murder is an assault on the divine image, it can only be punished capitally. It does not apparently occur to commentators to ask themselves, if they themselves do not demand the death penalty for every insult to their own honour, why should God?

because (i) you will certainly be executed if you do, or (ii) you run a risk of being executed if you do, or (b) whether it is saying to a community, (i) all murderers must be executed, or (ii) you ought to execute murderers, but you need not, or (iii) you can execute a murderer if you like. This does not sound like a text with a determinate meaning. There is no doubt that this text regards murder as a bad thing, but there is plenty of doubt about what it thinks should be done about it. Indeterminacy of course does not itself amount to a deconstruction. What makes the text self-deconstructive is that its claim is undermined by its content.

But this is not the end of the deconstructability of the text. The first case emerged from observing the tension between the form of the saying and its content, the second pair of deconstructions from an interrogation of the concept of killing ('shedding blood' in the terms of the text). The text professes to be against killing, but in fact it authorizes killing. Apparently it says, Do not kill, but in reality its message is, Kill! It even seems to be less interested in the killing that occurs (whenever, by whomever) than in the killing it itself sanctions. Humans no doubt go on killing, it says, but what you need to know is that you are required (or, permitted) to do killing yourself. In shifting the focus from the initial act of murder to the act of punishment or vengeance, it becomes not so much a prohibition of killing as an incitement to it. This is a strange deconstructive situation for an ethical text to find itself in, is it not?

The text does not disguise that the execution of a murderer is itself a killing. It uses exactly the same language for the murder and the judicial execution: the murderer sheds blood, his blood is shed. So the executioner is himself a shedder of blood, and there is nothing to distinguish him from the murderer—not in the language at any rate, and if not in the language, then where? This is not a linear sentence, then, this שֹׁפֵךְ דַּם הָאָדָם בָּאָדָם דָּמוֹ יִשָּׁפֵךְ; it is a circle, for every time that the sentence is completed it resumes, putting the implied subject of the second verb ('it shall be shed') in the position of the subject of the first ('whoever sheds'). To begin with, the executioner is hidden in the shadow of the passive voice, lurking at the end of the sentence, when he does his deed; but once it is done, the sentence begins to roll again, and this time the executioner is foregrounded; he is now the שֹׁפֵךְ, the shedder of blood, and the sentence concerns *him*. He is authorized to kill, but only at the cost of his own life.[15]

---

15. Westermann rightly recognizes that 'The death penalty carried out by the organs of state can also be murder', but he also claims that 'A community is only

And there is the ethical hint. If blood-revenge is permitted (or even required), but only at the cost of labelling it 'murder'—is it permitted? Somewhere, I mean to say, in among the words of a text that professes to authorize capital punishment, is the undoing of that authorization, at the very least its problematization. You can see from this case why I am beginning to wonder whether ethical initiatives might not originate at the points of deconstructibility of traditional ethics.[16]

c. *John 8.3-11*

> The scribes and the Pharisees brought a woman who had been caught in adultery, and placing her in the midst they said to him, 'Teacher, this woman has been caught in the act of adultery. Now in the law Moses commanded us to stone such. What do you say about her?' This they said to test him, that they might have some charge to bring against him. Jesus bent down and wrote with his finger on the ground. And as they continued to ask him, he stood up and said to them, 'Let him who is without sin among you be the first to throw a stone at her'. And once more he bent down and wrote with his finger on the ground. But when they heard it, they went away, one by one, beginning with the eldest, and Jesus was left alone with the woman standing before him. Jesus looked up and said to her, 'Woman, where are they? Has no one condemned you?' She said, 'No one, Lord'. And Jesus said, 'Neither do I condemn you; go, and do not sin again'.

My next examples are from narratives about Jesus, whom I regard as an arch-deconstructor. I had better apologize (in the sense of defend myself) for even referring to, let alone beginning with, a text that our editions and translations tell us most severely is not a text—not a text that has anything to do with the Gospel of John, not a text that is a part of the New Testament, not a biblical text at all, in fact. In case we have not got the message, commentators rub it in by reserving their commentary on

---

justified in executing the death penalty insofar as it respects the unique right of God over life and death and insofar as it respects the inviolability of human life that follows therefrom' (*Genesis 1–11*, p. 469). Is this an authorization of capital punishment, I ask myself, or is it not rather, deconstructively, a statement of the impossibility of offering a plausible ethical justification for it?

16. And also what I think of the statement of Luther's cited by Dillmann: 'Inasmuch as no human society is conceivable unless human life be regarded as sacred, it may be said with truth that the foundation is here laid for the social organisation of man' (in A. Dillmann, *Genesis, Critically and Exegetically Expounded*, I [Edinburgh: T. & T. Clark, 1897], p. 295).

these verses for the very end of their work,[17] or omitting to comment on it altogether.[18] Translations express their disapproval by relegating the text to a footnote (so RSV), putting it in square brackets (NAB, GNB, Moffatt), setting it off from the rest of the text with a line above and below (NIV), printing it at the end of the Gospel (NEB, who head it 'An Incident in the Temple'—so that we should not recognize it?).

'[M]issing from the best early Greek MSS'[19] is held to be a damning criticism. 'Present in the vast majority of Greek manuscripts' is not a phrase one encounters in the commentaries (though it is the truth); nor is it commonly remarked that this text is to be found in almost every copy of the New Testament ever printed.[20] These facts do not count against the current (but historically conditioned) supremacy of the text critics. They of course have their own, perfectly legitimate, programme to carry out, but there is no reason why that should include decisions about what is and what is not a biblical text. From the standpoint of the history of the text or of the physical reality of actual Bibles, it would be more correct to say apropos of this pericope, 'The best early Greek manuscripts are defective at this point'—and to force text critics to utter that sentence once a day for their presumption.[21]

It would not be seemly to cast doubt on the scholarly tradition of the

17. So, for example, C.K. Barrett, *The Gospel according to St John: An Introduction with Commentary and Notes on the Greek Text* (London: SPCK, 1967), pp. 90-93; J.N. Sanders, *A Commentary on The Gospel according to St John* (ed. and completed by B.A. Mastin; London: A. & C. Black, 1968), pp. 458-66.

18. So, for example, John Marsh, *Saint John* (The Pelican Gospel Commentaries; Harmondsworth: Penguin, 1968); Ernst Haenchen, *John, 2: A Commentary on the Gospel of John, Chapters 7–21* (trans. Robert W. Funk; Hermeneia; Fortress Press: Philadelphia, 1984), p. 22 (his editor writes: 'The author did not consider the pericope...to be an original part of the Fourth Gospel').

19. *New American Bible, in loc.*

20. The *New American Bible*, sponsored by the Bishops' Committee of the Confraternity of Christian Doctrine and translated by members of the Catholic Biblical Association of America, remarks that 'The Catholic Church accepts it as inspired Scripture', but manages, in the same footnote, to say five bad things about it (missing from the best early Greek manuscripts; found in different places in different manuscripts; many non-Johannine features of language; many doubtful readings; certainly out of place here).

21. Barnabas Lindars is something of an exception in beginning his commentary on the pericope on an upbeat note: 'By a happy chance this fragment from an unknown work has been preserved in the MS. tradition of John' (*The Gospel of John* [NCB; London: Oliphants, 1972], p. 305).

inauthenticity of this pericope. But I notice that it is a rare scholar who spares a moment to wonder whether there might not be a reason why the pericope is missing from the 'best' (? most authoritative, ? most authorized) manuscripts. A hermeneutic of suspicion is not, as it turns out, a merely modern affectation; Augustine put two and two together for himself when he roundly declared:

> Some of little faith, or rather enemies of the true faith, I suppose from a fear lest their wives should gain impunity in sin, removed from their manuscripts the Lord's act of indulgence to the adulteress.[22]

Was the passage missing, or was it excluded? Did it fall, or was it pushed?

No matter. It is enough for my purpose that this narrative, whether or not 'original' or 'authentic' (whatever those terms might mean), 'represents the character and method of Jesus as they are revealed elsewhere', as C.K. Barrett puts it.[23] For I want to argue that the 'method' of Jesus, especially in ethical matters, is a deconstructive one.

The essence of the story, from this point of view, is that express permission is given to execute the woman, but in such a form that it cannot be carried out. Jesus believes the woman is guilty as charged, for he tells her to 'go and sin no more' (v. 11). He believes the Mosaic law is applicable to her, and he upholds that law. Jesus is not against Moses, he is not against stoning. As far as Jesus is concerned, if one faultless man had stood there, he would have been entitled to stone her, and the others could then have joined in the stoning (could they not?), even though they themselves were not without sin. For Jesus says, 'Let him that is blameless (ἀναμάρτητος) among you cast the first stone'—but he does not say who should cast the second and the third.

But equally clearly, Jesus does not intend that the woman should be executed. If he does not condemn (κατακρίνω) her himself, even when he is in a position to do so, he cannot really want others to condemn her and carry out a sentence of death. Indeed, it is hard to see why the woman is brought to Jesus in the first place unless her accusers know that Jesus is not going to agree to her execution.[24] They know that, but

22. *De Conj. Adult.* 2.6.
23. Barrett, *John*, p. 491.
24. There are of course, 'historical' reconstructions ('speculations' is perhaps a better term) for why Jesus is being 'tested' by the Pharisees. J. Jeremias, for example, opined that it was illegal for Jews to carry out a death sentence at that time, and that agreeing to it would make him a revolutionary against Rome ('Zur

they also know that Jesus upholds the Mosaic law[25]—enough, that is, to make them eager to discover that in some respect he does not.[26] We readers, too, cannot imagine the Jesus of the Gospels consenting to the death of a woman for adultery.[27]

Jesus' response to the situation is to deconstruct the Mosaic law. Moses' law, like any law, relies on a distinction between wrongdoers and law-enforcers. Law-enforcers punish wrongdoers, criminals are punished by judges. As long as that binary opposition stands, societies can function as they have got into the habit of functioning. But suppose that there is something faulty about the opposition, and that law-enforcers are themselves wrongdoers. Suppose, that is, that the category 'judge', instead of being oppositionally related to the category 'criminal', is included within it. Then you have a classic deconstruction of the categories presupposed by a text. What follows, when the demarcation collapses, is that judges can no longer function as judges, not when they realize that they are—criminals!

Well, at least that is the *dramatic* consequence. It is not the 'real-life' consequence, for the judicial system in Judaea did not break down the moment Jesus performed his miracle of deconstruction. That real-life (non-)consequence is typical of deconstruction, of course, for the deconstruction of a binary opposition does not 'destroy' or 'abolish' or 'negate' or 'remove' the opposition. It only exposes its fragility, it only problematizes it, it only renders it unsafe and questionable, it only invites flexibility, it only encourages new arrangements, new conceptualizations. In the story world, the judges flee the scene, unable to lift a pebble; though they entered the story as a united block, they leave one by one, in a dissolve.[28] In the real world, on the other hand, all things continue

Geschichtlichkeit des Verhörs Jesu vor dem Hohen Rat', *ZNW* 43 [1950–51], pp. 145-50 [148-49]). But the text gives no hint of such a background.

25. If Jesus was notorious for his disregard of the Mosaic law, no one would be 'testing' (πειράζων) him to find out if he did in fact disregard it.

26. 'It brings into the open an existing conflict between the known teaching of Jesus and the requirements of the law' (Lindars, *St John*, p. 310).

27. '[I]t is unlikely', writes Mastin, 'that all that is involved here is an attempt by Jesus' enemies (who knew his merciful attitude toward sinners) to obtain a judgement from him which will enable them to accuse him as a transgressor of the Law' (in Sanders, *John*, p. 464), citing E.C. Hoskyns, *The Fourth Gospel* (ed. F.N. Davey; London: Faber & Faber, 1947), p. 569.

28. Cf. Thomas Wieser, 'Community—Its Unity, Diversity and Universality', *Semeia* 33 (1985), pp. 83-95 (86).

as they have since the creation—except that an ethical doubt has been inserted into the structure of the administration of justice, its Achilles heel has been exposed.

We are not done yet with the deconstructive possibilities of this text, though. It is not just a matter of how the character Jesus within the narrative deconstructs the law that he is confronted by, but also of how the narrative itself deconstructs itself.

A minor respect in which the text offers itself up to deconstruction is over the distinction guilty/righteous. In a word, the story hangs upon the Pharisees being both guilty and righteous. If they had not all been guilty, the woman would have died; it needed only one blameless man, and she would have been stoned to death. But, on the other hand, if they had not all been righteous—righteous in the sense of acknowledging their sin publicly, of telling the truth about their guiltiness, of not pretending they were blameless, indeed, of not disregarding the authority of Jesus (what *rights* does he have in the matter?, we wonder)—the woman would equally have been put to death. Just one man who would not confess his sin would have been enough to start the hail of stones. So, dramatically speaking at least, the woman's life depends upon the honesty of her accusers, upon their 'conscience' (συνείδησις) and their ability to be 'convicted' (ἐλέγχω) by it.

This deconstruction rubs against the grain of the text, no doubt. For it is in the interest of the text to show that Jesus is in the right, and that, ergo, his opponents are in the wrong. Indeed, Jesus always wins controversies with Pharisees. But here that clear-cut opposition between Jesus and Pharisees breaks down somewhat, as the text lets it slip that the woman's life, which Jesus is concerned to preserve, hangs less upon any action of his than it does upon the honest shamefaced confessions of the Pharisees. Jesus risks her life on their honesty. The Pharisees are still the villains of the piece, but they are not dyed-in-the-wool villains. If they are not ἀναμάρτητος, neither are they blackguards. The text does not explicitly acknowledge any goodness in the Pharisees, but it undermines itself secretly by its storyline.

A final deconstructive aspect of the narrative is of more moment. It is the deconstruction of Jesus' own deconstruction, and it goes like this. Jesus, I have argued, does not deny the woman's guilt or the applicability of the Mosaic law, but he saves her from stoning by deconstructing the opposition judge/criminal. Yet the narrative does not include *him* within the category of the criminal-judge, the Pharisee-sinner. Ex hypothesi, Jesus is the one ἀναμάρτητος on the scene. If, by his own profession, the one without sin should cast the first stone, then let him cast it! Is he free to rescind the law of Moses—and his own acknowledgment that it is indeed applicable in this case—on humanitarian grounds? Surely not! Or rather, if he is not going to support the law of Moses and carry it out by executing the woman, why did he not say so in the first place? If he resists the commandment of Moses, and does not believe adulterers should be stoned to death, why does he not reject the law rather than problematize it? Deconstructing the law of Moses does not render it invalid; it only gives one furiously to think. If he will not cast a stone, he must regard the law as invalid; and it is a waste of time to deconstruct a text that you have written off.

Which is to say, while the pericope professes to concern itself with the right of humans who are themselves sinful to execute judgment upon other humans, the issue turns out to be a quite different one: namely, the authority of Jesus vis-à-vis that of Moses, the question of whose word 'goes'. Is it Moses', who says, 'Stone her', or is it Jesus', who says, 'Neither do I condemn you'? The course of the narrative deconstructs its punchline, and vice-versa.

The last point is not, I think, an ethical one, but the first point, about the judge-criminal, is. What a deconstructive impulse—which I ascribe to the character Jesus—does in the matter of ethics is to call into question conventional ethics, especially those built into the fabric of society, and to hint at an ethic beyond ethics.

d. *Matthew 22.16-21//Mark 12.13-17//Luke 20.20-26*

> Then the Pharisees went and took counsel how to entangle him in his talk. And they sent their disciples to him, along with the Herodians, saying, 'Teacher, we know that you are true, and teach the way of God truthfully, and care for no man; for you do not regard the position of men. Tell us, then, what you think. Is it lawful to pay taxes to Caesar, or not?' But Jesus, aware of their malice, said, 'Why put me to the test, you hypocrites? Show me the money for the tax.' And they brought him a coin. And Jesus said to them, 'Whose likeness and inscription is this?' They said, 'Caesar's'. Then he said to them, 'Render therefore to Caesar the things that are Caesar's, and to God the things that are God's'. When they heard it, they marvelled; and they left him and went away.

> And they sent to him some of the Pharisees and some of the Herodians, to entrap him in his talk. And they came and said to him, 'Teacher, we know that you are true, and care for no man; for you do not regard the position

of men, but truly teach the way of God. Is it lawful to pay taxes to Caesar, or not? Should we pay them, or should we not?' But knowing their hypocrisy, he said to them, 'Why put me to the test? Bring me a coin, and let me look at it.' And they brought one. And he said to them, 'Whose likeness and inscription is this?' They said to him, 'Caesar's'. Jesus said to them, 'Render to Caesar the things that are Caesar's, and to God the things that are God's'. And they were amazed at him. The scribes and the chief priests tried to lay hands on him at that very hour, but they feared the people; for they perceived that he had told this parable against them.

So they watched him, and sent spies, who pretended to be sincere, that they might take hold of what he said, so as to deliver him up to the authority and jurisdiction of the governor. They asked him, 'Teacher, we know that you speak and teach rightly, and show no partiality, but truly teach the way of God. Is it lawful for us to give tribute to Caesar, or not?' But he perceived their craftiness, and said to them, 'Show me a coin. Whose likeness and inscription has it?' They said, 'Caesar's'. He said to them, 'Then render to Caesar the things that are Caesar's, and to God the things that are God's'. And they were not able in the presence of the people to catch him by what he said; but marvelling at his answer they were silent.

Here is Jesus again in deconstructive mode. He is presented with a binary opposition: God or Caesar. He responds in language that gives lip-service to the opposition, but that calls it into question nevertheless. His audience react with 'amazement' (θαυμάζω, Mt. 22.22; ἐκθαυμάζω, Mk 12.17; θαυμάζω, Lk. 20.26)—which is the signal that a deconstruction has been performed upon them. Jesus' own deconstructive reply is, however, itself open to deconstruction, so I shall argue.

The presenting form of the binary pair is the question: Is it lawful or not to pay taxes to Caesar? Are we to give or are we not to give? But these are not themselves the terms of the opposition. The question, Is it lawful (ἔξεστι)?, is not a real question, and it obscures the real question. For ἔξεστι ought to mean: '[I]s it warranted by anything in the Law or the Scribal tradition?'[29] But the law (and the scribal tradition, as far as I know) have nothing to say about Caesar, or about paying taxes to foreign rulers; at least, I can find no references in the commentaries to Jewish discussions of this theme.[30] Jesus and his opponents must both

29. A.H. McNeile, *The Gospel according to St Matthew* (London: Macmillan, 1915), p. 319.

30. Why is the matter not raised?, I wonder. I can learn from the commentaries much more than I need to know about where and when the poll tax was collected, and I am suffering from a numismatic overdose (cf., for example, H.J. Hart, 'The Coin of

know that paying tax is not forbidden, and therefore it is not 'unlawful'. There is thus a dishonesty in pretending that that is the issue.

The Gospel narrators, for their part, want to alert readers to the deviousness of the question, and they do so in five ways. They tell us that Jesus' interlocutors are out to 'entangle' (παγιδεύω, Mt. 22.15) or 'entrap' (ἀγρεύω, Mk 12.13) him. They say that his opponents are spies pretending to be honest (ἐνκαθέτους ὑποκρινομένους ἑαυτοὺς δικαίους, Lk. 20.20). They have the opponents of Jesus address him insincerely and sycophantically: they call him Teacher, they say that he is 'true' (ἀλήθης, Mt. 22.16; Mk 12.14) or 'speaks rightly' (ὀρθῶς λέγεις, Lk. 20.21), that he teaches the way of God truthfully, that he shows no partiality. They have Jesus evaluate his opponents' attitude as 'wickedness' (πονηρία, Mt. 22.18; πανουργία, Lk. 20.23) or 'hypocrisy' (ὑπόκρισις, Mk 12.15). They have Jesus address his interlocutors as 'hypocrites' (ὑποκριταί, Mt. 22.18). These are all tokens that the question presented is not the real question—which is to say, the opposition lawful/unlawful is not the issue.

Beneath the surface form of the question, beneath the presenting opposition lawful/unlawful, there is a more substantive opposition, and it is that opposition that Jesus will deconstruct. As Lohmeyer puts it, 'The question already hints at the distinction between a human and a divine order, a political and a religious command'.[31] The presupposition of the question, that is to say, is a disjunction between the rule of God and the rule of Caesar, an implication that obedience to the one implies disobedience to the other.

"Render unto Caesar" (A Note on Some Aspects of Mk 12:13-17; Mt. 22:15-22; Lk. 20:20-26)', in *Jesus and the Politics of his Day* [ed. E. Bammel and C.F.D. Moule; Cambridge: Cambridge University Press, 1984], pp. 241-48). But on the question, Is it lawful or not?—not a word. Not in a commentary, at any rate, but in a recent journal article, I do find an attempt to locate a biblical text that addresses the issue: David T. Owen-Ball, 'Rabbinic Rhetoric and the Tribute Passage (Mt. 22:15-22; Mk 12:13-17; Lk. 20:20-26)', *Novum Testamentum* 35 (1993), pp. 1-14, adduces Deut. 8.17-19 as 'Moses' warning against the use of one's wealth to serve other gods'. Quite apart from the fact that the divinity of the Roman emperor does not seem to be the issue in the tribute texts (and that Tiberius in any case declined divine honours), there is no connection in the Deuteronomy passage between wealth and serving other gods that I can see; so the alleged prooftext falls to the ground.

31. Ernst Lohmeyer, *Das Evangelium des Markus, übersetzt und erklärt* (Kritisch-exegetischer Kommentar über das Neue Testament, I/2; Göttingen: Vandenhoeck & Ruprecht, 17th edn, 1967), p. 252.

When a binary opposition is set up, and especially when it is a long-established distinction that has been inherited from the past, it is very difficult to ignore it, to challenge the terms of the debate. Jesus' opponents are looking for a yes/no answer, in the terms they have chosen (perhaps, to be fair, that have been chosen for them). Jesus offers them a both–and answer, and in so doing both accepts and negates the terms of the oppositional pair. He accepts the conceptualization God/Caesar, but he denies that the two terms are in opposition. It is *right* to pay taxes to Caesar and it is *right* to pay taxes to God. Paying tax to Caesar is not in opposition to the divine rule; giving God the things that are God's robs Caesar of nothing.

I do not know if other people would be happy to call a dislocation of a binary opposition such as this a deconstruction. But if a deconstruction is a 'teasing out of warring forces of signification within the text'[32] then that seems a good enough description of what Jesus is doing with the text of his opponents' questions. He is not doing a lot of 'teasing out' in patient philosophical mode, of course, for the Gospel narratives use the language of drama and rhetoric and debate; but the warring forces of signification are certainly his goal. With his 'both–and', he makes the lion to lie down with the lamb, even though, as the quip has it, the lamb will have an uncomfortable night of it.

His deconstruction of the (unspoken) terms of the binary opposition reduces his interlocutors to silence (Lk. 20.26); they walk away and abandon the conversation (Mt. 22.22). That is quintessentially the outcome of a deconstruction, for the rug is pulled from under your feet when the structure of your thought has been sabotaged (or even just problematized!); there is nothing more to say, and you might as well leave the room. There is an amazement too, if your arguments meet, not with a point-by-point refutation or even a global resistance, but with a riposte that, in a trice, changes the rules of debate. It is very interesting, and not at all surprising, that each of the Gospels concludes the pericope on the note of the *amazement* of Jesus' opponents.[33]

But, as I said, Jesus' own deconstruction is itself open to deconstruction. Though he has displaced the presenting opposition (lawful/unlawful),

32. Barbara Johnson, *The Critical Difference* (Baltimore: Johns Hopkins University Press, 1980); quoted by her in *Literary Theory Today* (ed. Peter Collier and Helga Geyer-Ryan; Cambridge: Polity Press, 1990), p. 18.

33. Commentators frequently remark on this testimonial to Jesus' cleverness, but not, of course, to his deconstructionism.

and then dislocated the resulting binary pair (God/Caesar) by rearranging their relationship from either/or to both–and, he still operates with a binary pair. And that in itself provokes deconstructionist suspicions.

Let us put those suspicions in the terms of the text. If Jesus' audience should render to Caesar what is Caesar's and to God what is God's, then they have divided the world into two spheres. What belongs to Caesar does not belong to God; what is God's is not Caesar's.[34] That seems to make everything clear and straightforward. But what if Caesar belongs to God? What indeed? For if one of the elements in a binary opposition can be shown to be in some sense included in the other, the opposition is thereby deconstructed.

Does Caesar belong to God? We could try answering that from first principles, which would make it pretty obvious that Caesar as a human being is as much a creature of God as anyone. Or we could answer it intertextually, by citing a text like Ps. 24.1, 'The earth is the LORD's and the fulness thereof, the world and those who dwell therein'—a text that would be familiar to all the characters in the Gospel narrative. Or we could try answering it from the narrative itself and its implicatures. If Caesar's image on the coin is the proof of his ownership of it, what is the proof of God's ownership? Is it the 'image of God' stamped upon humanity?[35] Then is Caesar made in the image of God, or is he not? If he is, he is God's.

34. The commentators fall over backwards to avoid this conclusion. Vincent Taylor, for instance, says that Jesus' reply 'does not mean that the worlds of politics and religion are separate spheres' and that 'Jesus held that the claims of God are all embracing', but also that 'obligations due to the State are within the divine order' (*The Gospel according to St Mark* [London: Macmillan, 2nd edn, 1966], p. 480); but he does very much *want* Jesus to agree with Paul over the proper Christian attitude to the State, and he has a personal investment in the issue in that he believes that submitting to Caesar's authority was in fact 'justified by the peace, justice and tolerance given to the world' by the Roman Empire. Hugh Anderson writes: 'Neither in this nor in his other sayings does Jesus give any indication that he considered the secular realm to have its own separate governing principles, so there is little to commend the view that he is here drawing a rigid line of division between the political and the religious spheres' (*The Gospel of Mark* [NCB; London: Marshall, Morgan & Scott, 1976], p. 275). It is not difficult to see how what the commentator *wants* to be true about the teaching of Jesus in general obscures the evidence of the text before his eyes.

35. So McNeile, for example, suggested (*The Gospel according to St Matthew*, p. 320). Similarly Charles Homer Giblin, SJ, '"The Things of God" in the Question concerning Tribute to Caesar (Lk 20:25; Mk 12:17; Mt 22:21)', *CBQ* 33 (1971),

Whichever way we look at it, Caesar owns nothing that God does not also own; perhaps we could even say, to which God does not have better title. And once we observe that Caesar belongs to God, the conceptualization of the two spheres collapses. If Caesar belongs to God, what of Caesar's possessions? Do they not also belong to God? And if Caesar owns nothing that God does not own, does Caesar own anything?[36] How then can anyone render to Caesar what is 'his'? *Nothing* is 'his'.[37]

The binary opposition, that is to say, is very unstable. So unstable, in fact, that we may well wonder whether the character Jesus, who is a dab hand at deconstructing oppositional pairs, does not set up this opposition precisely in order to watch it falling apart in the hands the moment anyone tries to work with it. S.G.F. Brandon, in fact, thought that in this saying Jesus, who would have regarded everything as God's by right, was absolutely prohibiting the payment of taxes to Caesar.[38] I think it is more subtle than that, as befits a truly deconstructive situation. The deconstruction does not settle the matter, as if it could shift us from one state of certainty to another. Deconstruction just exposes fragility, and leaves things more open to question. In this case, the deconstructability of the oppositional pair God/Caesar leaves us, I think, with this result: if you are looking for a text to authorize the payment of taxes, this is your text; if you are looking for a text to prohibit the payment of taxes, this is your text.

pp. 510-27 (521-22); Owen-Ball, 'Rabbinic Rhetoric', p. 10. Giblin relates the 'inscription' (ἐπιγραφή) to Isa. 44.5 (where 'I am God's' is inscribed on the hand) (' "The Things of God" ', pp. 523-24), and Owen-Ball to Exod. 13.9 (where the law is a sign on the hand and a memorial between the eyes).

36. Others, too, have asked this question. For example, Owen-Ball asks, '[W]hat can be said to belong to Caesar when one's entire life belongs to God?' But he responds lamely, 'Christians ought not to respond to civil issues without considering, first and foremost, their religious duty in the matter' ('Rabbinic Rhetoric', p. 14). Cf. also Michael Bünker, ' "Gebt dem Kaiser, was des Kaisers ist!"—Aber, Was ist des Kaisers?: Überlegungen zur Perikope von der Kaisersteuer', *Kairos* 29 (1987), pp. 85-98.

37. There is another way of performing (I would say 'prestidigitating' except that my OED does not acknowledge the verb) the deconstruction. If Marx is right, that religion is to be viewed as part of the ideological superstructure of the state, then it is Caesar that owns everything that is God's. This is equally a collapse of the two spheres' conceptualization.

38. S.G.F. Brandon, *Jesus and the Zealots* (Manchester: Manchester University Press, 1967), pp. 345ff. (I owe this reference to Anderson, *The Gospel of Mark*, p. 275.)

There are yet further deconstructions to which these texts lay themselves open. The first arises from my observation that everyone commenting on this pericope seems to accept its assumption that Caesar 'owns' the coins on which his image appears. 'According to ancient ideas', says Dennis Nineham, 'coins were ultimately the private property of the ruler who issued them'.[39] I find that very difficult to believe, though I can well believe in rulers wanting to put such an idea about. If anyone were to tell me that Caesar 'owned' coins with his picture on, I would find myself wanting to say, Not if they're in *my* pocket, he doesn't! Social and commercial life in the ancient world took no account whatever of such a theory, and even the business of paying taxes was discharged by most citizens, we may believe, without a nod to a principle of ultimate ownership. The narrative deconstructs itself—which is to say, opens itself up to undermining questions—by conducting its whole discussion without a glance in the direction of the real ownership of real money, and the evident fact that Caesar has only a *claim* to taxes, not a *right of possession* of other people's money.

Next there is the language about payment. When Jesus is asked about the tribute, the question is whether it is lawful to 'give' tax to Caesar (δίδωμι, in all three Gospels). But when he replies, he speaks of 'rendering', 'repaying', 'restoring' to Caesar what is his (ἀποδίδωμι, in all three Gospels). Is Caesar, according to Jesus, not to be 'given' anything but to be paid only what he is 'owed'? That then raises the question, And what *is* he owed? Does Palestine benefit *at all* from the taxes it pays? Some commentators feel obliged to think of some benefit that accrues from the taxes, so that Caesar can somehow 'earn' his taxes. 'The obligation to pay to Caesar some of his own coinage in return for the amenities his rule provided is affirmed', says Cranfield.[40] Now, what 'amenities' could Jesus have been thinking of?, we ask. Gymnasia? Or perhaps there were no amenities and no benefits accruing

---

39. Nineham, *Saint Mark*, p. 315. Nineham picked this idea up from A.E.J. Rawlinson (cited in C. Montefiore, *Rabbinic Literature and Gospel Teachings* [Hoboken, NY: Ktav, 1970], pp. 277-78): 'According to the ancient way of thinking, the authority of a ruler was co-extensive with the circulation of his money…and coins were regarded as being ultimately the private property of the sovereign whose image they bore'.

40. C.E.B. Cranfield, *The Gospel according to Saint Mark: An Introduction and Commentary* (Cambridge: Cambridge University Press, 1959), p. 372; similarly, Taylor regards the tax as 'justified by the peace, justice and tolerance given to the world' by the Roman Empire (*St Mark*, p. 480).

to the Jewish people from the taxes they paid, and Jesus means that it is simply and intrinsically 'just to demand payment from subject states as a general principle'[41]—as Leaney puts it; that is, emperors are 'owed' taxes because they are emperors. I would be surprised if Jesus held that as a general principle, and even more surprised if he thought it was 'just' that the Jewish people should be subject to the Romans. Now, if the text says that Caesar should be paid what he is owed, but gives no hint about whether he is, in fact, owed anything, the text faces two ways, undermining the confidence it projects.

Finally (for now), there is the problem that the text authorizes too much. If the reason why tribute should be paid to Caesar is because the coins have his image on them, why stop at the tribute? If every coin 'belongs' to Caesar, had they not all better be handed back to him forthwith? If I may keep one coin with Caesar's head on it in my pocket, why should I turn another, identical, coin over to him as his right? It begins to seem as if having Caesar's image and inscription on the coin has nothing whatever to do with the question of whether one should pay taxes—except in a suggestive, associative, symbolic, perhaps whimsical, satiric, even bitter, exasperated, hostile kind of way. A text that professes to give a reason for paying taxes but does not deliver on its promise is a deconstructive text. Perhaps texts in general are constitutionally incapable of delivering on their promises, and that is why deconstructibility is a feature of textuality in general, and not just of some texts. But all I wanted to argue at the moment was that this particular text is deconstructible in these particular ways, and that there is something specially interesting about ethical texts that deconstruct themselves.

This is, of course, a text that is 'about' far more than the payment of taxes. It is a rich ethical text, of almost infinite range. But it is an amazingly unstable text, which does not offer clear moral guidance. Its deconstructibility disenables it for incorporation into an ethical system; it will not serve as an ethical principle, not unless you are willing to entertain principles that face two ways, principles that lie down and roll over at a word, Möbius strips of principles, in which the outside is always already the inside ...

Where deconstruction touches upon ethics, I am concluding, it serves to render venerable verities shaky, to preclude systems, and to muddy

41. A.R.C. Leaney, *A Commentary on The Gospel according to St Luke* (BNTC; London: A. & C. Black, 1958), p. 252.

the waters. But at the same time, the problematization of ethical foundations does not imply the abandonment of them; rather, in making ethics more of a problem, it makes it more of a problem *for you and me*— which is to say, it tends to locate ethics in praxis, to remove it from the realm of ideas to the realm of lived experience, to make it the product of the human subject, to disaggregate it from the commonality, to foreground personal responsibility.

2. *The Ethics of Deconstruction*

It is so commonly alleged against deconstruction that it is itself unethical, or at least not interested in ethics, that a paper on ethics and deconstruction should perhaps address that question directly. I will review, in turn, some of the allegations that have been made against deconstruction on this issue, and some of the responses made by deconstructionists, and will conclude with four theses of my own which will (I hope) eventually tie the second half of this paper in with the first.

a. *Allegations*
I collect here a number of allegations against deconstruction on the ethical front:
   1. It is said that deconstruction is nihilistic, in that it

   removes all grounds of certainty or authority in literary interpretation...
   assert[ing] that the reader, teacher or critic is free to make the text anything
   he wants it to mean. [T]his is immoral because it annihilates the traditional
   use of the great texts of our culture from Homer and the Bible on down as
   the foundation and embodiment, the means of preserving and transmitting,
   the basic humanistic values of our culture.[42]

   2. It is dehumanizing, in that it does not treat the text as a human document. It proclaims the death of the author, and it abandons the idea of reading as an engagement of a human reader with a human author in favour of the 'text-as-such'. It 'denies access to the inexhaustible variety

---

42. J. Hillis Miller, *The Ethics of Reading: Kant, de Man, Eliot, Trollope, James, and Benjamin* (New York: Columbia University Press, 1987), p. 9 (this is, of course, not Hillis Miller's own view). See in this connection also, Walter Jackson Bate, 'The Crisis in English Studies', *Harvard Magazine* 85/12 (1982), pp. 46-53; Réne Wellek, 'Destroying Literary Studies', *The New Criterion* (December, 1983), pp. 1-8; E.D. Hirsch, *Aims of Interpretation* (Chicago: University of Chicago Press, 1976), pp. 11-13, 146-58.

of literature as a determinably meaningful text by, for, and about human beings'.[43]

3. It fails to acknowledge the difference between right and wrong, between reason and unreason,[44] being 'hostile to the very principles of Western thought'.[45]

4. It is particularly hostile to religious ideas and people.

> The radical indeterminacy of deconstructive criticism, which denies to any text a fixed and stable meaning, is scarcely compatible with the ways religious communities use their scriptures as a norm…Whether this style will flourish in biblical interpretation, or help unite and build up a religious community, is doubtful. Christian theology has certain metaphysical commitments which cannot easily be reconciled with these latest intellectual fashions.[46]

5. Deconstruction is atheistical, 'virulently anti-Christian, with its assault on the Logos-idea and its insistence that there is a great gulf fixed between language and reality'.[47] There is 'nihilism and skepticism behind most deconstructionism'.[48]

6. It offers no hope. Its vision of life is

> critically astute but morally impoverished. Metaphysics, epistemology, and ethics [are] dead topics, and philosophy and literature…nothing more than conversations to be carried on within the rotting corpse of Western belief…[T]he bad news is that there is no good news, and the good news

43. M.H. Abrams, 'How to Do Things with Texts', *Partisan Review* 44 (1979), pp. 566-88; cf. his *Doing Things with Texts: Essays in Criticism and Critical Theory* (ed. Michael Fisher; New York: Norton, 1991), p. 332; and 'The Deconstructive Angel', *Critical Inquiry* 3/3 (Spring, 1977), pp. 425-88 (= *Modern Criticism and Theory: A Reader* [ed. David Lodge; London: Longman, 1988], pp. 265-76).

44. Réne Wellek, *The Attack on Literature and Other Essays* (Brighton: Harvester, 1981), p. 99, speaking of the 'new apocalyptic irrationalism'.

45. *Newsweek* (15 February, 1988), cited by Johnson, 'The Surprise of Otherness: A Note on the Wartime Writings of Paul de Man', in *Literary Theory Today* (ed. Peter Collier and Helga Geyer-Ryan; Cambridge: Polity Press, 1990), pp. 13-22 (18).

46. Robert Morgan with John Barton, *Biblical Interpretation* (Oxford: Oxford University Press, 1988), pp. 256-57.

47. D.S. Greenwood, 'Poststructuralism and Biblical Studies: Frank Kermode's, *The Genesis of Secrecy*', in *Gospel Perspectives. III. Studies in Midrash and Historiography* (ed. R.T. France and David Wenham; Sheffield: JSOT Press, 1983), pp. 263-88 (278).

48. William S. Kurz, 'Narrative Approaches to Luke–Acts', *Bib* 68 (1987), pp. 195-220 (196).

is, surprisingly, that there has never been any good news. So we are liberated by knowing that we have no right to lament the loss of something we never had.[49]

7. The lives of certain prominent deconstructionists have called into question the moral value of deconstruction:

Moral questions have arisen because of widely publicized scandals involving the political affairs of post-modern philosopher Martin Heidegger and deconstructionist Paul de Man, both of whom have been linked to pro-Nazi, anti-Jewish, anti-humanist fascism. Their political involvements before and during the Second World War have raised serious moral questions not only about themselves but also about the political implications of their postmodern philosophies.[50]

8. As a philosophical enterprise, its guiding principles leave no room for ethics or at least call ethics very seriously into question:

The relationship between deconstruction and ethics is necessarily uneasy... Humanistic values...are grounded in what Derrida calls the framework of logocentric metaphysics, which deconstruction insistently calls into question...Deconstruction points to the inherent instability in the very idea of 'ethics'.[51]

9. Deconstruction is often represented as play, and play is not serious, so deconstruction is not ethical. In his famous 1966 paper, which introduced the United States to his deconstructionism, Derrida opposed to the 'saddened, *negative*, nostalgic, guilty, Rousseauistic' way of thinking a Nietzschean way that is

the joyous affirmation of the play of the world and of the innocence of becoming, the affirmation of a world of signs without fault, without truth, and without origin which is offered to an active interpretation. *This affirmation then determines the noncenter otherwise than as loss of the center.* And it plays without security.[52]

49. Roger Lundin, 'Deconstructive Therapy', *The Reformed Journal* 36 (1986), pp. 15-20 (15).

50. Lloyd Steffen, 'A Postmodern Ethic? The Case of Deconstruction', *Religious Humanism* 27 (1993), pp. 3-10 (6). On the de Man affair, see Barbara Johnson, 'A Note on the Wartime Writings of Paul de Man', preface to the paperback edition of *A World of Difference* (Baltimore: Johns Hopkins University Press, 1989 [1987]), pp. xi-xviii (= Collier and Ryan [eds.], *Literary Theory Today*, pp. 13-22).

51. Lisa D. Campolo, 'Derrida and Heidegger: The Critique of Technology and the Call to Care', *JAAR* 53 (1985), pp. 431-48 (431).

52. Jacques Derrida, *Writing and Difference* (trans. Alan Bass; Chicago:

10. Deconstructive critics are dishonest: they claim that all language is indeterminate, but the moment they speak they expect to be heard as having determinate things to say.[53]

11. There are no references to ethics in the indexes of standard books on deconstruction.[54]

b. *Responses*

To these charges of an unethical orientation of deconstructionism there have of course been several responses.

1. The first is the move of J. Hillis Miller, who wants to claim that deconstruction is 'nothing more or less than good reading as such'.[55] Good reading attends to the ethics of reading. And the ethics of reading is not a matter of discovering the ethical principles embodied in texts; rather, the ethical moment in reading is the ethical conviction one feels compelled to while reading, an ethical conviction that manifests itself in action, whether social or political.[56]

With the beginning of this argument I am in agreement. My difficulty with Hillis Miller's position as a whole is that I am not sure that I know what it is, since he does not write very well. For example,

> It is not because stories contain the thematic dramatization of ethical situations, choices, and judgments that they are especially appropriate for my topic [the ethics of reading], but for a reverse reason, that is, because ethics itself has a peculiar relation to that form of language we call narrative. The thematic dramatizations of ethical topics in narratives are the oblique allegorization of this linguistic necessity.

University of Chicago Press, 1978), p. 292 (= 'Structure, Sign and Play in the Discourse of the Human Sciences', in Lodge [ed.], *Modern Criticism and Theory: A Reader*, pp. 108-23 [121]).

53. Thus M.H. Abrams about J. Hillis Miller, in his 'The Deconstructive Angel', pp. 425-88 (= Lodge [ed.], *Modern Criticism and Theory: A Reader*, p. 274).

54. For example, Christopher Butler, *Interpretation, Deconstruction and Ideology: An Introduction to Some Current Issues in Literary Theory* (Oxford: Clarendon Press, 1984); Jonathan Culler, *On Deconstruction: Theory and Criticism after Structuralism* (London: Routledge & Kegan Paul, 1983); Art Berman, *From the New Criticism to Deconstruction: The Reception of Structuralism and Post-Structuralism* (Urbana: University of Illinois Press, 1988).

55. Miller, *The Ethics of Reading*, p. 10.

56. Miller, *The Ethics of Reading*, pp. 1-11 (ch. 1: 'Reading Doing Reading').

I feel sure it must be possible to make the point more lucidly without losing any of the subtlety; I also feel sure that if I cannot understand something after I have read it five times the fault is probably not mine.

2. The second is the move of Gary Phillips.[57] He argues that

> deconstructive reading calls for a certain kind of critical accountability on the part of readers to the Bible and enables a critical, destabilizing intervention within dominant critical practices, disciplines, interpretative traditions and institutions.[58]

He calls deconstruction's contribution to ethics an 'invigorating' of the ethical question by searching for 'subtler understanding of the ways texts refer, represent and bring about a different opening onto the world', but, above all, by demanding a 'hands-on, face-to-face encounter with the text' that stands as *other* to readers and their interests. Deconstructive reading does not allow us to keep a safe distance from the text,[59] but rather requires us to 'take responsibility for the text' by 'marking' the text with our own interventions, thus confusing the conventional boundary between author and reader. Deconstruction, as an engagement that is both affirming and analytic, is a response to 'the Other that lies beyond the Bible'; and the Other, which is the goal of deconstruction, is the name for that which 'escapes human control, grounding or anticipation'. The deconstructive process lays an ethical obligation upon readers to respond to the Other.

> By underscoring the radical 'otherness' of the Bible—marked in various ways by alternative meanings, readers, interpretative traditions, communities, practices, and so on—deconstruction works prophetically for a different kind of reading and writing *position* in the world. It does so by embracing the twin ethical aim characterized as a *responsibility to otherness* and a *responsibility to act*.[60]

---

57. Gary A. Phillips, 'The Ethics of Reading Deconstructively, or Speaking Face-to Face: The Samaritan Woman Meets Derrida at the Well', in E.S. Malbon and E.V. McKnight (eds.), *The New Literary Criticism and the New Testament* (JSNTSup, 109; Sheffield: JSOT Press, 1994), pp. 283-325.

58. Phillips, 'The Ethics of Reading Deconstructively', pp. 283-84.

59. Cf. Derrida's sentence that to read deconstructively you must be '"formed", "trained", instructed, constructed, even engendered, let's say *invented* by the work' (in Derek Attridge and Jacques Derrida [eds.], *Acts of Literature* [New York: Routledge & Kegan Paul, 1992], p. 74).

60. Phillips, 'The Ethics of Reading Deconstructively', p. 315.

I share Phillips's opinion that deconstruction 'invigorates' ethical questions (though not 'the ethical question'). But the difficulties I have with his approach are two: I do not care for his hypostatization of the Other, especially when it attains the status of capitalization.[61] No doubt there is plenty that escapes human control, plenty of diversity witnessed to by alternative meanings and interpretative traditions, but I can believe in nothing (= not a Thing) that can be denominated Otherness or the Other. The other difficulty I find in Phillips is in knowing whether the Bible is supposed to be *different* from other texts in this regard. Is the 'Other than lies beyond the Bible', the 'radical "otherness" of the Bible', the same sort of other or otherness that lies beyond all texts? And is the 'prophetic' work of deconstruction special to deconstructive reading of biblical texts, or is deconstruction 'prophetic' everywhere it casts its beady eye? I am nervous, in other words, that a religious agenda has slipped in under the covers.

3. A third approach is that made by Peter Kemp, who advocates a 'poetics of commitment' as a fix for the absence of an ethical dimension in the work of deconstructionists like Derrida. An ethic consistent with deconstruction would adopt a 'nevertheless' position: *despite* the deconstructive enterprise, we should never give up hope, even in the face of suffering and evil, he says.[62] A commitment to ethical values does not imply a knowledge of any universal truth; it is a way of living with the deconstruction of 'all forms of object cultivation'.[63] Although there seems to be no real space for ethics in philosophical deconstructionism—in that deconstruction, according to Derrida, operates on a pre-ethical plane—one could argue that that very affirmation implies an ethical justification of its own (why should we give priority to thought over action, regarding thought as 'pre-ethical'?). Furthermore, it could be suggested that Derrida himself, in foregrounding death as an issue in philosophy, implicitly invokes ethical questions. For him, the concept of 'presence'—which he categorizes as the hallmark of Western philosophy—rests on a suppression of the reality of death;[64] and he, of

---

61. Like Caputo, I do not find myself at home 'in the land where there are all and only Capitals, in the world where German nouns come true' (John D. Caputo, *Against Ethics: Contributions to a Poetics of Obligation with Constant Reference to Deconstruction* [Bloomington: Indiana University Press, 1993], p. 33).

62. Peter Kemp, 'Death and Gift', *JAAR* 50 (1982), pp. 459-71 (470).

63. Kemp, 'Death and Gift', p. 469.

64. 'The relationship with *my death* (my disappearance in general) lurks in this

course, wants to reinscribe death in the philosophical vocabulary, making Freud's death principle the fundamental principle for understanding life. Is he not in so doing making space for ethics within his philosophy of deconstruction?

4. In response to Peter Kemp, Lisa Campolo argues that the absence of ethics he perceives in Derrida's work is just the kind of 'lack' that deconstruction adopts as its target, just the kind of 'alienated longing for full presence' that Derrida would call into question.[65] Rather, deconstruction, at least in the person of Derrida, suspends and problematizes the traditional meanings of the terms 'ethical' and 'nihilistic'. Derrida has no intention to disregard or destroy humanistic values just because he wants to interrogate them. He believes we have a responsibility to the principles of reason and truth, and he affirms the hope of a new enlightenment.[66] This is not a positive ethical programme, but it is not hostile to ethics nor indifferent to it. In putting ethical signs *sous rature*, under the marks of erasure, Derrida both effaces them and leaves them visible[67]—and that is perhaps the best we can do these days with ethical signs.

5. Mark C. Taylor has spoken of an 'ethic of resistance' as the ethical stance of deconstruction.[68] What deconstruction entails is an insistence on the alterity that stands opposed to and resistant to structures. It is

> a way of coming to terms with the impossibility of liberation. The kingdom never arrives, there is no salvation; there never was wholeness, there never will be wholeness. The problem becomes, how does one linger with the wound, how does one linger with the negative without negating it? How does one carry on when there's no hope of overcoming in any kind of final way?[69]

That is to say, if I understand him correctly, that the ethical position the deconstructive enterprise engenders is that in ethics, as in theology and

determination of being as presence' (Jacques Derrida, *Speech and Phenomena and Other Essays on Husserl's Theory of Signs* [trans. David B. Allison; Evanston: Northwestern University Press, 1973], p. 56).

65. Campolo, 'Derrida and Heidegger', p. 432.

66. Campolo, 'Derrida and Heidegger', p. 446.

67. Jacques Derrida, *Of Grammatology* (trans. Gayatri Chakravorty Spivak; Baltimore: Johns Hopkins University Press, 1976), p. 23: 'That mark of deletion is not...a "merely negative symbol"...Under its strokes the presence of a transcendental signified is effaced while still remaining legible.'

68. As reported by Lloyd Steffen, 'A Postmodern Ethic?', pp. 3-10.

69. Steffen, 'A Postmodern Ethic?', pp. 8-9.

philosophy, the traditional fixed points of reference themselves become the objects of scrutiny rather than the guideposts to further ethical decisions.

c. *My Reflections*

Here are my own responses to, Is there an ethics of deconstruction?

1. If texts are indeed capable of deconstruction, and if, for example, the oppositions on which they rely are open to question, then I want to know about that—and I think that wanting to know is not just idle intellectual curiosity, but a kind of ethical courage, like wanting to know the worst from my doctor. I cannot bear to be kept in the dark about something that is the case, and I think it my duty to let other people in on secrets—especially secrets that important people would like to stay secret.

I do not particularly wish to prejudge whether such and such a text is deconstructible, or deconstructible in such and such a way; but if I have convinced myself that it is, then that is the way it is—for me. And I cannot imagine that pretending that that is not the case can be an ethical way of being.

I also observe that once I have seen how a text can be deconstructed, I find it very hard to forget the deconstruction. The deconstruction seems to be less something that one has done to the text than something the text has done to itself. The deconstruction is then an aspect of the text, something that one knows about the text, as one knows about its language and its rhetoric and its context and so on. Once I have noticed, for example, that the care of the shepherd for the sheep in Psalm 23 extends right up to the point where the sheep enters the 'house of the Lord'—and we all know what happens to sheep when they go to the house of the Lord—I have a new outlook on the image of the 'shepherd' which cannot be wished away.[70] If any of that is right, it is ethically *wrong* to ignore it.

I do not count it an especial intellectual virtue to demonstrate the deconstructibility of a certain text, and I should like to believe that there are often more interesting and more important things to say about texts than that they are deconstructible. But if it can be shown successfully to a reasonable number of people that a text deconstructs itself, that is for

---

70. I have considered some other ramifications of this deconstruction in my paper, 'Varieties of Indeterminacy', in R.C. Culley and R.B. Robinson (eds.), *Textual Indeterminacy, Part Two* (= *Semeia* 63 [1995]).

me a *fact* (by which I mean a mutually agreed perception), and I think of it as an ethical duty not to ignore facts. (Of course, if it is *your* fact and not mine, then it is not a fact *for me*, so I have no compunction about resisting and ignoring.)

2. What I find deconstruction does in the realm of ethics is to problematize traditional categories and distinctions. And what such problematization does is to weaken the authority of traditional ethics. And what such weakening does is to turn more ethical issues over to the decision of individuals. And what the taking charge of one's own ethical decisions does is to make one more of an ethical person.[71]

I would not want to say that to obey a law because it is a law cannot be an ethical act. But I do know that obeying a law can sometimes be an immoral thing to do, and sometimes it can be a way of avoiding an ethical decision of one's own. Being responsible for my own ethical decisions does not necessarily make me a better person, but it does make me more aware of ethical matters, and it does compel me to invest myself in ethical questions. The less I can rely on traditional decisions about ethical questions the more effort I have to spend on making my own. I argue therefore that deconstruction promotes ethical enquiry and ethical responsibility.

Of course, as I have observed before, to deconstruct a set of categories does not abolish those categories. Just because the distinction between right and wrong, between slave and free, between killing and executing, is hazier than people have thought, it does not mean that there is nothing 'in' those distinctions. Not necessarily. Whether I will go on operating with a set of traditional categories for the most part, or whether I will feel compelled to abandon them forthwith so soon as I have seen how grossly they deconstruct each other, is a matter that I will have to decide in each case on its own merits.

3. Deconstruction is the deconstruction of something. Without categories, oppositions or assertions there can be no deconstruction. Deconstruction is parasitic on traditional structures. It is not the same as making things up from scratch, and it is certainly not the same as working things out from first principles.

Deconstruction, in other words, starts from the way things are. It respects the historical formulation of ideas in systems of thought and in texts, and it honours the staying power of ancient and universal sets of

---

71. I am much taken by the argument of John D. Caputo, *Against Ethics*, who replaces the systemic term 'ethics' with the personal term 'obligation'.

ideas. It works with traditions, and even if its results are radical, its starting point is the given.[72]

In the realm of ethics, deconstruction pays tribute to the force of traditional ethics, and functions primarily to decentre ethics rather than to abolish it. That is to say, I see deconstruction as re-centring ethics around ourselves as decision-makers (fallible, inconsistent, committed), rather than around a system that is orderly, comprehensive and coherent.

4. Deconstruction invites a style of ethics that is in change and that leads to change. As we have seen in some of the examples from biblical texts, the openness of texts to deconstruction connotes the vulnerability of ethical systems to their own formulations. Ethical systems must change, must perhaps change into something other than ethical systems, precisely because they must be expressed in deconstructible language. But since, at the same time, ethical systems are the construct of power-holders in society, societies, too, open themselves to change whenever they devise an ethical system that expresses itself in (necessarily) deconstructible language. We saw that happening in the case of the runaway slave in Deuteronomy 23 and of the shedder of blood in Genesis 9. The moment the ethic is said (written), at that moment it becomes deconstructible, at that moment an agent for ethical and social change has been released into the community.

72. As, for example, with Nietzsche's 're-evaluation of all values'.

Theological Education as a Theory-Praxis Loop: Situating the Book of Joshua in a Cultural, Social Ethical, and Theological Matrix

Norman K. Gottwald

In a lecture some years ago, I proposed that 'it is the theological task of the church to grasp the theological representations in their social sites and praxis settings throughout Israelite–Jewish–Christian history and to focus all that critically re-worked content on a self-critical praxis of the church and its leadership here and now'.[1] In context, I was arguing that the seminary curriculum should be organized so as to further that theological task. This means that the customary divisions of the curriculum should be focused on church belief and practice in the present in such a way that all the disciplinary resources, and not simply the 'practical' subjects, contribute directly to the ongoing re-formation of the church.

I want to illustrate how I try to carry out that project in biblical studies by sharing the hermeneutic I use when I am teaching the Book of Joshua. There are several strategic moves involved. Since the point of this paper is to show a hermeneutical process rather than to substantiate particular judgments within the disciplines, what I propose is a kind of mapping of the inquiry that draws the disciplines together in the larger theological task.

The Cultural Matrix

The first task is to analyze the Book of Joshua according to appropriate critical methodologies in order to determine how its literary structure and theological claims functioned within the culture where it arose. Synthetic judgments about the cultural location and function of this

---

1. *The Hebrew Bible in its Social World and in ours* (Atlanta: Scholars Press, 1993), p. 247.

material are essential both for a coherent understanding of Joshua and for an assessment of its canonical authority.

In my analysis of the book I recognize a Deuteronomistic hand at work in shaping its component parts into one segment in the sequence of books from Deuteronomy through Kings. I understand this Deuteronomistic composition to be straddling late monarchic and exilic times. I perceive its cultural function as an attempt to explain the movement of Israel from its tribal beginnings through its monarchic experience and on into its colonial era. I accept the view that the book serves both an attempt at a reconstitution of monarchy and cult in the time of Josiah and an attempt to lay the groundwork for continuing Israelite life under colonial conditions. I further believe that in Joshua and Judges the Deuteronomist is drawing on older material broadly reflective of the conditions—although hardly the precise circumstances—of Israel's tribal beginnings, especially in their social and political contours. Within the book of Joshua as it stands, the overarching and controlling perspective on the tribal period is that of a threatened Judahite monarchy and cult which try to reform themselves but which fail to do so sufficiently to prevent their eventual collapse. The cultural problematic of the Deuteronomists is to clarify why the monarchy and cult failed and to suggest tentatively what might be salvaged from their ruins.

This means that the older materials displaying a tribal horizon are set in a frame with the following pre-understandings:

1. that inter-tribal Israel was in effect the polity of Israel/Judah in embryo, already a people unified in principle if not always in practice, and possessing sovereign territorial claims;
2. that the principled unity of inter-tribal Israel derived from its adherence to the deity Yahweh and, correspondingly, its frequent failures to embody this unity in practice stemmed from its periodic abandonment of Yahweh.

It is, in short, a pronouncedly monarchic political and monistic religious reading of tribal Israel. We see many signs that this reading is simplistically anachronistic, both in terms of the tensions and contradictions between the Deuteronomist framework and the filler traditions, and in terms of what we can ascertain from other biblical traditions; from archaeology and extrabiblical texts, and from comparative sociology and anthropology.

The Deuteronomistic pre-understanding implicit in Joshua is simplistic because an association of tribes is not an undeveloped or shadow version of monarchy. It has its own character, constituted and held together in a far looser and more consensual manner than a state polity. Likewise, the Deuteronomistic pre-understanding is simplistic because Israel's religion in the tribal period was not a slightly less developed form of the Yahwism of monarchic or colonial times. It had its own character; it was not an all-prevailing or monolithic entity in tribal times. The cult of Yahweh that eventually took center stage in Israel struggled with other cults, both in direct competition for adherents and in creative borrowing and transformation of elements of belief and practice. Consequently, just as the peoplehood of Israel was in the making in tribal times, so too was its religion in the making.

Furthermore, because the transition from monarchy to colonial status was such a wrenching experience for Israel, its sense of peoplehood and its religious identity underwent wrenching changes that require us to make as clear a demarcation between monarchic and colonial times as we make between monarchic and tribal times.

The result of these observations is that we must ask about the cultural function of the Joshua traditions in each of the major sociocultural horizons: the tribal, the monarchic and the colonial. How, then, we may ask, did these evolving Joshua traditions function in the three horizons?

Within the tribal horizon, the Joshua traditions tell us something about how an agrarian highland people managed to take root in the Canaanite highlands in the 12th and 11th centuries. Monarchic and colonial perspectives aside, they reflect a struggle of these highland peoples to secure a living space in the material, social and ideological dimensions of their corporate life. One aspect of this struggle was military—largely if not entirely of a defensive nature—against hostile city-states and emerging monarchies in their environs. A second aspect of this struggle was coalition building among various highlanders who were more or less a part of an emerging alliance of peoples who formed a precarious peace group attempting to develop economic, social, juridical and religious mechanisms to insure their viability in an inhospitable natural and sociopolitical environment. The cult of Yahweh appears to have been one of the energizing, legitimating and organizing means for these people to cooperate and experiment in community-building. Evidently, both the social movement and the Yahweh cult of early Israel arose interactively.

In that tribal horizon, the *claim to land*, stated positively, was a claim to use-rights of households and groupings of households for cultivation of the soil and for the breeding of animals. The same claim to land, stated negatively, was a denial of the right of external state polities or of internal elites to nullify or lay tribute to the use-rights of the associated households.

Accordingly, the *violence* expressed in the texts toward Canaanites and other outsiders, was not aimed, in the main, at annihilating or displacing prior populations, but was aimed rather at securing and defending the use-rights of cultivators and herders. The 'first violence' of the Canaanite and other neighboring elites was met by the 'counter-violence' of the Israelite agrarians. The plentiful references to violence within the community are of two types: instances of breach of the terms of alliance among the households, and juridically instituted or permitted violence to punish offenders against the rules of the alliance. This, of course, is a very different picture than that communicated by the monarchic and colonial forms of the evolving Book of Joshua.

Within the monarchic horizon, the constellation of the Joshua traditions tells us about the origins of the states of Israel and Judah viewed as a hierarchic polity in nuce, unified in principle, lacking only the single step of providing a king. At the same time, this polity is seen as devoted to Yahweh in principle, but not yet centralized and purified at Jerusalem, as it would be when the monarchy functioned as it should—and as the Deuteronomists believe it did, if only briefly under Josiah. Thus, Joshua is, in effect, the embryonic king, prototype of Josiah who is to come.

In that monarchic horizon, the *claim to land*, stated positively, was the right of Israel to mark off territory, over which its kings would have sovereignty so that its populace would owe allegiance and tribute to the monarch ruling in the line of David. The long apostasy of the northern Israelites would be ended by the reconstitution of the united kingdom under Josiah accompanied by the sole worship of Yahweh at Jerusalem. This same claim to land, stated negatively, denied the right of other state polities to encroach upon the territory of Israel or to lay its people under tribute.

Accordingly, the *violence* expressed toward the Canaanites is aimed at those viewed as the original possessors of the land who, according to notions of state aggrandizement, were properly annihilated or expelled from the territory that was to come under control of the Israelite monarchy. The plentifully attested violence within Israel was viewed as a defection from the pure cult of Yahweh as it was restored at Jerusalem by Josiah, and as represented in the Book of Joshua by fidelity or infidelity to the commands of Joshua—who functions as stand-in for the faithful king Josiah.

It is apparent from Deuteronomy and Kings that the Deuteronomists regarded impure religious practices and their adherents as virulent threats in Josiah's Judah, and in the corrupt Yahwistic worship in northern Israel. Thus, within the monarchic horizon, the Canaanites in Joshua serve a double role: they are, on the one hand, the original inhabitants who should have been totally annihilated but were not, and they are, on the other hand, surviving peoples within Israel who, while appearing to be Israelites, are apostates who deserve to be extirpated. Thus, some of the violence in Israel is seen as the deserved punishment meted out to these offenders against the pure cult of Yahweh.

We do not know, of course, how rigorously this mandated program of wiping out all Canaanite remnants was pursued under Josiah. Nevertheless, this is the conceptual picture of the monarchic book of Joshua. It is likewise the dominant understanding communicated with canonical authority to later Jews and Christians. While harsh and repugnant to moral sensibilities, it does present a plausible logic for those of us who do our interpreting as citizens of state polities that to this day operate with much the same rationale of territorial sovereignty and obedience to the state.

Within the colonial horizon, the Joshua traditions retain most of the content and aura of their monarchic ideology, but with altered nuances in their function. In particular, they serve as a narrative charter of the right of the restored Judahite community to determine who is a member on the basis of descent from the original Israelites faithful to Joshua. Nevertheless, important differences derive from the lapse of Israelite political independence and the emergence of religious identity that was able, over time, to adapt to diverse forms of communal life and polity.

One of these alterations of perspective is the ambivalence with which monarchy is viewed in the sweep of the Deuteronomistic History, such that we are left wondering at the close of the work whether the final redaction envisions a restoration of kingship. In any case, it seems to be preparing the cultural and religious ground for a continuing Israelite identity that can survive without monarchy, in part out of sheer necessity and in part out of the grim record of so many kings who failed in their religious duties.

Another alteration of perspective appears in the status of the *claim to land*. The restored Jewish community has no entitlement to exercise full political autonomy, to assert unqualified sovereignty over territory, and to exact tribute without interference from other powers. Israel no longer has its former power to annihilate or expel Canaanites from its midst, either those clearly non-Israelite or those who claim to be Israelites but believe and practice like Canaanites according to strict Yahwistic standards.

As a consequence, the *violence* of the book of Joshua inclines toward abstraction because its realization as a total program is impossible under the conditions of the Judahite restoration. Paradoxically, the mandated violence of Joshua grows more intensely religious as its political effectuality diminishes. The violence of Joshua enters into communal practice as a historic remembrance of the urgency to protect the integrity of the community by setting clear boundaries of membership and behavior. The violence of Joshua enters into the communal consciousness as a cipher expressing the ultimacy of religious claims that are, so to speak, 'worth killing for'.

What we see, I believe, in this trajectory of the Joshua traditions is a movement from violence as the defense of living space to violence as an instrument of the state, to violence as a way to insure religious purity and as a symbolic expression of the ultimacy of religious claims, pointing with lurid imagination to an ever-present threat of divine violence hanging over the Israelite community and over all peoples who interact with Israel.

The Social Ethical Matrix

With this cultural placement of the Joshua traditions in mind, we enter the social ethical matrix which entails several dimensions. One dimension is to ask what social ethical criteria are exhibited in the book of Joshua. A second dimension is to examine how the book of Joshua has impacted the social ethical beliefs and practices of later Jews and Christians. A third dimension is to determine what relevance or authority the book of Joshua has for social ethical belief and practice for the contemporary interpreter in an interpreting community.

This social ethical inquiry and reflection necessarily draws on the conclusions reached in the cultural inquiry and reflection. The cultural spaces of tribal, monarchic and colonial Israel shaped the social ethical discernment of their respective communities as they are expressed in the Joshua traditions. The cultural spaces occupied by various later Jewish and Christian communities shaped their ethical discernment of the Joshua traditions. The cultural spaces we as interpreters occupy shape *our* ethical discernment of the Joshua traditions.

It makes a difference whether we are tracing and evaluating the ethical claims of a peasant populace trying to secure its livelihood, or of a state trying to strengthen its authority and power, or of an ethnic enclave trying to maintain its identity and cohesion. And it makes a difference in the evaluation if we who are looking at the ethical issues do so as members of a peasant underclass, or as largely satisfied and socially integrated citizens of a state polity, or as an ethnic folk with an identity we want to preserve.

Nonetheless, in every cultural space, ethical questions insistently arise because they are constitutive of human life. Tribal, monarchic and colonial Israelites were engaged in ethical discernment as they developed and reflected on the Joshua traditions. Later Jewish and Christian communities were engaged in ethical discernment about their own lives as they read and responded to Joshua. Today, Peruvian and Haitian underclasses, North American and European governing elites, Serbian and Croatian ethnic communities are alike engaged in ethical discernment that interacts dialogically with the way they read their religious traditions, including the book of Joshua insofar as they read it at all or insofar as its claims are known to them indirectly.

These reflections bring me to two conclusions:

1. Within the social ethical matrix for evaluating Joshua we are not in the business of 'second guessing' the Israelites, or any one else for that matter. We are trying to understand their ethics in context. We are considering how like or unlike their situations were to our own or to the situations of others in our world. At bottom, the ethical crux for us has to do with what we conclude to be right and wrong on those matters which are ours to decide or concerning which we have influence. The cultural variability of all ethical reasoning, while it informs and chastens, does not relieve us of our irreducible moral responsibility.

2. Within the social ethical matrix, the ethical evaluations we make our own and take responsibility for are not derived from single texts or items in our tradition, such as the book of Joshua, but from a comprehensive construal about the meaning and value of human life in community. The biblical traditions are one source for our ethical construal, but even when considered in their entirety they are not the sole source. With specific reference to the Bible, we construe it ethically

by an intertextual reading in close dialogue with the operative ethical construal we have made of our own position in life as part of a particular community or communities.

At the level where we ask about the relevance and authority of Joshua for ethical belief and practice today, I think the crucial question is this: Understanding the social ethics of Joshua in their several contexts, do they in any way inform me about how I should understand similar ethical issues today and thus contribute to more carefully considered ethical decisions on my part? I say 'my part' to stress the personal responsibility integral to all ethics, but I should also say 'our part' since the combined interplay of individual ethical perspectives and decisions determines the ethical shape of the community in which I am but one moral agent.

Notice that, in this social ethical matrix, I have not put the stress on reaching particular ethical conclusions about Joshua but rather on the process involved in reaching any ethical assessment, whatever it might be. In classroom contexts, some version of these considerations will open up space in which the issues can be discussed and more self-aware ethical reflection on the Bible can be nurtured.

The Theological Matrix

In my judgment, all that I have said about the social ethical matrix applies as well to theological considerations; but there are some special twists in theological reflection. Let us examine the classic question about the book of Joshua that probably everyone who attempts to teach the book has heard more than once: Did God *really* tell the Israelites to kill all the Canaanites?

On one level, this question can be answered but it has to be answered in terms of the Israelite cultural spaces we examined earlier. This way of answering the question actually addresses a prior question which must be grappled with before the original question can be tackled. The prior question is this: Did the Israelites really believe that God told them to kill all the Canaanites?

In its tribal horizon, the early Israelites did not believe God was telling them to kill all Canaanites but only those who directly threatened them. In its monarchic horizon, the Deuteronomic reformers did believe that their ancestors were told to exterminate the Canaanites while recognizing that they had failed to complete the job, and thus that everyone in

Israel still exhibiting 'Canaanite' beliefs and practices should be killed. In its colonial horizon, the Deuteronomistic writer believed likewise that Joshua was commanded to kill the Canaanites and that Josiah was directed to stamp out Canaanite survivors, but the Deuteronomist concluded that even Josiah's efforts had not been adequate to outweigh all the prior apostasy in Israel's history. In the new circumstance of a totally disrupted community life, the Deuteronomist appears to have no new mandate to kill anyone.

In pressing the normative question, Did God really tell the Israelites to kill all the Canaanites?, the one asking is always uneasy about the killing, but this uneasiness may arise from a number of directions. The objections or reservations may arise from a prohibition against any killing (consistent pacifist stance), or from a prohibition against killing except in self-defense (partial pacifist stance), or from a prohibition against killing indiscriminately and/or a prohibition against taking over land from an already resident or sovereign people (just war stance), or from a prohibition against killing in the name of God (rejection of the holy war stance).

In addition, when people question whether God actually commanded the killing of the Canaanites, I think they are often also asking: If God did mandate killing the Canaanites, am I or others justified in feeling that we are entitled to kill in God's name? This leap from Joshua to the present is not always made, since there are theological routes that avoid linking Joshua's situation with ours, such as citing the exceptional circumstances of establishing the covenant community (thus making it 'a one-time' command) or believing that the love commandment and behaviour of Jesus supersede and abrogate any earlier biblical commands that contradict the revelation in Jesus Christ.

Each of the objections or reservations expressed concerning the annihilation of the Canaanites is rooted in some conception of the moral integrity of God. In particular, killing that is religiously motivated or justified seems to open the door to the legitimation of violence prompted by psychotic impulse, lust for wealth or power, revenge over historic grievances, psychosocial projections of evil onto others, or political agendas seeking diversion of attention from pressing social problems by rallying group support against a common external or internal enemy. We are familiar in our day with individuals, groups and nations that claim religious validation for their violence. In all such cases, the theological appeals must be decoded in order to find the substantive interests,

judgments, and motivations at work in the violence. In short, the theological claim must be deconstructed into ethical claims asserted within
particular cultural spaces such as I have proposed for the theologically
grounded mandates in the book of Joshua.

Conclusion

I have tried to sketch some of the theory-praxis 'loops' or 'spirals'
entailed in making cultural, ethical and theological sense out of the book
of Joshua. These are 'loops' or 'spirals' in the sense that we move
dialectically between theory and praxis in the text and theory and praxis
in our context, and the geometric metaphor for this movement is not a
straight line but a curving line that does not predictably cover the same
trajectory during each of its circuits. This 'looping' or 'spiraling' remains
ever open to new textual insight and to new contemporary experience.

This theory-praxis loop necessitates that our teaching of any academic
subject in the seminary curriculum be open to all the data and disciplines
relevant to the evaluation and appropriation of its content by the church.
To my mind, this means that we cannot wall-off the disciplines and
curricular units from one another in such a fashion that we are constantly telling students, in effect, that many of their most critical
questions about what we are studying really belong in another field.

How we are to achieve this intersection and convergence of the disciplines on the crucial issues facing the church is another matter. It
cannot be done by a mishmash of materials thrown together and taken
up in random order. It seems to me that the direction in which this process moves our curriculum planning is toward clarity about our modes
of reasoning. What are the methods of reasoning pursued in the church
and how do they relate to the methods of reasoning in our academic
disciplines? These modes of reasoning are recurrent and persistent amid
the mountains of factual details and the plethora of theoretical constructs
both in church and academy. These modes need to be the focus of what
we do in the classroom. Facts and theories will accumulate endlessly and
can never be comprehended in a single curriculum. Methods of
reasoning are less numerous and more stable throughout all the
disciplines and throughout all the issues that engage the church. It is on
these modes of reasoning that we might profitably concentrate our
attention in teaching biblical studies in a seminary context.

BIBLIOGRAPHY

Ahlström, G.W., *The History of Ancient Palestine from the Palaeolithic Period to Alexander's Conquest* (JSOTSup, 146; Sheffield: JSOT Press, 1993).

Albertz, R., *A History of Israelite Religion in the Old Testament Period*. I. *From the Beginnings to the End of the Monarchy* (Louisville: Westminster/John Knox Press, 1994).

Birch, B.C. and L.L. Rasmussen, *The Bible and Ethics in the Christian Life* (Minneapolis: Augsburg, rev. edn, 1989).

Chaney, M.L., 'Systemic Study of the Israelite Monarchy', *Semeia* 37 (1986), pp. 53-76.

Cross, F.M., *Canaanite Myth and Hebrew Epic* (Cambridge: Harvard University Press, 1973).

Davies, P.R., *In Search of 'Ancient Israel'* (JSOTSup, 148; Sheffield: JSOT Press, 1992).

Davies, P.R. (ed.), *Second Temple Studies: Persian Period* (JSOTSup, 117; Sheffield: JSOT Press, 1991).

Dearman, J.A., *Religion and Culture in Ancient Israel* (Peabody, MA: Hendrickson Publishers, 1992).

Frick, F.S., *The Formation of the State in Ancient Israel. A Survey of Models and Theories* (The Social World of Biblical Antiquity, 4; Sheffield: Almond Press, 1985).

Friedman, R.E., *The Exile and Biblical Narrative: The Formation of the Deuteronomistic and Priestly Works* (HSM, 22; Chico, CA: Scholars Press, 1981).

deGeus, C.H.J., *The Tribes of Israel: An Investigation into Some of the Presuppositions of Martin Noth's Amphictyony Hypothesis* (Amsterdam/Assen: Van Gorcum, 1976).

Gottwald, N.K., *The Hebrew Bible in its Social World and in ours* (Semeia Studies; Atlanta: Scholars Press, 1993).

—'The Interplay of Religion and Ethnicity in Ancient Israel', in M. Bradbury (ed.), *Religion, Ethnicity and Violence* (College Park, MD: University of Maryland Press, forthcoming).

—'Recent Studies of the Social World of Premonarchic Israel', *Currents in Research: Biblical Studies* 1 (1993), pp. 163-89.

—*The Tribes of Yahweh. A Sociology of the Religion of Liberated Israel, 1250–1050 BCE* (Maryknoll: Orbis Books, 2nd corrected printing, 1981).

Halbertal, M. and A. Margalit, *Idolatry* (Cambridge: Harvard University Press, 1992).

Jobling, D., 'Deconstruction and the Political Analysis of Biblical Texts: A Jamesonian Reading of Psalm 72', *Semeia* 59 (1992), pp. 95-127.

—'"Forced Labor": 1 Kings 2–10 and the Question of Literary Representation', *Semeia* 54 (1991), pp. 58-76.

Kelsey, D.H., *The Uses of Scripture in Recent Theology* (Philadelphia: Fortress Press, 1975).

Lemche, N.P., *Ancient Israel. A New History of Israelite Society* (The Biblical Seminar, 5; Sheffield: JSOT Press, 1988).

Nakanose, S., *Josiah's Passover: Sociology and the Liberating Bible* (Maryknoll, NY: Orbis Books, 1993).

Nelson, R.D., *The Double Redaction of the Deuteronomistic History* (JSOTSup, 18; Sheffield: JSOT Press, 1981).

—'Josiah in the Book of Joshua', *JBL* 100 (1981), pp. 531-40.

Noth, M., *Das Buch Josua*, Handkommentar zum Alten Testament (Tübingen: J.C.B. Mohr [Paul Siebeck], 2nd edn, 1953).

—*The Deuteronomistic History* (JSOTSup, 15; Sheffield: JSOT Press, 1981).

Ogletree, T.W., *The Use of the Bible in Christian Ethics* (Philadelphia: Fortress Press, 1983).

Schubeck, T., *Liberation Ethics, Sources, Models, and Norms* (Minneapolis: Fortress Press, 1993).

Schwager, R., *Must There Be Scapegoats? Violence and Redemption in the Bible* (San Francisco: Harper & Row, 1987).

Segundo, J.L,. *The Liberation of Theology* (Maryknoll: Orbis Books, 1976).

Smith, D.L., *The Religion of the Landless. The Social Context of the Babylonian Exile* (Bloomington, IN: Meyer–Stone Books, 1989).

Smith, M.S., *The Early History of God: Yahweh and the Other Deities of Ancient Israel* (San Francisco: Harper & Row, 1990).

Staub, E., *The Roots of Evil. The Origins of Genocide and Other Group Violence* (Cambridge: Cambridge University Press, 1989).

Stern, P.D., *The Biblical Ḥerem. A Window on Israel's Religious Experience* (Brown Judaic Studies, 211; Atlanta: Scholars Press, 1991).

DIVINE CHARACTER AND THE FORMATION OF MORAL COMMUNITY IN THE BOOK OF EXODUS

Bruce C. Birch

Throughout the Hebrew Bible, Israel is understood and presented as moral community. The term 'Israel' relates to different socio-political or institutional forms, some historical, some shaped by the canonical traditions (wilderness wanderers, tribal federation, nation, socio-cultural group, religious community). But in all of the traditions these forms reflect, Israel is the community which serves as the shaper of moral identity, the bearer of moral tradition, the locus of moral deliberation and the agent of moral action.[1]

It is also clear that the Hebrew Bible understands that Israel finds its focus as moral community in relation to its God. There are, of course, various descriptions, emphases and perspectives on this relationship, but ethics in the Hebrew Bible are theocentric. Even the wisdom tradition, with its emphasis on human capacity to seek wisdom and learn from experience, understands the source of wisdom and the order of all things to be in God.

Further, the existence of the canon itself implies that the story of Israel as moral community in relation to God is intended to play a crucial role in the shaping of subsequent generations of moral community in continuity with the biblical communities themselves. The formation and preservation of Hebrew traditions as a canon of scripture clearly shows the intention of extending the shaping influence of those traditions into the future. Since both church and synagogue continue to regard this canonical collection as scripture we can say that ancient intention was realized with some success.[2]

---

1. See Bruce C. Birch and Larry L. Rasmussen, *Bible and Ethics in the Christian Life* (Minneapolis: Augsburg, rev. and expanded edn, 1989), pp. 120-40, for a discussion of these functions in moral community.

2. It goes without saying that conceptions of the authority claimed for the canon

Thus, understanding of the *formation of Israel as moral community* is of crucial interest both to scholars concerned with the ethics of ancient Israel as presented in the canonical traditions and to the churches and synagogues who still claim Israel's story as Scripture. These latter seek to draw on that story as a resource for contemporary ethics and as a shaping influence on their own lives as moral communities.[3]

Exodus as Formative Story

It is the Exodus story that is crucial to understanding Israel's origins and formation as a distinctive community. The Book of Exodus, although composed of traditions originating in different periods of Israel's life, now stands as the definitive narrative telling of this originating and formative story. This Exodus story is drawn upon and alluded to in literature throughout the canon as testimony to its centrality—however, it is to the Book of Exodus itself that we must return to understand these Exodus motifs and allusions.

Theological and ethical readings of the Exodus story in this century have largely focused on Israel as a people called into being and shaped by the activity of God. God delivered Israel out of bondage in Egypt, overcoming the power of an oppressive Pharaoh and leading them dramatically through the midst of the sea to new life, just when all seemed lost. This divine activity continues in the leading of Israel through the dangers of the wilderness to encamp at Mt. Sinai where God initiates a covenant relationship and gives Israel the law. God has taken the initiative to act on Israel's behalf, and it is in response to what God has done that Israel comes into being as the community of God's people.

This emphasis was, of course, popularized earlier in this century by the salvation history (*Heilsgeschichte*) theologies which stressed the saving acts of God in history as the central focus of the Old Testament faith story. The Exodus story of deliverance was usually the first and the initiating episode in this drama of God's saving activity.[4] Although sub-

---

of Scripture vary. For a discussion of the issue of authority related to Christian ethics, see Birch and Rasmussen, *Bible and Ethics*, pp. 141-58; see also the discussion of the function of the canon in biblical ethics, pp. 171-81.

3.   This article necessarily relies, at a number of points, on my own previous work on the Hebrew Bible as a resource for Christian ethics, *Let Justice Roll Down: The Old Testament, Ethics, and Christian Life* (Louisville: Westminster/John Knox Press, 1991). This essay is also greatly informed by a recent reading of Eckardt Otto, *Theologische Ethik des Alten Testaments* (Stuttgart: W. Kohlhammer, 1994).

4.   Representative of this emphasis are Gerhard von Rad, *Old Testament*

sequent scholarship has broadened the focus in Old Testament theology, salvation history perspectives still have enormous ongoing influence in church readings of the Old Testament.

More recently, the Exodus story has received particular attention in various liberation theologies. Many of these have been influenced by salvation history emphases. The focus is on what God has done in saving/ liberating Israel from oppression and slavery. What is new, however, is the drawing of stronger theological and ethical implications for present socio-political circumstances. What God has done in liberating Israel, God can do for those who suffer in oppression today. The activity of God in Exodus becomes the basis for hope in the present and a summons to join in God's liberating activity.[5]

The emphasis in these formulations is on divine conduct—what God has done. Correspondingly, the emphasis in understanding Israel as community, especially as moral community, has been on Israel's conduct. Israel's ethics have thus been generally characterized in terms of its doing God's revealed will. It is Israel's moral conduct that has been of interest. Thus, many who have come to the Book of Exodus with an interest in ethics have focused on the Decalogue and the role of the law. The concern has been to see whether such guidelines for the moral conduct of Israel can make a contribution to our own moral decisions and actions. Some, particularly in the liberation theologies, have been interested in the ethical issues of participation in God's liberating activity (e.g. Moses as agent of God's liberation) but the emphasis has still been on ethical conduct in response to what God has done.

The deliverance at the sea and the final defeat of Pharaoh's power is, of course, the literary climax of the story, but centering on God's saving action in that moment has been the customary theological focus as well. But this moment finds its meaning in a broader context expressed in the Exodus story, and this is significant for the story as formative of moral community—Israel's or ours.

Theology, I (New York: Harper and Row, 1962 [1957]), and G. Ernest Wright, *God Who Acts* (London: SCM Press, 1952). This approach was popularized and widely influential in churches through works such as Bernhard Anderson, *The Unfolding Drama of the Bible* (New York: Association Press, 1957).

5.   See, for example, the use of Exodus themes in James Cone, *A Black Theology of Liberation* (New York: J. Lippincott, 1970), George V. Pixley, *Exodus: A Liberation Perspective* (Maryknoll, NY: Orbis Books, 1987), and José Serverino Croatto, *Exodus: A Hermeneutics of Freedom* (Maryknoll, NY: Orbis Books, 1981).

Walter Brueggemann, in an address to the Society of Christian Ethics, observed that 'it is conventional in theological interpretation of the Exodus to focus on God's powerful deliverance. In fact it is the hurt of Israel that is the driving force of the Exodus tradition'.[6] He is right in the sense that Israel's suffering is the crucial context for understanding the unique nature of this story. But even when Israel's hurt is noticed and voiced (which Brueggemann rightly notes as significant in this story) it would make no difference in its life or to the wider world apart from a God who responds to that hurt. 'Israel understood that its voiced hurt was definitional for the character of Yahweh.'[7] It is in relation to Israel's hurt that we discover in this story something of who God is and that makes all the difference in understanding what God later does. What God does in delivering Israel finds its meaning as activity consistent with who God has revealed the divine self to be. It is the character of God as revealed in the Exodus story that provides the categories for understanding the exercise of divine power. And it is the character of God as crucial to the power of this story to shape moral community that has been underemphasized.

In the remainder of this article I will first comment briefly on recent work on character and community in contemporary ethics. I will then turn to a discussion of the character of God as disclosed in key texts within the Exodus story. Finally, I will discuss the ways in which Israel is shaped as moral community in relationship to the God revealed in the Exodus story.

Character and Community in Contemporary Ethics
In recent years discussion in religious ethics has focused considerable attention on the understanding and interrelationships of character, community and story. Although none of these concepts is new, each is enjoying renewed attention alongside more customary attention in religious ethics to moral conduct (decision making, action and consequences) and to the self as moral agent (where some attention to story is also appropriate). Richard Bondi suggests that two assumptions permeate these more recent discussions: 'that human beings are creatures formed in communities marked by allegiance to a normative story, and that this

6. Walter Brueggemann, 'The Rhetoric of Hurt and Hope: Ethics Odd and Crucial', *Old Testament Theology: Essays on Structure, Theme, and Text* (Minneapolis: Fortress Press, 1992), p. 74.
7. 'The Rhetoric of Hurt and Hope', p. 77.

formation can best be discussed in the language of character.'[8]

When we speak of 'character' we point to the moral identity or being of a person or group that has been shaped into a distinctive pattern. The elements often encompassed in the reference to character include motives, dispositions, perceptions and intentions. Character and its elements form the fertile soil out of which all moral decisions and actions spring. Moral agents, whether individuals or groups, can always be discussed in ethical terms related to both character and conduct. This is true, for our purposes, of both God and Israel.

But formation of character always takes place in relation to community—whether those communities we intentionally chose or those we are a part of without our choosing. And the medium for this shaping of character in community is encounter with the stories those communities tell. 'The proper topic of the language of character is the self in relation to the world...Central to this formation [of character] is the impact of powerful stories with their accompanying symbols and visions of the good life...Yet because the self is always in relation, and stories come only out of community, other people play a vital role in the formation of an individual's character...Character is formed in response to stories told in community.'[9] The Book of Exodus is such a powerful, formative story. It is unusual because it is both a witness to the experiences out of which the story originated and a testimony to generations of Israel as moral community who have been shaped by encounter with the Exodus story and have made it their own.

Recent work in Christian ethics has been especially interested in the role of community in the moral life. Lisa Cahill describes this development among ethicists and biblical scholars as a 'turn to the community':

> First, the concerns of ethicists have moved from trying to assimilate biblical morality to the model of deductive argumentation to an interest in Scripture as foundational to the formation of communities of moral

8. Richard Bondi, 'The Elements of Character', *The Journal of Religious Ethics* 12 (1984), p. 201. Other key works that have informed this discussion are Stanley Hauerwas, *Character and the Christian Life* (San Antonio: Trinity University Press, 1975); *A Community of Character* (Notre Dame: University of Notre Dame Press, 1981); *The Peaceable Kingdom* (Notre Dame: University of Notre Dame Press, 1983); Gene Outka, 'Character, Vision and Narrative', *Religious Studies Review* 6 (1980), pp. 110-18; Larry Rasmussen, *Moral Fragments and Moral Community* (Minneapolis: Fortress Press, 1993). See also my forthcoming article 'Moral Agency, Community, and the Character of God in the Hebrew Bible', *Semeia* (1995).

9. Bondi, 'The Elements of Character', pp. 212, 215.

agency. Second, *biblical scholars* have become more explicitly aware of the social repercussions of [biblical faith], and also more interested in drawing social and moral analogies between the biblical world and our own.[10]

This emphasis on community has made recent scholarship on biblical ethics more aware of the biblical text as both evidence for the formation of moral community in Israel or the early church, but also as intended to influence the moral formation of later generations of the community. The Book of Exodus shows evidence for Israel's remembering of its originating story and for its reinterpreting of that story as subsequent generations make it their own. At both of these levels we are witnessing the shaping of the community's own moral character as it encounters this formative story.[11] For Israel this encounter with the Exodus story involves encounter with the Exodus God.

The Character of God in the Book of Exodus
The Book of Exodus not only witnesses to the decisive action of a delivering God but reveals the character of God out of which this action comes. This story becomes formative for Israel not simply because they are the beneficiaries of divine action, but because they have come into ongoing relationship with the God who stands behind that action. In a curious way these stories are also formative for God's character. Character requires relationship and community. God has no character that matters in the world until there is a community to which God is related and that can give witness to the experienced character of God.[12] In the Book of Exodus there are crucial episodes that reveal elements of the character of God precisely at the point we see God initiating ongoing relationship with a community. 'I will take you as my people, and I will

10. Lisa Sowle Cahill, 'The New Testament and Ethics: Communities of Social Change', *Interpretation* 44 (1990), p. 384. On this strong renewed interest in community as context for the moral life, see also Stephen E. Fowl and L. Gregory Jones, *Reading in Communion: Scripture and Ethics in Christian Life* (Grand Rapids: Eerdmans, 1991).

11. See my fuller discussion of these issues in my forthcoming article, 'Moral Agency, Community, and the Character of God in the Hebrew Bible'.

12. One could argue that God as Creator is in relationship to the whole of the natural world and that this reveals divine character. But creation in general does not give witness to the character of God as Creator so much as to imply a Creator. The character of God as Creator becomes explicit when there arises a community to give praise to God as Creator and to tell stories of divine creative activity.

be your God' (Exod. 6.7a). We will look at texts out of three of those episodes.[13]

1. *Exodus 3.7-8.*

> [7]Then the Lord said, 'I have observed the misery of my people who are in Egypt; I have heard their cry on account of their taskmasters. Indeed, I know their sufferings, [8]and I have come down to deliver them from the Egyptians, and to bring them up out of that land to a good and broad land, a land flowing with milk and honey, to the country of the Canaanites, the Hittites, the Amorites, the Perizzites, the Hivites, and the Jebusites.

Along with its precursor in Exod. 2.23-25, these verses constitute one of the most important statements in the Hebrew Bible about the nature of God and is especially informative in terms of the moral character of God.

This self-revelation of God is motivated by the cry of the Israelites out of their pain in slavery (2.23). Their 'groan' and their 'cry' 'rose up to God', and God responds. Here is the truth of Brueggemann's claim that the Exodus story focuses not on divine power but on Israelite hurt. God may take the initiative to relationship with Israel in this story, but that initiative is preceded by the voiced hurt of Israel—a cry of pain with no expectation that any would hear. I wish to argue that there would be no way to move from Israelite hurt to divine deliverance unless we learn it is in the character of God to be moved by this cry of pain. God is one whose regard, care and eventual saving action can be mobilized by human cries of pain, and from slaves at that. God is one who can allow the human experience of suffering to set the agenda and take the role of respondent.

God's response is stated in a series of bold first-person verbs in 3.7-8 that reveal much of the divine character. These verses are a part of God's first direct speech in Exodus and are programmatic for much that follows: God 'sees', God 'hears' and God 'knows'. These same three verbs appeared in 2.24-25 but the statement here is fuller and more revealing. Each verb here has as its object Israel's hurt. God sees

---

13. In dealing with particular Exodus texts I am particularly indebted to three commentaries for their rich theological reflections: Brevard S. Childs, *The Book of Exodus: A Theological Commentary* (OTL; Philadelphia: Westminster Press, 1974); Terence E. Fretheim, *Exodus* (Interpretation Commentaries; Louisville: Westminster/ John Knox Press, 1991); and Walter Brueggemann, 'The Book of Exodus: Introduction, Commentary, and Reflections', in *The New Interpreter's Bible*, I (Nashville: Abingdon, 1994), pp. 675-981.

'afflictions'. God hears 'cries'. God knows 'sufferings'. Whereas God saw only Israelites in the statement of 2.25, now, in direct speech to Moses, God acknowledges them as 'my people'. Seeing and hearing the hurt of Israel certainly suggests a kind of caring regard for human suffering as an aspect of God's character, but the third verb may suggest something more. It has been often observed that the verb יֵדַע has a broader range of meaning than our usual association of knowing with cognition. Many have suggested that the verb 'to know' must be understood as relational and participatory. One participates in relationship to the reality of that which is known. Thus, it is remarkable that God should use this verb related to Israel's suffering. God chooses to enter into and participate in Israel's suffering. This remarkable self-revelation of divine character might be thought of as the *vulnerability of God*.[14] God chooses to establish relationship with Israel at the point of their greatest need, at a time when they were slaves without standing in the world, in the midst of pain that allowed no more than an outcry.

That this precedes the exercise of God's power in deliverance is crucial to understanding what motivates God's saving activity and how that action is to be understood in the world. The three verbs we have discussed are followed by three more, not paralleled in 2.23-25. 'I have come down...to deliver...and to bring them up' (3.8; cf. also 3.17). The divine character, revealed in identification with Israel's suffering, becomes the basis of divine action. God enters the arena of human experience to act in ways that make a difference in Israel's suffering. God's announced deliverance declares in advance a divine intention expressive of solidarity with Israel in its suffering and of divine resolve to transformation of their situation.

2. *Exodus 6.1-8.*

> Then the Lord said to Moses, 'Now you shall see what I will do to Pharoah: Indeed, by a mighty hand he will let him go; by a mighty hand he will drive them out of his land'.
>
> [2]God also spoke to Moses and said to him: 'I am the Lord. [3]I appeared to Abraham, Isaac, and Jacob as God Almighty, but by my name "The Lord" I did not make myself known to them. [4]I also established my covenant with them, to give them the land of Canaan, the land in which they

---

14. See Birch, *Let Justice Roll Down*, pp. 119-20, and *To Love as we are Loved* (Nashville: Abingdon, 1992), pp. 29-48. Also Terence E. Fretheim, *The Suffering of God: An Old Testament Perspective* (OBT; Philadelphia: Fortress Press, 1984), pp. 127-37.

resided as aliens. [5]I have also heard the groanings of the Israelites whom the Egyptians are holding as slaves, and I have remembered my covenant. [6]Say therefore to the Israelites, "I am the Lord, and I will free you from the burdens of the Egyptians and deliver you from slavery to them. I will redeem you with an outstretched arm and with mighty acts of judgment. [7]I will take you as my people, and I will be your God. You shall know that I am the Lord your God, who has freed you from the burdens of the Egyptians. [8]I will bring you into the land that I swore to give to Abraham, Isaac, and Jacob; I will give it to you for a possession. I am the Lord"'.

This text has been called 'the fullest self-disclosure of God that is offered in the exodus narrative'.[15] What is disclosed of the character of God here centers around the revelation of the divine name and the meaning of this for relationship with Israel. Obviously, this text is preceded by the revealing of God's name in 3.14-16, both in the present sequence of the book and in the historical development of the narrative. I have chosen to focus on ch. 6 because it is a fuller statement of the theme, and because it is significant that this priestly text gives witness to the importance that a generation in exile gives to the identity and character of Yahweh as mediated by the revelation of God's name. When all else appeared to have failed, especially the saving activity of God, Israel held on to the name of Yahweh as the guarantee that God's character, and the faith built in relationship to that God, had not changed.[16] This priestly, exilic remembering and reclaiming of the Exodus story of God's self-revelation of the divine name is now incorporated into the story itself and becomes part of its formative power for still later generations.

Verse 2 opens this passage with the self-introductory formula 'I am Yahweh' and the formula is repeated in vv. 6, 7 and 8. Zimmerli's study of this formula has shown that this spare phrase is God's way of making available to Israel through Moses God's own self and what God intends in relation to Israel. Verses 3-8 are only exposition of the declaration in v. 2.

The focus in Exodus 6 is not on the meaning of the name Yahweh (unlike 3.14-15 in which the debate over the meaning of Yahweh remains problematic), rather it is the significance in the act of revealing

---

15. Brueggemann, 'The Book of Exodus', p. 733.

16. It is especially Walther Zimmerli's study of the self-revelation formula 'I Am Yahweh', in Exodus 6 and Ezekiel 20 that is the foundation for all subsequent work on this theme ('Ich bin Yahweh', in *Gottes Offenbarung: Gesammelte Aufsatze*, I [TB19; Munich: Chr. Kaiser Verlag, 1969], pp. 11-40; ET *I Am Yahweh* [Atlanta: John Knox, 1982], pp. 1-28).

the divine name and what that discloses about God's character in a willingness to risk God's own self in relationship. To give one's name is an act of intimacy that establishes relationship.

> Naming entails a certain kind of relationship. Giving the name opens up the possibility of, indeed admits a desire for, a certain intimacy in relationship...Naming entails vulnerability. In giving the name, God becomes available to the world and is at the disposal of those who can name the name. This is a self-giving act of no little risk, for it means not only that God's name can be honored, but also that it can be misused and abused...When God's name is given, this means life, distinctiveness, concreteness, intimacy, accessibility, communication, historicality, identifica-
tion and vulnerability. One can easily see how speaking the name of God became for Israel a speaking of God's self.[17]

Several additional aspects of God's self-revelation flow from this announcement of name and identity. The first is the tie of God's identity as Yahweh with the promise to the ancestors. God had 'appeared' to the ancestors but was not 'known' to them (v. 3). Full relationship was not yet established; specifically, God had not yet revealed the divine name and they called on God by another, less personal name. But God had made a commitment, a covenant, with Israel's ancestors (v. 4) and in their time of suffering God had 'remembered' that covenant (v. 5). The revelation of God's name in Exod. 3.14 is also identified with the God who appeared to the ancestors, but the reference is less explicit about covenant or promise made with the ancestors (3.6, 15, 16). The notice in 2.23-25 had included 'remembering' as one of God's responses to Israel's outcry and this motif is now a quality identified with the revealed name of Yahweh. Yahweh is a God who remembers and keeps commitments. Even though Israel has not fully known God until this moment, God has honored the relationship begun with the ancestors. The divine character includes the trustworthiness of God's commitment to relationships. This was probably an especially important theme to emphasize in this story as it was told to a generation of exiles who worried that God had abandoned them.

Based on this divine remembering, God now issues a powerful new promise in vv. 6-8. The formula of self-identification, 'I am Yahweh', stands at its beginning, its middle and its end. God's promise is totally encompassed with God's very being as the guarantee of its reliability. In three strong verbs God promises first to 'free', 'deliver' and 'redeem'

17. Fretheim, *Suffering of God*, pp. 100-101.

Israel (v. 6). God finally promises to 'bring' Israel to the land, and to 'give it to you for a possession' (v. 8). In between, and also undergirded by the 'I am Yahweh' formula, is the announcement of covenant relationship between God and Israel: 'I will take you as my people and I will be your God' (v. 7a). It is not so much a promise as a statement that relationship is made available. God has already 'known' Israel's suffering. Now God offers to 'be known' as the one with power to free them. 'You shall know that I am Yahweh, your God, who has freed you' (v. 7b). God experiences Israel's hurt and invites Israel to experience God's power. The formula here obviously anticipates the covenant making at Sinai, but suggests that the relationship formalized at Sinai is already begun in the self-revelation of God's character in relation to suffering Israel.

> God's very character is to make relationships, bring emancipation, and establish covenants. The covenantal formulation of v. 7 suggests not only that Israel is now always Yahweh connected, but also that Yahweh is always Israel connected, and will not again be peopleless. Moreover, the fact that this symmetrical formula has most currency precisely in the exile means that at the time of the deepest rupture of faith, this relatedness persists. The God of Israel is defined by that relatedness.[18]

3. *Exodus 34.6-7.*

> [6]The Lord passed before him, and proclaimed,
> 'The Lord , the Lord,
> a God merciful and gracious,
> slow to anger,
> and abounding in steadfast love
> and faithfulness,
> [7]keeping steadfast love for the
> thousandth generation,
> forgiving iniquity and
> transgression and sin,
> yet by no means clearing the
> guilty,
> but visiting the iniquity of the
> parents
> upon the children
> and the children's children,
> to the third and the fourth
> generation'.

18. Brueggemann, 'The Book of Exodus', p. 737.

This well-known and remarkably self-revealing speech by God appears in the context of covenant reaffirmation following the golden calf episode. It is undoubtedly an important and carefully shaped statement that capsulizes and forms the basis for much of Israel's reflection on the character of God. Many texts return to this formulation and make use of its various parts (e.g. Num. 14.18-19; Deut. 7.9-10; Ps. 145.8-9; Nah. 1.2-3; Joel 3.21; Jon. 4.2; Neh. 9.17).[19] This is a rich and complex text which we cannot fully explore here. We include it as an important witness to the continuing reflection on the character of God which follows the climactic deliverance at the sea in the Book of Exodus. God's saving action in delivering Israel from Egyptian bondage gives Israel a freedom which can now be exercised by entering into full covenant relationship with that liberating God. However, God's saving action finds its context in the Exodus story not only in preceding disclosures of the divine character but in Israel's subsequent learning about the character of the God who has delivered them and to whom they are now related. 'Thus the speech of vv. 6-7 is Yahweh's self-disclosure, revealing to Moses the fullness of God's character and intentionality. Nowhere before this speech has anyone been privileged to hear directly a disclosure of what is most powerful and definitional for God's own life.'[20]

God's proclamation begins with the repetition of the divine name Yahweh (v. 6 is perhaps a third utterance of the name in v. 5; cf. also 33.19). What follows is, in a sense, an elaboration of the content of that name and the qualities of the divine self that bears it. This text builds upon and deepens what we know of the meaning of that name from Exod. 3.14-17 and 6.1-8.

The recital which follows consists of categories that delineate the moral content of God's character and make clear that relationship with God requires one to know and take into account these qualities of the divine self. We do not have space to deal individually with the meaning of each of these important terms. There are ample commentaries and treatises on them all. We will simply note that the recital uses seven terms to indicate qualities of God's graciousness and generosity (especially important in the wake of Israel's sin with the golden calf). These are: merciful, gracious, slow to anger, abounding in steadfast love,

19. See Phyllis Trible, *God and the Rhetoric of Sexuality* (Philadelphia: Fortress Press, 1978), pp. 1-5.

20. Brueggemann, 'The Book of Exodus', p. 946.

faithfulness, keeping steadfast love and forgiving (vv. 6-7a). Cumulatively, these make a powerful statement of God's capacities and desire to sustain covenant relationship and to act in ways that maintain and restore the partner to wholeness. But these seven terms of grace are followed by two statements of God's judgment. The recital affirms that God will not acquit guilt, and God will visit iniquity (i.e. invoke covenant sanctions) against the community even into future generations (v. 7b). God is not lightly wronged. The grace offered is not cheap grace. 'Iniquity' appears in each half of this recital. It may be forgiven (v. 7a), but it will exact consequences (v. 7b). This is a moral tension in the affirmation of God's character that many have considered contradictory and wanted to resolve. But the juxtaposition itself is an important statement about God's character. Those who would live in relationship to this God must reckon both with God's grace and judgment. The community of faith resolves this tension one way or the other at its own peril and at the risk of blurring its identity as God's community. The easy grace of a constantly forgiving God and the retributionist picture of God as a stern enforcer of moral codes are both distortions of the God revealed here. The God of this recital given to Israel will retain sovereign freedom: 'I will be merciful to whom I will be merciful' (33.19). To covenant with this God is to live confident of divine grace but in constant repentance before the exercise of divine judgment—a people with constant resources for hope but an endless capacity for self-examination. Fretheim reminds us that there 'is no predictability or inevitability about the divine grace. This serves as a reminder that the community of faith ought not live close to the margins of God's patience' (cf. Rom. 6.1).[21]

4. These texts, and others that could be explored, make clear the important affirmations concerning God's character which surround and give meaning to the climactic action of God's liberation of Israel from Egyptian bondage. Deliverance is significant because it is not an isolated random action of some powerful God about whom nothing else is known. It is significant because it is expressive of the character of a relationship making God. The liberating action of God is consistent with the character of God revealed as the foundation of hope while still in bondage, and the basis of on-going relationship when deliverance is followed by covenant making. God's action alone would not have been enough to form Israel as an on-going moral community. The Exodus

21. Fretheim, *Exodus*, p. 307.

story which helps to form that community would not have been possible with the bald report of the sea experience alone. (Perhaps Amos 9.7 suggests the truth of this. Philistines and Aramaeans are said to have experienced the delivering hand of God, but no stories arose to acknowledge this, and no communities were formed to live in relation to this God.) Moral community is not possible simply by experiencing what God has done; the community must come to know who the God is that has done these things. Having argued for the importance of witness to divine character alongside of divine action in the Exodus story, I can turn to some brief remarks on the significance for understanding Israel's formation as moral community.

Israel as a Community of Character

I have argued that as a community of faith Israel is shaped not only by what God has done, but by who God is revealed to be. Behind the act of deliverance at the sea is a trustworthy God whose character is revealed and witnessed in other texts within the Book of Exodus and who invites Israel into relationship. It is the story of the Exodus experience with this God that makes on-going relationship as God's people possible. The Book of Exodus is the cumulative evidence of such storytelling.

Stanley Hauerwas argues that narrative is the most suitable form for the community to remember and reinterpret its own past. It is in the telling of its stories that a community of character is formed.[22] Israel's character is significantly formed by its remembering and reinterpreting of God's self-revelations, delivering actions, and relationship forming initiatives in the Exodus story. This is not without tensions and complexities, for there is no harmonious, single, official version of this remembered Exodus story. In fact, the Book of Exodus is the cumulative evidence not only of originating memory but of community reclaiming and reinterpreting that memory.

It must be remembered that the community is not shaped by the text or the story *per se* but by the belief that the narrative is a truthful (not the equivalent of historical) witness to the reality of the community's actual encounter with God in historical time and space. Narrative (stories) mediates this encounter to new generations of the community, but does not create it. The community, from Israel to the present, believes that alongside the continuous telling of the stories is the continuous possibility of actual relationship to the God about whom the stories are told.

22. Hauerwas, *Peaceable Kingdom*, p. 39.

1. For Israel, *new identity is the necessary context for formation as moral community*. Israel as moral community is formed in response to what God has already done, and who God has already revealed the divine self to be. The Exodus story makes witness to this divine activity and self-disclosure available for the on-going shaping of the community. The result is not a new set of prescribed moral behaviors, but a new identity in relationship to God. It is out of this new identity that obedience to God's will can meaningfully flow. The shaping of the community's moral character will provide the meaningful context out of which moral conduct can flow. When some textbooks and curriculum materials move quickly and superficially from God's power in delivering Israel to God's giving of commandments, the impression emerges of an ethics based on God as the one who has the power to set the rules. Broadened attention to the character of God leads us to consider more fully the character of Israel. It is here that relationship can be most fully understood and the context for moral behavior established. Before moving too quickly to commandment and obedience we will be drawn to consider the moral significance of texts that define a new identity for Israel. For example, Exod. 19.4-6 prefaces the covenant making stories not with the language of obligation arising out of God's deliverance. Deliverance leads instead to new relationship and identity out of which obedience can have meaning: 'You have seen what I did to the Egyptians, and how I bore you on eagle's wings and brought you *to myself*' (v. 4). The language is of intimacy, not stern command. Now arises the possibility of a new identity as God's 'treasured possession out of all the peoples' (v. 5). Israel can be shaped in response through covenant to become 'a priestly kingdom' and a 'holy nation' (v. 6).

2. *For Israel, ethics arises not out of obedience to external code but by entering into the life of God*. Traditional uses of the Hebrew Bible in Christian ethics have focused on the revealing of the divine will as the basis for Israel's ethics. Israel's moral norms were primarily sought in commandment and law with some attention given to the concept of covenant, but even this was primarily understood in juridical terms. Even more sophisticated and helpful treatments of moral resources from the Hebrew Bible have tended to focus on commandment as the primary basis for Israel's ethics, and therefore have characterized ethics in pre-exilic Israel as almost entirely deontological.[23]

23. E.g. Thomas W. Ogletree, *The Use of the Bible in Christian Ethics* (Philadelphia: Fortress Press, 1983).

Although obedience to God's revealed will and the role of commandment are important in the Book of Exodus, a singular focus here as the basis of Israel's ethics separates moral obligation from the person of God. My contention, stated at the start of this section, is that in the Book of Exodus ethics arises not as a matter of obedience to an external model or code of morality but by entering into the life of God. A number of scholars have argued a similar point in the recent literature, and a much richer picture of the basis for ethics in the Hebrew Bible is emerging. John Barton suggests that the 'Old Testament is not primarily to give information about morality...but to provide materials which, when pondered and absorbed into the mind, will suggest the pattern or shape of a way of life lived in the presence of God...Ethics is not so much a system of obligations as a way of communion with God'.[24] Brevard Childs argues that 'divine command rests, of course, on a prior understanding of God...who continues to make his will known for his people. Nor can this will ever be separated from the person of God'.[25]

A fuller understanding of Israel's ethics arising out of relationship to God and encompassing character and conduct will lead to a broader set of categories for understanding the source of Israel's moral norms. I will list three of these ways of thinking about moral norms, all of which are attested in the Exodus traditions and in the wider canonical traditions. (A fuller discussion would require a further investigation than this article affords.)

Moral norms arise out of *knowing God*: 'I will take you as my people, and I will be your God. You shall know that I am Yahweh, your God' (Exod. 6.7). The experience of God in relationship, which knowing implies, is at the heart of covenant. The moral categories associated with covenant then flow out of intimate relationship to God and not out of external codes of law: 'Did not your father eat and drink and do justice and righteousness? Then it was well with him. He judged the cause of the poor and needy; then it was well. Is not this to know me? says the LORD?' (Jer. 22.15b-16).

Moral norms arise out of *imitating God*. I have written in some detail

24. John Barton, 'Approaches to Ethics in the Old Testament', in J. Rogerson (ed.), *Beginning Old Testament Study* (Philadelphia: Westminster Press, 1982), pp. 128, 130.

25. Brevard S. Childs, *Biblical Theology of the Old and New Testaments: Theological Reflection on the Christian Bible* (Minneapolis: Fortress Press, 1993), p. 677.

elsewhere about the importance of *imitatio dei* as an important source of Israel's moral norms.[26] The desire to imitate God arises naturally out of relationship to God who models qualities essential to our relationships with others. Imitation of God can focus on qualities of God or on specific actions of God; i.e. on character or conduct: 'You shall be holy, for I the LORD your God am holy' (Lev. 19.2); '[God] executes justice for the orphan and the widow, and...loves the strangers, providing them with food and clothing. You shall also love the stranger, for you were strangers in the land of Egypt' (Deut. 10.18-19).

Moral norms arise out of *obeying* God. This has been the most common category used to understand Israel's morality and hardly needs illustration. The Decalogue, Deuteronomy's constant references to commandments and statutes, various prophetic summons to obedience—all are ample witness to the importance of the revelation of God's will as a guide to moral behavior in ancient Israel. The importance of obedience to God's will cannot be challenged. However, God's commandments do not appear in Exodus for the first time, apart from an encompassing story that relates Israel (and those who read these texts as Scripture) in other morally significant ways to the God who does the commanding. Attention to some of these other dimensions of moral relationship between God and Israel is essential to a full understanding of the ways in which the Hebrew Bible plays its role as an ethical resource.

---

26. Birch, 'Moral Agency, Community, and the Character of God in the Hebrew Bible'.

NATIONALISM AND THE HEBREW BIBLE

Mark G. Brett

> Nationalism is in this sense like class. To have it, and to feel it, is the only way to end it. If you fail to claim it or give it up too soon, you will merely be cheated, by other classes and other nations.[1]

The question of national identity is currently a burning issue in almost every political region. Ethnic nationalisms pose a challenge within many states, while multi-national confederations have another kind of deconstructive potential. The significance of these issues can hardly be over-estimated, and the need for ethical reflection on constructions of national identity (amongst which xenophobic nationalism is only one kind) should be manifest to all but the most extreme postmodernists for whom the discussion of ethics no longer has meaning.[2] The purpose of this paper, however, is neither to analyse postmodern philosophy nor to recommend a programme of 'applied ethics'. The purpose is to explore the analogies between social ideas in the Hebrew Bible and social ideas in the contemporary world which, in certain defined senses, can be included under the heading of nationalism. This exercise of analogical imagination has both descriptive and normative dimensions and is designed to be a contribution to 'practical ethics'[3] insofar as we are

---

1. From *Second Generation*, a novel by Raymond Williams; quoted in T. Eagleton, 'Nationalism: Irony and Commitment', in T. Eagleton, F. Jameson and E. Said, *Nationalism, Colonialism and Literature* (Bloomington: Indiana University Press, 1990), p. 23. Cf. Gerald West's comments on 'exclusive black nationalism', in *Biblical Hermeneutics of Liberation: Modes of Reading the Bible in the South African Context* (Pietermaritzburg: Cluster, 1991), pp. 75 and 209 n. 19.

2. For a critique of this strain of postmodernism, see Z. Baumann, *Postmodern Ethics* (Oxford: Basil Blackwell, 1993).

3. This terminology is borrowed from Thomas Ogletree, *Hospitality to the Stranger: Dimensions of Moral Understanding* (Philadelphia: Fortress Press, 1985), p. 11, but I do not thereby subscribe to the details of his distinctions between fundamental, symbolic and practical ethics.

focussing on social and cultural factors which have shaped the moral frameworks of Judaism and Christianity.

There are a number of motivating assumptions behind this essay which, for space reasons, cannot be defended here in detail. Most of my conclusions, it should be said, are logically separable from these background assumptions, but it may nevertheless be helpful to begin by highlighting them since they indicate the possible significance of the project. First, I assume that both Christians and Jews will regard the Hebrew Bible as an essential ingredient of their identities and that it is therefore incumbent upon us to explicate, however critically, the moral visions to be found in the Scriptures which we share. In spite of the diversity of attitudes to the Bible, we can at least agree that through these writings we converse with 'significant others' who have shaped us, and with whom we must engage, even if it is our destiny to outgrow them.

Secondly, I assume that such conversations with the Hebrew Bible can be formulated in *relative* independence of the later developments of our respective religious traditions, although the later developments will have a considerable bearing on the applied ethics which we adopt. It would be important to recognise that we cannot be independent of traditions in which we participate *unconsciously*; these can be 'bracketed' only when they have been explicitly identified (this point is part of the 'hermeneutical humility' which has been advocated by philosophers as different as Hans-Georg Gadamer and Karl Popper). Nor should we underestimate the scholarly vocation to evaluate the history of the Bible's influence, for example, in the construction of 'the divine right of kings' or of modern Zionism. But here I have in mind a simpler point: the applied ethics of Christians will naturally pay serious attention to the New Testament and church history, while in the case of Jews, Mishnah and Talmud would need to be considered. Nevertheless, in both religious traditions, it would be possible to formulate an ethical vision with warrants drawn primarily from the Hebrew Bible.[4]

Thirdly, I assume that a Jewish or Christian moral vision, however difficult to communicate in the public realm, may have significance (for

---

4. In an age of post-Holocaust theology, it is especially important for Christians to appreciate the integrity of the Hebrew Bible and to avoid any pre-emptive Christological hermeneutics. See further M.G. Brett, 'The Political Ethics of Postmodern Allegory', in M. Daniel Carroll R., D.J.A. Clines and P.R. Davies (eds.), *The Bible in Human Society: Essays in Honour of John Rogerson* (JSOTSup, 200; Sheffield: Sheffield Academic Press, 1995), pp. 67-86.

better or for worse) beyond the confines of those particular religious traditions. Even if there is no persuasive ethical argument for established churches in the modern world, it does not follow that public discourse should be 'secular'. In an important analysis of multiculturalism, Charles Taylor has identified two quite different accounts of the public sphere in Western democracies: on the one hand, there is a politics of universalism which emphasises the equal dignity of all citizens and an equalizing of rights, while on the other hand, there is a politics of difference which emphasizes the uniqueness of social identities (e.g. aboriginality, ethnicities and gender) and the fact that these identities have been constructed through dialogue with 'significant others'. Characteristically, the politics of difference emphasizes the necessity for redistributive programmes and affirmative action.[5] The first approach—universalism—operates with a homogenizing presumption of 'difference-blind' liberalism, usually insisting that the particularities of cultural commitment should be privatized. The second approach claims that such supposedly difference-blind principles usually turn out to be a reflection of one hegemonic culture, or, at the very least, a restricted range of cultures.[6] It seems to me that the attempt to privatize religious cultures is potentially dangerous since it stifles conflicts which will appear in other ways,[7] and the second approach is more defensible ethically insofar as it recognises that some social histories of marginalisation cannot be rectified within existing political frameworks.

Clearly, any explicit use of the Bible in a multicultural society will be

5.   C. Taylor, 'The Politics of Recognition', in A.Gutman (ed.), *Multiculturalism and "The Politics of Recognition"* (Princeton: Princeton University Press, 1992), pp. 25-73. The dialogical construction of identity has been a key theme in the social research influenced by George Herbert Mead and in the literary research influenced by Mikhail Bakhtin. See further Taylor, *The Sources of the Self* (Cambridge, MA: Harvard University Press, 1989); *idem, The Ethics of Authenticity* (Cambridge, MA: Harvard University Press, 1991).

6.   Taylor, 'Recognition', pp. 43, 62. Cf. J. Derrida, *The Other Heading: Reflections on Today's Europe* (Bloomington: Indiana University Press, 1992), p. 19: 'We must thus be suspicious of *both* repetitive memory *and* the completely other of the absolutely new; of *both* anamnestic capitalization *and* the amnesic exposure to what would no longer be identifiable at all'. To mix Taylor's metaphor with Derrida's, one could say that difference-blind liberalism is politically amnesic.

7.   J. Moltmann, 'Covenant or Leviathan: Political Theology for Modern Times', *SJT* 47 (1994), pp. 19-41 (esp. pp. 38-39), reflecting on the German experience under Hitler; see further Moltmann, *Politische Theologie—Politische Ethik* (Mainz: Grünewald, 1984).

confronted by the problem of how biblical 'authority' can be construed in public discussion. It might be thought, for example, that the Hebrew Bible reflects a single tradition which should be placed on an equal footing with any other. If Taylor's account of multiculturalism is correct, however, then we are not well served by a political stance which suggests, for apparently good ethical reasons, that all cultures are equally valuable; such a stance is both condescending in that it offers a pre-emptive judgment of worth without actually engaging with the other, and paradoxically it is ethnocentric in suggesting that we already have the standards to make such judgments. Authentic judgments of value allow the possibility that in actually engaging with the other our original standards may be transformed.[8]

Having asserted the potential value of the Hebrew Bible in constructing contemporary moral visions, it is also necessary to recognise that any use of the Bible has to be, in some sense, commensurable with the particular context of use. The nature of this commensurability will always be controversial; the differences between biblical times and our own are, of course, considerable. Historians and cultural relativists will insist that such differences never disappear. Nevertheless, this paper will suspend the justifiable disbeliefs of cultural relativists and proceed cautiously, by analogies, towards a hermeneutical 'fusion of horizons'.

I will be concerned with three basic questions under the heading of 'nationalism', and in each case there is an ancient and a modern aspect to be considered. First, in what respects can the concept of nationalism be applied to the study of ancient Israel, and in what respects should it be seen as a uniquely modern concept? Second, how do concepts of nationalism function in the contrasts between universalism and particularism in biblical theology? Third, what are the implications of nationalism for specifically ethical issues such as the treatment of strangers?[9]

8. Taylor, 'Recognition', pp. 67, 70; *idem*, 'Understanding and Ethnocentricity', in his *Philosophy and the Human Sciences* (Cambridge: Cambridge University Press, 1985).

9. See W. Brueggemann, *Interpretation and Obedience* (Minneapolis: Fortress Press, 1991), ch. 13; S.E. Fowl and L.G. Jones, *Reading in Communion: Scripture and Ethics in Christian Life* (London: SPCK, 1991), ch. 5; M. Ignatief, *The Needs of Strangers* (New York: Viking, 1985); J. Kristeva, *Strangers to Ourselves* (New York: Columbia University Press, 1991); *idem*, *Nations without Nationalism* (New York: Columbia University Press, 1993); E. Levinas, *Totality and Infinity* (Pittsburgh: Duquesne University Press, 1969); Ogletree, *Hospitality to the Stranger*; P.J. Palmer, *The Company of Strangers* (New York: Crossroad, 1983).

These questions might seem, *prima facie,* to be unrelated, but they do in fact overlap. In reviewing, for example, the extensive literature on the tension between universalism and nationalism in Second Isaiah (particularism and nationalism are often used interchangeably), it is interesting to note how often scholars express concern about the danger of anachronism in using the term 'universalism', but they are rarely concerned with this danger in the case of the term 'nationalism'. Both terms, as we shall see, suffer from the threat of anachronism and from equivocating usages, and both terms raise problems concerning the treatment of strangers.

Defining Nationalism
Nationalism is a contested concept.[10] Different definitions will, no doubt, elicit different configurations of social reality, and the most one can hope for, perhaps, is to find a heuristic strategy which is both productive and not idiosyncratic. Here we will primarily follow the definition of one sociologist, Liah Greenfeld, both because her work articulates more widely spread ideas and because it provides a useful heuristic strategy for constructing analogies between modern nationalism and the literature of ancient Israel.

In her major work, *Nationalism: Five Roads to Modernity,* Greenfeld rightly begins by resisting a simply pejorative connotation of the term 'nationalism', suggesting instead that an even-handed study should investigate national identity in all its forms, some, but not all of which, have been xenophobic. She also resists any simple definition of nationalism which would focus on particular features or factors, such as common territory, common language, statehood, shared traditions and history or race. Particular forms of nationalism may indeed combine any number of these features, but taken by themselves, such factors would not distinguish *national* identity from other kinds of social identity.[11]

10. See N. Harris, *National Liberation* (London: I.B. Tauris, 1990), p. 276: 'We cannot say in general what any particular nationalism means in isolation from the specific conflicts of a given situation. The nationalist tradition can swing from the extreme right to the extreme left, can be the voice of the landlords or the landless'.
11. For example, the language of ancient Israel did not divide it from many of its immediate neighbours; some have argued that classical Hebrew is but one dialect of the same Canaanite language which includes Moabite, Edomite, Ammonite, Phoenician, Ugaritic and perhaps even the creole of Amarna letters. W.R. Garr has put forward the view that Hebrew belongs on a continuum of dialects with Phoenician at one end and old Aramaic at the other. Isa. 19.18 speaks simply of 'the language of Canaan',

The specificity of nationalism, Greenfeld argues, derives from the idea of a 'people' which is seen as the bearer of sovereignty and the basis of collective solidarity. The 'people' are seen as larger than any concrete community but as fundamentally homogeneous in that they are perceived as 'only superficially divided by the lines of status, class, locality, and in some cases even ethnicity'.[12] Greenfeld makes a good case for thinking that it is only this principle of perceived social homogeneity which justifies viewing the variety of nationalisms as expressions of the same general phenomenon.

If we follow the line promoted by Greenfeld, however, it would appear that there are links between nationalism, modernity and democracy, and a key question which therefore emerges is whether it is possible to speak of nationalist tendencies in ancient religious traditions. Is it rather the case, as much recent work has suggested, that it would be misleading to speak of nationalism before the eighteenth century?[13] It is instructive to notice that it is precisely Greenfeld who (in agreement with those 'modernists' who are willing to see antecedents of national consciousness only a century or two earlier) points out the role of biblical interpretation in early English Protestantism and thereby in the rise of English nationalism in the sixteenth century.

It was the Hebrew Bible that supplied the model of a chosen and

and we find no tradition concerning linguistic origins outside the promised land. The question of language might have played some small role in the envisioning of Israelite territory insofar as the scope of the promise of land to Abram in Gen. 15.18—from the border of Egypt to the river Euphrates—encompasses precisely the territories in which the Canaanite language was spoken: Edom, Moab, Ammon, and Aram. Thus, what is envisaged is a linguistically unified territory, and at least 1 Kgs 4.21 claims the expanse between the border of Egypt and the river Euphrates as the scope of Solomon's territory, although texts like 1 Kgs 11.23-25 would suggest that the claim was an ideal one. It may be the case that a unity of language played a role in the envisioning of the promised land, but we should beware of accounts of the united monarchy which slip and slide without qualification between the terms 'nation' and 'empire'. See W.R. Garr, *Dialect Geography of Syria-Palestine, 1000–586 BCE* (Philadelphia: University of Pennsylvania, 1985), p. 229; B. Waltke and M. O'Connor, *An Introduction to Hebrew Syntax* (Winona Lake: Eisenbrauns, 1990), pp. 8-9; J. Mauchline, 'Implicit Signs of a Persistent Belief in the Davidic Empire', *VT* 20 (1970), pp. 287-303.

12. L. Greenfeld, *Nationalism: Five Roads to Modernity* (Cambridge, MA: Harvard University Press, 1992), p. 3.

13. For a brief overview, see A.D. Smith, *The Ethnic Origins of Nations* (Oxford: Basil Blackwell, 1986), ch. 1: 'Are nations modern?'

godly people, 'a people which was an elite and a light to the world because every one of its members was a party to the covenant with God'.[14] The Bible provided a language of nationality which encompassed all levels of society, as opposed to the earlier uses of the term 'nation' which designated either groups of foreigners or cultural elites.[15] At the same time, Greenfeld emphasizes that it was not so much the Hebrew Bible in itself which was the catalyst for English nationalism. There were a whole range of factors which coincided: for example, the practice of reading became a religious virtue in a Bible-focused society and literacy was remarkably widespread in sixteenth-century England;[16] Protestant doctrines such as the priesthood of all believers nurtured a novel sense of individual dignity; when this dignity was infringed upon by Queen Mary, her persecutions had the unintended effect of ensuring an identification of Protestantism and national causes. Martyrdom and exile became catalysts of national consciousness, both for elite groups and for the wider populous. After Mary, the monarchy had to be seen as representing the national interest or it lost its legitimacy. John Poynet, a Bishop of Winchester who died in exile in 1556, was able to write that 'Men ought to have more respect to their country than to their prince, to the commonwealth than to any one person. For the country and the commonwealth is a degree above the king'.[17]

Greenfeld's view is that the birth of nationalism is to be found in sixteenth-century England in the interaction between religious and political movements which included a widespread appropriation of the idea of being an elect people, reflecting the influence—at least initially— of the theology of Israel. What turned out to be more important for the subsequent history of nationalism, however, was not so much the religious dimension but the perception of being part of an essentially

14. Greenfeld, *Nationalism*, p. 52.

15. G. Zernatto, 'Nation: The History of a Word', *Review of Politics* 6 (1944), pp. 351-66.

16. L. Stone, 'The Educational Revolution in England, 1540–1640', *Past and Present* 28 (1964), pp. 41-80.

17. W.S. Hudson, *John Poynet: Advocate of Limited Monarchy* (Chicago: University of Chicago Press, 1942), p. 61. Cf. B. Anderson, *Imagined Communities: Reflections on the Origin and Spread of Nationalism* (London: Verso, 1983, 2nd edn, 1991), pp. 15-16, who defines 'nation' as 'imagined political community...It is imagined as sovereign because the concept was born in an age in which Enlightenment and Revolution were destroying the legitimacy of the divinely-ordained, hierarchical dynastic realm'.

homogenous people. The explicit religious dimension had subsided by the eighteenth century, even in English political philosophy,[18] and when the French adopted the originally English idea of nationhood it was by a complex process of *ressentiment*; a mixture of envy and critique in which they presented the ideas of liberty and equality as indigenous French contributions to nationalism.[19]

Religion, from Greenfeld's perspective, was simply one factor in the birth of nationalism; what is more remarkable is the spread of nationalism and its role in the fostering of a modernity which ironically turned against religion. Greenfeld suggests only parenthetically that there were 'proto-nations' in the ancient world, notably among the Jews and the Greeks, but their versions of nationalism 'never spread beyond the borders of these individual societies'.[20] Whatever we might think of Greenfeld's overall theses, her work provides a fresh impetus for re-examining the history of Israel from the perspective of national identity. Her emphasis on the capacity of nationalism to minimize social segmentation is particularly suggestive,[21] but there is one aspect of her definition which begs the question. She suggests that belonging to a national group is a matter of explicit acknowledgment, by the people concerned, of the marks that define that group: 'An essential characteristic of any identity is that it is necessarily the view the concerned actor has of himself or herself...It cannot be presumed on the basis of any objective characteristics...Identity is perception'.[22] The question arising here is a constant one for social historians: Whose perception? What evidence do we have for the views of 'the concerned actor'? As we turn to studies on ancient Israel we should bear these questions in mind.[23]

18. See H.G. Reventlow, *The Authority of the Bible and the Rise of the Modern World* (London: SCM Press, 1984).

19. Greenfeld, *Nationalism*, pp. 14-17, 177-80.

20. Greenfeld, *Nationalism*, p. 495 n. 9.

21. Cf. Steven Grosby's emphasis on the connections between 'trans-tribal people' and 'trans-local land' as constitutive characteristics of nationality, in his 'Kinship, Territory and the Nation in the Historiography of Ancient Israel', *ZAW* 105 (1993), p. 15.

22. Greenfeld, *Nationalism*, p. 13.

23. Cf. E. Hobsbawm, *Nations and Nationalism since 1780: Programme, Myth, Reality* (Cambridge: Cambridge University Press, 1990), p. 11; cf. L. Colley, 'Whose Nation? Class and National Consciousness in Britain 1750–1830', *Past and Present* 113 (1986), pp. 96-117.

Nationalism in Israel

Was the transition from tribalism to the Davidic-Solomonic state a transition to nationhood? It has been frequently emphasized that the
divisions between north and south lay just below the surface of this state,
and one might even question whether the 'imagined' cultural unity
extended any further than the urban court and its associated elites. In his
recent study on *Early Israel*, Robert Coote suggests that, as a social
reality, the term 'nation' belongs mainly to the industrial era, yet he also
asserts that the idea of nation was a mystification projected in Israel by
the royal court, the main function of which was to maximize the intake
of taxes.[24]

There may well be a kernel of truth to this view, but the logic of
Coote's argument has not been drawn out with sufficient clarity. If
Greenfeld is correct, all ideas of nationalism are 'mystifications' insofar
as they perceive complex societies as fundamentally homogenous and
only superficially divided by lines of status and class. This could be
described negatively as 'mystification' or more neutrally, perhaps, as
'imagined community'.[25] Nationalism is not about 'objective' social
reality; it is about the perceptions of the actors involved. In other words,
even if this particular mystification really did maximize the intake of
taxes then the *possibility* remains, for example, that the Israelites generally saw taxes as a necessary evil which served the national good,
especially through the maintenance of a standing army under the
monarchy.

Moreover, it is precisely this possibility which is presented in the story
of the people's request for kingship in 1 Samuel 8. In spite of Samuel's
warning about the evils of monarchy, including taxation, the people
reply that they want a king—like all the other nations (*gôyim*)—so that
he can lead their battles. In short, military aggression is perceived here as
a greater threat to the common good than the evils of monarchy.
Indeed, the very perception of an inter-tribal 'common good' may have
arisen precisely out of the threat of external aggression, notably from the

24. R. Coote, *Early Israel* (Minneapolis: Fortress Press, 1990), pp. 24-25, 159-
60.

25. See B. Anderson, *Imagined Communities*, p. 16: 'regardless of the actual
inequality and exploitation that may prevail in each, the nation is always conceived as
a deep, horizontal comradeship.' As Anderson points out, the weakness in the
common suggestion that nations are 'invented' or 'fabricated' is the implication that
there exist 'true' communities which are somehow natural.

Philistines. In more recent attempts to explain the rise of the Israelite state, the Philistine threat has been largely displaced by other socio-economic factors such as population growth and the regional diversification of the economy.[26] But we should be careful to distinguish here between explanations of statehood devised by modern historians (etics) and the perceptions of the actors involved (emics). If we are interested in a question like the birth of national identity, which is essentially a question about native perceptions, we are primarily dependent on textual evidence, such as we find in the biblical texts and in ancient inscriptions, and not so much on archaeological reconstruction of material conditions. Assuming for the moment that the Samuel traditions are our earliest witnesses to the dynamics of nascent kingship,[27] then 1 Samuel 8 is potentially relevant to the task before us.

We need to pursue the politics of this narrative a little further. It falls in a stream of tradition which is commonly regarded as anti-monarchic, yet it depicts the monarchy as arising through popular will. One would think that anti-monarchic strategists would be reluctant to concede the existence of such widespread support for a king (unless, of course, they embodied such elitist attitudes that they tended to see popular views as *ipso facto* usually wrong). Accordingly, one might see some plausibility in the suggestion that precisely because of the anti-monarchic tendency of this tradition, 1 Samuel 8 provides evidence that tribal unification under a king was broadly perceived to be in the common interest. In other words, such a story might be considered evidence not only for the rise of a monarchic state but also for the rise of a nation; i.e., in this case, a large social group which is seen by actors involved as only superficially divided by lines of status, tribal identity or tribal territory.

Such an argument is, however, fraught with difficulties. The emphasis of 1 Sam. 8.20 is on the king as military leader, and although there is much evidence that states can be forged through wars,[28] there is no difficulty in finding biblical material which points to the *disunity* of

26. See especially I. Finkelstein, 'The Emergence of the Monarchy in Israel', *JSOT* 44 (1989), pp. 43-74.

27. See F. Crüsemann, *Der Widerstand gegen das Königtum* (Neukirchen–Vluyn: Neukirchener Verlag, 1978); K. Whitelam, 'Israelite Kingship: The Royal Ideology and its Opponents', in R.E. Clements (ed.), *The World of Ancient Israel* (Cambridge: Cambridge University Press, 1989), pp. 119-39.

28. See C. Tilly (ed.), *The Formation of National States in Western Europe* (Princeton: Princeton University Press, 1975); A. Giddens, *The Nation State and Violence* (Cambridge: Polity, 1985).

Davidic-Solomonic times. For example, the story of the split between the northern and southern kingdoms in 1 Kings 12 seems to indicate that even if the rise of monarchy was associated with a popular idealism (and the extent of this popularity is unknown), the reign of Solomon had descended into a rule characterised more by brute force than by ideological incorporation. Issues of tribe and territory continued, apparently, to work against any over-arching sense of social homogeneity. The unity of a coercive state should not be immediately identified with the social and cultural solidarity of nationalism.[29]

Taking a different methodological tack, one could also enquire whether native perceptions of a shift in social identity might be reflected in the semantic contrast between early Israel as a 'people' ('am) and monarchic Israel as a 'nation' (gôy) 'like all the nations' (1 Sam 8.5, 20).[30] Aelred Cody's judgment on the subject is essentially in agreement with the earlier work of Rost and Speiser: 'while 'am throughout the Old Testament refers to a people or nation in its aspect of centripetal unity and cohesiveness, gôy is linked inseparably with territory and government'.[31] Thus, one might want to argue that the use of the term gôy in reference to Israel reflects a native perception of 'national' identity, even if the resulting concept of society bears little resemblance to nationalism in any modern sense. Ron Clements takes a step in this direction by arguing that 'Since Israel did not attain full territorial control of Canaan and independent political status until the reign of David, it is from this period that its historical existence as a gôy is to be dated'.[32]

This argument, however, poses some methodological puzzles. Weisman, for example, has pointed out two important exceptions to the common generalizations about gôy: first, in Gen. 46.3 God assures Jacob that his family will grow into 'a great nation' (gôy gādôl) in Egypt; second, the creed in Deut. 26.5 also speaks of becoming a gôy gādôl in

29. On the distinctions between 'state' and 'nation' see, for example, L. Tivey, *The Nation State* (Oxford: Martin Robertson, 1980), Introduction; J. Breuilly, *Nationalism and the State* (Manchester: Manchester University Press, 2nd edn, 1993), especially pp. 366-424.

30. See L. Rost, 'Die Bezeichnungen für Land und Volk im alten Testament' (1934), in *Das kleine Credo und andere Studien zum Alten Testament* (Heidelberg: Quelle & Meyer, 1965), pp. 76-101; E.A. Speiser, '"People" and "Nation" in Israel', *JBL* 79 (1960), pp. 157-63.

31. See A. Cody, 'When is the Chosen People Called a Gôy?', *VT* 14 (1964), pp. 1-6.

32. R. Clements, "גוי gôy', in *TDOT*, II, p. 430.

Egypt. In other words, these texts presuppose that it is possible to be a 'nation' without territory and sovereignty; in each case, being a *gôy* is an accomplished fact before the exodus from Egypt is envisaged.[33] Such exceptions do not negate the common associations of sovereignty and territory, but they introduce a meaning of the term *gôy* which leaves it much less clearly distinguished from *'am*.[34] This possibility is noted by Clements, but he later concludes that any usage of the term in reference to pre-monarchic Israel is 'anachronistic'.[35] But if a Deuteronomic author can conceive of a *gôy* without territory and monarchy (as in Deut. 26.5), what does it mean to say that this conception is anachronistic? Does Clements mean that there was an early period when *gôy* could only imply territory and sovereignty (and therefore no pre-monarchic Israelites could have used it to describe themselves) and then it later acquired another possible meaning which did *not* imply territory and sovereignty (and therefore monarchic Israelites could use it anachronistically in reference to earlier periods)? What evidence could support such a hypothesis? Surely, all we can say with any degree of certainty is that *gôy* is a polysemous term[36] which may, or may not,

33. Z. Weisman, 'National Consciousness in the Patriarchal Promises', *JSOT* 31 (1985), p. 68. An 'imagined' territory is clearly the common feature of all the patriarchal promises, but Weisman's point here is that, in these particular texts, the status of *gôy* is already achieved in Egypt. It is also interesting to note that amongst the patriarchal promises it is only the so-called P traditions which specifically refer to a future monarchy, and it is precisely these (Gen. 17.6; 35.11) which undermine the unique status of Israel by speaking in the plural of 'nations' and 'kings' (p. 66).

34. Weisman goes further and suggests a comparison between Gen. 46.3 (which he regards as distinctively 'Elohistic') and the 'Elohistic' promise to make Ishmael a *gôy gādôl* (Gen. 21.13, 18) without suggesting that this includes possession of national land: 'it may well be asked, therefore, whether E does not represent an earlier stage than J in the formation of national consciousness in Israel' (Weisman, 'National Consciousness', pp. 65-67). Weisman does not further explicate the significance of the marked differences between the patriarchal 'nation' promises in E, J and P, and whatever one might think about its source-critical assumptions, his work does illustrate a diversity of national conceptions even within the book of Genesis. His wise avoidance of dating questions may suggest, however, that these conceptions are, in fact, largely undatable.

35. Clements, '*gôy*', pp. 427, 430.

36. In theoretical linguistics, there is a more technical meaning of 'polysemy' which would distinguish it from 'vagueness' or 'generality'. I am not aware of any biblical studies which would allow us to conclude that *gôy* is polysemous in this precise sense, so I will leave the details of a linguistic analysis as a matter for further

carry connotations of territory and sovereignty, depending on the linguistic context. When this term was first used in relation to Israel is an open question which cannot be decided on semantic grounds alone.

If, on the other hand, we are looking for examples of nationalism in something like a modern sense (which frames any monarchic sovereignty with popular sovereignty), we may be on more promising ground if we focussed our attention on the seventh century.[37] According to an old orthodoxy of historical research, it is in this century that we find the programme of social unification and homogenization promoted by king Josiah and inspired by the book of Deuteronomy.[38] It is in the book of Deuteronomy that we find a balance of judicial, priestly, prophetic and monarchic powers which effectively limits the power of kings (Deut. 17.14-20) within the context of the common good under Yahweh. As Baruch Halpern puts it, 'In erecting a central judiciary, a priestly order, and a prophetic office as positions independent of the monarchy, this remarkable document...limits the monarch's power to arrogate to himself all authority in the national regime'.[39] This description forms a remarkable contrast with, for example, the universal obedience demanded in Thomas Hobbes' theory of the state, in which the king was to have all authority to interpret Scripture, preach, ordain, and censor any public

research. The distinction between 'vagueness' and ambiguity (here equivalent to polysemy) is to be found in R.M. Kempson, *Semantic Theory* (Cambridge: Cambridge University Press, 1977), pp. 128-34. This has been reformulated as a distinction between 'generality' and ambiguity by D.A. Cruse, *Lexical Semantics* (Cambridge: Cambridge University Press, 1986), ch. 3.

37. So Grosby, 'Kinship, Territory and the Nation'; M. Liverani, 'Nationality and Political Identity', *ABD*, IV, p. 1035. The views of Grosby and Liverani undermine the outdated sociology which underlies the earlier work of G. Buccellati, *Cities and Nations of Ancient Syria* (SS 26; Rome: Instituto di Studi del Vicino Oriente, 1967).

38. The details of such an historical claim are now much disputed, but whatever position one adopts on questions of editing and dating, the ideas found in the texts can still be described as 'nationalist'. For a review of recent research that illustrates the inter-connections between redactional hypotheses concerning Deut. and Dtr and the historicity of Josiah's reform, see B. Gieselmann, 'Die sogenannte josianische Reform in der gegenwärtige Forschung', *ZAW* 106 (1994), pp. 223-42.

39. B. Halpern, *The Constitution of the Monarchy in Israel* (Missoula: Scholars Press, 1980), pp. 234-35; cf. F. Crüsemann, *Die Tora: Theologie und Sozialgeschichte des alttestamentlichen Gesetzes* (Munich: Kaiser, 1992), pp. 235-322, who, with conscious reflection on modern analogies, regards Deuteronomy as a constitution with a vision of 'Theokratie als Demokratie' (pp. 273, 287).

prophecy.[40] Some have even suggested that Deuteronomy's theology and law are cast in conscious opposition to the Davidic monarchy.[41] The Deuteronomic tradition also systematizes the specific self-description of Israel as the 'people of Yahweh',[42] claiming a unique vocation over against other peoples (yet being careful to moderate a sense of superiority: Deut. 7.7-8; 8.17-18; 9.4-5). All this 'imagines' a popular solidarity, whatever the socio-historical background might have been.

It is also worth noting, in this context, that Deuteronomy was enveloped in the introduction to the so-called Deuteronomistic History, which John Van Seters has celebrated as a genuine example of history writing precisely because (unlike writings from all the other *gôyim*) it communicates a *national* identity:

> Insofar as any of the other Near Eastern nations express a concept of identity through their historiographic forms, it is in the person of the king as the state. In Dtr the royal ideology is incorporated in the identity of the people as a whole..., so that the leaders of the people must always be obedient to the Mosaic covenant...The doctrine of Israel's election as the chosen people of Yahweh set the nation apart from other peoples...All other callings and elections, whether to kingship, priesthood, or prophecy, were viewed in association with the choice of the people as a whole. Many

40. Thomas Hobbes, *Leviathan* (New York: Collier, [1st edn, 1651] 1962), pp. 340-41; 395-98; on Hobbes' use of the Hebrew Bible, see Reventlow, *Authority of the Bible and the Rise of the Modern World*, pp. 194-222; J. Milbank, *Theology and Social Theory* (Oxford: Basil Blackwell, 1990), pp. 9-26; for a contemporary reflection, see J. Moltmann, 'Covenant or Leviathan?', pp. 19-41.

41. See Clements, *God's Chosen People* (London: SCM, 1968), pp. 45-49. Stronger claims about the resistance to monarchy in Deuteronomy have been made by Frank Crüsemann. See '"Und die Gesetze des Königs halten sie nicht" (Est. 3.8): Widerstand und Recht im Alten Testament', *Wort und Dienst* 17 (1983), pp. 9-25; "Damit er dich segne im allem Tun deiner Hand" (Dtn. 14.29): Die Produktions- verhältnisse der späten Königszeit, dargestellt am Ostrakon von Mesad Hashavjahu, und die Sozialgesetzgebung des Deuteronomiums', in L. and W. Schottroff (eds.), *Mitarbeiter der Schöpfung: Bibel und Arbeitswelt* (Munich: Kaiser, 1983), pp. 72-103.

42. G. von Rad, *Das Gottesvolk im Deuteronomium* (BWANT, 47; Stuttgart: Kohlhammer, 1929); N. Lohfink, 'Beobachtungen zur Geschichte des Ausdrucks *'am yhwh*', in H.W. Wolff (ed.), *Probleme biblischer Theologie* (Munich: Kaiser, 1971), pp. 275-305. See also the discussions of popular rebellion depicted in 2 Kgs 11.14; 21.24, in Crüsemann, *Die Tora*, pp. 248-51, 275, 322; J.A. Soggin, 'Der judäische *'am-hā'āreṣ* und das Königtum im Juda', *VT* 13 (1963), pp. 187-95. Cf. Buccellati's view that the *hapiru* rebellions, on the other hand, were anti-monarchic but not 'nationalistic', *Cities and Nations of Ancient Syria*, pp. 71-72.

of the Near Eastern historiographic documents that have to do with kingship deal with the special election of the king to rule, and even recount the divine providence by which he gained the throne and was victorious over his enemies. But nowhere outside of Israel was the notion of special election extended to the nation as a whole, such that the complete history of the people could be viewed in this way.[43]

Disregarding Van Seters' questionable arguments concerning the genres of historiography, one would have to agree that this account of the Deuteronomistic History has much in common with the sentiments of sixteenth-century English nationalists who placed strict limits on the role of the monarchy and elevated the status of the whole people. In other words, it would not be entirely anachronistic to regard some features of Deuteronomy and the Deuteronomistic History as nationalistic in something like a modern sense.

It would still be possible to question, however, the extent to which such beliefs permeated the whole of Israelite society. In many ways, this question is unanswerable, since we do not possess a great deal of written evidence outside of the biblical texts which would count as relevant evidence of popular beliefs concerning corporate identity. Certainly, Van Seters wants to emphasize that the formation of traditions—in particular, historiography—is the activity of intellectual elites, not communities as a whole.[44] We do know that Deuteronomistic theology was engaged in a polemic against certain forms of popular religion, such as the worship of the goddess Asherah as YHWH's consort. But this does not count as evidence against the view that popular religion held to something like the theology of the people's election. (Indeed, it would be arguable that the 'temple sermons' in Jeremiah 7 and 26 are directed against a popular over-confidence in the election, at least, of Zion.) It might be the case, as is now commonly argued, that an early edition of the Deuteronomistic History (*Dtr* I) served the purposes of Josiah's programme of national unification, and at this level at least, it may have been a projection of courtly interests.[45] But one could hardly argue that

43. Van Seters, *In Search of History: Historiography in the Ancient World and the Origins of Biblical History* (New Haven: Yale, 1983), pp. 359-60.

44. E.g. Van Seters, *Prologue to History: The Yahwist as Historian in Genesis* (Louisville: Westminster Press/John Knox, 1992), p. 35.

45. One might well ask how a book like Deuteronomy, with severe reservations about kingship, could be turned to Josiah's advantage. This is ironic but not inconceivable: Dtr's praise was not for kingship in general but for Josiah in particular, who was remarkably unlike any king before or after him (2 Kgs 23.25). An

the Deuteronomistic History in its exilic version (*Dtr* II) was a mystification projected by the royal court, since there *was* no royal court in exile with interests to legitimate. The theological task of the exile was precisely to provide some sort of explanation of a national tragedy which included the failure of the monarchy.

But if *Dtr* is said to have national interests, then, according to Van Seters, the historians who responded to it with the Yahwist document in the Pentateuch can be credited with a more universalistic theology, comparable with the inclusive features of Second Isaiah.[46] At the very least, it should be borne in mind that even if we succeed in identifying a nationalist strand of Deuteronomistic tradition within the Hebrew Bible, it would be important to recognise the reactions against it. And this leads us on to the contrasts in discussions of biblical theology between universalism and particularism. As we shall see, some traditions commonly regarded as universalist also possess nationalist features, and the reverse seems also to be true.

Universalisms and Particularisms

There is a substantial literature on the tension between universalism and particularism in biblical theology, and very often, particularism has been equated with nationalism. It is commonly suggested that Israelite religion during the period of the monarchy was predominantly a nationalistic and territorial faith while the destruction of the temple ensured the rise of a more universalistic faith. A bridge to this universalism has been seen in the treasonable preaching of prophets like Jeremiah and Ezekiel who proclaimed that Judah should surrender its sovereignty to foreign aggressors. Universalism, so this story goes, was anticipated especially

analogy, perhaps, may be drawn with English history insofar as Queen Elizabeth was so regarded as a liberator from Catholic oppression that 'The association of the national sentiment with the person of the queen attenuated and slowed down the development of the democratic implications of English nationalism' (Greenfeld, *Nationalism*, p. 65).

46. Van Seters, *Prologue*, p. 331. In addition, one could note that the Priestly tradition shows signs of a surprising internationalism in the patriarchal promises which see the descendants as a plurality of nations and kings (Gen. 17.6-8; 28.3-4; 35.11-12; 48.3-4). See Weisman, 'National Consciousness', p. 66. Cf. the stimulating studies of N. Habel, 'Peoples at Peace; The Land Ideology of the Abraham Narratives' in Habel (ed.), *Religion and Multiculturalism in Australia* (Adelaide: AASR, 1992), pp. 336-349; *idem, The Land is Mine: Six Biblical Land Ideologies* (Minneapolis: Fortress Press, forthcoming).

by the challenge to beliefs in the inviolability of Zion and consummated by the prophetic visions of salvation for the nations. Views such as these have been promulgated not only by Christians but also by a number of popular Jewish authors.[47] In a notable defence of Christian pacifism, John Howard Yoder has argued that the NT conception of peoplehood intensifies the prophetic critique of national identity to the extent, for example, that holy war is no longer conceivable, even if it was so in Early Israel: '[T]he relativizing of the given ethnic-political peoplehood is completed...There is no one in any nation who is not a potential son of Abraham'.[48]

There are a number of reservations that one can express about such abstract contrasts between nationalism and universalism. Let us concede, for the moment, that the Deuteronomic tradition, for example, contains some features which could be associated with national identity. Does it follow that Deuteronomy contains a simple contrast between Israel and other nations? The laws concerning resident aliens (*gērîm*) are sufficient evidence against this, since they repeatedly enjoin the Israelites to treat aliens well since they themselves were once slaves in Egypt. These laws envisage *gērîm* as displaced people who have entered into dependent relationships within a household. Some *gērîm* were evidently from another tribe, but Exod. 12.48 makes clear that they can also be foreigners who became 'like one born in the land' when they underwent circumcision and kept the law. The treatment of the *gērîm* varies in the different law codes, but the overall picture clearly indicates that such aliens occupied a social position between the native born and the foreigner (*nokrî*) who had no settled status in the society. Under certain conditions, resident aliens were allowed full participation in Israelite religious festivals (Deut. 16).[49] In terms of comparison with nationalisms

47. See J. Magonet, *A Rabbi's Bible* (London: SCM Press, 1991), pp. 136-37, citing the rabbis Victor Reichert and Isodore Epstein.

48. Yoder, *The Original Revolution* (Scottdale: Herald, 1977), p. 103.

49. Aliens are not explicitly mentioned in the law of passover, one of the three festivals mentioned in Deuteronomy 16, but it is doubtful whether this silence necessarily implies exclusion (contra C. Van Houten, *The Alien in Israelite Law* [JSOTSup, 107; Sheffield: JSOT Press, 1991], pp. 88-91). In any case, the legislation in Exod. 12.48 explicitly allows aliens to participate in the passover. If this law was, in fact, a late, Priestly revision of Deuteronomic practice, as implicitly suggested by Van Houten, it would be a remarkable development in a tradition customarily judged to be exclusivist. In this connection, it would be important to consider the stimulating argument recently advanced by Mary Douglas that Priestly theology in Numbers can

from the modern period, one might wish to conclude that the laws concerning aliens associate Deuteronomy more with civic nationalism than with ethnic nationalism,[50] i.e., the emphasis in the construction of national identity seems to be more on shared tradition than on blood ties.[51]

If, on the one hand, the particularism in Deuteronomy needs careful qualification, the putative universalism of the Isaiah tradition is no less straightforward. On the one hand, Second Isaiah proclaims that the servant figure will be a 'light to the nations' (or 'light of the nations', 42.6; 49.6), that the nations wait for the servant's justice and *tôrāh* (42.4), that the 'islands' hope for the *tôrāh* and salvation of Yahweh, whose justice will be a light to the peoples (51.4-6). On the other hand, Second Isaiah envisions nations coming to Israel in chains (45.14) and kings licking the dust of Israel's feet (49.23).

A few scholars have seen such irreconcilable contradictions in these traditions that they find it necessary to identify several layers of editing. It may well be true that Second Isaiah is not always consistent, but it is probably also true that some diachronic reconstructions of the text have avoided an uncomfortable key to the unity of the material, namely, that Second Isaiah is more nationalistic than it appears. In line with such an uncomfortable solution, Whybray interprets the justice (*mishpaṭ* in 42.1) which the servant brings to the nations as a universal rule 'which will

be read as a critique of the marriage policies in Ezra and Nehemiah; in short, priestly theology may not be as exclusive as commonly imagined. See Douglas, *In the Wilderness* (JSOTSup, 158; Sheffield: JSOT Press, 1993), esp. chs. 12–13. Cf. R. Rendtorff, 'The *gēr* in the Priestly Laws of the Pentateuch', in M.G. Brett (ed.), *Ethnicity and the Bible* (Leiden: Brill, forthcoming).

50. On civic nationalism versus ethnic nationalism see L. Greenfeld, *Nationalism*, Introduction; for a parallel distinction between 'territorial' and ethnic nations, cf. A.D. Smith, *Ethnic Origins of Nations*, ch. 6; similarly, E. Gellner, 'Nationalism and Politics in Eastern Europe', *New Left Review* 189 (1991), pp. 127-34.

51. I would suggest that this is true even of the ban on indigenous peoples in Deut. 20.16-18; the overriding motivation is not racial xenophobia but shared tradition (20.18; cf. 7.4). On the intractable ethical problem of the ban, see J. Barr, *Biblical Faith and Natural Theology* (Oxford: Clarendon Press, 1993), ch. 10. At the very least one would have to say that Deuteronomy's xenophobia is inconsistent: in addition to the laws concerning aliens, it should be noted that foreigners are not excluded by the law in 21.10-14, nor by the laws of assembly in 23.7-8. Even Ammonites and Moabites might be considered for membership in the assembly after the 'tenth generation' (23.2). This phrase is evidently a redactional addition, but a seventh-century context for such a law would place it clearly ten generations distant from Mosaic times.

mean salvation for Israel but submission for the other nations'.[52]
Similarly, Orlinsky emphasizes that texts like 52.10 demonstrate no
more than that the nations are the helpless witnesses to God's exclusive
love for Israel. Commenting on 42.6 and 49.6, he suggests that

> Israel will be 'a light of nations' in the sense that Israel will dazzle the
> nations with her God-given triumph and restoration; the whole world will
> behold this single beacon that is God's sole covenanted people.[53]

Reacting against such 'nationalist' interpretations of Second Isaiah,
Antony Gelston has recently suggested that this tradition contains three
kinds of universalism: first, YHWH is affirmed as the only true sovereign
of all creation and all humankind; second, there is the expectation that
this truth will be recognized by the gentiles; third, that there is a universal offer of the experience of salvation. It is this third claim which is
perhaps the most controversial in recent work on Second Isaiah, but it
seems to me Gelston has built a good case for it, beginning with Isa.
45.20-25.[54]

A major difficulty with Gelston's work, however, is not so much
exegetical as conceptual. Even granted his claim about the universal
offer of salvation, he still has not grasped the significance of the basic
point made by Harry Orlinsky over two decades ago: much of the
eschatological prophecy which is apparently universal in its scope has
Zion as the focus of its expectation, and all the other nations are
envisaged as flowing towards this territorial centre (in addition to
Second Isaiah, see the parade examples in Mal. 2.10; Isa. 2.2-4; 56.7).
Orlinsky has rightly argued that we should see such visions as

---

52. N. Whybray, *Isaiah 40–66* (NCB; London: Marshall, Morgan & Scott,
1975), p. 72.

53. H. Orlinski and N. Snaith, *Studies on the Second Part of the Book of Isaiah*
(VTSup, 14; Leiden: Brill, 1967), p. 117 ; cf. Orlinski, 'Nationalism-Universalism and
Internationalism in Ancient Israel', in H.T. Frank and W.L. Reed (eds.), *Translating
and Understanding the Old Testament* (Nashville: Abingdon, 1970), pp. 206-36. Cf.
F. Huber, *Jahwe, Juda und die anderen Völker beim Propheten Jesaja* (BZAW, 137;
Berlin: de Gruyter, 1976).

54. A. Gelston, 'Universalism in Second Isaiah', *JTS* 43 (1992), pp. 377-98. One
should also note, however, Gelston's qualification that the universal offer of salvation
'by no means precludes the continued subordination of the nations to Israel'. Cf.
D.W. Van Winkle, 'The Relationship of the Nations to Yahweh and to Israel in Isaiah
xl-lv', *VT* 35 (1985), p. 457: the 'tension between universalism and nationalism may
be resolved by recognizing that for Deutero-Isaiah the salvation of the nations does
not preclude their submission to Israel'.

nationalist-universalist rather than internationalist.[55]

Second Isaiah can also be related to the discussion above concerning the definition of nationalism, since it is precisely here that we find the idea of the Davidic covenant 'democratized' (55.1-5).[56] The only monarch in this vision is the Persian 'messiah' Cyrus (45.1), and, unlike Deuteronomy, there is no separation of powers for Israelite kings or priests envisaged; there is only a 'servant' who is an agent of imagined solidarity. All this has been observed by Norman Gottwald who, nevertheless, resists any implications of egalitarianism. He argues that the social subtext is more significant; Second Isaiah imagines the exiled community as a 'purified, aristocratic oligarchy who, within the structure of the Persian political imperium, will have a free hand to develop the internal life of restored Judah' over against the 'indigenous Judahites' who escaped exile and remained behind in the land.[57] In short, the vision of second Isaiah is here reduced to a strategy for preserving the identity of the former Judahite ruling elite.[58]

If Gottwald is correct in this thesis, however, then Second Isaiah is not 'nationalist' in the more precise sense which includes some notion of popular sovereignty. Ezekiel's programmatic vision for the restored community included a prince with sharply reduced powers (Ezek. 45.7-12), but Gottwald infers that even this would have endangered the pro-

55. The parallel of Isa. 2.2-4 in Mic. 4.1-4 is a different matter. Orlinsky conflates the two without discussion ('Nationalism-Universalism', pp. 218-19), but Mic. 4.5 concludes the oracle with what is arguably an internationalist saying. Most commentators regard this verse as contrary to what precedes it, and therefore redactional. But it is a highly significant re-interpretation which seems to say that the nations *visit* Jerusalem not so much because it is an imperial centre but because wise advice may be gained there which will help to resolve political problems at home. What is found in Jerusalem, it should be stressed, is not weaponry but only instruction (*tôrāh*) and word (*dābār*).

56. Isaiah 55.1-5 is a *locus classicus* for this idea, but Edgar Conrad's work on the subject has advanced much broader form-critical and literary arguments which lead in the same direction: see Conrad, 'The Community as King in Second Isaiah', in J.T. Butler *et al.* (eds.), *Understanding the Word* (JSOTSup, 37; Sheffield: JSOT Press, 1985); *idem*, *Reading Isaiah* (Minneapolis: Fortress Press, 1991).

57. Gottwald, 'Social Class and Ideology in Isaiah 40-55: An Eagletonian Reading', *Semeia* 59 (1992), pp. 51, 54.

58. Contrast T.W. Ogletree, *The Use of the Bible in Christian Ethics* (Philadelphia: Fortress Press, 1983), p. 65: 'In these texts exclusiveness no longer concerns Israel's struggle for identity among the nations; it is linked instead to principles entrusted to Israel for the peaceful gathering of the whole human family'.

Persian stance of Second Isaiah: 'a Judahite restoration without a native prince would "sit better" with the Persians'. The motive was to preserve the interests of an elite group *under imperial rule*; national sovereignty was apparently not at issue.

But we may doubt whether Gottwald is correct on this point. Isa. 54.2-3 would surely have been more offensive to Persian interests than Ezekiel's modest prince: 'Enlarge the place of your tent...For you will spread abroad to the right and to the left, and your descendants will possess the nations'. The vision is, indeed, 'empire wide', and the powerful centre of this imagined empire is Zion. Carol Newsom rightly points out that Zion is the 'destination' of YHWH in Second Isaiah (e.g. 40.1-10),[59] and in 49.17-21, Zion is depicted as surprised by the return of children born to her in exile; she is urged to make room for them, and there is no hint of social division.[60] Could such a vision still be motivated by a conscious will to 'social' power over the people of the land who never went into exile? This seems unlikely; John Milbank has rightly argued that in the biblical world the 'social' was never conceived as a separable, more fundamental reality in isolation from ideological strategies.[61] Nevertheless, it *is* arguable that imperialist visions such as we find in Second Isaiah can be a reflex of certain forms of nationalism,[62] or, in Orlinsky's terms, national universalism. In short, Isaiah might still be read as a type of nationalism which includes an

59. Contra John Milbank, whose concept of 'nomadic' Zion fits better with Lam. 1.3, 7 than with Second Isaiah. Zion may be 'elastic', as Milbank suggests, but it is anchored to a territorial centre. Milbank has followed Deleuze and Guattari in wrongly conflating Isaiah with 'nomad' and ark theology. See Milbank, '"I will gasp and pant": Deutero-Isaiah and the Birth of the Suffering Subject', *Semeia* 59 (1992), pp. 59-71; G. Deleuze and F. Guattari, *A Thousand Plateaus: Capitalism and Schizophrenia* (London: Athlone, 1987), pp. 111-48.

60. C. Newsom, 'Response to Norman K. Gottwald, "Social Class and Ideology in Isaiah 40–55"', *Semeia* 59 (1992), pp. 76-77.

61. Milbank, 'Deutero-Isaiah and the Birth of the Suffering Subject', pp. 62-63; *idem, Theology and Social Theory*, pp. 101-143. It does not follow, however, that the discourses of modern social sciences must be prohibited from formulating 'social' explanations. Milbank seems to believe that what ancient discourses have joined together, no other discourse may put asunder, but this only holds true for emic studies. Whether the conflict between emic and etic discourses must be construed in Nietzchean, agonistic terms, as argued by Milbank, is a matter for further debate.

62. See, e.g., Said's comments on Ruskin's 1870 Slade Lectures at Oxford, in *Culture and Imperialism* (London: Chatto and Windus, 1993), pp. 123-26; cf. Anderson, *Imagined Communities*, pp. 80-103, 137.

imperial periphery, and such a reading would not necessarily be anachronistic.

Orlinsky argued, with some justification, that the seeds of internationalism are not to be found in Second Isaiah but in a Hellenistic text, Isa. 19.18-25, where we find a highway envisaged between Assyria and Egypt: 'Israel will be the third with Egypt and Assyria, a blessing in the midst of the earth, who the lord of Hosts has blessed, saying, "Blessed be my people (*'amî*) Egypt, and Assyria the work of my hands, and Israel my heritage"'. Here, at least, the centrality of Zion has been deconstructed.

Contemporary Reflections

There are many issues arising from this discussion which the space available does not permit us to explore. Nevertheless, I want to conclude with a few, somewhat tentative, reflections. The first area of concern would be the implications of our discussion for Jewish and Christian appropriation of Israelite moral visions. A crucial question arising is whether the Hebrew Bible can be saved from charges of malign nationalism.

The book of Isaiah is a good illustration of the complexity of the issue. On the one hand, it reflects no militant nationalism in the prophetic challenge to Ahaz and Hezekiah to trust in YHWH's sovereignty rather than their own military preparations (e.g. Isa. 7.1-9; 30.15-16; 31.1-3; 37.1-7). And if nationalism is primarily 'a principle which holds that the political and national unit should be congruent',[63] then Isaiah's vision of the loss of political sovereignty is also not nationalist (e.g. 1.21-31). In this and other passages, Isaiah reflects an ethical impulse characteristic of the canonical prophets: the political and the national unit will be congruent, if and only if the people practice justice. Justice is explicated particularly in terms of defending the cause of the widow and orphan (1.23). In the prophetic material of the eighth century, the resident alien is not yet included amongst the marginalized as a focus of concern,[64] but certainly in the later Isaiah tradition, not just the alien but the 'foreigner'

---

63. E. Gellner, *Nations and Nationalism* (Oxford: Basil Blackwell, 1983), p. 1.

64. F. Crüsemann, '"You know the Heart of a Stranger" (Exod. 23.9): A Recollection of the Torah in the Face of New Nationalism and Xenophobia', *Concilium* 4 (1993), p. 98. Note, however, that the treatment of *gērîm* does become a touchstone of justice for Jeremiah (Jer. 7.6; 22.3; cf. Ezek. 22.7) who similarly sees it as amongst the necessary conditions for possessing the land.

(*nēkār*) is included among those who will offer acceptable sacrifices (Isa. 56.3-7; cf. 66.18-21).

However radical such theology may have been in its own context, a modern appropriation of this material would need to recognise the imperialist overtones with which it is associated; these are negative over-tones for us, even if they were not so in the ancient world. Enemies are still subjugated if they do not conform to YHWH's demands (e.g. Isa. 45.14; 49.23), and the nations are envisaged, in eschatological peace-fulness, as flowing up to Jerusalem (Isa. 2.1-5). Such peace and univer-sality is based ultimately upon conformity; Zion is the centre about which all else is oriented.

But there are at least two points to make in response to this problem. First, the visions of Second Isaiah issue from an experience of exile. There is no imperial force which can give sanction to them. These oracles are not so much imperialist as counter-imperialist: they imagine a social future which is in some sense shaped by the Babylonian empire but which rises up against it with hope and not with weapons. If this kind of social vision arises from an erstwhile elite, then they are an elite who have no powers of state. And we can surmise from the conflicts depicted in Isaiah 56–66 that the inheritors of Second Isaiah's tradition did not secure imperial patronage; such went to the bearers of the Ezra-Nehemiah traditions.

Secondly, the Hebrew Bible included much material with no real interest in 'the national story'. This is true of the wisdom books, and it is striking that the sceptical character of Job was canonized in spite of his foreignness (Job 1.1). The book of Jonah satirises a prophet with narrowly ethnic dispositions, and the book of Ruth imaginatively legalizes a Moabitess who dared to say 'your people (*'am*) will be my people' (1.16). These are all familiar examples which will appeal to the liberal sentiments of a modern, civil republican. We should also note that Rabbinic tradition—with a more comprehensive use of scripture—developed the concept of the Noahide covenant, incumbent on all humanity. This clearly envisaged gentiles having a proper relationship with God,[65] and we could conclude that Judaism became 'universalist' at the level of the Noahide covenant and 'particularist' at the level of the

65. See D. Novak, *The Image of the Non-Jew in Judaism* (New York: Edwin Mellen, 1983), pp. 14-28; cf. Novak, *Jewish Social Ethics* (Oxford: Oxford University Press, 1992).

Mosaic covenant.[66] Such an approach can hardly be judged imperialist; it neither deprives foreigners of moral agency nor compels them to adopt Jewish values.[67]

This traditional Rabbinic solution has much to commend it, but in many ways it simply emphasizes the need for critical reflection on the diversity of biblical politics. The Bible in itself provides no explicit guidance in evaluating its own diversity. There are many ways in which we need to be critical of the moral resources of the Hebrew Bible, and the tension inherent in Second Isaiah is a case in point; if we inherit the dream of *mishpaṭ* and *tôrāh* for the nations, we still need to debate the precise shape that such justice will take. Deuteronomy provokes a similar ambivalence. It provides a vision of life which satisfies deep human needs for community while demanding respect for the marginalized and for the alien. It does this by defining Israel as the story of aliens who were liberated from Egypt—'a primal inscription of foreignness'[68]—and by articulating an imagined community with minimized distinctions of status, class, and even, to some extent, of ethnicity. Yet Deuteronomy 20 also prescribes, retrospectively,[69] an ethnic cleansing of any real competitors in the promised land—men, women and children; the defence of the national interests entails violence on a scale which is contrary even to the most hawkish formulation of 'just war' theory (although it is quite consistent with recent memory in Dresden and Hiroshima). In short, Isaiah and Deuteronomy provide moral resources which can be seen as both nationalist and anti-nationalist; they can be appropriated only through a critical dialogue with other elements of biblical and subsequent tradition.

Another issue to explore would be the parallels between arguments concerning the fate of national identities in a postmodern age and the fate of Jewish identity after the Babylonian exile, when its nationhood was no longer expressed in a state. I have in mind the sociological theories of postmodernity which see nationhood as being deconstructed,

66. See Jon D. Levenson, 'The Universal Horizon of Biblical Particularism', in A. LaCoque (ed.), *Commitment and Commemoration: Jews, Christians and Muslims in Dialogue* (Chicago: Exploration Press, 1994).

67. Cf. John Barton's argument concerning 'natural morality' in Amos, in *Amos's Oracles against the Nations* (SOTSMS, 6; Cambridge: Cambridge University Press, 1980).

68. Kristeva, *Nations without Nationalism*, p. 23.

69. For a plausible account of the composition of this chapter, see M. Fishbane, *Biblical Interpretation in Ancient Israel* (Oxford: Clarendon Press, 1985), pp. 199-209.

on the one hand by economic and cultural internationalism, and on the other hand by a reactive search for more immediate identities, notably, ethnic identities.[70] A parallel suggests itself in the fact that a racialized ethnic strategy was tried by Ezra and Nehemiah in their prohibition on foreign marriages, although there were no clear precedents for this in the earlier legal traditions—not even in Priestly legislation. There is no evidence that Ezra and Nehemiah envisage the possibility of foreign conversions, articulated both in the earlier Deuteronomic and Priestly laws concerned with resident aliens, and in later Rabbinic tradition. The ban on foreign marriages (and, as several authors have suggested, the associated attempt to narrow the definition of who counts as 'foreign') stands out as a failed option for the construction of social identity, perhaps motivated by a struggle over land rights.[71] Ezra and Nehemiah form a striking contrast to Ezekiel's exhortation to allot resident aliens an inheritance within the boundaries of the land (47.22-23).[72]

Nationalisms are always open to deconstruction. This point has been stressed especially in recent, poststructuralist social science and literary theory, but the main issue is not a new one. 'Forgetting', said Ernest Renan in 1882, 'I would even go as far as to say historical error, is a crucial factor in the creation of a nation, which is why progress in historical studies often constitutes a danger for nationality'.[73] Renan had

70. See, e.g., B. Smart, *Postmodernity* (London: Routlege & Kegan Paul, 1993), pp. 56-61; S.I. Griffiths, *Nationalism and Ethnic Conflict: Threats to European Security* (Oxford: Oxford University Press, 1993), p. 127: 'The emergence of the "globalization" phenomenon is, paradoxically, strengthening local and ethnic allegiances around the world'.

71. See Mary Douglas, *In the Wilderness*, chs. 12–13; T. Eskenazi, 'Out from the Shadows: Biblical Women in the Postexilic Era', *JSOT* 54 (1992), pp. 34-36. A comprehensive discussion of the recent literature can be found in T.C. Eskenazi and K.H. Richards, *Second Temple Studies. II. Temple Community in the Persian Period* (JSOTSup, 175; Sheffield: JSOT Press, 1994); especially the essays by H. Washington, D. Smith-Christopher, T.C. Eskenazi and E.P. Judd.

72. It is surely ironic that when later Judaism emphasized descent through the mother rather than the father, the resulting model of peoplehood could be understood as familial but not narrowly racial; see Levenson, 'The Universal Horizon of Jewish Particularism'. Anderson argues that modern racism arises more from ideologies of class than of nation (*Imagined Communities*, p. 136; cf. B. Moore, *Social Origins of Dictatorship and Democracy* [Boston: Beacon, 1966], p. 436).

73. Renan, 'Qu'est-ce qu'une nation?'; lecture delivered at the Sorbonne, 11 March 1882 (trans. M. Thom in H.K. Bhaba [ed.], *Nation and Narration* [London: Routledge & Kegan Paul, 1990], pp. 8-22, 11).

in mind the kind of forgetfulness which allowed old conflicts and linguistic diversity to be subsumed under the social dream of the French Revolution—a nation of citizens equal in dignity and status.[74] If it is true that this process of homogenization has links with ideas of modernity and the 'maturity of reason', as several authors have argued, then it is intriguing to note that the consequences of the postmodern 'unmasking' of reason have been described by Umberto Eco as a kind of 'neo-medievalism'—the development of micro-societies and minority neighbourhoods, with an associated increase in ethnic conflict and social fragmentation.[75]

Liah Greenfeld insightfully concludes her book by suggesting that 'national identity is fundamentally a matter of dignity'. This is true of the earlier European attempts at nation building, of colonial struggles, of post-colonial reconstruction, and of social problems internal to many contemporary states.[76] Identity is partly shaped by the recognition, or mis-recognition of others; individuals and groups can suffer damage when a confining or demeaning picture is reflected back to them. The assertion of dignity, when rising in response, is often still partly shaped

74. See Anderson, *Imagined Communities*, pp. 199-201; P. McPhee, *A Social History of France 1780–1880* (London: Routledge & Kegan Paul, 1992); *idem*, 'A Case-study of Internal Colonization: The *Francisation* of Northern Catalonia', *Review: A Journal of the Fernand Braudel Center* 3 (1980), pp. 399-428. For feminist critiques of revolutionary fraternity, see J.B. Landes, *Women and the Public Sphere in the Age of the French Revolution* (Ithaca: Cornell University Press, 1988); L. Hunt, *The Family Romance of the French Revolution* (Berkeley: University of California Press, 1992).

75. See U. Eco, *Travels in Hyperreality* (London: Picador, 1987); B. Smart, *Postmodernity*, pp. 30-31; cf. the conclusion of Smith, *Ethnic Origins*, who remarks on the practical limits to 'an infinite regress of ever smaller ethnic nationalisms': 'In seeking to match *ethnie* with their own homelands and, preferably, states, nationalism encounters the suspicion, if not hostility, of powerful state elites intent on upholding the prevailing pattern of bureaucratic states linked by networks of economic, diplomatic and military ties' (p. 221). See also E. Hobsbawm, 'Some Reflections on "The Break-up of Britain"', *New Left Review* 105 (1977), pp. 3-23.

76. See, e.g., P. Gutkind and I. Wallerstein (eds.), *The Political Economy of Contemporary Africa* (Beverly Hills: Sage, 1976), ch. 1; Harris, *National Liberation*; T. Nairn, *The Breakup of Britain: Crisis and Neo-Nationalism* (London: New Left Books, 1977); J. Eddy and D. Schreuder (eds.), *The Rise of Colonial Nationalism: Australia, New Zealand, Canada and South Africa first Assert their Nationalities 1880–1914* (Sydney: Allen & Unwin, 1988); A. Nandy, *The Intimate Enemy: Loss and Recovery of Self under Colonialism* (Delhi: Oxford University Press, 1983).

by the original oppression, but it can build strategically important solidarities.[77] The story of Israel can be read in this way not so much as the history of a race but as a series of counter-assertions of dignity: the exodus solidarity 'half-created' by Egypt; the united monarchy half-created by the Philistines; the Deuteronomic constitution half-created by Assyria;[78] the imagined empire of Second Isaiah half-created by Babylon. The construction of nationalism was simply one feature of this long, culturally-mediated conversation about what it means to be a community before God.

In spite of its 'primal inscription of foreignness', some of Israel's conversation is thoroughly ordinary in its capacity to defend ethnic, national or imperialistic interests, but some of it is extraordinary in its capacity to love the stranger. Even the national imaginations of Deuteronomy and Second Isaiah can still inspire us: these traditions are essentially in agreement with the classical prophetic view that justice is a necessary condition of Israel's identity. We may no longer agree with the shape of Israel's justice, and, for example, we will need continuing reflection on how the inscription of foreignness can be more radically applied in our own national identities. A major challenge for contemporary politics, it seems to me, is not that societies set out to construct an imagined *homogeneity*, whether in terms of civic or ethnic nationalism (and it is important to see that ethnicity is also a construct);[79] more important is the question of how the *diversity* within us shapes the national conversation.[80] And as the Hebrew Bible itself suggests, we

77. Cf. Harris, *National Liberation*, p. 276: 'In the struggle between Congress and the British Raj, whether or not 'Indians' existed as a political conception was a key issue in dispute. Congress won on this score not because it was correct in its judgment that Indians existed, but in the gamble that the British had half-created them—and they could be fully created in action'. The same is true of many post-colonial states, but Harris's comment on Sri Lanka is particularly significant: 'In the long history that lies behind the civil war in Sri Lanka, we can see multiple layers of oppression generating nationalist responses—the British on the Ceylonese, the Sinhalese ruling order on the Tamil' (p.221).

78. See N. Lohfink, 'Culture Shock and Theology', *BTB* 7 (1977), pp. 12-22; revised as 'Pluralism', in Lohfink, *Great Themes from the Old Testament* (Edinburgh: T. & T. Clarke, 1982), pp. 17-37.

79. See Smith, *Ethnic Origins*, p. 16: '[E]thnicity is largely "mythic" and "symbolic" in character, and because myths, symbols, memories and values are "carried" in and by form and genres of artefacts and activities which change only very slowly, so *ethnie*, once formed, tend to be exceptionally durable'.

80. See, for example, the recent attempts to reconstruct Australian identity by

should not suppress the voices in that conversation which are anti-nationalist; a living tradition will be 'an historically extended, socially embodied argument, and an argument precisely in part about the goods which constitute that tradition'.[81] If the public realm is to be saved from mere bureaucracy, the same will also need to be true—*mutatis mutandis*—of a living nation.

recovering the contributions of aboriginals, women, and ethnic minorities, notably in P. Grimshaw, *et al.*, *Creating a Nation* (Melbourne: McPhee Gribble, 1994); S. Genew, 'Denaturalizing Cultural Nationalisms: Multicultural Readings of "Australia"', in Bhaba (ed.), *Nation and Narration*, pp. 99-210. For a theological reflection, see John Thornhill, *Making Australia: Exploring our National Conversation* (Newtown: Millenium, 1992).

81. A. MacIntyre, *After Virtue* (Notre Dame: University of Notre Dame Press, 1981), p. 207.

ETHICS AND THE OLD TESTAMENT*

Philip R. Davies

Books about biblical ethics for the most part deal with what the Bible prescribes, directs, advises or implies about the Christian's code of conduct[1] (Jews do not use their Scriptures in quite this way because they have a postbiblical tradition of *halakhah*). 'Ethics' in such books tends to be represented as a list of 'rights and wrongs', a code of behaviour. However, such a procedure rarely raises the question *why* certain behaviour is right or wrong, perhaps because the fact that it is (apparently) endorsed in the Bible answers that question. But ethics as it has been couched philosophically for some time now is not about the *what* but the *why*: and even more recently, about what it means to say that something is 'good'. Can 'biblical ethics' make any contribution to modern formulations of the problem of ethics?

Let us dispose of one way in which the Bible *cannot* help. For many people the Bible furnishes a source of advice, or command, on how those who venerate it as scripture should behave. Ethical living amounts to obedience to the prescriptions. Now, obedience, generally speaking, is regarded as a virtue, and disobedience as a vice, and certainly in the area of 'biblical ethics', obedience is high on the list of requirements; the readers of the Old Testament in particular will frequently come across the word 'hear' (שמע) which also means 'obey', while the words 'command' and 'commandments' (צוה, מצוה) are spread through not only large areas of the Pentateuch, Prophets and Psalms but are found in most other biblical books, as well. Certainly, obedience to Elohim, Yahweh,

---

*   I am using the term 'Old Testament' because the reception history which influences this reading is a Christian one. However, the Hebrew text underlying my discussion is the Masoretic Text, i.e. the (Jewish) *Tenakh*.

1.   Examples of the sort of books I am referring to are the following: W.C. Kaiser, Jr, *Toward Old Testament Ethics* (Grand Rapids: Zondervan, 1983), and T.L.J. Mafico, 'Ethics (OT)' in *ABD*, II, pp. 645-52. By comparison with Mafico, P. Perkins's companion essay in *ABD*, II on New Testament ethics (pp. 652-65) is reflective and analytical.

and kings and prophets and priests is presented as one of Israel's highest duties and as what we would call 'ethical behaviour'. Yet obedience is clearly an ethically neutral response. It *can* lead to what might be regarded as ethical behaviour, but equally it can lead to unethical actions. In the case of Auschwitz guards or of civil servants working for a corrupt regime (such as we conspicuously have in many countries of the world, including the United Kingdom), obedience would be regarded by many persons outside the system itself as unethical. To be regarded as an ethical act, obedience must have an ethical motivation; the decision to obey must be based on an ethical choice. That is why we do not regard obedient dogs as behaving ethically and why obedient concentration camp guards were executed after the end of the 1939–45 war. Like the slave in Deuteronomy who chooses to remain a slave, the necessity of an *ethical decision to obey* actually contradicts the notion of obedience that many people have, which is that obedience involves a suppression of independence of will.[2] I have raised the question of obedience and its ethical neutrality not merely as a fanfare but because it leads into the opening part of my paper, which is a fairly wide-ranging (and thus probably superficial) account of ethics in the Old Testament

The Old Testament is not much of a resource for ethics because it usually resorts to invoking obedience to commands, be they from a deity, a prophet or a parent. That may well be because this literature reflects a system of communal rather than individual ethics. Possibly our interest in, and definition of, ethics does not correspond to the Bible's own. But since we are concerned with the Bible as a modern text, addressing or being addressed to modern issues, this circumstance is really irrelevant. In any case, I think we can see, with the aid of a little probing, that the Old Testament (with which I am mainly concerned) *does* provide a basis for ethical thinking, and indeed, opens with a set of fundamentally ethical questions. Let me therefore begin by considering, in the light of Gen. 1–3, the *possibilities* for ethics in the world of human thought and action.

Genesis 1, describing the creation of one world by one god, emphasizes that this god 'saw that it [whatever he created] was good'. What could this assertion possibly mean? Only the god is there to pronounce

---

2.   Whether a 'promise to obey' or an oath of allegiance is ethical is a question I do not have time for here, but obviously deserves discussion. My own view is that it is unethical because it commits one to the possibility of a situation where one has either to break such an oath or commit a crime or wrong.

the verdict: by what criteria does this god call something 'good'? A possible solution—a frequently given answer— is that both 'evil' and 'good' in the OT are relative and not absolute, that they mean, in that well-known biblical phrase, 'evil/good *in the sight of X*'; i.e. something of which a subject (usually a god) approves or disapproves. Thus the statement that Elohim said the world was good would mean that it pleased him, that he was happy with his work. But obviously, since there are no value systems independent of this sole creator god prior to the creation of that species, humanity, which can also categorise things as 'good' or 'bad', the declaration 'I am happy with it' must mean the same as simply 'being good'—objectively, as it were.

A digression: Some biblical theologians have suggested that the chaos which lies beyond the ordered creation, the seas that have been pushed above and below the biosphere, and the underworld beneath it, function as the realm of evil, with evil effectively defined as disorder. That view might reflect the role of the goddess Tiamat in the Babylonian Creation Epic, who represents the salt water and is linguistically and conceptually present in the word *tehom* in Genesis 1 ('the deep'). Indeed, there are biblical references to a fight between Yahweh/Elohim and a primordial beast, either personifying the sea or depicted as a sea monster, in the act of world creation.[3] These extra-biblical and biblical texts imply a potentially dualistic world in which evil exists independently of the god, but is vanquished (not eliminated) in the process of creating an orderly cosmos. I take the view, however, as do the majority of commentators, that the writer of Genesis 1 wishes to exclude this well-known mythical dimension and to affirm a unitary world. Nevertheless, the geographical encoding of the realm of the good and the bad, which the dualistic view of Genesis 1 implies, is a worldview that I think can be detected elsewhere in the books of the Old Testament.

With this digression over, let us move from a world from which ethics is absent, because everything is good, to Genesis 2–3, the Eden story. Whether we ignore source-critical arguments and read these chapters in the light of ch. 1, or instead construe chs. 2–3 as an independent creation account, the human (later to become humans) has no consciousness of evil, or of good—either because nature and goodness are synonymous (invoking ch. 1) or because such knowledge is locked up in a tree which the human is forbidden to touch.

We might ponder the question: Where does this knowable evil in the

3.   Isa. 27.1; 51.9; Ps. 74.13 (EV).

tree's fruit come *from*? Metaphysically or theologically, the conclusion seems to follow that the god has created it and put it somewhere into the world where it can be accessed by means of this tree. So the world is not entirely good; it contains an evil which can be known about. But, to return to what I observed about 'evil' and 'good' earlier, there can be no evil unless the god has deliberately created something that displeases him. And why would he do that? There are indeed possible answers to this question, but, putting aside the conundrum for now, we can instead focus on another feature. This very prohibition itself creates a world of ethics. If the first 'evil' act to occur is disobedience on the part of humans, we have the problem that I mentioned earlier; that disobedience is itself ethically neutral. How should humans know or think it is good to obey? Besides which, there can be no disobedience until there are commands. Similarly, in a world where there are no laws, there cannot only be no crime, but no concept of crime. The insertion of a command into the relationship between maker and creature creates the possibility of obedience or disobedience, and thus also—from the perspective of human writer and reader—something that can be, and will be, construed as *evil*, even though that will be 'evil in the sight of the god'. The command not to eat the fruit of this one particular tree thus *creates the possibility of evil* while appearing to be preventing the realisation of evil (something the knowledge of which potentially exists, and therefore itself potentially exists) through eating! Just as Elohim created the world by his word to the elements (Genesis 1), so Yahweh created evil by his word to the humans (Genesis 2)! If we take this line of interpretation, there does not have to be any 'knowledge of (good and) evil' locked up in the fruit of the tree at all. It could be locked up in the secret of disobedience. It would follow that the text is equating the seeds of evil with disobedience to the command of the deity, and setting us on a particular ethical track in which good is obeying and evil is disobeying. The text would in this case be somewhat 'proto-Deuteronomistic'.

But I am not ready to draw this conclusion yet. Even if I were, I would find myself personally opposed to that point of view. For although I do not believe in gods, I believe they are symbols of authority which claim absolute power (or more precisely instruments by which some other agent claims authority). And I reject such symbols, and such authority.

I am unsure how the writer of the story regards the matter of the origin of evil, but I will try and interpret the text, of which I am very fond, in such a way that I get the author to agree with me (whether that sort of manoeuvre is ethical or not!). No narratorial judgment on the human act is in fact offered. But it may be possible to infer an authorial point of view by probing further into the telling of the story. To begin with, the decision of the woman here is not really between obeying and not obeying, but between obeying a deity and obeying other things—the promptings of the snake and the verdict of one's own senses, both of which, of course, are as much creations of the deity as his command. In turn, the decision of the man is to eat what his woman offers: whether he is aware of what it is we are not told, but the god appears to think so—and again, the agent of his disobedience, the woman, is the god's own creation, indeed, the god's own idea.

The woman's choice, which is paramount here, is also between two propositions: she will die the day she eats (says the god), and she will become like the god (says the snake). Her choice is dictated not by a negative impulse to disobey but by a real dilemma, and she follows the evidence of her own desire, the pleasant appearance of the tree, and the eloquence of the snake. And as it happens, she apparently chooses the true proposition (the words of the snake) rather than the false one (Yahweh's), since her eyes *are* opened and she does *not* die 'that day'.[4] Indeed, it is Yahweh himself who acknowledges that she has chosen the true proposition.

The god then, apparently, punishes and prevents further encroachments on his monopoly of power. But the objects of his curse are all his own creatures, whom he has himself endowed. It is surely clear that the narrator is presenting a god who deliberately creates the possibility of disobedience by issuing a command, and ensures that the command will be disobeyed by having in place the agents and instruments that will ensure its transgression—attractive fruit and central location of the tree, perceptive and persuasive snake who happens to know about the tree's fruit and its properties, woman who will 'help' man. It is quite inevitable that the humans will acquire the godlike knowledge of good and evil which will turn them into ethical beings. That is, of course, the point of the story. But the narrator is not telling of a 'fall', or even about the perversion of the god's intentions, but of the birth of humans as ethical agents and the *fulfilment* of the god's intentions.[5] Yet, according to the

---

4.   Even less truly if 'that day' means 'that moment', as is quite possible!

5.   I have argued elsewhere (in 'Making It: Creation and Contradiction in Genesis', in M.D. Carroll R., D.J.A. Clines and P.R. Davies [ed.], *The Bible in Human Society: Essays in Honour of John Rogerson* [JSOTSup, 200; Sheffield: Sheffield Academic Press, 1995], pp. 249-56) that Elohim's intentions for humans in

actions assigned to him, Yahweh must ensure that the responsibility for the original individual decision rests with the human, that ethics itself is born from a free choice.

I suppose that if one treats this story as an allegory of child-rearing one can unravel the paradox: before they are old enough to act ethically, children are subject to commands from their parents, who may punish disobedience. But here, too, obedience is a *pre-ethical* response, and punishment for disobedience ethically reprehensible, even though parents usually indulge in it. It was recognized in the society that produced this tale that children make choices before they are aware of the categories of good and evil (see e.g. Isa. 7.15); the author presents these Edenic humans, apparently, as the primordial children, commanded by the parent. Disobedience of the parent is no evil from the perspective of the child, even though parents, having ethical responsibility, are tempted to impute it to their children. Only when 'opening of the eyes' takes place, though, do human decisions become ethical ones. And from that point onwards, obedience (the rule of the child, the pre-ethical condition) is no longer possible as an ethical mode of existence. Obedience has to be chosen, subjected to ethical reflection and ethical principles—whatever they are.

The story thus ends with humans having acquired a sense of right and wrong, superficially by eating the fruit of the tree, but at a deeper level by having been obliged to make a choice between conflicting commands and desires. The storyteller, I conclude, wishes to argue that evil is not something that comes from heavenly beings (as some Jewish authors maintained)[6] but from human decisions. This author is, like the author of Genesis 1, a monotheist who wishes to entertain no dualism in the universe. 'Evil' is therefore the result of discrete human decisions. Put into the terms of a modern agenda, the criminal is responsible for his or her own acts, not the state, nor the parent, nor the system. This writer looks to me to be antagonistic to a view that sees obedience to the law as the basis of Judaism. Recently, the Eden story has been understood as a wisdom text,[7] and I am inclined to agree with that verdict, as I am

Genesis 1 (filling the earth and subduing it, multiplying) are possible only if the disobedience occurs, resulting in the paradox that disobedience is planned by the god who gives orders, in order that his intention will be fulfilled.

6.   The myth of the fall from the sky of some heavenly beings is concealed in Gen. 6.1-4 but narrated fully in 1 Enoch 1–6 and Jubilees 1–11.

7.   See the comments in J. Blenkinsopp, *The Pentateuch. An Introduction to the First Five Books of the Bible* (New York: Doubleday/London: SCM Press, 1992), pp. 65-67.

inclined to regard it as one of the latest stories to be inserted into the historical narrative which it now adorns.[8]

Let me now turn to some other ethical systems in the Bible and examine them in the light of Genesis 1–2. I am not assuming, by the way, any chronological priority of Genesis or any parts of it over any other parts of the Old Testament. This is a synchronic exercise.

Leviticus

I referred earlier to the suggestion that Genesis 1 is not so much about the creation of a material world but the creation of an *ordered* one, with chaos represented by water, and death, represented by the underworld, geographically surrounding the biosphere of order and life. It is in Leviticus, if we follow the kind of anthropological analysis pursued by Mary Douglas,[9] that we find that same conceptuality replicated onto the mini-cosmos of the people of Israel. The biosphere is the camp, within which order and life are sustained; outside the camp is the place beyond the concern of the god, where the dead are buried and the unclean are banished. Within the camp, the proper categories of purity and impurity are observed, corresponding to the careful ordering of air, sea and land in the world's creation. The categories of good and evil are not explicit here, but they are implicitly mapped onto the categories of order and disorder and of inside and outside.

Here we find a representative of that strand of OT ethics that, unlike Genesis 2–3, makes the social unit the locus of ethics. Individual cleanness or uncleanness, individual defilement, affects the viability of the entire community. Correspondingly, it is not free decision-making that constitutes good behaviour but subservience to the demands of the deity, which are absolute. This society represents the values of that least ethical community, the totalitarian state, with its big brother, the all-holy uncompromising sacrifice-consuming despot as the invention of a fascist clique. The idealized society of Leviticus is no Utopia except for the ritually pure and the utterly obedient, a haven of hierocracy. But its perceptual ordering of the natural world as a part of its strategy of social power is a wonderful model of ideology at work.

8.   See my *In Search of Ancient Israel* (Sheffield: Sheffield Academic Press, 2nd edn, 1995), pp. 142-43.

9.   M. Douglas, *Purity and Danger* (London: Routledge and Kegan Paul, 1966); cf. G. Wenham, *Leviticus* (NICOT; Grand Rapids: Eerdmans, 1979), who adopts Douglas's approach.

Proverbs

With Proverbs the relationship between the three categories of nature, good and knowledge, prominent in Genesis 2–3, are again played off. The view of Proverbs (see ch. 8) is that the natural and the ethical are one and the same: the god who made the world made it with wisdom, and through wisdom humans should interact with it. There is a moral order just as there is a natural one. Because of this inbuilt order, it is possible to know by observation and deduction what is good and what is not. And experimental verification is possible because good and evil are rewarded and punished. Because ethics can be discerned by knowledge (and recommended by parental experience), good behaviour can be called wise and bad behaviour foolish. Being good and being wise are virtually synonymous. Although it may seem that being good is a matter of listening to the voice of the father (and sometimes the mother), the appearance is deceptive. Obedience alone does not bring wisdom, but discernment. The proverbs themselves are generalisations, not dogmas. They are illustrative of the ethical universe, but only by intellectual acuteness can one achieve wisdom, and thus richness and long life. We are all open-eyed, can see good and evil, but still have to choose. We are, again, responsible for our own individual decisions. The counter-argument (deployed by the *śāṭān* in the opening of the prose narrative of Job) that virtue and materialism become synonymous in this ethical system is hard to overcome, but there are few ethical systems that do not, in the end, proclaim some reward for virtue; be this reward the bosom of Abraham or Nirvana or the eternal rule of the saints. Yet this observation hardly alleviates the strength of the objection to any notion of ethics that is not disinterested. It might nevertheless bring to our attention the fact that the one book in the Old Testament (Ecclesiastes) to have come to such a conclusion achieved a scriptural status by the skin of its teeth. Religious systems do not often trust people to be disinterestedly ethical: obedience is a safer virtue to preach.

Kings

The 'Deuteronomistic' book of Kings, like Leviticus, addresses not each human as the locus of ethics but the community, whether or not represented by the king. The individual reward and punishment of Proverbs is here substituted by the national reward of prosperity and destruction. Moreover, evil is primarily described in terms of obedience to a covenant in which cultic propriety is paramount, in which the place of worship is as important as its object. In those parts of the prophetic books that have been created—such as Kings—by those we call 'Deuteronomists', there is the frequent call to obey the covenant and not 'do what is right in your own eyes'. This interesting phrase suggests a *discouragement* of ethical discourse. Unable or unwilling to develop, like Proverbs, a system of ethics, however flawed, the Deuteronomists invoke a legal obligation: your deity has done this and demands that you do this: if not, the land he gave you will be forfeit. This literature may well be endorsing the ethics of patronage, which sustains many sub-cultures in the world (the examples I have in mind are too obvious to need mentioning) and supports what might be seen as a kind of morality. But the trade-off between 'respect' and compliance on the one hand, and 'protection' on the other, with 'favours' on both sides, tends to strike most people as an unethical rather than an ethical contract (because it is based on inequality? What is the point of any religion where the adherent and their god are *equals*!).

The Prophets

I ought to consider the prophets, since it is they who carry the torch for much of what is regarded as OT 'ethics'. Where they are concerned with ethics (which is by no means their primary concern) they claim that oppression of the underprivileged is wrong (as do the legal books of Deuteronomy and Leviticus), and commend the practice of justice (as does the wisdom of Proverbs). There is little in their actual content—in the virtues that they call for—that distinguishes them from laws or wisdom writings. Indeed, throughout the OT, what actually counts for good behaviour hardly varies at all. I could add that it hardly varies from the principles of right behaviour found in every other ancient near eastern civilization. It is precisely where many biblical scholars see the high ethical watermark of the OT that I fail to see coherence, founda-tional principles, or ethical reflection. One finds Zion theology, the holiness of the god, the hatred of the god, the marital status of the god, the vengeance or inscrutability of the god, his monopoly, authority and much else being used as a reason for doing what the prophet says: much religion, little ethics and not a lot of consistency.

Indeed, so long as any social system presents its members with a set of rules of conduct which it claims to have divine origin and which must simply be obeyed on pain of punishment, I cannot see that we are dealing with ethics at all; rather with a totalitarian system in which individual will and freedom exist only to be sacrificed to the supreme authority of someone's deity. On the contrary, where systems of behaviour are customary, or traditional, interpreted by elders and by the members of society, slowly evolved, learnt, internalised, we have a better model of an ethical society because the rules elicit to a greater extent the consent of those who obey them, and indeed, those who obey them also make them. I imagine that among the Iron Age inhabitants of Palestine this is, in fact, how ethics were evolved. There is no need to equate the biblical system with any real ancient society.

So is it perhaps the *absence* of a transcendental deity that makes ethics ethics? Or is it only in the presence of a transcendental authority that there can be objective good and evil? To go back to Genesis, should the expulsion from Eden be seen as expulsion from the rule of the father and the once-for-all entry into a human world construed not by fear of god but by ethics? Or is it the beginning of the eternal submission of will to the paternal command, with the added twist that obedience has to be coerced because of human freedom?

I might consider other possible ethical or quasi-ethical systems in the Old Testament (or the New, where I see the apostle who claims freedom from the law issuing his own laws!), but I have made the point I wished: that there are various ethical systems or models suggested or even expounded here, and that most of them are not ethical at all, while those that are ethical are flawed. My point is, however, that this is not other than we might expect, and we need not expend our indignation on writers and writings that address a different society. Where our annoyance needs to be directed is against those who, while proclaiming a concern for ethics (Christian or otherwise), refuse to engage ethically with the Bible, which in very many cases means resisting it.

Many biblical scholars—ultimately, most, I fear—not only fail to criticise such systems in their Bible but even fail to identify them and analyse them. There is a tendency in some quarters to purvey them as values for our modern world. As well as consider the 'ethics' of the Bible, we might also, in the fashion of the postmodern era, consider the ethics of interpretation itself, and especially the manner in which its moral authority is invoked as a pretext for systems of belief and behaviour that deserve to be resisted. What *is* the ethical responsibility of a modern biblical exegete? I do not wish to instigate another debate here, but I do not see how a responsible exegete can pretend to a neutral or objective position. My own anti-religious approach to ethics is, I hope, clear enough, and I expect that others in this volume will feel as happy to expose their own prejudices too.

AND THE DUMB DO SPEAK:
ARTICULATING INCIPIENT READINGS OF THE BIBLE IN
MARGINALIZED COMMUNITIES

Gerald West

When it comes to understanding the alleged silence of the poor and oppressed—their apparent accommodation to the ideology of the dominant—we find thick and thin accounts of ideological hegemony. The thick version emphasizes the role of ideological state apparatuses—such as education systems, the church, and government structures—in controlling the symbolic means of production, just as factory owners monopolize the material means of production. 'Their ideological work secures the active consent of subordinate groups to the social arrangements that reproduce their subordination.'[1] The thin theory of hegemony makes less grand claims for the ideological control of the ruling class. What ideological domination does accomplish, according to this version,

> is to define for subordinate groups what is realistic and what is not realistic and to drive certain aspirations and grievances into the realm of the impossible, of idle dreams. By persuading underclasses that their position, their life-chances, their tribulations are unalterable and inevitable, such a limited hegemony can produce the behavioral results of consent without necessarily changing people's values. Convinced that nothing can possibly be done to improve their situation and that it will always remain so, it is even conceivable that idle criticisms and hopeless aspirations would be eventually extinguished.[2]

Such analyses of domination argue that 'when oppressed people live in silence, they use the words of their oppressors to describe their

---

1. J.C. Scott, *Domination and the Arts of Resistance: Hidden Transcripts* (New Haven and London: Yale University Press, 1990), p. 73. For a detailed account of this phenomenon, see A. Memmi, *The Colonizer and the Colonized* (London: Souvenir Press, 1965).
2. Scott, *Hidden Transcripts*, p. 74.

experience of oppression. Only within the praxis of liberation and in dialogue with what Antonio Gramsci called "organic intellectuals" is it possible for the poor to break this silence and create their own language'—organic intellectuals enable an articulation.[3] So, within liberation theologies, whether they be Latin American, black, womanist or feminist, the role of the intellectual is crucial in breaking 'the culture of silence'.

Because 'the logic of domination represents a combination of historical and contemporary ideological and material practices that are never completely successful, always embody contradictions and are constantly being fought over within asymmetrical relations of power',[4] organic intellectuals, who can learn with the poor and marginalized while simultaneously helping them to foster modes of self-education and struggle against various forms of oppression, are able to point to the spaces, contradictions, and forms of resistance that raise the possibility for social struggle. However, oppressed people's accommodation to the logic of domination may mean that they actively resist emancipatory forms of knowledge.[5]

James Scott problematises both thick and thin versions of ideological hegemony, and so too the role of the intellectual. In his detailed study of domination and resistance we find a more nuanced analysis of ideological hegemony, arguing that theories of hegemony and false consciousness do not take account of what he calls 'the hidden transcript'.[6]

> Every subordinate group creates, out of its ordeal, a 'hidden transcript' that represents a critique of power spoken behind the back of the dominant. The powerful, for their part, also develop a hidden transcript representing the practices and claims of their rule that cannot be openly avowed. A comparison of the hidden transcript of the weak with that of the powerful and of *both* hidden transcripts to the public transcript of power relations offers a substantially new way of understanding resistance to domination.[7]

The crucial point of Scott's detailed argument is that '[t]he public transcript, where it is not positively misleading, is unlikely to tell the

---

3.   P. Frostin, *Liberation Theology in Tanzania and South Africa: A First World Interpretation* (Lund: Lund University Press, 1988), p. 10.

4.   H.A. Giroux (1985), 'Introduction', in P. Freire, *The Politics of Education* (London: Macmillan, 1985), pp. xi-xxv (xii).

5.   H.A. Giroux, 'Introduction', pp. xviii-xxiii.

6.   Scott, *Hidden Transcripts*, pp. 85-90.

7.   Scott, *Hidden Transcripts*, p. xii.

whole story about power relations. It is frequently in the interest of both parties to tacitly conspire in misrepresentation'.[8] So, social analysis which focuses on the public transcript, as most social analysis does, is, at the same time, focussing on the formal relations between the powerful and weak,[9] but is not attempting to 'read, interpret, and understand the often fugitive political conduct of subordinate groups'.[10] A focus on the hidden transcript, where it is accessible in the rumours, gossip, folktales, songs, gestures, jokes and theatre of the poor and marginalized, or the more public infrapolitics of popular culture,[11] reveals forms of resistance and defiance. 'Unless one can penetrate the official transcript of both subordinates and elites, a reading of the social evidence will almost always represent a confirmation of the status quo in hegemonic terms'.[12]

Put differently in the words of the Ethiopian proverb with which Scott opens his study, 'When the great lord passes the wise peasant bows deeply and silently farts'. Theories of ideological hegemony look at the obvious, the public transcript of the bowing peasant. Scott draws our attention to what is hidden, the silent fart.

But is there still not a case for Gramsci's notion of the dominated consciousness of the working class? For Gramsci, hegemony works primarily at the level of thought as distinct from the level of action. Scott turns this around. He considers 'subordinate classes *less* constrained at the level of thought and ideology, since they can in secluded settings speak with comparative safety, and *more* constrained at the level of political action and struggle, where the daily exercise of power sharply limits the options available to them'.[13] So, he argues that 'subordinate groups have typically learned, in situations short of those rare all-or-nothing struggles, to clothe their resistance and defiance in ritualisms of subordination that serve both to disguise their purposes and to provide them with a ready route of retreat that may soften the consequences of a possible failure'.[14] This is because most protests and challenges—even quite violent ones—'are made in the realistic expectation that the central features of the form of domination will remain intact'. Consequently,

---

8. Scott, *Hidden Transcripts*, p. 2.
9. Scott, *Hidden Transcripts*, p. 13.
10. Scott, *Hidden Transcripts*, p. xii.
11. Scott, *Hidden Transcripts*, p. 198.
12. Scott, *Hidden Transcripts*, p. 90.
13. Scott, *Hidden Transcripts*, p. 91.
14. Scott, *Hidden Transcripts*, p. 96.

'[m]ost acts of power from below, even when they are protests—implicitly or explicitly—will largely observe the 'rules' even if their objective is to undermine them'.[15] He believes that 'the historical evidence clearly shows that subordinate groups have been capable of revolutionary thought that repudiates existing forms of domination'.[16] However, because the occasions on which subordinate groups have been able to act openly and fully on that thought are rare, the conflict will usually take 'a dialogic form in which the language of the dialogue will invariably borrow heavily from the terms of the dominant ideology prevailing in the public transcript'. We therefore must 'consider the dominant discourse as a plastic idiom or dialect that is capable of carrying an enormous variety of meanings, including those that are subversive of their use as intended by the dominant'.[17]

Given Scott's analysis, the role of the intellectual in enabling articulation is less clear. Subordinate groups are already engaged in forms of resistance, and what is hidden is hidden for good reason, so any attempt to penetrate the disguise is dangerous. And when dignity and resistance demand an irruption or an articulation, this must be done in ways determined by the dominated. Oral culture as a popular disguise is a good example of the point I am making here. The oral culture of subordinate groups offers seclusion, control, and anonymity, and is therefore a useful vehicle for ideological resistance.[18] Each enactment is unique as to time, place, and audience, as well as different from every other enactment. Gossip, rumour, folktales, songs, gestures, jokes and theatre are taken up, performed or learned at the option of the audience and, over time, their origins are lost altogether:

> It becomes impossible to recover some *ur* version from which all subsequent renditions are deviations. In other words, there is no orthodoxy or center to folk culture since there is no primary text to serve as the measure of heresy. The practical result is that folk culture achieves the anonymity of collective property, constantly being adjusted, revised, abbreviated, or, for that matter, ignored. The multiplicity of its authors provides its protective cover, and when it no longer serves current interests sufficiently to find performers or an audience, it simply vanishes forever.[19]

15. Scott, *Hidden Transcripts*, p. 93.
16. Scott, *Hidden Transcripts*, p. 101.
17. Scott, *Hidden Transcripts*, pp. 102-103.
18. Scott, *Hidden Transcripts*, p. 160.
19. Scott, *Hidden Transcripts*, p. 161.

It could be argued that written forms of communication, largely the territory of the intellectual, are more effectively anonymous. Anonymous circulars, for example, can be prepared, produced, and circulated in secret. However,

> once a text is out of the author's hands, control over its use and dissemination is lost. The advantage of communication by voice (including gestures, clothes, dance, and so on) is that the communicator retains control over the manner of its dissemination—the audience, the place, the circumstances, the rendition. Control, then, of oral culture is irretrievably decentralized.[20]

To illustrate more fully, we can consider the well known story of Isaac, Rebekah, Esau and Jacob in Genesis 27. What was probably a trickster tale,[21] told by women, has become the property of the patriarchs. A female story has been coopted and controlled by the fathers. The trickster tale, a common form of cultural resistance among subordinate groups,[22] celebrates the guile and cleverness of the woman, Rebekah. The woman is a character in a story that is obviously a story about supposedly male issues, including lineage, succession, blessing, and inheritance. However, by inserting this narrative into an apparently innocuous context, other women could identify with the protagonist, who manages here to outwit and ridicule her more powerful adversary.

Within this relatively veiled context women are able to express *publically* a form of resistance. Such tales would not only be told off-stage in the women's quarters as a way of socializing a spirit of resistance, they would also have a place in public discourse because of their disguise. The story has a form which is both acceptable to men and empowering for women. Clearly, such a tale also has an instructive and cautionary side. Identifying with Rebekah, women, including young women, learn that in a context of overwhelming male domination, safety and success often depend upon channeling resistance into forms of deception and cunning.[23] While it may seem 'that the heavy disguise this reply wears must all but eliminate the pleasure it gives', it 'carves out a public, if provisional, space for the autonomous cultural expression of

20. Scott, *Hidden Transcripts*, p. 161.
21. See A.J. Bledstein, 'Binder, Trickster, Heel and Hairy Man: Re-reading Genesis 27 as a Trickster Tale Told by a Woman' (unpublished paper, Society of Biblical Literature, 1991).
22. Scott, *Hidden Transcripts*, p. 162-66.
23. See Scott, *Hidden Transcripts*, p. 164.

dissent. If it is disguised, it is at least not hidden; it is spoken to power. This is no small achievement of voice under domination'.[24]

However, this trickster tale has almost been lost to us because it has been inserted into a literary context which is so completely concerned with supposedly male issues that we easily miss this form of female resistance. The hidden transcript has had to disguise itself and to speak warily, and so reading 'the dialogue from the public and oral traditions of subordinate groups', particularly when these have been incorporated into a larger more ideologically diverse written corpus, requires 'a more nuanced and literary reading'.[25] This is the danger of the written text. But this is also an opportunity for the intellectual, in this case the socially engaged biblical scholar, to serve the poor and marginalized.

Although Scott does not go on to develop what he means by 'a more nuanced and literary reading', this phrase resonates with work that is being done in the interface between socially engaged biblical scholars and readers of the Bible in poor and marginalized communities. Remarkably, in contexts like Brasil and South Africa, biblical scholars are continually being 'called' by ordinary readers of the Bible. This trust of intellectuals is reserved, however, only for those whom the people choose to speak with. The biblical scholars who are part of this 'contextual Bible study process' are committed to doing biblical studies with and from the perspective of the poor and oppressed. So, there has always been a clear recognition by intellectuals of their role as servants. Their contribution may be distinctive and different, but it is not in any way better or more significant. While not all of these biblical scholars are organic intellectuals, they all at least work closely with organic intellectuals.

But what is the usefulness of the socially engaged biblical scholar? Why is it that ordinary poor and marginalized readers of the Bible find their participation in the Bible reading process useful? Scott's concern for 'a more nuanced and literary reading' of the public transcript provides a helpful clue. Socially engaged biblical scholars involved in various liberation theologies agree in at least four crucial areas. They agree that the Bible must be read from the perspective of the poor and marginalized, that the Bible must be read *with* the poor and marginalized, that the Bible reading is related to social transformation and that the Bible must be read critically. What Scott is pointing to in his

24. Scott, *Hidden Transcripts*, p. 166.
25. Scott, *Hidden Transcripts*, p. 165.

phrase 'a more nuanced and literary reading' is, at least in part, I would argue, a critical reading in the sense that biblical scholars use the term 'critical'.

While biblical scholars do differ on the nature of this critical reading, some favouring a historical-sociological perspective, others a literary point of view, and still others a symbolic, thematic, and metaphoric approach,[26] all these modes of reading offer *a* critical reading of the biblical text; although their respective emphases differ. Another important related similarity is that the appropriation of biblical elements, whether behind the text, in the text, or in front of the text, is a *critical appropriation*. A *critical* reading and appropriation of the biblical text is the primary concern from the side of (organic) intellectuals involved in the interface between an engaged biblical studies with its socially committed trained readers of the Bible and ordinary poor readers of the Bible.

The historical and cultural struggles of the poor and marginalized must be the starting point of biblical interpretation in liberation hermeneutics. But, as I have argued, their readings of the Bible must also be critical. Why? So that, Frostin argues, the poor can 'create their own language'.[27] In his critique of black theology in South Africa, Itumeleng Mosala makes a similar point when he argues that black theology has not been able to develop organic links with the popular struggles of, especially, the black working class people who are the most exploited section of the black community.

> In the meantime the oppressed black masses relentlessly continue their struggle against apartheid and capitalism—with or without the leadership and cultural equipment of black theology. As one might expect, however, many forms of resistance that the oppressed create for themselves remain open to co-optation and undermining by the dominant classes. The latter are able to co-opt and undermine the discourses of the oppressed on the grounds of intellectual and theoretical superiority. Needless to say, the oppressed are very often unable to contest this claimed intellectual and theoretical superiority. In the realm of religious practice, this state of affairs underscores the absolute necessity of a theoretically well-grounded and culturally autonomous black theology of liberation.[28]

---

26. G.O. West, *Biblical Hermeneutics of Liberation: Modes of Reading the Bible in the South African Context* (Maryknoll, NY: Orbis Books/Pietermaritzburg: Cluster Publications, 2nd edn, 1995 [1991]), pp. 131-73.

27. Frostin, *Liberation Theology*, p. 10.

28. I.J. Mosala, *Biblical Hermeneutics and Black Theology in South Africa* (Grand Rapids: Eerdmans, 1989), pp. 2-3.

James Cochrane argues incisively that Mosala's concerns for a critical reading of the Bible raise

> the practical matter of facilitating a critical consciousness among oppressed people in order that they may be assisted in taking up the chains of the[ir] oppression and breaking them. This is crucial because—as in the best work of the independent black-led trade unions—it concerns the empowerment of people who have been dispossessed and dehumanized. Moreover, it contributes to the process of building the communicative competence necessary for a democratic society free from domination and [the] maximizing of the participation of its citizens. Mosala recognizes that critical consciousness and democratic activity is not spontaneous (though always potential), but are learned…One may say, therefore, that Mosala represents an approach which has taken praxis into itself as the most penetrating way of uncovering the strategies of domination.[29]

Now all of this makes sense if we accept either the thick or the thin version of hegemony. But, what if Scott is right, and the poor and marginalized already have a finely honed critical consciousness? Is there still a need for a specifically critical reading of the Bible, or do subordinate groups already read the Bible critically? Bible study work in Brasil and South Africa has shown that while poor and marginalized ordinary readers do have a general critical consciousness towards society and texts, they do not have the historical, sociological, literary, or symbolic tools to be critical of the biblical text in the same way as biblical scholars.[30] There may appear to be some affinities between the readings of the poor and the modes of reading of biblical scholars, but the situation is more complex. While there are certainly similarities with critical modes of reading, we must recognize that something fundamentally different is going on in the modes of reading of the ordinary reader. Ordinary readers read the Bible pre-critically. They read it precritically because they have not been trained in critical modes of reading. Ordinary readers do not have access to the resources of critical biblical scholarship. So, in this carefully defined sense, ordinary poor and marginalized readers do not read the Bible critically.

29. J.R. Cochrane, 'Struggle and the Christian Story: The Exploitation of Truth as a Challenge to Tradition', (unpublished paper, 1989), p. 30.

30. West, *Biblical Hermeneutics of Liberation*, pp. 198-200. See also Scott, *Hidden Transcripts*, p. 116 and V.L. Wimbush, 'The Bible and African Americans: An Outline of an Interpretative History', in C.H. Felder (ed.), *Stony the Road we Trod: African American Biblical Interpretation* (Minneapolis: Fortress Press, 1991), pp. 81-97.

What Scott's analysis does help us to understand, however, is the remarkable readiness of ordinary readers in poor and marginalized communities to use the critical resources of biblical studies in addition to their own critical resources. They seem to recognize a need for 'a more nuanced and literary reading' of the Bible and their traditions of interpretation. Let me illustrate this.

The Institute for the Study of the Bible (ISB) was invited by a women's group in Umtata, a rural town in South Africa, to facilitate a workshop on 'liberating ways of reading the Bible as women'. The group consists of a majority of black women, most of whom are from Umtata, with a few from rural areas, and a few white women from Umtata.

Although the theme of the workshop was determined by the Umtata women's group, as well as the programme, the ISB was asked to suggest some texts for Bible study. Mark 5.21–6.21 was one of the texts used. The text was chosen because two of the main characters are women. Besides this, there was no clear sense of where the Bible study group might go with the text. No exegesis was done in preparation, and only three questions were used to facilitate the Bible study process.

> Question 1: Read Mark 5.21–6.1 and discuss in small groups what this text is about.
> Question 2: If this text is about women, what is it saying?
> Question 3: In what way does this text speak to us today?

Question 1 was designed to encourage participants to read the text carefully and closely. Question 2 had a similar purpose, but also invited readers to probe behind the text to the society that produced the text. The final question, question 3, drew the text and readers' context together in an act of appropriation.

My role as facilitator was to provide what Cornel West calls 'enabling forms of criticism'.[31] In this case the process entailed, first, encouraging participants to read the text fully and closely (Question 1), and then, second, providing some resources for reflection on the type of society that produced the text (Question 2). The resulting discussion, first in groups and then in plenary report-back, produced the basic elements of form and content that constitute the reading that follows below. There is nothing in the final form of the reading that did not have its beginning in that first Bible study group among ordinary African women readers.

But the process of the reading's production did not end there.

---

31. C. West, *Prophetic Fragments* (Grand Rapids: Eerdmans, 1988), p. 210.

Subsequent to the Umtata women's workshop, a local Anglican church asked me to preach on the subject of 'Compassion and women'. I declined to preach, but offered to do a short workshop instead. The same format was used as with the Umtata women's group, but this time the ordinary readers were mainly white, about sixty percent women and forty percent men. Their responses, too, have shaped this reading, just as the responses of the Umtata women's group shaped the responses of the local church participants.

I then did the workshop with a Master's class in the School of Theology, University of Natal, Pietermaritzburg. This time the responses of trained readers were allowed to shape the Bible study, but only in ways that were 'accountable' to the shape that had emerged 'from below'. This was not difficult or forced because most of the responses of these trained readers, half of whom are women and half of whom are black, supported and strengthened the reading of the ordinary readers. The readings of the trained readers might have been more systematic, but the contextual Bible study process produced substantially similar responses.

The final stage in the development of the reading presented here included some systematic structuring and further textual and sociological support for the reading that had already emerged from the contextual Bible study process. Once again, it was wonderful and remarkable to discover how, for example, reference to the Greek text reinforced and supported the reading that had initially emerged from ordinary poor African women readers.

Initial responses to the first question—concerning what Mark 5.21–6.1 is about—included the following: healing, compassion, faith, love, hope, despair, suffering, power and other similar themes. When the groups had reported back with these responses, I then asked the plenary group as a whole whether they thought the text could also be about women. There was an immediate buzz as participants began to explore this option with each other. I therefore asked them to go back into their small groups to discuss the question more fully and to support their discussion with careful reference to the text.

The resultant report-back from the groups was remarkable. Participants argued that a careful reading of the text did indicate that the story is about women. The groups supported this reading by relating the following arrangements. First, the story of the two women is a literary unit, delimited by the geographic shifts in 5.21 and 6.1. Second, although the central character appears initially to be a man, Jairus, the central characters in the story are, in fact, two women. Jairus does initiate the action, but is then ignored as first the woman with the flow of blood and then Jairus' daughter move to centre-stage. The actual absence of the first woman, Jairus' daughter, emphasizes her narrative presence. The plot depends on her presence. Similarly, the woman with the flow of blood (ῥύσει αἵματος), the second woman, is foregrounded even though she seeks to be self-effacing (ἐλθοῦσα...ὄπισθεν). And while Jesus is still speaking to the second woman, the first woman is again presented (v. 35).

It is almost as if the narrator himself (herself?) is interrupted—the narrative certainly is—by the unnamed woman with the flow of blood. The careful narrative introduction of Jairus, a named male with power (εἷς τῶν ἀρχισυναγώγων; v. 22), is first interrupted, and then deconstructed, by the unnamed woman with no power.

Third, that the plot and sub-plot are carefully connected is stressed by the repetition of 'daughter' (θυγάτηρ), in v. 34, with reference to the second woman, and in v. 35 with reference to the first woman. The ambiguity of 'your daughter' ('Η θυγάτηρ σου), referring to Jairus and possibly to Jesus, in v. 35, reinforces this connection. The women, and so their stories, are also linked by repetition of 'twelve years' (vv. 25 and 42). It has also been suggested by some readers that 'twelve years' may, in the case of the young woman, be an allusion to the onset of menstruation and so the beginning of fertility. The flow of blood for the younger woman meant life was possible, but the flow of blood for the older woman meant that life was no longer possible. The young woman of twelve years of age is a narrative reminder of the child(ren) that the older woman has not been able to bear. Here is another link between the two stories. There is also a parallel structure to each episode. In each case, the woman is defined by her social location; in each case the woman is in need; in each case, Jesus responds to her need; in each case, the woman is unclean; in each case, there is contact, touching, between Jesus and the woman; in each case, Jesus speaks to the woman; in each case, there is healing and restoration of the woman to the community.

We agreed, then, that this text is about women. This does not mean, of course, that the text is not also about other things, as well. But it is clearly, and probably primarily, about women.

At this point in the workshops we moved on to the second question: If this text is about women, what is it saying? Small group discussion and report-back on this question generated a clear understanding of the issues involved but also many questions of a historical and sociological nature, so I offered historical and sociological resources as they were requested. Participants then returned to their small groups before the final plenary report-back.

Participants argued that both women in the story are initially identified in terms of patriarchal social systems, and not in their own right. They are not named, they are described in terms of their location within two central social systems. The first woman is defined by the patriarchal system of first-century Palestine. She is defined in terms of her relationship to a male, her father. The second woman is defined by the purity system of first-century Palestine. She is defined in terms of her uncleanness, her flow of blood. Both women, in other words, are situated in social systems that determine how the world in which they live relates to them.

But Jesus responds differently. Having heard the story of the second woman, he embraces her uncleanness by affirming her faith and healing. Her twelve years of uncleanness and social alienation are ended when he is healed and restored to the community. The acceptance and affirmation of Jesus, together with her faith, bring freedom from her religious, economic (v. 26), sexual, and social suffering (μάστιγος). The nameless, self-effacing woman has become a part of the Jesus movement; has become 'daughter'. Jesus has literally empowered her! (ὁ Ἰησοῦς ἐπιγνοὺς ἐν ἑαυτῷ τὴν ἐξ αὐτοῦ δύναμιν ἐξελθοῦσαν; v. 30).

There will still be times when this woman will not be able to worship in the temple, when she will not be able to be touched, when she will be unclean, when she will be marginalized by the patriarchal purity system. But that system has been challenged by her story.

Things go similarly with the first woman. Not only does Jesus touch her unclean dead body (v. 41), he also refers to her in her own right rather than as the property of the father. Her father and 'some men' (so certain English translations) refer to her in the patriarchal genitive (vv. 23 and 35). Jesus relates to the young woman as a subject, not as an object (vv. 39 and 41; τὸ παιδίον and Το κοράσιον respectively). Significantly, the narrator adopts Jesus' subject designation (τὸ παιδίον) in v. 40, in his (her?) implicit refusal to relate to the young woman as the property of her father, rather than the patriarchal language of Jairus and his men. He even goes so far as to reverse the genitive of possession. Instead of defining the young woman as possessed by her father, as an object (see v. 23 where Jairus refers to her as 'My little daughter'; Τὸ θυγάτριον μου), the narrator now designates her as a subject, possessing her father and mother (v. 40; τὸν πατέρα τοῦ παιδίου καὶ τὴν μητέρα).

There will still be times when this young woman is defined in terms of her social location within a patriarchal household, when she will be described with the possessive case, when she will be treated as an object by the patriarchal system. But that system has been challenged by her story.

The final question related text to present context: In what way does this text speak to us today? There were a variety of responses to this last question. In one group, for example, women began to explore ways of lobbying the new government to make health care for women a priority. In another group, the women decided to design a series of Bible studies that would make men in their congregations more conscious of structures and attitudes that oppress women. Overall, women experienced the Bible study as empowering. In the words of one participant, 'This Bible study has stopped me from throwing my Bible into the toilet and flushing it away'.

As I have already indicated, this workshop did not produce the above reading 'as is'. The reading, in its final form, is the product of a longer process, but the basic shape and substance of the reading emerged from this group.

We can now return to our earlier discussion. The contextual Bible study process that produced this reading is suggestive in a number of respects. Contextual Bible study begins with the needs and concerns of poor and marginalized communities. The question or questions that shape the Bible reading emerge from below, not from above. So, in actual contextual readings of Mk 5.21–6.1 the life interests of the participating group determined the theme; in each case, the theme focussed on 'women'. In the three workshops in which this text was used, the theme was related to the needs and concerns of women. Trained readers did not dictate the theme, it emerged from the life experience of ordinary readers.

The ISB is committed to working with organized communities or groups who can 'talk back' and who have the identity, structures, and resources to 'own' the workshop process. In other words, the ISB deliberately chooses to work in those contexts in which it is possible for the positions of the subject within both the ISB staff and the community participants to be vigilantly foregrounded.[32] The relationship between trained and ordinary reader is that of subject to subject and not subject to object. The trained reader reads the Bible 'with' and not 'for' ordinary readers.[33]

Within such a framework of accountability to Bible study groups of ordinary readers, trained readers can participate fully in the Bible study process. So, for example, in this workshop, I, as a trained reader, suggested that this text, along with a number of other texts identified by the groups, might be relevant to the chosen theme of 'women'. The advantage of a text like Mk 5.21–6.1 is that it is not usually perceived as a text primarily about women. Consequently, reading this text in this way 'surprises' the readers, and facilitates a more critical reading. The danger with well known texts is that we think we already know what they mean; we 'domesticate' and 'tame' them. The disclosive power of the 'untamed' and 'undomesticated' text is a contribution that trained readers can make to the contextual reading process. And this was the effect: on an initial reading, most readers did not recognize that the text was primarily about women. But once this was suggested and supported from a careful reading of the text there was great excitement and expectation.

In any reading of the Bible, in the interface between trained and ordinary readers, there is a great deal that ordinary readers can discover and recover in texts using their own resources, provided there is some facilitation of this process. So, in the workshops the Bible was read communally, in small groups. My role was to facilitate a more critical reading, by bringing to the reading process resources to enable 'a more nuanced and literary reading'. For example, instead of me providing evidence from the text to support the suggestion that the text was about women, it was usually sufficient to give one or two examples from the text and then to ask the groups to find additional examples. My task was then to summarize and systematize their arguments. Contextual Bible

---

32. G. Spivak, 'Can the Subaltern Speak?', in G. Nelson and L. Grossberg (eds.), *Marxism and the Interpretation of Culture* (London: Macmillan, 1988), pp. 271-313; J. Arnott, 'French Feminism in a South African Frame?: Gayatri Spivak and the Problem of "Representation" in South African Feminism', *Pretexts* 3 (1991), pp. 118-28.

33. G.O. West, 'Difference and Dialogue: Reading the Joseph Story with Poor and Marginalized Communities in South Africa', *Biblical Interpretation* 2 (1994), pp. 152-70, 154-55.

study, then, is committed to corporate and communal reading of the Bible in which the trained reader is just another reader with *different* resources and skills, not *better* resources and skills.[34]

As already indicated, the contextual reading process is also committed to critical readings of the Bible. While ordinary readers do have critical resources, these are not the specific critical resources of biblical studies. Ordinary readers, by definition, read the Bible pre-critically, while trained readers read the Bible critically (or post-critically).[35] Once again, creative facilitation can enable ordinary readers to read more critically than is their usual practice, producing 'a more nuanced and literary reading'. In the reading of Mk 5.21–6.1 I concentrated on providing resources for two critical modes of reading. What I call a close and careful (literary) mode of reading was used in order to substantiate the suggestion that the text was primarily about women. The use of narrative transitions to delimit the literary unit, the reading of the whole text to discern its structure, the careful and close reading of the component parts, the return to reread the text as a whole in the light of the reading of the parts, and the continual attention to the internal relationships within the text, including reference to plot, character, them, repetition, and other literary devices, are all elements of this mode of reading.[36] And while ordinary readers are not familiar with these literary resources for reading in any systematic way, they are able to recognize and appreciate their usefulness and integrate these resources into their own modes of reading.

The mode of reading I call 'behind the text', a historical and sociological mode, was used to situate this text in its first-century context. The implicit use of historical-critical tools to delimit the text, and to locate it historically, and the reconstruction of aspects of the sociological setting of the text, including reference to the patriarchal and purity systems, are elements of this mode of reading.[37] Once again, while

34. Being able to say 'different, not better' with integrity requires some form of conversion experience. Postmodernism can provide, I would suggest, resources for this conversion; see G.O. West, 'No Integrity without Contextuality: The Presence of Particularity in Biblical Hermeneutics and Pedagogy', *Scriptura* S/11 (1993), pp. 131-46.

35. The term 'post-critical' is not usually used to mean 'anti-critical', rather it is used to indicate modes of reading which move beyond historical-critical methods.

36. G.O. West, *Contextual Bible Study* (Pietermaritzburg: Cluster Publications, 1993), pp. 30-36.

37. See West, *Contextual Bible Study*, pp. 25-30.

ordinary readers are not familiar with these historical and sociological resources, they are able to recognize and appreciate their usefulness and integrate these resources into their own modes of reading.

It should be noted that these critical resources were not used as the way into the text. The Bible study began with a life interest of the participants. The generative theme determined by the group—in this case the theme of 'women'—was the initial mode of reading. This mode of reading is similar to what I have elsewhere called 'reading in front of the text',[38] although as practiced by ordinary readers it is usually not a critical mode of reading. But a thematic approach does provide a useful way into the text, particularly as it draws on the needs and questions of the participants. The role of the other modes of reading is then to develop and elaborate what is initiated through this thematic approach to the text.

The range of experience that groups of ordinary readers bring to their reading of the Bible is various and vast. Creative facilitation, including asking questions instead of simply providing information, can draw on the resources of ordinary readers and in so doing empower them to construct their own critical and contextual readings. Ordinary readers have no problem being contextual,[39] but they do require resources from trained readers to read the Bible in a more nuanced and critical way. The task, however, in contextual Bible study is not to do the reading for ordinary readers, nor to simply uncritically accept their readings. Rather, our task is to read the Bible *with* ordinary readers. This requires that we vigilantly foreground our respective subject positions, and that we become explicit concerning the power relations implicit in the reading process.[40]

The key contribution of critical resources to the contextual Bible study process is that it enables ordinary readers themselves to articulate 'the hidden transcript' and not only 'the public transcript', both in the Bible and in their own traditions of interpretation. Critical tools and skills also provide ordinary readers with a means for articulating what is incipient and subjugated.[41] While the first response in many Bible study groups is

---

38. West, *Contextual Bible Study*, pp. 36-40.

39. J.A. Draper and G.O. West, 'Anglicans and Scripture in South Africa', in F. England and T.J.M. Paterson (eds.), *Bounty in Bondage* (Johannesburg: Ravan, 1989), pp. 30-52.

40. West, 'Difference and Dialogue', p. 154.

41. For a discussion of what J.R. Cochrane terms 'incipient theologies' see his

often the 'missionary response' or the dogmatically 'correct' response—the public transcript—critical modes of reading enable ordinary people from poor and marginalized communities to begin to articulate readings and theologies that are incipient, and even perhaps elements of readings and theologies that are deliberately hidden from public view. The latter is clearly dangerous; what is hidden from the dominant is hidden for good reason, and can and should only be openly spoken in a context of trust and accountability. But within such a context, the intersection of contextual and critical resources enables the recognizing, recovering, and arousing of dangerous memories, subjugated knowledges and hidden transcripts.

The more systematic, critical, reading of the contextual Bible study process provides ordinary readers with the resources to situate the text both within its literary and linguistic context and within its historical and sociological context, and in so doing enables both ordinary and trained readers to appropriate the text more critically. Situating the text in these ways prevents a simple correspondence between text and present context. And reading the Bible with ordinary readers encourages the trained reader to complete the hermeneutic cycle and risk appropriation; albeit a critical appropriation.

What is particularly exciting and challenging about reading the Bible *with* ordinary readers is that it is quite legitimate for ordinary readers and trained readers to emerge from the reading process with different elements of interest. The readings produced in this interface affect ordinary and trained readers differently, and this is not surprising because we come to the text from different places, and after the reading encounter return to our different places. Our subjectivities as trained and ordinary readers are differently constituted, and so the effect that the corporate reading has on our subjectivities will be different. However, and this is extremely important, we will have been partially constituted by each other's subjectivities.[42] And this should always be a constituent element of the contextual Bible study process: a desire to be partially constituted by those from other communities. For me, this means choosing to be partially constituted by working with poor and marginalized communities.

'Conversation or Collaboration?': Base Christian Communities and the Dialogue of Faith', *Scriptura*, forthcoming.

42. West, 'No Integrity', p. 144, and see also S.D. Welch, *A Feminist Ethic of Risk* (Minneapolis: Fortress Press, 1990), p. 151.

The finished product which is this article was not produced by ordinary readers. It is, in its final form, my reading. But this is a reading that had its birth among ordinary black women who were struggling to hear God speak to their needs and questions.[43] What they have taken away from the Bible study workshop and how they will use it, I do not fully know. For example, one of the woman in the Umtata women's group summed up her group's discussion with the words: 'The problem is that men don't bleed; men must bleed!' What this means for that group of women and what they will do with this reading is theirs; it belongs to their context. Clearly, the participants found the reading process and its product to be empowering. I, too, have learned much from reading this text with ordinary readers and I have found the process empowering. But I recognize that what I have learned and how I have been empowered may be different from what ordinary readers have learned and how they have been empowered. That is the joy of reading the Bible *with* ordinary readers; by vigilantly acknowledging who we are, we are free to bring and share what is important to our respective subjectivities and take and use what is empowering for our respective subjectivities. And that this may be different for trained and ordinary readers respectively is further acknowledgement of our differences. Yet the reading process has enabled us to be partially constituted by the other; and it is 'the other' who is usually absent from biblical studies.[44]

The subtext of this article, which I will now state in the text, is that biblical studies and other trained readers need 'the other', particularly those 'others' from the margins, in our readings of the Bible. Our readings may be critical, but they are not truly contextual without the presence of ordinary readers. We trained readers also need to be ready to hear that we might have resources which are needed by poor and marginalized communities. Some of our biblical training may be useful and empowering to such communities.[45] The contextual Bible study

43. It has, as I have mentioned, also been shaped by other hands on the way, including responses I received when I presented aspects of these workshops in a paper to the New Testament Society of South Africa.

44. D. Tracy, *Plurality and Ambiguity: Hermeneutics, Religion, Hope* (San Francisco: Harper and Row, 1987), p. 79.

45. The cautionary tone is intended: 'People ask us for bread and we offer them a handful of theories about each verse of John 6. They ask questions about God and we offer them three theories about the literary form of one Psalm. They thirst for justice and we offer them discussions about the root of the word *ṣedâqâ* ('justice' in Hebrew). I am examining my conscience out loud, and the reply I hear is: the one must be done

process in which we read the Bible *with* ordinary readers provides a way of reading together in which we partially constitute each other without effacing difference and the power relations that come with difference.[46] Together we can resource each other so that we can read the Bible both contextually and critically.[47]

without neglecting the other' (L. Alonso Schöckel, cited in R.S. Sugirtharajah (ed.), *Voices from the Margin: Interpreting the Bible in the Third World* (Maryknoll: Orbis Books, 1991), p. 70. I would rephrase the last sentence to read: 'the latter must be done to serve the former'.

46. West, 'Difference and Dialogue', p. 154.

47. The financial assistance of the Centre for Science Development of the Human Sciences Research Council, the University of Natal, and the British Academy towards this research is gratefully acknowledged.

THE BIBLE AND THE RELIGIOUS IDENTITY OF THE MAYA OF GUATEMALA AT THE CONQUEST AND TODAY: CONSIDERATIONS AND CHALLENGES FOR THE NONINDIGENOUS

M. Daniel Carroll R.

This essay operates at two levels. At the most obvious, the discussion focuses on the topic expressed in the title. This essay, however, is not designed simply to provide the reader with an interesting description of the Maya of Guatemala. This case study of a particular people within a specific Central American country is also an attempt to illustrate a fundamental issue in the use of the Bible by Christian communities in ethics.

Christian communities do not exist in a vacuum, but rather in complex social and cultural contexts that, in a myriad of ways, impact Christian identity itself and the choice, interpretation, and utilization of biblical texts for ethics. An appreciation of how Christian identity has been shaped, and the Bible utilized in context, is foundational to subsequent attention to systemic ethical frameworks and to specific ethical issues. Readers, therefore, must be aware of this subtext of the commitment to contextual realism in ethics even as they follow the presentation of the nature of Mayan Christian identity vis-à-vis the Bible.

In the years ahead, the nature of Guatemalan socio-political life and of the Christian Church in this beautiful, though long-suffering, Central American nation will largely depend on seriously engaging for the first time with the Maya, who comprise over half of the population. My own ignorance as a non-Maya Christian living and working in Guatemala has motivated the research for this piece. It is hoped that this brief look at what being a Maya Christian has meant and now signifies, and the role of the scriptures in establishing this identity, can serve as a basis for dealing with the many new challenges to the theological thinking and ethical decision making of the non-Maya Christian in Guatemala.

Approaching the Context

Guatemala stands at a crucial juncture in its history. The thirty year internal armed conflict is nearing resolution, and the first tentative steps are being made to a more just and participatory democracy. At the same time, several factors are converging that now permit greater prominence to the Maya. It is no longer possible to continue to ignore the indigenous, a culturally rich tapestry of over twenty different groups and languages. The Maya have suffered the most loss and displacement during the years of violence (Falla) and have endured centuries of economic exploitation. Increasingly, diverse elements among the indigenous are gaining greater visibility in local and national politics, seek a voice in the peace negotiations between the government and the guerrilla coalition, and demand vindication of their languages and traditions. These developments have also become the focus of worldwide attention, due in no small measure to the selection of the Quiché woman Rigoberta Menchú for the Nobel Peace Prize in 1992. This choice deliberately coincided with the 500th anniversary of the coming of the Spanish to the Americas, and her election became a symbol of the struggle for indigenous rights in the Americas and around the globe.

The Christian Church, both Roman Catholic and Protestant, has often marginalized the Maya. The stirrings of the larger indigenous population, however, are also finding expression among Maya Christians of all stripes. On the one hand, indigenous Christians are wrestling with what it means to be both a Christian and Maya, and their greater involvement is beginning to impact local church communities and national bodies. On the other hand, many Ladinos and foreign personnel are beginning to face the reality of sharing authority with the indigenous in ecclesiastical structures and of broadening the doing of theology to embrace the contributions of the Maya.

Two insights from the discipline of interpretative anthropology can provide greater conceptual clarity to this introductory essay. The first is a particular way of looking at the nature of culture and cultural identity. Ideally, a fuller study would differentiate between the various schools of thought regarding other definitions of culture and would deal in a thorough theoretical manner with the multiple mechanisms of cultural change. We start from the interpretative premise that cultural identity refers to the collective identity that a social group possesses and transmits over time to successive generations. This cultural identity is grounded in interrelated codes of meaning embracing values, behavior, world view, and a multitude of symbols in all sorts of spheres. Culture involves, to use Geertz's phrase, webs of significance. While from an interpretative perspective culture might seem at first glance to be fixed, the truth is that cultures also constantly interact with forces in the political, social and economic realms. Cultural identity, in other words, is both stable and dynamic, as it recreates and adjusts itself in the interplay with these other influences (Geertz 1973, 1984; Carroll R. 1992: 49-71; Schreiter: 39-74). An important part of the cultural identity of the Maya is the religious component.

A second helpful notion that can be drawn from interpretative anthropology is the emic-etic distinction. Simply put, 'emics' refers to what anthropologists call the 'native point of view', whereas 'etics' speaks of the conceptual categories and analysis of the scientific observer. With the former, the goal of cultural study is to present descriptions and explanations of cultural phenomena in ways that are meaningful and appropriate to the people in question; with etic accounts, it is to provide testable and verifiable procedures to facilitate comparative studies, especially those dealing with infrastructural causes of these phenomena (Harris: 32-56; Headland, Pike, Harris; Carroll R. 1992: 54-63). Both perspectives are valid and can be mutually informing and enriching. In terms of our topic, this differentiation will help remind the nonindigenous, however interested in or sympathetic and committed to the Maya, not only to pursue conclusions about Mayan religious identity grounded in scientific socio-political and economic research of Guatemalan national life, but also to listen to the Maya themselves regarding that identity.

Three different case studies will focus on different contexts and point out some lessons to be learned in considering the relationship of the Bible to the religious identity of the Maya: the efforts of Bartolomé de las Casas on behalf of the indigenous during the colonial period and the perspectives of ecumenical and evangelical Protestant Maya Christians in contemporary Guatemala.

Bartolomé de las Casas: The Arrival of the Bible

The Spanish arrived in the 'New World' at the end of the fifteenth century fresh from the victories over the Moors and the uniting of the kingdoms of Castille and Aragon under Isabel and Ferdinand. Emboldened with a messianic sense of being the nation chosen to further the Roman Catholic faith and eager to possess the proverbial wealth of the 'Indies', the *conquistadores* launched the invasion of the Americas in the name of the crown and Santiago, St James, the patron saint of Spain.

The conquest of the indigenous peoples in combination with the preaching of a Christian tradition sparked fierce theological debates in Spain, and these in turn had implications for both royal and ecclesiastical policies in the colonies. There was no single view regarding either the humanity of the indigenous or the most appropriate manner by which to propagate the Catholic faith. Religious orders took different sides in the struggles over theological definitions, territorial allotments and funding by the crown (Todorov; Mires; Rivera; Núñez; Schwaller; Wilson). Of those who defended the integrity and cultural rights of the indigenous during the colonial period, no other name stands out as prominently as Bartolomé de las Casas (1474–1564; Las Casas 1992: 9-58, 185-208; Gutiérrez).

Las Casas traveled to Hispaniola in 1502 to farm the land that Columbus had given his father. Though ordained a priest in 1507, it was not until he was deeply convicted by the admonitions of Ecclus. 34.18-22 in preparation for his sermon for Pentecost in 1514 that he made the decision to dedicate his life to fighting to change the values and structures of Spanish colonial life. In 1522 he joined the Dominican order.

Las Casas had witnessed firsthand the utilization of the Catholic faith to theologically legitimate the conquest through the *requerimiento* and the setting up of the colonial arrangements of the *encomienda* (or *repartimiento*) and the *reducción*. The *requerimiento*, a document in Spanish that was read aloud upon contact with the indigenous, demanded the native population to submit to the crown and the Catholic faith on pain of death if refused (Mires 49-58; Rivera 32-41). The *encomienda* (from the Spanish verb *encomendar*, to entrust) entailed granting concessions to towns and broader indigenous areas to Spanish overlords and clergy. The *reducción* involved the concentration of scattered indigenous populations in towns. Both proposed social structures were designed to aid civil administration, tax collection, and the recruitment of labor, as well as to 'civilize' and christianize the indigenous (Mires: 107-31, 179-204; Hawkins 54-80; Rivera 113-31). This 'ideal' hardly matched the realities of colonial life. The indigenous were exploited and enslaved to work the mines for precious metals and to farm the plantations. The destructiveness of the colonial era is well known: the harsh socioeconomic system, coupled with massive epidemics of diseases brought by the Spanish, quickly decimated the indigenous population (Gutiérrez 637-41; Lovell and Lutz).

In order to counteract this colonial cruelty, Las Casas worked tirelessly to lobby the crown for substantive changes. He was able to receive permission to conduct an experiment of peaceful evangelization in a part of the territory which the Spanish had not been able to vanquish (1537). This 'Land of War', Tuzulutlán, Las Casas renamed Vera Paz ('true peace'), the name to this day of two states in Guatemala (Alta and Baja Verapaz). He convinced the Spanish monarch to promulgate the 'New Laws' (1542), which strove to neutralize the *encomienda* (Mires: 97-131; Rivera, passim), and wrote a series of works defending indigenous rights. The Dominican spent years working on the *Historia de las Indias*, a massive study presenting to the Spanish people a different picture of indigenous cultural life than that promoted by the exploiters.

His use of the Bible is best exemplified in *The Only Way to Draw All People to a Living Faith* (Las Casas: 61-182). In this work Las Casas presents arguments based on papal pronouncements, tomes of ancient philosophers, and Church tradition for evangelizing in a peaceable manner so as to win the willing consent of the indigenous to the Catholic faith. *The Only Way* is also heavily sprinkled with biblical references. For example, Las Casas appeals to the New Testament examples of Jesus and Paul, who provide models for acts of charity and of preaching that touch both the heart and mind; Christ's weapons are not the ways of violence, but rather a gentle spirit (Mt. 11.29-30) and a powerful word that can convert the soul (2 Cor. 10.4-5). He cites Isa. 42.1-4, 52.7, and 61.1 as defining texts for evangelization efforts, while at the same time thundering condemnation on the Spanish by comparing them with the shameless shepherds of Ezek. 34.2-4 and Zech. 11.4-5. For Las Casas, the Spanish actually owe restitution to the indigenous (Exod. 20.15; Rom. 13.7; Lev. 19.13) and are in danger of eternal damnation because of their barbaric deeds (Mt. 19.17). Las Casas closes the treatise with a quote from Proverbs: 'When someone's ways please God, God makes even their enemies to be at peace with them' (16.7).

In *The Only Way* the indigenous are, first of all, declared to be wholesome and intelligent humans (Las Casas: 63-66). Though the indigenous are pagan, they are not like other hostile infidels like the Moors who require violent treatment, but rather exhibit developed and rational forms of government and threaten no harm to Christianity (Las Casas: 66-67, 114-16: Rivera: 213-15). These pagan peoples will be able to

understand by gentle persuasion the Christian message incarnated by
godly missioners (Mt. 5.16; 1 Thess. 2.7-8; 2 Tim. 2.24). The opposite
way is military coercion, which forces the non-Christian to listen to a
contradictory message:

> What pagan soul would want to hear about our faith and Church if he or
> she is horribly harmed by the cruel weight of war, the brutal, unbearable
> waste of war? The voice of war is not calm; its face is not kind; it has no
> modest bearing, no peaceable language; it does not attract, does not con-
> vince with charm. War is a frightful chorus of yells... War is all curse and
> catcall; it is the grating, fearsome screech of weapon on weapon left and
> right and dead men falling... War is weeping and wailing everywhere.
> What balm or blessing will it take to make victims of war willing and able
> to learn religious belief? (Las Casas: 121)

These eloquent words stand in stark contrast to the reasoned defense of
the conquest by the Spanish jurist Juan Ginés de Sepúlveda (Sepúlveda;
Todorov: 146-60). Framed in Socratic dialogue form, his argumentation
is based on classic just war theory, on the basis of which the more
developed and spiritual nation has the divine right to subjugate and
enlighten inferior peoples. What is more, the indigenous sins of idolatry
and human sacrifice make judgment necessary.

Sepúlveda's work is full of biblical citations, imagery, and allusions.
His choice of passages and his political commitments, however, are very
unlike Las Casas's. For Sepúlveda, the Bible substantiates the right of
appointed authorities to punish sin (Rom. 13.4), different treatment for
enemies in warfare (Deut. 20.10-14) and the legitimacy of slavery with
spiritual goals (Col. 3.22-4.1; 1 Pet. 2.16).

Sepúlveda also utilizes the biblical text to impute a different identity on
the indigenous. In his understanding, the natives are like the fools who
must serve the wise (Prov. 11.29), like the sinners of the Flood and
Sodom and Gomorrah who are destroyed in divine wrath, and like the
idolatrous Canaanites who suffer at Joshua's hand. Only through the
generosity and patience of the Spanish can the indigenous hope to come
to the Catholic faith. Sepúlveda would even question the fullness of their
humanity:

> ... with perfect right the Spaniards rule over these barbarians of the New
> World and surrounding islands, who, in regards to wisdom, cleverness,
> virtue and humanity are as inferior to the Spanish as children to adults and
> women to men; there is as big a difference as between a fiery and cruel

people and a merciful one, as between the most prodigiously intemperate and the self-controlled and restrained, and I could even say as between monkeys and men (Sepúlveda: 101; my translation).

It is appropriate to begin our reflections as nonindigenous on Maya religious identity with this brief look at Las Casas. In some ways he is a model of theological and ethical praxis. Because of his commitment to the poor and to the marginalized, the Dominican has been heralded by some as a precursor of Latin American Liberation Theology (e.g. Mires: 217-18; Gutiérrez; Rivera: 267-71). Even though an 'outsider', he devoted years to the study of the indigenous cultures. One can appreciate this effort to blend the etics of his theology and philosophical training with an attempt to approach the emics of indigenous cultural and religious identity so as to somehow comprehend and respect their view of life and the world, even while trying to bring them within the Christian fold. He also toiled to offer alternative structures and theological perspectives to a hegemonic Church and sacrificed the greater part of his life at the Spanish court to change imperial foreign policy. There was much of value in the actions taken by this nonindigenous cleric— actions which alleviated the suffering of the indigenous in the colonies, helped force the rethinking of theological categories and convictions both at home and in the 'New World', and impacted government. In all of this, the Bible was a powerful tool by which Las Casas tried to forge a very different world.

At the same time, however, one should not idealize Las Casas. To begin with, he never did totally shed his deep belief in the providential mission of the Spanish on the continent (Todorov: 175-201; Rivera: 55-62), though at the end of his life he prophesied judgment upon Spain for the prostitution of its divine election (Las Casas: 194-95; Rivera: 254-57). What is more, for a time he lobbied to bring African slaves to take the place of the indigenous—a decision he deeply regretted later (Las Casas: 201-208; Rivera: 180-95). Herein lie other lessons for the nonindigenous: the need to be aware of the temptation of a messianic calling, in which one arrives with foreign answers and programs, even as one identifies with the indigenous. While Las Casas indeed used the Bible *for* the indigenous, he also very quickly labeled them pagan and was an instrument in the imposition of a particular kind of Christian religious identity. It is evident, then, that, although narrative theology is correct in calling the Bible an identity document for the Christian community (Hauerwas;

Carroll R. 1992: 143-75), the identifying process is inseparable from the realities of power and context.

The conquest consisted not only of the military clash between two cultures, but of a battle between their gods (Todorov: 63-123; Rivera: 154-68, 258-71). Extant texts describe the desperate theological reflections of the indigenous, who tried to make religious sense of their defeat and loss and struggled to come to grips with being forced to accept a new identity (León-Portillo). A new religious identity, with its customs, costumes, and celebrations, was, in fact, put in place. What relationship did/does this indigenous post-colonial religious identity have with the original Maya culture? The conquest obviously was a defining moment for Maya culture, but there is no agreement concerning this cultural entity that emerges from the sixteenth and seventeenth centuries and that endures to this day. Some from the ideological Left would say that what exists today as the so-called indigenous culture is wholly the creation of the Spanish, and that the future of the indigenous lies with shedding these trappings and joining the resistance of the proletariat (Martínez Peláez); others propose that the indigenous culture is an indigenous creation shaped in response to the overlord Spanish culture (Hawkins). More classic views include the idea that what exists is a mixture of the Spanish and the Maya, or the theory that pre-Columbian survivals can still be seen today. Whatever the case might be, the nonindigenous must appreciate that any talk of Maya religious identity must deal with the colonial period, for the present religious context of the Maya finds its roots there.

From another angle, anthropologists and Christian theologians continue to debate whether the resulting hybrid of Catholic and indigenous religions is an alien syncretism and, if so, to what degree it reflects Christian faith. Other related issues, such as the possibility of divine revelation within the pre-Columbian religion, also occupied the work of colonial clergy and anticipated modern discussions (Todorov: 202-54; cf. Schreiter: 122-58). These topics will surface again later, though this essay cannot attempt their resolution. At this point it is enough to say that the life of Las Casas forces the nonindigenous interested in the Maya to begin to examine personal commitments and to be cognizant of the role of history and context in biblical interpretation and in the defining of religious identity.

*Ecumenical Protestant Maya: The Bible in Dialogue
with Indigenous Rights*

Today the religious identity of the Maya Christians is in no way homogenous. The Maya can be subdivided in broad terms into three groups (Scotchmer 1995): (1) The Traditionalists, who are identified with town patron saints and festivals, the *cofradías* (a male religious order charged with honoring these saints and organizing important local religious events), the shaman-priest, a hierarchical social structure focused on the *principales* (the elders) and certain rituals linked, to some degree, to the ancient Maya; (2) the more orthodox Roman Catholics of Catholic Action or the charismatic groups; and (3) the Protestants. This essay will focus briefly on two subgroups within the last category, the ecumenical and the evangelical wings of Maya Protestantism.

Ecumenical Maya Protestants in Guatemala can be well appreciated within the more encompassing framework of the indigenous rights movement, as these share several similar concerns with the indigenous rights movement. This movement, if it can be properly called such, is not so much an organized effort among the Maya, but rather more of a way of referring to the general direction of the labors of different Maya organizations (Bastos and Camus; Smith 1991; Cojti 1992, 1995). Umbrella groups, such as the Consejo de Organizaciones Mayas de Guatemala and the Academia de Lenguas Mayas de Guatemala, seek to coordinate these activities.

The key issue for these organizations is Maya identity. The Guatemalan state is considered to represent and perpetuate a modern form of colonialism that would want to eliminate or minimize this cultural identity (cf. Smith [ed.] 1990):

> A country is colonialist and imperialist when, among other things, it monopolizes and controls other peoples, practices linguistic and cultural oppression through championing its own ethnic characteristics or by prohibiting the teaching and use of unofficial languages, tries to assimilate the oppressed peoples under the pretext of recognizing them as having equal rights and access to power, and exploits the dominated peoples economically (Cojti 1992: 1).

At the political level, what is sought is some kind of regional autonomy. The hope is to obtain the sort of national unity which would allow for cultural pluralism and a measure of self-determination. Though constitutionally the Maya are equal to the Ladino, this legal status is not reflected, for instance, within the day-to-day process of law and the allotment of government funding and personnel for education and social services. Some of the related commitments of the movement include the promotion of indigenous languages (with an attempt to unify the Maya alphabet), the elimination of forced military recruitment, and the achievement of basic economic demands. An important goal is to secure congressional ratification of United Nations Convention 169 regarding indigenous rights.

On a national level this movement, although in many ways sympathetic to the positions of the Left, has not identified wholeheartedly with the traditional Left in Guatemala for two principal reasons. First, the Left has usually been more interested in class and economic discourse rather than cultural issues (Smith 1990); second, certain factions of the Left opted for guerrilla warfare, an opposition strategy foreign to the Maya. At the same time, the movement does visualize some common cause with nonindigenous human rights organizations and labor unions, both at a national and continent-wide level (INCEP). This solidarity, of course, finds its most visible symbol in the person of Rigoberta Menchú.

How representative among the Maya population is this movement? Up to now, even its leaders admit that the participants are few. Most of the indigenous are perceived to lack a clearly defined consciousness and are not politically organized (Cojti 1992). As Carol Smith points out:

> Three types of people currently make up the movement, almost all of them literate, self-proclaimed Maya: students and intellectuals; community-based professionals (teachers, agronomists, health workers); and members of local NGOs [nongovernment organizations] and cooperatives, often supported by foreign sources...Few Maya nationalists are 'men of maize'—the illiterate peasants, plantation workers, traders, and artisans who make up the majority of Guatemala's native people (Smith 1991: 30).

To say this, however, is not to try to minimize the movement or its goals, but rather to put it within perspective—within the realities of national life. The issues that these organizations are raising are important, even if the majority of the indigenous population might not be aware of them, understand them or even agree with them. The danger, of course, is that a pan-Mayan program run by an elite might lose touch with local Maya communities and overlook the cultural diversity of the different Maya peoples in its quest for a pan-Maya identity (Smith 1991; Warren: 206-13; Watanabe 1995: 35-41).

Though some of the indigenous movement would disqualify Christianity as one among several foreign imperialist impositions (Cojti

1992: 3,16), ecumenical Maya Protestants view their faith in a different light and want to champion its relevance, even as they attempt to reformulate its categories and praxis. Because of the contemporary challenges to Maya identity and life, these Protestants question the hermeneutical approaches and the theology inherited from the missionaries (Scotchmer 1995: 44-50). I mention two fundamental concerns.

To begin with, this perspective desires to vindicate the religious and cultural values of the pre-Columbian Maya. Although Tamez writes of the indigenous of Mexico, one of her articles will serve as an example of this indigenous Protestant point of view (Tamez; cf. the Roman Catholic, Richard). She goes back to pre-Aztec religion, to an earlier vision of Quetzalcoatl of the Náhuatl, to demonstrate that this was a single supreme deity of love and peace. The Aztecs perverted these beliefs and transformed Quetzalcoatl into a warlike and bloody god.

With several New Testament texts as a biblical foundation, she posits the possibility of finding divine revelation in the native religion before the coming of the Spanish. The word of God cannot be limited, in other words, to the Bible, but is also found in other cultures. The key is the divine commitment to life, and this is the bridge to the god of the Bible.

Tamez does not see a contradiction with native polytheism if the deities are for the fullness of human life in all of its dimensions, as there the true god is revealed (Tamez: 43, 49-51). Others, however, claim that the attribution of polytheism to the natives is a Western fabrication (Colop *et al.*: 13). Some have pointed to important themes that can link the biblical text with indigenous religion: the biblical concept of bread as a connection to corn (Chaj Hernández), a holistic faith which does not separate the spiritual from the material, the centrality of the earth and nature, the plurality and the unity of god and the call for justice. Taylor reports the attempt to initiate the doing of theology from the cultural values of the sun (Taylor). In sum, the Bible is utilized as a vehicle to stretch back across the centuries in order to establish a continuity of indigenous identity by serving as a guide to common concerns and theological themes crucial to indigenous life.

As the indigenous movement rejects certain elements of the positions of the Left in Guatemala, so too some ecumenical Maya Protestants would disagree at points with Liberation Theology (Taylor: 20-34). Once again, the crux is the priority of ethnic identity and a life closely tied to nature instead of a discourse more focused on class and economics. The nature and goal of social transformation, therefore, take a different shape. Opposition strategies are less confrontational than some of the positions taken by several liberationists; time is on the side of the Maya, who will not only adapt, but will also survive. Some also are inclined to join with other ecumenical rights groups in the Americas (Colop *et al.*; Tamez).

Several lessons for the nonindigenous can be gleaned from the ecumenical perspective. First, this wing of Protestantism will not allow any attempt to contextualize the Bible for the religious identity of the Maya to ignore the religious traditions of the past, both oral and written. The topics of pluralism and revelation thus resurface. Second, it is evident that this identity cannot be isolated from the larger issues of indigenous rights, which are so central to the future of national social and political life.

Third, the nonindigenous must have a realistic picture of the actual representativeness of ecumenical Maya Protestants. Even as Liberation Theology reflected the perspectives and practice of few Christians on the continent, a fact that liberation theologians now admit (e.g. Berryman; cf. Stoll 1990: 308-21; Carroll R. 1992: 137-39), this ecumenical position would speak for only a minority of Mayan Protestants. Their views are 'popular', not in a demographic sense (Carroll R. 1994), but because they speak to pressing needs of the Maya. They represent, that is, a certain kind of emics; a 'native point of view' that is considering social and theological items of which all Protestants must be aware and with which all must deal.

Fourth, Taylor's essay provides an outstanding example for a nonindigenous scholar. He has listened carefully to the Maya and even incorporates a Mayan Christian leader's reactions to his thoughts into the footnotes. Concerning this need to actually try to get at the 'native point of view' and to subject oneself to the scrutiny of the indigenous in the doing of research, Taylor appropriately warns the outsider: 'almost always [the Mayan] concerns are lost in the voices of us benevolent, maybe even emancipatively-inclined intellectuals' (Taylor: 4; cf. Watanabe 1995: 25-29).

Evangelical Protestant Maya:
The Bible's Various Roles in a Context of Change

Evangelical missionaries arrived in Guatemala over a century ago by invitation of the Liberal reformer and president General Justo Rufino Barrios. The nature of the earliest 'founding' missions and the character of their early efforts have marked in some degree the conservative temper of Guatemalan evangelicalism. The reactionary tenor of some evangelicalism in this country also has been due in part to the negative stances taken by the Roman Catholic hierarchy toward the evangelical presence and expansion. Earlier stereotypes, however, of evangelical organizations as the vanguard of North American imperialism utilized by the C.I.A. and funded by the U.S. government, and of evangelicals as imported 'sects' destructive of Guatemalan family and cultural life, are beginning to be replaced by more balanced approaches which recognize the variety among evangelicals (Martin; Cleary; Berryman) and that are more circumspect of ideological charges (though these cannot be totally dismissed: Stoll 1990). Recent years have witnessed impressive growth, especially among the historic Pentecostal and the neo-Pentecostal denominations, and estimates of how much of the total population is evangelical now vacillate between 20 and 30 percent. The number of Maya evangelicals could be as high as one million (Scotchmer 1991: 9).

The characterization by some anthropologists and social scientists of evangelical Protestantism as the noxious agent of modernization and the political Right has also been applied to the indigenous culture. However, newer anthropological studies of religious change among the Maya of Guatemala (whether wrought by evangelicals, Catholic Action or the more politically committed) take a disparate view. An 'essentialist' perspective on culture—which locks on to a particular configuration of that culture as timeless, pristine, and coherent and qualifies any change as necessarily detrimental—is yielding to a more dynamic comprehension of cultural identity. Yet more materialist explanations can be too deterministic. As John Watanabe points out:

> Cultural essentialists correctly stressed the importance of ongoing differences in interpersonal relations, attitudes, and values in shaping distinct Maya communities, but they tended to assume a static view of Maya culture itself: distinguished by dress, language, livelihood, place of residence, economic status, and local institutions, the Maya themselves would disappear as they acculturated to Ladino ways. Conversely, historicists rightly perceived the colonial trappings and dialectical nature of the opposition between Indian and Ladino, but they often reduced this opposition to an artifact of colonial domination: Maya culture and community became, at best, empty tokens of ideological resistance; at worst, blind, ultimately pernicious, self-deception or false consciousness. Implicitly or explicitly, both approaches portrayed the Maya as fundamentally passive—either the stoic survivors of a fading past or the hapless victims of an unjust present.

In the end, whether through acculturation, proletarianization, or even
revolution, the Maya would inevitably succumb to the Ladino world
(Watanabe 1992: 8).

Interaction, adaptation, resistance, assimilation, invention, creativity:
these are the words that would describe the complex relationship
between Maya cultures and the Ladino world over the centuries (Smith
[ed.] 1990; Wilson). What one witnesses at a local level are a wide range
of Maya responses to the distinct pressures of particular contexts. Maya
identity is tied more to place and community than to a fixed transcendental list of pan-Maya characteristics. Cultural identity is inevitably
and fundamentally local, and in each place race, color, stature,
occupation, customs, language, dress, education, concepts of origins and
religion come together in particular and unique ways. Field research
among the Maya in different parts of Guatemala and southern Mexico is
yielding data that demonstrate that the evangelical message responds to
Maya needs of various kinds and that conversion to this form of
Christian faith yields a religious identity distinct from the Traditional and
the orthodox Roman Catholic, but which the indigenous still consider to
be Maya.

David Stoll has studied the stories of the evangelical Maya in the Ixil
Triangle in the Quiché department, one of the areas hardest hit by the
awful violence of the war (Stoll 1993; cf. Green). What indigenous
support there was for the guerrillas had been based on reaction to army
excesses, not ideological convictions. This support was withdrawn once
it became evident that the guerrillas could neither provide the promised
food or protect them from the army. The evangelical churches offered a
neutral space between the army and the guerrillas within which the
indigenous could rebuild their civil society, hold together their families,
and receive aid for the widows and orphans. Neutralism became a
strategy for survival. What is more, the Ixil had been making political
and economic gains in the area towns in a peaceable manner and did not
seek the recourse to violence. Social changes were afoot: ethnic tensions
between Ladino and the Ixil were subsiding as both groups had suffered
together the cost of war and as Ladinos simply left the area; new civil
organizations were sprouting up in the shape of cooperatives; many
indigenous were migrating to other regions due to population growth
and land shortages. That is, Maya strategies of resistance and of dealing
with the hardships differed from those of the militant Left and Right,
and within a volatile context the evangelical church provided a refuge.

This research has forced Stoll to question his own prejudices and political idealism:

> If we give due weight to the commentaries of noncombatants, the popular character of peasant-based insurgencies is likely to be transitory. Once a population has been ravaged by war, what prevails is a hunger for stability, even on blatantly disfavorable terms. This puts scholars like myself who identify with the Left in an uncomfortable position. If subordinate groups usually do not want to pay the cost of defying dominant ones, where do we find a revolutionary subject to support in our work? (Stoll 1993: 305)

Kay Warren describes the changes in the town of San Andrés Semetabaj in the department of Sololá (Warren 1992, 1993). Here, too, the violence prompted changes in the social context and in communal relations. Stories of conversion to evangelical faith utilized traditional Kakchikel imagery and narrative elements. Although evangelicals were shunning traditional *costumbre* (Catholic Action was reviving but desacralizing the rituals), these indigenous Christians still considered themselves to be Maya.

Sheldon Annis's work looks at San Antonio Aguas Calientes (Annis). Here violence was not the paramount cause for social rupture. Instead, evangelical faith appeared to respond better to new economic pressures, which were manifesting the inadequacy of agriculture methods that are interwoven with the traditional belief system. The festivals are left behind; holidays are no longer full of drinking; the *cofradía* taxes are no longer applicable. The new faith provides a different manner of looking at work and orients individuals and families to other practices and customs (cf. Scotchmer 1991: 277-300, 377-95; Goldin and Metz; Goldin). Religious identity is changing, and cultural identity is being reshaped to meet the realities of a new context.

In Zinacantán and Chamula in the Chiapas highlands of southern Mexico, where Maya evangelicals are 40 percent of the population, Garrard-Burnett's investigation suggests that evangelical growth be classified 'not as a medium of transition [to Westernization], but as a modern-day means of asserting Indian identity; as a mechanism by which indigenous peoples can assert ethnic differentiation in such a way as to use their "otherness" to their advantage' (Garrard-Burnett: 4). A cultural precedent for change and authenticity lies in the *cofradía*, which itself is an indigenous adaptation and creation from the last century that arose in response to new economic pressures. Today, the evangelical religious identity asserts its Mayaness by the use of the vernacular in worship services, the development of heterodox doctrines with some affinities to Maya cultural beliefs (cf. Scotchmer 1986, 1989, 1991; Watanabe 1992: 185-216), and the role of indigenous leadership within local (primarily) neo-Pentecostal groups.

Among Maya evangelicals the Bible is a key symbol of conversion. The Bible is carried to services; it is placed in a prominent place in the homes, and texts appear on the walls of homes and churches. The Bible is not a religious relic or totem for rituals as with many Traditionalists, but is to be read, memorized and preached. It represents a final written word from God, a powerful symbol within an oral culture which now makes magic, the shaman, divination and the priest unnecessary mediations to the divine (Scotchmer 1989: 297-300; 1991: 244-323). Evangelical Maya have usually not been involved in larger socio-political issues, though there are exceptions to the rule at local (Garrard-Burnett) and national levels. Still, the evangelical emphasis on the biblical teaching of the image of God (Scotchmer 1991: 300-310; Ortiz Ch.: 176-185) and the high value placed on education of both males and females (Scotchmer 1991: 361-77) have provided avenues for asserting the worth of indigenous life and culture vis-à-vis the dominant Ladino society.

For the nonindigenous, this look at evangelical Maya serves to underline the importance of not losing sight of the familial and the parochial. This is a different perception of the emic than that of the ecumenical Maya. Here, variety and complexity are the catchwords, and everyday life of discreet communities the context. The outsider must tune the ear to hear the different local native stories and appreciate the many different contributions of the Bible in helping the indigenous to face the ethical and cultural challenges of violence and change.

At the same time, though change is inevitable, some trends among evangelical Maya need to be scrutinized, too. What should be done with traditional rituals? What, if anything, of Maya identity is lost, and why are once certain customs disdained and proscribed? Evangelical reactions to the other religious expressions among the Maya once again bring the issues of pluralism and revelation to the table.

Conclusion

This essay is an attempt by a nonindigenous Christian in Guatemala to offer some introductory thoughts on some basic issues concerning the establishment of the religious identity of the Christian Maya and the role of the Bible in that process. The twin concerns of Christian identity and the function of the Bible do generate theological reflection in difficult areas, like the relationship between ideology and faith, religious pluralism, and the nature of divine revelation. At the same time, in light of the most basic purpose of this essay, these two fundamental issues especially demand thoughtful circumspection in order to be able to begin to move in a constructive and sensitive manner into other realms of Christian ethical discourse in Guatemala. It is hoped that these observations on the complexities of a specific Latin American situation will encourage serious consideration of contextual realism in ethics in other contexts around the globe.

BIBLIOGRAPHY

Annis, S.
1987   *God and Production in a Guatemalan Town* (Austin: University of
            Texas Press).
Bastian, J.-P.
1993   'The Metamorphosis of Latin American Protestant Groups: A
            Sociological Perspective', *Latin American Research Review* 28/2,
            pp. 33-61.
Bastos, S. and M. Camus
n.d.   *Quebrando el silencio. Organizaciones del pueblo maya y sus
            demandas (1986–1992)* (Guatemala: Facultad Latinoamericana de
            Ciencias Sociales).
Berryman, P.
1994   *Stubborn Hope: Religion, Politics, and Revolution in Central America*
            (Maryknoll: Orbis; New York: The New Press).
Carroll R., M. Daniel
1992   *Contexts for Amos: Prophetic Poetics in Latin American Perspective*
            (JSOTSup 132; Sheffield: JSOT Press).
1994   'Lecturas populares de la Biblia. Su significado y reto para la
            educación teológica', *Kairós* 14, pp. 43-61.
Chaj Hernández, J.B.
1992   'El maíz: un paradigma teológico para la pastoral indígena', *Vida y
            Pensamiento* 12/1, pp. 5-25.
Clearly, E.L.
1992   'Evangelicals and Competition in Guatemala', in E.L. Clearly and
            H. Stewart-Gambino (eds.), *Conflict and Competition: The Latin Church
            in a Changing Environment* (Boulder: Lynne Rienner), pp. 167-95.
Cojti C., Demetrio
1992   'The Mayan Movement in Contemporary Colonial Guatemala'. Paper
            given in Los Angeles at the annual meeting of the Latin American
            Studies Association.

1995 'Colonialismo mestizo y anticolonialismo maya. Primeros desencuentros', *Siglo Veintiuno* (Guatemala, 16 February), pp. 12-13.

Colop, M., A. Castañeda and G. de la Cruz

1990 *500 años de resistencia. Hacia una pastoral indigena* (San José, Costa Rica: Centro Evangélico Latinoamericano de Estudios Pastorales).

Falla, R.

1992 *Masacres en la selva. Ixcán, Guatemala (1975–1982)* (Guatemala: Editorial Universitaria).

Garrard-Burnett, V.

1994 'Protestantism as a Popular Movement Among Indigenous Peoples in the Trans-Maya Region of Mexico and Guatemala'. Paper given in Atlanta at the annual meeting of the Latin American Studies Association.

Geertz, C.

1973 *The Interpretation of Cultures: Selected Essays* (New York: Basic Books).

1984 'Culture and Social Change: The Indonesian Case', *Man* NS 19, pp. 511-32.

Goldin, L.R.

1993 'Uneven Development in Western Guatemala', *Ethnology* 32/3, pp. 237-51.

Goldin, L.R., and B. Metz

1991 'An Expression of Cultural Change: Invisible Converts to Protestantism among Highland Guatemalan Mayas', *Ethnology* 30/4, pp. 325-38.

Green, L.

1993 'Shifting Affiliations: Mayan Widows and *Evangélicos* in Guatemala', in V. Garrard-Burnett and D. Stoll (eds.), *Rethinking Protestantism in Latin America* (Philadelphia: Temple University Press), pp. 159-79.

Gutiérrez, G.

1992 *En busca de los pobres de Jesucristo. El pensamiento de Bartolomé de las Casas* (Lima: Instituto Bartolomé de las Casas/Centro de Estudios y Publicaciones).

Harris, M.

1979 *Cultural Materialism: The Struggle for a Science of Culture* (New York: Vintage Books).

Hauerwas, S.

1980 'The Moral Authority of Scripture: The Politics and Ethics of Remembering', *Interpretation* 34, pp. 356-70.

Hawkins, J.

1984 *Inverse Images: The Meaning of Culture, Ethnicity and Family in Post-colonial Guatemala* (Albuquerque: University of New Mexico Press).

Headland, T.N., K.L. Pike and M. Harris

1990 *Emics and Etics: The Insider/Outsider Debate* (Frontiers of Anthropology, VII; Newbury Park: Sage Publications).

INCEP (Instituto Centroamericano de Estudios Políticos)

1993 *Identidad y derechos de los Pueblos Indigenas. La cuestión étnica 500 años despué* (Guatemala: INCEP).

Las Casas, B. de
1992   *The Only Way to Draw All People to a Living Faith*, (ed. Helen Rand Parish; trans. Francis Patrick Sullivan; New York: Paulist Press).
León-Portillo, M.
1992   *Visión de los vencidos. Relaciones indígenas de la Conquista* (Mexico: Universidad Nacional Autónoma de México).
Lovell, W.G.and C.H. Lutz
1992   'Conquest and Population: Maya Demography in Historical Perspective'. Paper presented in Los Angeles at the annual meeting of the Latin American Studies Association.
Martin, D.
1990   *Tongues of Fire: The Explosion of Protestantism in Latin America* (Cambridge: Basil Blackwell).
Martínez Peláez, S.
1972   *La patria del criollo. Ensayo de interpretación de la realidad colonial guatemalteca* (San José, C.R.: Editorial Universitaria Centroamericana).
Menchú, R.
1985   *Me llamo Rigoberta Menchú y así nació mi conciencia* (Mexico: Siglo Veintiuno Editores).
Mires, F.
1987   *La colonización de las almas. Misión y conquista en Hispanoamérica* (San José, C.R.: Departmento Ecuménico de Investigaciones).
Núñez, E.A.
1992   'Luces y sombras del sistema colonial español', *Kairós* 10, pp. 71-89.
Ortiz Ch., I.
1992   'Dignidad e identidad indígena: una crítica evangélica sobre los 500 años', *Boletín teológico* 47/48, pp. 157-85.
Richard, P.
1992   'Hermeneútica bíblica india. Revelación de Dios en las religiones indígenas y en la Biblia (Después de 500 años de dominación)', *Revista de Interpretación bíblica latinoamericana* 11, pp. 9-24.
Rivera, L.N.
1992   *A Violent Evangelism: The Political and Religious Conquest of the Americas* (Louisville: Westminster Press/John Knox).
Schreiter, R.J.
1985   *Constructing Local Theologies* (Maryknoll: Orbis Books).

Schwaller, J.F.
1992   'The Clash of Cultures', *Latin American Research Review* 27/3, pp. 227-43.
Scotchmer, D.
1986   'Convergence of the Gods: Comparing Traditional Maya and Christian Maya Cosmologies', in E.G.H. Gosen (ed.), *Symbol and Meaning Beyond the Closed Community: Essays in Mesoamerican Ideas* (Studies on Culture and Society, I; Albany: Institute for Mesoamerican Studies), pp. 197-226.
1989   'Symbols of Salvation: A Local Mayan Protestant Theology', *Missiology* 17/3, pp. 293-310.

1991   'Symbols of Salvation: Interpreting Highland Maya Protestantism in
            Context', unpublished PhD thesis (State University of New York at
            Albany).
1995   'Blood or Water? Mayan Images of Church and Mission from the
            Underside', unpublished paper.
Sepúlveda, J.G. de
1986   *Tratado sobre las justas causas de la guerra contra los indios* (1550)
            (Mexico: Fondo de Cultura Económica).
Smith, C.A. (ed.)
1990   *Guatemalan Indians and the State: 1540 to 1988* (Austin, TX:
            University of Texas).
Smith, C.A.
1990   'Conclusion: History and Revolution in Guatemala', in Smith (ed.)
            1990, pp. 258-85.
1991   'Maya Nationalism', *NACLA Report on the Americas* 25/3, pp. 29-33.
Stoll, D.
1990   *Is Latin America Turning Protestant? The Politics of Evangelical
            Growth* (Berkeley: University of California Press).
1993   *Between Two Armies: In the Ixil Towns of Guatemala* (New York:
            Columbia University Press).
Tamez, E.
1991   'Quetzalcóatl y el Dios cristiano: alianza y lucha de dioses', *Vida y
            Pensamiento* 11/1, pp. 31-54.
Taylor, M.
1992   'Toward a Revolution of the Sun: Protestant Mayan Resistance Amid
            Guatemala's "Eternal Tyranny"'. Paper given in San Francisco at the
            annual meeting of the Society of Biblical Literature.
Todorov, T.
1984   *The Conquest of America: The Question of the Other* (trans. R. Howard;
            New York: Harper & Row).
Warren, K.B.
1992   'Transforming Memories and Histories: The Meanings of Ethnic
            Resurgence for Mayan Indians', in Alfred Stepan (ed.), *Americas: New
            Interpretive Essays* (New York: Oxford University Press), pp. 189-
            219.
1993   'Interpreting *La Violencia* in Guatemala: Shapes of Mayan Silence &
            Resistance', in Kay B. Warren (ed.), *The Violence Within: Cultural and
            Political Opposition in Divided Nations* (Boulder: Westview Press),
            pp. 25-56.
Watanabe, J.M.
1992   *Maya Saints & Souls in A Changing World* (Austin: University of
            Texas Press).
1995   'Unimagining the Maya: Anthropologists, Others, and the Inescapable
            Hubris of Authorship', *Bulletin of Latin American Research* 14/1,
            pp. 25-45.
Wilson, R.
1994   'Shifting Frontiers: Historical Frontiers of Identities in Latin America',
            Bulletin of Latin American Research 14/1, pp. 1-7.

'THE GOSPEL, THE POOR AND THE CHURCHES': ATTITUDES TO POVERTY IN THE BRITISH CHURCHES AND BIBLICAL EXEGESIS

Chris Rowland

I

For a period of two years between 1992 and 1994 I was involved with members of Christian Aid in the planning, gestation and birth of a project entitled *The Gospel, the Poor and the Churches*.[1] It started life as a contribution of Christian Aid to discussions about the Decade of Evangelism, as well as a means whereby the organisation could signal to the churches the central importance it attached to its work within the churches and the need to persuade them of solidarity with the poor as a central feature of mission, a theme at the heart of this conference. It was decided to commission a reputable sociological research institute (*Social, Planning and Community Research*) to carry out an investigation of the attitudes of British Christians to poverty. After much discussion it was decided that the institute should embark on a piece of qualitative research; that is (to quote the report's outline of its method), 'an attempt to present the social world, and perspectives on that world, in terms of the concepts, behaviours, perceptions and accounts of the people it is about'. The report tells us nothing about the prevalence of attitudes within the churches but does enable us to see the spectrum of opinion that exists. Although there has been a systematic presentation of the material, we are allowed to hear the attitudes and reactions of Christians on every page as they seek to respond to the researchers' questions. It is a rich treasury of opinion which illuminates the present state of the church and enables one to catch a glimpse of how we all view the relief of poverty.

---

1. *The Gospel, the Poor and the Churches* published by Christian Aid in May 1994 and available from them at P.O. Box 100, London SE1 7RT.

The researchers did not determine the responses or the choice of responses and organised their findings on the basis of the information they assembled. So, although they went to a range of different churches, they found that the material they assembled compelled them to present a typology of the variety of Christian responses. The types are as follows:

1. *Personal-literal*: this person's faith focuses on the need for individual conversion. The Bible is read in a literalistic way and is the main source of authority. Key indications of appropriate behaviour includes prayer, Bible reading and treating others with patience and love.

2. *Personal-questioning*: similarly, personal commitment is important but room is left here for personal experience which is allowed to foster questioning. Here, greater priority is given to addressing issues of social and individual morality.

3. *Institutional-literal*: for this group the teaching of the Church is central and is usually accepted without question. Living out faith can include broader social issues but is mainly concerned with personal morality.

4. *Institutional-questioning*: for this group, as for the previous, membership of worshipping community is central and the demands of that community and the wider church are given a high priority. Nevertheless, experience and individual conscience is important. Greater emphasis is placed on addressing broader social and political issues than on personal morality.

5. *Individual-unreflective*: the defining characteristic of this particular type is an individual's morality and how it is that she or he lives life everyday. Beliefs and dogma are considered to be of secondary importance as compared with individual morality. Attending church has a pragmatic purpose as it is necessary to keep the individual on the right track. There is little sense of common belief and practice and communal obligation.

6. *Corporate analytical*: interpreting the Christian message must take place in relation to contemporary existence. But that task is one that is complex, and the approach to faith and life needs a corporate context for understanding and engaging a shared practice. Members of this group interpret the Christian message in relation to everyday life; the investigation of the social and corporate dimensions of faith is essential.

General definitions of poverty included the following: basic needs unmet (e.g. food, shelter, livelihood, health and education), limitations on choices and lack of power and control. There emerged differences in the understanding of poverty in the UK as compared with the Third World and in the way in which poverty should be defined either relative to context or in absolute terms:

Reference points	UK	Third World
Poverty in relation to local context	Poverty in relation to 'normal' living standards in UK	Poverty in relation to 'normal' living standards in Third World
Poverty compared across contexts	Poverty may be acknowledged but is considered 'minor' in relation to poverty in the Third World	'Real' poverty is found in the Third World and is the standard of measurement
Poverty in absolute terms (starvation)	Poverty is not acknowledged in the UK as 'genuine' or 'real' poverty	Poverty is measured in relation to the most extreme cases in the Third World (i.e. people who are starving)

Although the broad definitions of poverty applied equally to the UK and the Third World, the specific qualifying circumstances necessary to be poor in each area differed. As one might anticipate, the suggestions offered about the causes of poverty varied and included decline in individual morality, fate, the growth of materialism and lack of Christian values in society, as well as the more politically aware assessments which pointed to underlying structural and political causes. What was apparent was the different causes offered for poverty in the Third World and UK. In the latter it was seen more as the result of the individual's fault. The researchers give an impression of the different stances on poverty which are based on a variety of factors: definitions of poverty; perceptions of the origins of poverty; whether poverty is attributed to personal, environmental, or economic and political causes; whether poverty is seen in terms of unmet needs or unequal access to choices and rights; and the extent to which parallels are acknowledged between the First and Third Worlds. In the survey, people who are concerned about malaise in political life tend to adopt structural stances (i.e. attentiveness to underlying trends which play a part in social conditions); concern about declining standards in personal morality is linked to blaming views of poverty. Whereas the laity are represented in all positions, there are no clergy in the most unsympathetic groups.

There was a variety of understandings of the purpose of the church. Some favoured a more ecclesiastical and inward-looking view focussed on fellowship and maintenance or the promotion of ecumenism, while others favoured a more outward-looking, 'secular' understanding of the church's task in playing its role in social concerns. Poverty was not a major concern for all, and frequently was in competition with other, more pressing, 'Christian' concerns. There was a range of positions on the centrality of dealing with poverty in the church's life: from 'the church is here primarily to preach the gospel' to one which advocated the abolition of poverty as being the central concern of Christian life (often found as part of a range of issues concerned with the relief of human need and injustice):

The Church's Priorities

Evangelism and internal welfare	Concern is with falling numbers, spiritual development of members, pastoral needs of local community and direct evangelism
Evangelism and state of nation	Concern is with perceived moral decline in society, fellowship, pastoral needs of local community and indirect evangelism
Evangelism and social concern in a material world	Concern is with relevance of church and of religion itself in a secular, material age, indirect evangelism and addressing broader social issues
Practical social concern	Concern is with broader social issues addressing them through provision of practical help
Prophetic social concern	Concern is with broader social issues addressing them by speaking out against inequality and injustice

In the following table six basic positions on poverty are identified: (i) a comprehensive view of world poverty; (ii) similar to (i) but with a less overarching outlook; (iii) a harsher attitude towards the poor in the UK who as individuals are seen to be responsible; (iv) little sense of an overview with reluctance to recognise poverty in the UK; (v) and (vi) poverty the fault of the poor either in the Third World or the UK:

Positions on Poverty

	(i)	(ii)	(iii)	(iv)	(v)	(vi)
	Underlying economic & political structures (UK & 3W)	Underlying economic & political factors (UK & 3W)	Individual choice/fault (UK) & underlying structures (3W)	Unforeseen circumstances	Individual choice/fault (UK & 3W)	Entirely individual choice/fault (3W); no poverty in UK
Explanation of origins	Political & economic structures in 3W & UK with joint responsibility between West and 3W govts.	Political & economic factors in 3W & UK with joint responsibility between West and 3W poverty never considered to be fault of individuals	Political & economic factors in 3W with joint responsibility between West and 3W. In UK origins relate to individual choice & fault	3W people are thought to be 'victims of circumstances' while in UK origins may also be related to 'personal failings'	individual choice or fault in UK & 3W (govts. play a part)	fault of 3W govts. & people
Definition of poverty	structural or summary definitions with similarities noted between UK & 3W poverty	symptomatic or summary definitions with less clearly defined view	symptomatic or summary definition with poverty seen as distinctly different in UK & 3W	symptomatic definition of poverty	symptomatic definition with only reluctant acknowledgment of UK poverty	symptomatic absolute definitions of poverty (starvation). Poverty not recognised in UK
Secular concerns	political malaise	political malaise & discrete problems	discrete problems	moral malaise & discrete problems	moral malaise & discrete problems	moral malaise & discrete problems
Experience of poverty	linked to extensive 3W experience/ some local exposure	commonly linked to extensive local exposure	linked to negative experiences of poverty in UK & more positive impressions of 3W	little or no first-hand exposure to poverty	little or no personal exposure to poverty	little or no personal exposure to poverty

When asked for the Christian teaching on attitudes to poverty, most responded with favourite ideas, like love one's neighbour, you will be judged by your actions for the poor (dependent on Matthew's account of the Last Judgement in Mt. 25.31-46) or your preference should be for the poor. There was little evidence of much more than a selective series of quotations from the Christian tradition and hardly any evidence of a more sophisticated theological explanation of the causes and responses. Some thought that there was no specifically Christian message, and an oft-quoted text was Mark 14.7: 'the poor you always have with you'; a text whose meaning was seen to be rather obscure.

It was apparent that the sources of knowledge about poverty were mainly the media rather than Christian teaching. Not one person spontaneously said that the church was the source of their knowledge about poverty. Striking television images were at the top of the list: 'the news comes on when one's having one's meal and adds to the difficulty'. Church goers would appear to be no different from the general public in the character and source of their knowledge. Those who were best informed and most committed often had personal exposure via an overseas visit or working in a Third World country.

One of the most interesting parts of the research was the findings of the investigation of the differing ways in which people in the churches coped with the issue of poverty. Most church goers are *not* hard-hearted. The level of feelings are intense across the spectrum, but how people deal with the feelings differs. On the one hand, there was an *active coping stance*. People in this group expressed the following feelings: anger at unfairness; a desire to help; shame at the differences between rich and poor; admiration of the poor. They responded in the following ways: by seeking more information; acknowledging personal responsibility; focussing on the human aspect of particular situations of poverty; taking inspiration from the poor for their own lives; believing that however small their contribution it could help to alleviate poverty; emphasising things that were succeeding; and, through all of this, converting negative energy into positive action.

On the other hand, there was the *passive coping stance*. People in this group expressed smiliar feelings: anger; a desire to help (though qualified by a sense of helplessness); a sense of being greedy; despair or panic; horror and distress. The enormity of the situation with which they were confronted led them to react as follows: avoidance of the plight of the poor; refusal to believe the reports; placing of responsibility elsewhere so that they were relieved of it; a belief that the poor had given up trying to help themselves and so were less deserving of assistance; leaving it in God's hands; making poverty an abstract problem rather than an immediate human need; avoiding issues of local poverty; focussing on others who do even less themselves; emphasising failed initiatives ('Does it really make any difference when money is wasted or aid projects come to nought?'). If anything, the 'passive copers' had stronger feelings of anguish. The act of 'switching off' is one of despair.

In conclusion, the researchers drew the threads of the research together by outlining the correlation between different positions and the various types of Christian allegiance:

Overall Stances

1. *Low tolerance*: corrupt Third World governments and the poor were to blame for poverty; solutions lie in greater aid and the encouragement of greater self-reliance; by and large, poverty is a subject usually avoided.

2. *Reluctant acknowledgement*: responsibility for support lies mainly with governments and charities rather than churches; poverty is just one of many concerns facing churches; there is a tendency to avoid poverty.

These first two groups tend to be literal or unreflective in their religious allegiances, and concerned about evangelism and internal welfare.

3. *Neutral sympathy*: the poor are victims and deserve our charity; poverty is one among many concerns for the church.

Passive copers tend to be found in this group, and personal-literal, individual-literal, and individual-unreflective modes of allegiance predominate.

4. *Analytical sympathy*: structural analysis of the social world is a necessary preliminary response leading to advocacy of solutions for economic and political change; there should be a general Christian responsibility for the poor.

Passive copers, personal-literal, personal-questioning, and institutional-literal are all found in this group.

5. *Compassionate criticism*: structural origins for the origin of poverty are recognised ; there is a particular responsibility of the poor in this country for their own poverty; there is a clear mandate for church involvement and a 'bias to the poor' is needed and should be a key priority for individuals and churches.

This perspective is found particularly among clergy [2] and among the institutional-questioning group and those with first-hand knowledge of poverty.

6. *Comprehensive Concern*: structural origins of poverty are recognised and comprehensive solutions advocated; the church has a major role in such activity, so there is need for a 'bias to the poor'; poverty is no fault of the poor.

This group tend to be made up of active rather than passive copers. Characteristic of this group is their questioning attitude to beliefs, with personal-questioning, institutional-questioning and corporate-analytical groups all represented.

Neither social position nor denominational membership were thought to be significant factors in determining the different attitudes. Key influences include a person's world view, perception of the church's mission and the nature of their experience of poverty. In general, an individualist outlook combined with a literal approach to belief tends to characterise people who adopt unsympathetic or neutral stances in relation to poverty and for whom relief of poverty has a relatively low personal priority. By contrast, a corporate outlook combined with the questioning or analytical approach to doctrine tends to be found among people who see the need to explore the structural origins and socio-economic solutions to poverty and for whom poverty is a central issue of concern. Views on the mission of church tend to vary depending on the extent to which poverty is perceived as central for the church.

We have in the report some flesh put on the bare bones of our hunches and our anecdotal evidence. We are shown the range of views on poverty and reminded of the range of types of beliefs which are found, not just in different churches but in the same church. We cannot go on teaching without being sensitive to the very different needs which are to be found in our midst, as well as in society as a whole. Not only is there diversity of view but also an absence of any widespread evidence

---

2. The clergy were more likely to give a high priority to poverty issues and to be found in the more sympathetic positions and to be absent from the most negative positions (it was striking that in the non-conformist churches which were part of the survey the ministers were often corporate-analytic while their congregations were personal-literal, personal-questioning or individual-unreflective types). Nevertheless, the clergy frequently answered questions on behalf of their congregations or in other ways *in role*. They spoke of their concerns for the poor but were unwilling to 'burden' their congregations with too frequent reference to the issue.

of ability, either among clergy or lay people, to offer an explanation of why, as a Christian, one should want to behave in particular ways towards others. Linked with this is the almost complete dominance of non-ecclesiastical sources for knowledge of and understanding of poverty. What is true in respect to attitudes to the poor is probably the case in other areas of life also.

Some reservations about the results should be noted. It is a pity that none of the views recorded is further contextualised. The impression one has is of individuals wrestling with these issues alone rather than as part of communities, however fragmented. It would have been good to have had further indication of why the researchers thought that class made little difference to attitudes. This is of particular interest to those seeking to assess the extent to which social context determines the particular use of the Bible that is adopted. Also, there is a lack of attention to the process involved in producing the reactions of passive and active coping. Perhaps the way in which poverty is presented disposes receivers to be angry and passive because there is little help offered to enable a recipient of the information to respond with anything other than anger or despair. Little attention is paid in the report itself to the effects on the process of assembling the information because the attitudes of the people interviewed might have been influenced by the interviewers' presence. There is no attempt made to reflect on how people might have reacted and answered *to them*. Finally, much of the report concentrates on what people *say* and not what they actually *do*: how did the interviewee's behaviour differ from their attitudes?

The findings of this report demand a careful and circumspect assessment. What follow are some initial reactions. The first demand is for a sense of realism about the task. If this report is at all accurate, then it is necessary to enable use of the Bible in ethics to seek to recognise how little the discourse of Christian tradition informs current practice (at least in this particular area, but there is evidence to suggest that this would extend to matters of personal morality also). That will probably cause little surprise. Anecdotal evidence suggests that even religious 'professionals' tend to ignore what they learned about the content and use of the tradition in training in preaching and pastoral work. This seems to be borne out by the study. It is important for the biblical theologian to be realistic about the sort of contribution she or he can make.

II

Although there was little evidence of a systematic presentation of an argument in favour of the preferential option for the poor, respondents often made reference to passages of Scripture. One of the favourites was 'the poor you always have with you' (Mark 14.7). The report states that people 'commonly referred to this verse but neither the clergy nor the laity were clear as to its precise meaning and varying interpretations were made'. Here are a couple of examples:

> I think...Jesus did also say, The poor you will always have with you...I found it very depressing, but I also found it encouraging that you really just keep going, you know...I found it quite depressing actually...I thought, why do these people have to go on the dole ? But actually perhaps they don't; perhaps we could work...to a better world. Perhaps there will be a better world if we keep on working towards...the poor who are always with us...sharing together. And why shouldn't we be poor together; yeah, and any way, then he said something about 'blessed are the poor in spirit'—so maybe...it's a growing thing somehow. Hmmmmm! (Laity)

> Well you see, the first thing that comes to mind with the Bible [is] Christ said that, the poor will always be with you, and I've wrestled with that one...I believe that Christ realised that he could not get everyone to share so there are always going to be those people who have less than others; I don't know whether that's true. On the other hand I feel that Christ would never have accepted anything other than the ultimate of everyone sharing in everything, so I don't know to be honest...(Laity)

> The poor are always with us, that is the old Victorian maxim. And I think that is true, because communities are like that. But I'm beginning to feel over some months that there is more that we could and should be doing. I don't quite know what it is. (Laity)

> Christ does tell us that the poor will always be with us. He does tell us that we should help the poor, but I would probably put limiting factors on that. (Laity)

The first quotation epitomises that tortuous attempt to articulate a Christian response to the challenge of poverty which the research suggests was typical of many respondents. There is no doubt about the extent of the concern about poverty among church goers, though why this should be, from a theological point of view, and what should be done about it, is much less clear. In *one* sense, the quotations above are all examples of contextual theology, where the Bible has merged into experience. It is a form of theologising to which I am committed. If (as I happen to believe) all interpretation, in one form or another, manifests the agenda of the modern world, what is the problem with interpretations which adapt a fatalistic attitude in the light of Mark 14.7? Do we just have to admit that where you are and work determines the way you read the Bible and leave it at that?

One contribution of the professional interpreter is to assist with the use of Scripture. In all these cases one can note the way in which the text has been taken out of context, but such a criticism, of course, itself depends upon a hermeneutical method which rejects atomistic exegesis. Attention to the wider context has not been part of the hermeneutical method adopted by Jews and Christians down the centuries. Those who use Mk 14.7 in this way have a long list of patristic and other writers on their side. And yet such use has, within mainstream Christianity, been subordinated to other principles (for example, the rule of faith). The use of Scripture in the liturgy places a question-mark against the wrenching of isolated verses out of their immediate context. Even if hearers of Mk 14.7 might not be expected to know the whole of the Marcan context (of which more in a moment), there is a legitimate expectation that they should attend to the story of the anointing, read, as a whole, liturgically.

Then there is the contribution of the professional interpreter of providing allusions to other parts of the Bible. Most readers of the verse who have access to marginal references will note that the words used by Jesus are very similar to those in Deuteronomy 15. In the light of Deuteronomy, Jesus is alerting his hearers to an ongoing obligation. Because of human hardness of heart there will not be a removal of poverty, and so there is a demand for continuous and vigilant action on behalf of the poor and needy. Thus the saying is not an admission of defeat, but a reminder that day in and day out there is to be no grudging attitude, nor 'villainous thought', in order to avoid one's obligation. As long as the poor are there, the demand continues.

There are hints in Mark that this obligation is not being met. Indeed, the particular concern with the widow advocated by the Torah (e.g. Deut. 14.29 and 16.11) is ignored by those scribes who devour widows' houses (12.40). Immediately following that condemnation is the isolated story of the poor widow who gives her whole livelihood to the Temple, an institution which in the very next verses Jesus predicts is destined for destruction (13.2) and judgement (15.38). Is this a condemnation of a religio-political system (and its values) which prompts her action and leaves her a debtor rather than a beneficiary, as the Torah demanded?[3]

Many readers of Mark 14 consider that the disciples have a point: was not giving to the poor precisely what Jesus had enjoined to do the rich man in 10.21? If we have to make choices, shouldn't the poor be given first priority over this costly 'wastefulness' (Mark 14.4)? Here the passage stresses the appropriateness of the action, not necessarily because it was a gesture shown to Jesus but because it was the fulfilment of an obligation to a human person, who, according to the beginning and end of this particular story, was being plotted against by a close companion as well as the political authorities. When he died, he was not honoured in death—something the memories of Jesus' death indicate was omitted at the time of his burial. It is not a choice between waste and the poor, for Jesus is presenting himself as one who is about to die, 'one of the poor—the guest of a leper, headed for death',[4] to whom respect should be shown. That respect is given in advance by the woman, the ultimate act of consideration for a human person in death.

> To give money to benefit the poor but to refuse to comfort and assist the one right beside you is as wrong as ignoring the agony of the poor of the world in order to concentrate on personal concerns. *Both* public acts of almsgiving *and* private acts of sympathy and compassion are part of the religious life—neither one substitutes for the other—and one should not be harassed for doing either.[5]

Also, the carelessness with regard to money here is not out of line with the attitude to money elsewhere in the gospel. Throughout the gospel there is an implicit question about the financial and conventional norms which so dominate the horizon of hearers of Mark's narrative and of hearers of the gospel today (4.18-19; 6.8; 10.17; 12.14-15; 12.41; 14.11). The life of discipleship involves battling with the snares of wealth. It is all part of an alternative perspective on life which Mark's gospel portrays, and is best summarised in 10.42-43 where the disciples want to sit and rule but are only offered baptism and a cup. They have to understand that there is to be a contrast between their nascent, alternative culture and that of the rulers of the earth: 'it shall not be so among you' (10.42). Understanding may come about only by leaving everything and following Jesus (1.20; 4.10; cf. 14.10)—something that

3. Ched Myers, *Binding the Strong Man* (Maryknoll, NY: Orbis Books, 1988).
4. *Binding the Strong Man*, p. 359.
5. Mary Ann Tolbert, in *The Women's Bible Commentary* (London: SPCK, 1992), p. 271.

one rich man finds very difficult to do (10.22)—and may come only when one takes up the cross (8.34 cf. 10.40-45).

III

Another text which was alluded to in the report is Mt. 25.31-46 (a fundamental text for liberation theologians and papal encyclicals, too, of course). The following quotation from *The Gospel, the Poor and the Churches* is not untypical of use of this text:

> ...We as Christians know that God is a God of judgement, not a God of love (or) not only a God of love. He's a God of judgement and every one of us in this room one day will stand in front of his throne of judgement and answer to what we have done with our life and what we have done to [*sic*] the life of the poor around us. (Laity)

It is quite clear that this passage is being interpreted here in a way which has wide currency in the contemporary church but which differs markedly from the exegetical consensus. Let me say immediately that while I am disposed towards the former view for a variety of reasons— which I am prepared to admit are conditioned in part by an agenda which is external to the text—I want to stay with my prejudices because prejudice in interpretation *may* be able to throw light on the text and enable me to read it from a different perspective.

In a stimulating article Francis Watson[6] has explored the interface between this aspect of theology and conventional exegesis, ancient and modern, in which he doubts whether this famous text can be appropriately used to justify an option for the poor and outcast. In the essay he wrestles with the concerns that have been around at least since Johannes Weiss: that there is an unbridgeable gulf fixed between theological ethics and exegesis. It is a rich resource and would take too long to do justice to. One paragraph deserves quoting in full as I want to explore the issues it represents in depth:

> In the conventional exegetical procedure the apparent literal sense of this text has to be subordinated to other texts scattered throughout the gospel, a procedure justified by appeal to authorial intention understood as a means of imposing relative unity on apparently heterogeneous material. What appears to be the literal sense of the parable is sacrificed for the sake of the unity of the whole as it is imagined to have existed in its authors mind.

6. Francis Watson, 'Liberating the Reader', in *idem* (ed.), *The Open Text* (London: SCM Press, 1993).

'Matthew' may indeed have understood the parable in the restricted sense, but his intention remains a hypothetical entity insufficiently externalised in the actual wording of the text as it stands. In other words, we may appeal to the letter of the text against the author who, absented from his text in the very act of writing, can only be speculatively reunited with his text by an allegorical or spiritualising reading which seeks to penetrate the letter of the text in pursuit of the more fundamental entity that it is said to conceal: here, an imperfectly expressed authorial intention to which the entire text of the Gospel of Matthew is to be subordinated. But what if the author refuses to play this game? What if, as we tell him what he should have said to make his meaning clearer, he simply refers us back to the text with the words, What I have written, I have written? The hermeneutical principle of the absence of the author from the text is a useful way of countering the reductionist tendency to confine textual meaning to the reconstructed circumstances of origin.[7]

Watson's thesis of setting the text against the author provokes a variety of reflections. There is an implicit criticism of the subservience to the absent author which may at times lead to neglect of the details of the text itself. Watson's major concern is to explore the validity of the liberationists' use of Mt. 25.31-46 as an inclusive challenge to all to minister to the heavenly Son of Man in the needy in the present age. He points to features in the text which deconstruct the neat characterisation of the Matthean community on the basis of a simple relationship between text and life and the water-tight notion of purpose which is bound up with a clearly enunciated authorial intention. His hermeneutical strategy is to read Mt. 25.31-46 as prolegomenon to the Passion narrative in which the earthly son of man shows himself in solidarity with the weak and vulnerable.

The force of the exclusive interpretation[8] of 'brethren' depends on the data of the text : brethren are frequently disciples; the elect seem to have already been separated from the nations in 24.31 and the end of the mission discourse in 10.42 seems to indicate that the little ones—so similar, in many ways, to the least of the brethren of v. 25—who are to receive the cup of water, are the disciples. In 10.42 there seems to be an interpretative guide to the identity of the brethren.

One can see why Mt. 10.42 has been seen as the hermeneutical key that unlocks the interpretation of Mt. 25.31-46. Giving a cup of cold

7.   'Liberating the Reader', p. 65-66.
8.   Well set out, for example, in G. Stanton, *A Gospel for a New People* (Edinburgh: T. & T. Clark, 1992).

water to the little ones echoes quenching the thirsty. What is more, the little ones and the least of these my brethren, have been linked at least from the time the Western manuscript tradition replaced μικρῶν τούτων by ἐλαχιστων. Several factors need to be considered. First of all, we note the change of person in 10.41 as compared with the previous verse. If the disciples are still being addressed, why the change? Secondly, the parallel with Mk 9.41 is instructive. Mark's version identifies those who are to receive the drink of water with the disciples: 'Whoever gives you a drink of water because you belong to the messiah, I tell you, will not lose their reward'. Even if we suppose that Matthew is not directly dependent on Mark here and has used an independent tradition that he has preferred to Mark; still it is true that the Matthaean version makes no explicit link between the little ones and the disciples. I recognise that such a comparison, standard fare in Gospel study, is a form of canonical criticism which may not be entirely appropriate for a narrative approach, and that another interpretative manoeuvre is being embarked on here. At the very least we can see in Mark a stage in the identification of children with disciples. Luke 17.1 has not yet reached it and I am not convinced that Matthew has either.

So one might question whether it is obvious that the little ones here are disciples. Matthew 18 has often seemed to point in the direction of an identification of disciples with the little ones, but even there one may have pause for thought. In ch. 18, children are offered as the models to those who are called to be disciples because they are the ones whose particular perspective allows them to recognise Jesus when others who should have known better fail to recognise him (21.16; cf. 11.25-26). So the reference to little ones in 18.5 cannot readily be equated with the twelve disciples[9] (though it is intimately linked with the understanding of the character of true discipleship, for which the child is held up as the type).

If we follow Watson's principle of setting the letter of the text against an allegorising interpretation[10] that allows the 'hidden' story of com-

---

9. Despite the Christian flavour of the words in 18.6, the phrase τῶν πιστευούτων εἰς ἐμέ is unique here in Matthew, where belief and confession are not confined to disciples (who are portrayed as betraying and forsaking Jesus). Πιστευω is only used in this type of phrase in a variant at Mt. 27.42. Elsewhere (8.13; 9.28; 21.22; 21.25, 32; 24.23, 26) it seems to have the force of trust rather than membership of a community of faith based on a christological confession.

10. Some forms of historical criticism that rely on the reconstruction of another

munity and author to place constraints upon the literal sense of the chapter, the identification of the μικροι with Christian disciples in ch. 18 becomes less clear. While that other dimension of interpretation may make us sensitive to the imagined needs of Matthew and his world, the letter of the text does not *demand* the 'ecclesial' interpretation as the only possible reading, and it presses us to recognise that whatever 'internal' concerns may be inherent in the narrative and in its hypothetical original setting, the literal sense challenges the reader to identify with the child as an example of messianic humility. Meg Davies has put the point well with regard to Matthew 18: 'making children exemplary for disciples does not imply that [disciples] should become childish, but that they should assume the social powerlessness of children. Children had no economic independence and were dependent on their parents for their survival. The disciples' leadership was not to mimic the powerful but the powerless'.[11]

I am not saying that I can demonstrate that Matthew's Gospel is more inclusive in its attitude to the weak and outcasts than much mainstream exegesis has allowed. The points made by opponents of the inclusive interpretation are weighty and reflect strands in Matthew's narrative. My point is rather different and echoes the point made by Francis Watson: the text of Matthew, through all the vicissitudes of its narrative, does not allow the reader to rest confident that she or he can be assured of ultimate vindication. Possibly, Matthew the evangelist wanted to say this (though I am not convinced that this was the case). In contrast with the eschatological passages from contemporary texts, which seem to manifest a self-assured belief in the ultimate salvation for their readers, Matthew's gospel is much more ambiguous in refusing to allow its readers to be complacent in the face of judgement.[12]

---

story 'behind' the literal sense of the text (authorial intention, community struggles, historical Jesus etc.) have an uncanny resemblance to ancient allegorical exegesis. The major difference, of course, is the referent of the hidden story. See the suggestive comments of J. Barr, 'The Literal, the Allegorical, and Modern Biblical Scholarship', *JSOT* 44 (1989); cf. B. Childs, 'James Barr on the Literal and the Allegorical', *JSOT* 46 (1990).

    11. *Matthew* (Sheffield: JSOT Press, 1993), p. 127.

    12. 'Jewish and Christian writers turned to apocalyptic in periods of historical crisis and trauma. Apocalyptic regularly functions as consolation for groups which perceive themselves to be under duress. Apocalyptic language is also often used to reinforce attitudes of group solidarity among minority groups at odds with society at large; clear lines are drawn between "insiders" and "outsiders". This is the social

If Mt. 25.31-46 was the high point of the New Testament's teaching on attitudes to the poor, it might appear to endorse the view that alleviation of the symptoms of poverty was all that was required, and a challenge to the causes of poverty was not to be contemplated. To put it another way, Helder Camara's oft quoted dictum ('If I give food to the poor they call me a saint; if I ask why the poor have no food they call me a communist') might seem to apply to the New Testament teaching—but only its first part. There is charity in plenty but the critique of an unjust society seems to be absent from its pages. Or, to put it in the words of Meg Davies, elsewhere in this collection the New Testament is replete with 'a charity of consumption' but lacks any recipe for 'a charity of production'.[13] Such charity would not begin to be addressed until the emergence of a coenobitic monasticism within Christianity.

We should not neglect the apocalyptic tradition in Revelation and elsewhere. What we have in the apocalyptic texts is what I have described elsewhere as an unmasking of reality in which the true character of institutions is revealed.[14] It is something that is not confined to Revelation alone and is to be found also in the virulent critique of wealth in the later chapters of 1 Enoch.[15] The critique of Babylon in Revelation 18 is an *economic* critique,[16] and that of the Temple in Mark's Gospel is arguably one that does not fail to stress its part in ignoring the needs of the needy like widows.[17] Similarly, the political

setting of the passages from 4 Ezra, 2 Baruch and 1 Enoch...It is also the social setting of the book of Revelation which announces judgement and doom for the powerful and complacent and in so doing provides hope of ultimate vindication for the powerless and oppressed people of God. Mt. 25.31ff. comes from a similar social setting and was intended to function similarly for the first recipients of the gospel', Stanton, *Gospel*.

13. Cf. Rowland, *Christian Origins*, p. 368 n. 6, and G. de Ste. Croix, *The Class Struggle in the Ancient Greek World* (London: Duckworth, 1981), p. 419.

14. E.g. in *Liberating Exegesis* (London, 1990), pp. 131-33; also K. Wengst, *Pax Romana and the Peace of Jesus Christ* (London: SCM Press, 1988).

15. Discussed in the context of Luke's Gospel in P.L. Esler, *Community and Gospel in Luke–Acts: The Social and Political Motivations of Lucan Theology* (Cambridge: Cambridge University Press, 1987). See also, Moxnes, *The Economy of the Kingdom. Social Conflict and Economic Relations in Luke's Gospel* (Philadelphia: Fortress Press, 1988) and L. Johnson, *Sharing Possessions* (Philadelphia: Fortress Press, 1981).

16. R. Bauckham, 'The Economic Critique of Rome', in L. Alexander (ed.), *Images of Empire* (JSOTSup, 122; Sheffield: JSOT Press, 1991), pp. 47-91.

17. C. Myers, *Binding the Strong Man*; F. Belo, *Materialist Readings of the*

dimension of the language about the powers and the change which is wrought via Christ's redemption has been stressed in recent study.[18] Nevertheless, we are still at the level of protest with little of the detailed prescription for a charity of production that would enable a different pattern of production and exchange.

The Gospel, the Poor and the Churches is a survey of attitudes and we need to recognise that there is evidence to suggest that there is a gap between attitudes and behaviour. So, whatever their attitudes, people dig into their pockets in a very generous way when confronted by human need. The position of manifest concern is one that the aid agencies and the high profile given to the tragedies in Eritrea, Somalia and Rwanda have done much to form. While there is clearly enormous concern about the poor (more particularly abroad than at home) people often find themselves at a loss to know how to respond theologically. Now in using the term 'theological', I am not meaning at a level of sophistication appropriate to monographs and journals. Rather, I am thinking of the incapacity of people to respond as they would like, as ordinary followers of Christ. It is the frustration that is the lot of anyone who longs to be more literate and articulate, to be able to understand in a way in which instincts nurtured in the heart of the Church would suggest. The dearth of theological resources known to be available or able to be retrieved is striking, and represents a serious challenge to all of us in theological education. Familiar passages from Scripture may be quoted, but the allusions are peripheral to the basic instinct to be concerned and to want to do something. The backing of the tradition is often elicited from memory by enquirers who possess an inkling of the extent of the biblical or theological basis for the position adopted. Paul had to write and offer a rationale to the Corinthians and Romans for the Collection for the poor in Jerusalem. Many contemporary Christians are searching for a language to explain, justify and understand a much more ready response. That something must be done is not in doubt. But why (and how)? Ours may not seem to be the situation of those first Gentile Christians, for whom the whole concept of an international collection for

Gospel of Mark (Maryknoll, NY: Orbis Books, 1981); M. Clévenot, *Materialist Approaches to the Bible* (Maryknoll, NY: Orbis Books, 1985).

    18. E.g. W. Wink, *Naming the Powers* (Philadelphia: Fortress Press, 1984); *Unmasking the Powers* (Philadelphia: Fortress Press, 1986); and *Engaging the Powers* (Philadelphia: Fortress Press, 1993).

the poor (rather than the rich) would have been quite foreign, and, as a result, needed a Paul to explain to them why it should be done. But perhaps like them we need to be persuaded that such international concern is theologically and morally grounded?

As attempts are made to offer some explanation, we know that the appeal to favourite proof-texts will not do. Something more profound is required. We find in the biblical texts often apparently conforming and compromised texts alongside the clarion-calls to liberation and option for the poor. The temptation to read the texts in ways which suit us is one thing which exegesis has always sought to avert. Such a remedy to deal with self-indulgent reading is a necessary companion to the slow task of exploring whether and in what way Scripture can inform the judgements of people who long to act in defence of the poor, and to be in solidarity with them, or even have only the vaguest inkling that the ordering of the world is unjust but cannot quite articulate why.

THE NEW TESTAMENT AND THE ETHICS OF CULTURAL
COMPROMISE: *COMPROMISO* WITH THE GOD OF LIFE
OR COMPROMISE WITH THE IDEOLOGY OF POWER?

Sharon H. Ringe

These reflections about the interaction of the Bible and ethics grow out
of issues raised by students and people in local congregations representing various Protestant churches in the United States. The reflections
themselves have evolved dialogically, as I have worked with members of
these communities as a Euro-American, middle class, feminist clergy-
woman and seminary professor, whose world has been altered by time
spent accompanying students and other church workers in Central
America and in the multi-cultural urban areas of the United States.

Many of the people who have posed the questions that shape these
reflections are longing for help with questions of identity and lifestyle:
Who are we? and How should we live?[1] Both of those are fundamentally ethical questions that the Bible has been understood to address
through the years by virtue of being both stable (providing an anchor or
a center that is not at the mercy of the small tremors and tectonic shifts
of history) and adaptable (capable of being read afresh when new
circumstances demand it). For many people, however, the process of
seeking such guidance in and from the Bible is no longer working.
People whose core beliefs acknowledge in the Bible a sufficient guide for
faith and practice, and who want to turn to the Bible to sort out life
choices, find that it deserts them or even betrays them. It deserts
because the world it assumes is so foreign to the one in which we live.
What can the Bible tell us as we wrestle with issues in bio-medical ethics,
for instance, or as we try to sort out the legacy of colonialism and
empire in the ferocious tribal warfare that is tearing up the continent of
Africa, eastern Europe and island nations of the Caribbean? The Bible

---

1. James A. Sanders, *Torah and Canon* (Philadelphia: Fortress Press, 1972),
pp. ix-xx.

betrays because within the construct of its own worlds it articulates values that deny what we know to be true, for example, about human wholeness and able-bodiedness, about gender equality and gender relationships, about social institutions like the family (whose contours are in flux in modern Western society, to say nothing of among other cultures) or slavery (which is an accepted institution according to the writers of both testaments), and about the interdependent relationship of humankind and the rest of the created order.

It is tempting just to walk away from the Bible when we are wrestling with the truly thorny problems that plague us, and to claim other foundations for our ethical decisions. In particular instances, I would do just that. But as we think through the larger dilemma of the relationship among culture, values, and the Christian gospel—a dilemma which underlies many of the specific questions we face—some of the phenomena evidenced in the development of the books of the New Testament itself can perhaps provide lenses through which to clarify our task, and with that understanding free us for more creative choices.

To begin with, each book in the New Testament is contextually rooted. That is true of Paul's letters that identify with considerable precision what questions or behaviors prompted Paul to write, and it is true of the Gospels that frame the Jesus story to respond to the particular needs, questions, longings, problems and hopes of each Gospel writer's community. Jesus' own ministry—both words and actions—likewise took culturally specific forms, and addressed specific socio-historical concerns peculiar to rural Galilee of the first third of the first century. That news is hardly going to send reporters scrambling for their modems. But more is at stake than costumes and customs, sandals and cloaks, and reclining at table and broadcasting seed before you plow it under. The question cannot be trivialized into a contrast between 'bathrobe-pageant Christianity' and life in the real world.

Neither context nor reality is a neutral term. Both entail the question of perspective or point of view. *Whose* world of rural Galilee of the first third of the first century underlies what we can recover of Jesus' ministry? *With whom was he identifying*, and what was good news to them? And, to ask the tougher question, *does that perspective shift* as we move from Jesus to various parts of the New Testament? With what social groups or economic classes was Luke or Matthew identifying? What categories of people benefit as these early Christian theologians appropriate and interpret the meaning of Jesus for their day? In the process, what happens to the meaning of 'gospel'?

Note that I am not setting up the alternative of some pure essence of 'gospel' that is good, as opposed to culturally compromised contaminations of that essence that are bad. There is no such thing on earth as a pure gospel that does not have specific historical, social, and cultural roots and consequences, and that is not expressed in finite, limited, and thus culturally specific language. In any case, the gospel story is carried in actions set somewhere at some specific time. The question is not *whether* the gospel is culturally compromised, but only *to which* cultures it is compromised. That is true of the gospel Jesus brought. It is true of the various early Christian communities that codified it in oral traditions and written forms. It is equally true of every interpretation or expression of the gospel, including every paraphrase in word, music, paints or film ever since. And this complexity of cultural engagement addresses only the level of the production of versions of the gospel.

Before any of these culturally embedded expressions can become resources for the subsequent quest for meaning and guidance, they must be interpreted, and that also is not an objective or value-neutral process. It is a process rooted in cultural specificity of both methods and purposes, whether those be the allegedly value-neutral disciplines of historical criticism (which, in fact, embody the ideology of the post-enlightenment university), or the overtly engaged analysis of feminist scholarship or of the Base Christian Communities of Latin America. Persons from different socio-economic or ethnic contexts, of different genders, and with different life experiences or histories bring different questions, concerns, and insights to any situation, including to any text. The text itself may be the same, but the reading and meaning can shift dramatically. That is the premise of the flourishing of increasingly specific perspectival readings that are enriching the discipline of biblical studies on the current scene, as issues of the reader's identity, previously invisible or ignored, assume a new importance. Whatever we conclude about the perspective *in* the story, we also have to examine the perspective *on* the story. Just as all expressions of the gospel are contextual, so are all interpretations. It is not a question of whether contexts are granted a voice in the process of interpretation, but only which contexts find places at the table of conversation, and how widely one is prepared to seek out the voices that have been silent or silenced in the history of interpretation in the church and the academy.

All of this stands as a long introduction to the study of the New

Testament and cultural compromise. That study draws us back to the New Testament in our ethical quest, not for its specific content, but to try to understand how the intersection of culturally rooted producer (proclaimer of the gospel or writer of a Gospel) and culturally rooted interpreter can open up or close off a space for God's healing presence in the world—a space where God's persistent longing for a covenant of justice and peace can be realized. The long introduction is appropriate, in part because the agenda is complex, but also because the first half of that inquiry, *compromiso* with the God of Life, draws the Western church and academy into unfamiliar territory. English speakers tend to hear 'compromise' as cutting a deal, giving in on some things in order to get agreement on others, going along in order to get along. The Spanish word, however, pushes our imaginations. In addition to 'compromise', *compromiso* means commitment, and in what we might call the liberation church or the church of the poor, it means, in particular, commitment to the cause of the poor and all marginalized people relegated by the institutions of their society to the category of non-persons. To say someone is *muy comprometido* means that he or she can be counted on to understand, support, and stand in solidarity with struggles for land, for bread, for shelter, for health care, for education, and struggles to put an end to the official terrorism of the national security state and to heal the destruction of decades of violence. To say that someone *no tiene mucho compromiso* means the person cannot be counted on to stick to the cause when things get hard or costly, that she or he has made peace with the value system and institutional demands of the ruling elites.[2]

It is in that sense that this first part of the discussion speaks of cultural compromise—*compromiso* with those on the margins, exploring the meaning and dimensions of gospel seen from below. It appears from what we are able to learn about the ministry and teaching of Jesus that he, indeed, was a part of, and committed to, just such classes and communities of people. Some of the 'life of Jesus' research that has enjoyed a resurgence in the past few years is content with resuscitating the old mania to recover Jesus' very own words, and adjudicating history by counting colored marbles (a reference, of course, to the well-known

---

2.   Compromise and commitment come together in the word (whether the noun *compromiso* or the verb in its active and reflexive forms, *comprometer* and *comprometerse*), but the context in which the word is used always clarifies which meaning is intended.

mechanism for voting used by the Jesus Seminar to adjudicate the historical authenticity of a saying or pericope). Other expressions of that newest quest have embodied efforts at the socio-economic and cultural analysis of clues to the world in which Jesus moved.[3] Scholars involved in these studies do assess Gospel traditions for their relative age, in order to see what they can disclose about Jesus and his world, but these scholars also draw on disciplines of comparative sociology, archaeology and cultural anthropology in order to understand the texts.

Their integrity as scholars both reflects and supports the wisdom of persons on the margins who know that the history of the high and mighty is a story in which they are merely the grammatical as well as the political objects, and not a story in which they matter as subjects of the verbs of their own lives. Such scholars have demonstrated that the gospel proclaimed in word and action by Jesus was a religious truth precisely because it was about an agenda for all of human life. It spoke a good news that was a counter-voice to the good news proclaimed by the empire, to herald another military victory (an extension of the dominion of Rome, and the subjection of yet more people) or a birth in the imperial family so that the regime could continue. Jesus' good news was, instead, the promise of a fresh beginning for Galilean peasants trapped in the cycle of taxation that ate up, by most accounts, 65-80% of their harvest, and forced them off their own lands into tenancy, indebtedness and indentured servitude.

Jesus' gospel practice apparently brought healing from physical and psychological ravages of poverty and domination, and embodied open commensality in place of patterns of exclusion that rejected people who were ill or physically different from the so-called norm, or people too poor to practice all the protocols that would prevent their becoming impure. That gospel rejected the preference for the public life of temple and market place over the intimacy and relationality of hearth and

---

3.   See for example Marcus J. Borg, *Meeting Jesus Again for the First Time: The Historical Jesus and the Heart of Contemporary Faith* (San Francisco: Harper & Row, 1994); John Dominic Crossan, *The Historical Jesus: The Life of a Mediterranean Peasant* (San Francisco: Harper & Row, 1991); John P. Meier, *A Marginal Jew: Rethinking the Historical Jesus* (2 vols.; New York: Doubleday, 1991 and 1994); Richard A. Horsley, *Jesus and the Spiral of Violence: Popular Jewish Resistance in Roman Palestine* (San Francisco: Harper & Row, 1987); and, with a particular concern for the circumstances of women during the early years of the Christian movement, Elisabeth Schüssler Fiorenza, *In Memory of Her: A Feminist Theological Reconstruction of Christian Origins*(New York: Crossroad, 1983).

home—in other words, it rejected the patriarchal ideology that valued men higher than women, and that valued the well-to-do who could afford such distinctions more than the poor for whom the family's survival required everyone's full effort both in and out of the home. Jesus' gospel came to a climax in an account of Jesus' arrest by representatives of the empire and their local collaborators as a threat to the social order, and his condemnation to death in administrative hearings designed not to determine guilt or innocence, but to take care of a problem. As that gospel is recounted, it ends with the affirmation of a verdict different from that of the political and religious elites—a verdict of life in all its fullness instead of death in all its horror—as the last word. In that sense, the resurrection is not something unexpected that happened to Jesus' corpse, but the perfectly consistent affirmation of God's sovereign will that the divine project of justice and peace that defined Jesus' life on earth, and which is known in microcosmic victories of *pan y techo* (food and shelter for destitute people), as well as in the macrocosmic expression of the reign of God, will finally carry the day.

The investigation that enabled us to uncover this gospel of those on the margins, of *compromiso* with the God of life, drew on both careful and imaginative scholarly tools, and the insights and questions that have entered the discipline of biblical interpretation with the work of Euro-American women, of women and men of color from the northern latitudes and from the two-thirds world, and of those women and men from dominant cultures whose work has been transformed by the church of the poor. Such persons and communities have brought questions that directed attention to the impact of the gospel on those marginalized groups, not merely as 'the oppressed'—passive recipients of harmful actions by the powerful. Rather, these readers and reading communities have enabled the discovery and recovery of these ancestors on the margins, also as active partners of the gospel, who dared to live out its implications in lives of courageous resistance. Their readings, like the resistance of which they speak, always entail reading against the grain, for between us and the gospel of *compromiso* are layers of social, political, ecclesiastical and theological compromise with the values of the dominant cultures—the cultures of wealthy and powerful minorities in every context.

At issue in the working out of these compromises are important values supporting them, like the community's surviving to fight another day, instead of being wiped out by more powerful forces of economic, political or military empires. But at issue, too, is what is compromised or bargained away when—like potatoes in a soup—concerns of power, security and prestige threaten to pull out that *compromiso* that is the 'salt' of the gospel—source of its unique flavor, its healing power, and its ability to irritate the rich and powerful. Some extended examples from the New Testament will serve to illustrate this dynamic.

In the time of Jesus, crosses were a penny a dozen on the Palestinian landscape. Crucifixion was the preferred means of execution by the various Roman functionaries charged with keeping order in their corner of the empire. It was a torturous death, and a humiliating one, fitting for those of the lower classes or for members of the elite on whom one wanted to heap scorn as well as retribution. Crucifixions usually came in clusters—object-lessons for on-lookers, warning them not to get involved in whatever brought down their neighbors. Many Jews met such deaths, and their religious leaders—in particular, the temple leadership in Jerusalem—were well aware that any acts of brigandage or economic or political terrorism against their occupying forces brought the Roman sandal down even more viciously on their people's necks. For the long term good of the people for whom they were responsible, the religious elites were often eager to silence any whose action would draw negative attention on Jewish citizens, especially those of the upper classes.

Jesus appears to have run afoul of just such concerns. All four Gospels implicate the religious leaders in some way in the administrative process that led to his condemnation, but just what their role was is less clear. Did they instigate the proceedings against Jesus, and get the reluctant collusion of Rome, as the Gospel accounts portray? Or were they pressured into it, used as investigative agents by a Roman administration that had already decided that Jesus had to be executed, but that wanted collaborators within the Jewish population to bear the responsibility? Or did the temple leaders recognize that a popular movement such as the one that formed around Jesus would have disastrous consequences—a judgment borne out several decades later? Whether they agreed with his purposes or not, for the sake of the people's survival, and in order not to have the price exacted by the Roman administration against the whole people get any worse, did these leaders perhaps choose to get him (and other trouble makers) out of the picture?

Rather than portray them totally as unwilling victims, however, we need to acknowledge also that they would have had reasons of self-interest to want to silence Jesus. After all, these members of the religious elite were enjoying considerable profit from the imperial system—both directly, in the Roman protection of systems of religious taxation and of the elaborate economic infrastructure surrounding the temple, and indirectly, from the economic and political stability that the empire brought and, for a time at least, from the distance of immediate warfare. Christians have been quick to condemn their collusion in Jesus' death as cowardly, greedy, and just plain evil. But it is important to recognize the ambivalence of their situation. What choice did they really have, given that all the power was on the Roman side of the ledger? Indeed, less than forty years after Jesus' death, the first Roman-Jewish War proved conclusively the futility of directly opposing Rome: the temple was demolished, the holy city was destroyed, and many people were killed, and as a consequence the history of Judaism and of the off-shoot Christian religion was forever changed. Had such movements as that of Jesus been allowed to flourish unopposed, the end would likely have come sooner.

Besides, the church has made similar compromises with power virtually from the beginning, and continues to do so. It is easy to recognize modern parallels to the bind in which the Jewish leaders were caught at the time of Jesus, as we observe news reports of the choices made by religious leaders in parts of the world under foreign domination, or under the internal terror of civil war or of a national security state. Whatever the leaders' own sympathies, they have to consider their responsibilities for all the people entrusted to their care Besides, in many cases they have at least the possibility of enjoying privileges and protections if they cooperate with the army or the state, and so they do. They turn over rebel leaders and clergy who join their groups or merely provide them shelter or other support. They arrange for church groups and community organizations to be infiltrated by informers who feed names and plans to the authorities. Those who do not join in this collaboration, like Oscar Romero, are recognized as martyrs, and their funerals themselves become occasions for renewed slaughter and repression.

I want to suggest that—in ways that are less dramatic, perhaps, but sometimes equally deadly—the same kind of compromises are made within the texts of the New Testament themselves, and those compromises hold a mirror in front of our own less than exemplary reflections as we engage in our reading of those texts, as well. Three examples illustrate how the radicality of the gospel has been both preserved and betrayed under pressures of survival in, and accommodation to a succession of cultures of dominance: Paul's interaction with Christians at Corinth as seen in 1 Corinthians; the transformation of images and ideology of that letter in the new context reflected in the letter to the Ephesians; and the accommodation of the story of Jesus to similar pressures, as seen in the Gospel of Luke.

From what we are able to tell from Paul's letters, he was himself a person caught in the transitions and competing pressures that characterized much of the Hellenistic world. He was apparently a Roman citizen, which gave him a certain security of position and status in the empire, but he was ethnically and religiously a Jew—a member of a minority group, part of whose identity required a degree of separation from the dominant society.[4] He came from, and lived his life in, the Diaspora—outside of Israel, and not directly under the sway of the temple ritual or of the temple economy. Even before the cataclysmic events of the war in 66–70, he apparently lived a pharisaic type of Judaism, normed by faithful observance of the law, in response to God's gracious covenant. In fact, Paul may have been a missionary of Judaism, taking advantage of his itinerant life as an artisan to interpret his religion to those who did not know it. As an artisan, he would have been taking advantage of the *pax romana* to travel widely, plying his trade. We should not, however, see him as a first-century business traveler going first class from one luxury accommodation to the next. As a tentmaker he would have been either a worker in leather or a weaver—neither an easy job. Both would have put him in contact with members of the urban poor who worked in the artisans' stalls (as well as with the occasional merchant of luxury goods of related types, like Lydia, a merchant who traded in purple cloth and dyes). There, in the artisans' workshops, he would have had occasion to exchange news about others in these guilds whose paths had crossed his at other points in his travels, and he would have been able to engage in conversation about ideas—philosophies—and about religion, as people wove, stitched and talked together. Several times, his way of life, the company he kept and the suspicions these evoked from authorities interested in law and order, apparently landed him in jail.

---

4. Elsa Tamez, *The Amnesty of Grace: Justification by Faith from a Latin American Perspective* (trans. Sharon H. Ringe; Nashville: Abingdon, 1993), pp. 47-64.

Paul was thus prepared for what he identifies as his encounter with the risen Christ by knowing life already as a Jew, an artisan and a prisoner. Language and imagery from those three arenas of life gave him the raw material to express the good news he came to know of God's grace freely given, independent of any human social honor or behavioral merit. And that gospel, in turn, provided him new content for those conversations in the weavers' stalls. The people who responded to his preaching of God's values—values which countermanded the meritocracy that established a person's worth by one's wealth, or by one's social or legal status, and which established justice (justification or righteousness) by God's generosity and grace, and not according to a person's ability to meet legal criteria—would have come from a variety of social locations in the cities where he preached, but especially and predominantly from those on the margins. Others who heard and responded may have been wealthy, but, even in their privilege on the economic front, they would often have known the pain of exclusion or marginalization by some other criteria such as ethnicity or legal status, or the trades they practiced.

But, it seems, some of these better-off Christians—*los bien acomodados* (those who were 'accommodated', or adapted to their cultural, social, and economic environment, and more or less comfortable with its mores)—were caught in the middle. The case of the Corinthian Christians is a good illustration.[5] Wealthy people who opened their homes for community gatherings, furnished food for the common meal, or otherwise underwrote the costs of the local community (as well as contributing to the support of missionaries like Paul) knew well the etiquette of Corinthian society. They were used to moving in a society where groceries would include meat from local markets, which would probably have begun as an animal sacrificed at an altar of one of the many gods worshipped in that multi-cultural port city. But they thought nothing of it; it was just food. Poor Christians, on the other hand, were bothered by that meat, because the only meat they ate came directly as part of festivals to official deities, festivals at which attendance was

---

5. See the discussions in Wayne A. Meeks, *The First Urban Christians: The Social World of the Apostle Paul* (New Haven: Yale University, 1983), pp. 9-110; Gerd Theissen, *The Social Setting of Pauline Christianity: Essays on Corinth* (ed. and trans. John H. Schutz; Philadelphia: Fortress Press, 1982), pp. 69-174; Ben Witherington III, *Conflict and Community in Corinth: A Socio-Rhetorical Commentary on 1 and 2 Corinthians* (Grand Rapids: Eerdmans, 1995), pp. 1-35.

compulsory. The religious connection of the food was clear, and problematic.

Furthermore, according to the etiquette of their day, members of the wealthy class would be expected to treat social peers differently from the way they would treat social inferiors. Their usual guests on social occasions would have been only other rich people. When they hosted meals that included persons from different social and economic classes (such as gatherings of trade guilds or—by extension—the Christian gatherings for worship and common meals), the peers of the wealthy hosts would expect their accustomed elaborate meals, including meat. The others would expect less costly and elaborate foods—bread, grains and vegetables—served to them not in the intimate dining rooms, but in more public halls and atria of the hosts' homes, depending on their class. Christian servants, for whom the dinner parties of the wealthy usually meant only more work, may have received only the symbolic food of bread and wine that followed the prayer designating it not as an ordinary meal, but as the Lord's supper.

Apparently, through the visit of 'Chloe's people' and at least one letter from the community, Paul got wind of such practices as these (1 Cor. 11.17-34), as well as of other controversies stemming from the highly stratified and culturally polymorphous society, and his letter to the Christians at Corinth addresses such practices as having serious implications for the gospel. In the process of addressing these issues, Paul tries to sort out the interrelationship of gospel and culture. He focuses most closely on the behavior of the 'strong'. Among these were included the economically advantaged, who tended to presume on their experiences of social privilege, and persons who were boasting about their intellectual wisdom or spiritual gifts. In both cases, Paul's counsel emphasized choices sensitive to the needs of the 'weak'—the poor or those with less claim to honor or privilege. The 'strong' were reminded about the image of the body of Christ, in which the whole body suffers if any part is harmed, and in which all parts are of equal worth and interdependent.

With all of its problems, the Christian community in Corinth, under Paul's guidance, constituted a collection of house churches without the help of fixed standards and guidelines, in a place of religious pluralism and economic stratification and competitiveness. In that context, the house churches were called to a counter-cultural posture of affirming social commonality, open commensality, and the inclusion of a variety of economic and social groups as full participants or members of one religious community—one 'body' of Christ on earth.

In a later generation, the church at Ephesus faced different problems. That community to which the letter was principally addressed, though it appears to have functioned also as a circular or cover letter to accompany a collection of copies of Paul's letters, looks back at least one generation at Paul. Instead of 'making the path while walking on it' (*hacer el camino al andar*), which was how Paul's letters functioned in his own day, for the writer of Ephesians those letters were themselves authoritative words that needed only to be interpreted and applied to the new context. They were key expressions of the evolving standards or norms to which congregations were held by their leaders. These congregations had become largely settled congregations of residents in a place less oriented to the transient and socially suspect trade guilds. The church at Ephesus—and such a singular form of the word is appropriate, unlike its anachronistic use to refer to earlier gatherings of house churches in a given city—was needing to work out its identity as an institution of the Empire, of whose social fabric and relationships it was now a part. It was also working out the terms, means and style of its long-term survival. Questions of order and doctrine that established clear limits on the variety of beliefs and practices that had marked an earlier period became more important than opening out one's understanding of the meaning of one's faith or of the basis of people's participation in the community. In this letter, then, written by a follower of Paul, the image of the church as 'the body of Christ' is transformed to that of the church as 'the body' only, with Christ as the head to direct and control the body. No longer did the image emphasize equality and interdependence, but order and orthodoxy (or what would become that as the church moved toward the uniformity of one church, with one Scripture and one creed, under one bishop).[6]

In addition, as the church became an institution of the society, it came to include more and more people with some investment in the status

---

6. E. Elizabeth Johnson, 'Ephesians', in C.N. Newsom and S.H. Ringe (eds.), *The Women's Bible Commentary* (Louisville: Westminster Press/John Knox, 1992), pp. 338-42; David L. Balch, 'Household Codes', in D.E. Aune (eds.), *Greco-Roman Literature and the New Testament: Selected Forms and Genres* (Atlanta: Scholars Press, 1988), pp. 25-50; Craig S. Keener, *Paul, Women and Wives: Marriage and Women's Ministry in the Letters of Paul* (Peabody, MA: Hendrickson, 1992), pp. 139-224.

quo—those with something to lose economically and in terms of social status. At the same time, with the disintegration of the formerly strong Roman administration, which now allowed local rulers to act out their insanity on the populations they were to govern, it was increasingly important that Christians not be seen as a threat to the good order and stability of their society. In that context, Christian identity underwent a shift in the basic social unit by which its life was organized. In terms that are conveniently similar, but widely different in meaning and social implications, the church's basic unit shifted from the *house church* to the *household*. Given the centrality of the household as the economic base of the empire (center of both production and consumption), as well as the household's role as an ideological mirror of the hierarchical structure of the empire, a focus for good Christian behavior came to be the well ordered household. Not surprisingly, then, this letter (as well as Colossians and 1 Peter) included Christian 'household codes', or tables of obligations and responsibilities for members of the household under the dominance of the *pater familias*. These codes mirrored those found in secular writings, albeit with some accountability for members of dominant groups and with emphasis on the model of Christ, allegedly to mitigate the severity of the patriarchal system, but without questioning its fundamental hierarchy.

How great a shift there has been from the initial counter-cultural movement attributed to Jesus in Galilee, or even from the persistent reminders of Paul not to use one's 'strength' as an excuse to ride roughshod on those less privileged! Something was clearly gained in terms of the long term survival and cultural integration of the church, and perhaps a measure of that had to happen, or the Christian movement on the way to becoming the Christian church as an institution might not have survived. But the question must be raised whether in the process of compromise for the sake of the survival of the church and, in particular, Christians, the survival of the gospel itself was threatened.

In fact, the Gospels of Matthew, Mark, Luke and John pose the same question about the gospel of Jesus, even as they purport to relate the story of Jesus. From what we can determine, Jesus' immediate followers came from the marginalized classes of artisans and fishers who often came to such occupations when they lost ownership of farmlands and were forced into some form of dependency or clientage. Among them were also poor people of the villages or cities, including women forced into prostitution in order to survive, and those whom illness or physical or emotional disability forced into reliance on charity. They were the 'outcast of Israel', whose straitened circumstances made survival questionable and removed them from the possibility of participating in organized religion, whether by observing even basic demands of the law, making required sacrifices at the temple, or paying their temple taxes. They were individuals and members of households who had little investment in the institutions of their society, and they were people drawn to the gospel of open commensality, cancellation of debts and healing of illness that was summarized in the phrase 'the reign of God'.

These followers can be recognized in and through the Gospel witnesses to Jesus, but they are glimpsed behind layers of interpretation and the imposition of other concerns stemming from the life of the early church. Recognizing them is like trying to recognize the physical likeness underlying an icon, with its layers of varnish and decoration in gold and precious gems. Just as that adornment is crucial to the very meaning and beauty of the icon, so also the processes of interpretation that obscured whatever traces of Jesus' own life and ministry that may still be visible are crucial to the chronicle of the earliest Christian communities, and to our own wrestling with the challenge of ethics and the New Testament.

The Gospel of Luke was written at about the same time as the letter to the Ephesians (80–85 CE) in another city of the Diaspora (perhaps one of the relatively safe and prosperous cities of southern Greece). By the author's own admission, that Gospel was an attempt to produce 'an orderly account of the events that have been fulfilled among us, just as they were handed on to us by those who from the beginning were eyewitnesses and servants of the word' (Lk. 1.1-2). Often regarded as the Gospel for poor people and for women, Luke preserves such concerns masked by commitments to propriety befitting that Gospel's honorable and 'most excellent' audience.[7] Women figure prominently in the Gospel, but in their place. Women as bearers of children contribute to the divine plan, and thus one finds the positive portrayal of Mary, Elizabeth and Anna in the double-strand of narratives of annunciation, birth, naming, and childhood of John and Jesus. In those first two

---

7. See Jane Schaberg, 'Luke', in Newsom and Ringe (eds.), *The Women's Bible Commentary*, pp. 275-92; Itumeleng J. Mosala, *Biblical Hermeneutics and Black Theology in South Africa* (Grand Rapids: Eerdmans, 1989), pp. 154-89; and the essays in Jerome H. Neyrey (ed.), *The Social World of Luke–Acts: Models for Interpretation* (Peabody, MA: Hendrickson, 1991).

chapters of the Gospel, time itself is calculated by the rhythms of pro-creation, but by the beginning of ch. 3, public events of the religious and political hierarchies mark the passage of time. Later in the Gospel, women receive healing at Jesus' hand, and they are praised for supporting the movement and for serving at table (Lk. 4.39; 8.3). In the important story of Mary and Martha (Lk. 10.38-42), however, Martha is ridiculed for her concern for hospitality, and Mary's passive listening at the feet of Jesus leads to a lack of commission to pass on the story, like those received by the male disciples. (Similarly, in the Book of Acts, the work of women as missionaries and teachers, so often praised in Paul's letters, is reduced to a brief comment on the work of Priscilla in Acts 18.[8]) In Lk. 14.25-35, husbands are not on the list of family members to be 'hated' or left behind by faithful disciples, suggesting that women believers were to stay at home, protected from the risk to the security of their family status, but at the same time prevented from the full measure of discipleship.

Luke's rather traditional and socially conservative perspective on women's roles appears to be echoed by his perspective on wealth, possessions and people who are poor. In that arena, the economically and socially revolutionary imagery, which in earlier layers of the tradition attacked systems of taxation and indebtedness, has been reduced to a form of charity or almsgiving. What remains is a curiously mixed message—a 'liberal' call to persons of privilege to be socially responsible. The radicality of the Gospel persists in that the almsgiving that is commended does not refer to the gift of the few idle coins that the wealthy jingle in their pockets, but rather to the redistribution of the excess that allows one group to have too much while others lack the basic necessities of life. It is now a gospel *about* problems of poverty and poor people, but it is directed *to* those who have wealth to redistribute. Its point of view on social institutions and human relationships is no longer from below, but from high enough on the social ladder to represent a stake in the system's survival.

What is amazing is the persistence of the power—the 'salt'—of the gospel, despite cultural compromises, especially those that our ancestors made and that we continue to make with the ideology of power. It is crucial, however, to ask if such choices were made in order to survive under threat, to adapt the gospel to new realities, or to make it accessible

8.   Gail R. O'Day, 'Acts', in Newsom and Ringe (eds.), *The Women's Bible Commentary*, pp. 305-312.

and understandable to readers of a new generation and context, or if the gospel has been sold out for the sake of the comfort of the privileged. It is easy to recognize and criticize the compromises to which the text is transparent, but it is harder to recognize when we make the same compromises in our own readings.

The question is not whether there is compromise with cultures into which the gospel is received, but the question is rather on whose behalf compromise or *compromiso* is made. The strength and durability of the gospel to make its claim in spite of efforts to tame it to the perspective of privilege is a source of encouragement. So, too, is the gospel's power to draw us out from the centers of comfort and power where we normally reside, to the margins where we are met by the invitation of the Risen One to break bread at the open table where all are welcome, and to find a home where there are no inferiors and no outsiders.

THE ETHICS OF BIBLICAL VIOLENCE AGAINST WOMEN

J. Cheryl Exum

> If God is male, then the male is God.
> Mary Daly, *Beyond God the Father*

> What is an essentially simple act of identification
> when the reader of the story is male
> becomes a tangle of contradictions when the reader is female.
> Judith Fetterley, *The Resisting Reader*

Feminist criticism has made us more aware of the problem of the prevalence of violence against women in the Bible,[1] from mass violence against anonymous women—as in cases of war where we frequently find the command to destroy completely entire cities, including women and children (e.g., Deut. 2.34; 7.1-5; Josh. 6.21; 8.24-25; Judg. 21.10-14; 1 Sam. 15.3) and where the rape or humiliation of captive women is taken for granted (Judg. 5.30; Lam. 5.11; Amos 4.2-3; 7.17)—to individual cases, such as the rape, murder, and dismemberment of the Levite's wife in Judges 19; the rapes of Dinah (Gen. 34), Tamar (2 Sam. 13), and ten of David's wives (2 Sam. 16.21-22); the abduction of the dancers at Shiloh (Judg. 21.19-23); the sexual appropriation and later expulsion of Hagar (Gen. 16; 21); the slaughter of Cozbi the Midianite (Num. 25). And so on.

It is not my intention to chronicle instances of biblical violence against women. Rather I want to examine a particularly pernicious form of biblical violence against women where the perpetrator is not a collective, such as an army plundering cities, nor particular 'evil men' but the deity himself—sexual violence where God appears as the subject and the object of his abuse is personified Israel/Judah/Jerusalem.[2] The fact that

---

1. My discussion is limited to the Hebrew Bible, but there is ample problematic material in the New Testament; see, *inter alia*, Thistlethwaite 1985; Ellwood 1988: 20-23. The occasional transliterations of Hebrew that appear in this essay are not scientific.

2. I use the term 'his' for God since God is a character in these texts who is

this is metaphorical violence does not make it less criminal. Indeed, it is extremely injurious: because God is the subject, we—that is, female as well as male readers—are expected to sympathize with the divine perspective against the (personified) woman. The examples of biblical sexual violence discussed below are illustrative and representative rather than comprehensive. All of them come from the prophetic books and the book of Lamentations, where this particular kind of imagery has its locus. (What this says about prophecy and the prophets in general is a larger ethical issue.)

In dealing with the ethical problems raised by passages in which a male deity is pictured as sexually abusing a female victim, we cannot confine ourselves to the issue of gender bias in representation, which we can describe and account for as the product of an ancient patriarchal society where the subordinate position of women was taken for granted. We also need to consider gender bias in interpretation. How should we respond to these texts, and what is our responsibility as readers and consumers of these violent images? These texts make claims upon their readers, and their claims will be experienced differently by female and male readers. Male readers (if the commentators are any example; see below) do not find it difficult to identify with the divine perspective portrayed in these texts and thus to defend a righteous and long-suffering God for punishing a wayward and headstrong nation. Female readers, on the other hand, are placed in a double bind. On the one hand we are asked to sympathize with God and identify with his point of view. To the extent we do so, we read these texts against our own interests (see Fetterley 1991). On the other hand, by definition we are identified with

male identified, and I capitalize 'God' as though it were a proper name when referring to this character. *Foreign* cities or nations personified as women are also sexually abused by God; e.g., Nineveh in Nahum 3.5-6; Babylon in Isa. 47.1-3 (cf. 23.13-18); Edom in Lam. 4.21-22. Because in these cases the accused woman is not God's wife and there is no covenant to give him rights of ownership over her body, they raise a different set of issues from those discussed here. In some cases, the city/woman's sexuality is deliberately construed as a threat to the (male) god's male-identified people, for whose seduction she is blamed. Others represent a(n insulting) feminization of Israel's enemies, upon whom retaliation can be enjoyed and described in a sexually degrading manner. These passages share the fear of and fascination with female sexuality that motivates the passages discussed in this essay. On the use of sexual imagery to describe military conquest in the Hebrew Bible, see Thistlethwaite 1993; Gordon and Washington 1955. Gordon and Washington deal specifically with the image of the conquered city as a raped woman.

the object that elicits scorn and abuse. This involves acceptance if not of guilt, then at least of the indictment of our sex that these texts represent.

Gender Bias in Representation

These texts contain shocking and scandalizing language. Not surprisingly, most translations tone them down. Many terms, because they are rare or because their sexual meaning is obscure or only allusive, are difficult to translate. Pinning down specific meanings for rare words, however, is not crucial for our understanding of these passages, for their misogynistic import is clear enough.[3] By way of analogy, we have only to think of the power of our own language to convey sexual innuendo and to give common words vulgar connotations to recognize that the semantic field of many of these terms is broader than any one particular lexical meaning.

The first to employ the husband/wife metaphor for God's relation to his people, Hosea uses his marriage to Gomer, 'a wife of harlotry', to illustrate God's covenantal dealings with an idolatrous Israel (prominent in chs. 1-3, the harlotry theme runs through the whole book). In ch. 2, the indictment of the unfaithful woman slips into an indictment of the land personified as a harlot, whom God threatens to strip naked and slay with thirst (v. 3). After a description of her shameful behavior with her lovers and his response, God describes how he will publicly humiliate her.

---

3.   *Contra* Carroll 1986: 134, 180. Though Carroll recognizes the ideological bias of prophetic polemic and the pornographic (a term he uses) nature of this material, he cautions that 'biblical condemnation of sexual activity, whether real or metaphorical, is a balanced matter of condemning male as well as female behaviour (epitomized in Hos. 4.14). If feminine images of sexuality appear to be more numerous, that is because it is masculine behaviour which is being condemned: "whoring after..." is a male activity' (p. 180). This is, in my opinion, precisely the problem. The prophetic condemnations are aimed principally at men but the use of imagery of *female sexual* sin and female sexual abuse as a means of representing male *social* and *political* sins and their consequences reflects, in my view, a devaluation and denigration of women. These texts rely on a rhetorical strategy of abusing men verbally in the worst possible way—by placing them in the humiliating inferior female position—in order to shock them into changing their behavior. To say, as Carroll does (p. 134), that 'Without knowing the psychological make-up of the biblical writers it is not possible to evaluate the degree to which their writings may be characterized as misogynistic or otherwise' seems to me to be inquiring after the author's intention (conscious or subconscious). I am more interested in the effect on the reader, and I experience this material as defamatory, insulting, and, ultimately, misogynistic.

9[11]Therefore I will take back
my grain in its time,
and my new wine in its season;
and I will snatch away my wool and my flax,
which were to cover her genitals.[4]
10[12]Now I will expose her genitals[5]
in the sight of her lovers
and no one shall rescue her from my hand.

It is important to recognize that the point of view here is male. Hosea describes the nation's unfaithfulness in terms of unrestrained female sexual freedom. The woman's decision to pursue other lovers—in other words, her control of her own body—which is threatening, is visualized as rampant promiscuity, which is not tolerated. Given the carefully circumscribed social position of women in ancient Israel, it is hard to imagine a real woman getting away with such free and open behavior. I find it difficult therefore to see the bizarre exaggerated sexual appetite described here as anything other than a male fantasy of female desire—a fantasy born out of fear of female sexuality and fascination with it. The punishment for sexual 'transgression' or 'wantonness' is sexual abuse, which is also crudely fantasized in terms that conjure up the atrocities inflicted upon women prisoners of war. It is the male's job to restrain the female's freedom/wantonness and to punish the woman whose behavior brings dishonor upon him.[6] God is the wronged party here; he is male-identified and portrayed as the abusive husband. Sexual abuse is presented as justified by the woman's guilt.

Isaiah too calls Jerusalem a harlot (1.21; cf. 57.3-13). Language of sexual humiliation similar to Hosea's appears in Isa. 3.16-24, where the object of God's sexual abuse is at first real women, the women of Zion (Jerusalem). The imagery in this passage is fluid,[7] and by

4. The word *'erva* is a euphemism for genitals; cf. Gen. 9.22-23; on the relation of vv. 9 and 10 [Heb. 11 and 12], see the discussion in Andersen and Freedman 1980: 246-248.

5. The word I translate 'genitals' here is *nablut*, a hapax. For this translation, see Wolff 1974: 31, 37 n. 52. Andersen and Freedman (1980: 248) dispute the meaning of the Akkadian cognate cited by Wolff. They note, however, that something concrete is meant by the image and conclude that it is 'likely that the woman is to have her naked body put on display as obscene'.

6. See the discussion in Yee 1992: 197-198.

7. Cf. Susan Ackerman 1992: 162: 'Indeed, the identification of women, in particular the women of Jerusalem/Zion, with Jerusalem/Zion itself was made so facilely that a prophet could slip almost without notice from describing one to the other.'

v. 25 the daughters of Zion have become Zion herself.

> [16]Because the daughters of Zion are haughty
> and walk with outstretched necks,
> glancing provocatively with their eyes,
> tripping along as they go,
> rattling their bangles with their feet,
> [17]the Lord will make bald
> the heads of the daughters of Zion,
> and the Lord will bare their cunts.[8]

What exactly is these women's guilt? It appears that humiliation is punishment for pride and the possession of luxury items (described and stripped away in vv. 18-23). But where did the women get this finery in the first place? From their own economic endeavors, or from their husbands and fathers? 'The flamboyant behaviour of the women attracted the prophet's attention and indignation, when contrasted with the abject poverty that existed in the city', observes R.E. Clements (1980: 50). But surely there must be more to their guilt than this, so Clements does what biblical commentators usually do when no clear cause for divine punishment suggests itself—he surmises that the problem lies with an improper religious attitude: 'Trust in human beauty could signify a lack of regard for God' (1980: 51). Can behavior be the *cause* of poverty? Otto Kaiser apparently thinks so:

> The more extravagant they are, the more they lead the men on into illegal profiteering at the expense of those who are socially weaker. In various ways, either by their own attitude to the ordinary man in the street, or by the consequences for the economic behaviour of their husbands, they are undermining the internal unity and health of the people of the covenant. They are judged not because they adorn themselves, but because they break down the order of the people of God through their whole attitude.[9]

Not only are women to blame for the crimes of men, in Kaiser's view the breakdown of the entire social fabric can be attributed to these women's *attitude*!

8.   The meaning of v. 17 is obscure and my translation conjectural. The word *pot* in 1 Kings 7.50 refers to the sockets in which the door pivots turned (BDB, p. 834); assuming the word refers to a hollow place in which something turns, I take it as an obscene reference to the woman's vagina (cf. RSV, 'the Lord will lay bare their secret parts'); an alternative reading is 'the Lord will lay bare their foreheads'. On the difficulties, see the commentators.

9.   Kaiser 1972: 48; similarly, Watts (1985: 47) speaks of 'pride that makes destruction necessary'.

Not what androcentric ideology considers wanton behavior but simply what it suspects as glancing provocatively or 'ogling' is sufficient to bring the most vile abuse upon these women. At whom are they glancing provocatively, and why is it threatening? The female gaze is postulated in order to be condemned, while readers are invited to assume the text's male gaze at the women's genitalia. The intrusive textual gaze remains fixed upon the female body and its humiliation in the following verses, where the images are resolved in a picture of Zion as a ravaged woman.

> [24]Instead of perfume there will be stench,
> and instead of a belt, a rope,
> and instead of well-set hair, baldness,
> and instead of a rich robe, a girding of sackcloth,
> instead of beauty, shame.[10]
> [25]Your men will fall by the sword
> and your heroes in battle.
> [26]And her entrances will lament and mourn,
> ravaged she will sit upon the ground.

Like his prophetic predecessors, Jeremiah also refers to Israel's unfaithfulness in terms of illicit female sexual activity (e.g., 4.30; 22.20-23; and 2.33-3.20, where she is even said to have taught wicked women her ways, 2.33). The irrationally jealous husband imagines that his wife will have sex with anyone.[11] Jer. 2.23-24 masks male fear of and fascination with female desire by crudely caricaturing the woman as a young camel or wild donkey in heat.[12] In Jer. 13.22, when Jerusalem questions her harsh treatment by her lord, she is told:

> It is for the greatness of your iniquity
> that your skirts are lifted up
> and your genitals[13] are treated violently.

It is the woman's fault; abuse is deserved. Jerusalem will be raped by Babylon (13.20-27), and God not only endorses it, he participates in the attack.

---

10. MT lacks 'shame'; restoring *bšt* with 1QIs[a]. LXX and Vulg. lack the stichos.

11. Ellwood (1988: 10-11) observes that this is a trait God shares with the battering husband.

12. I am not convinced that the actual mating behavior of camels need inform the metaphor (Holladay 1986: 100). For discussion of the pornographic nature of this passage, see Brenner 1993.

13. Hebrew *'aqebayik* is literally, 'your heels'; like Hebrew *raglaim*, 'feet', it is a euphemism for genitals; see Carroll 1986: 303; Holladay 1986: 414.

> And I too will lift up your skirts over your face,[14]
> and your genitals will be seen (v. 26).

Since God has seen her 'adulteries', 'neighings' (another reference to female lust as insatiable) and 'lewd harlotries', it is presented as fitting that he should repay her in kind by exposing her genitals for all to see (as in the Latin *pudenda*, the Hebrew word *qelonek*, 'disgrace, dishonor', expresses the typical view of the female sex organs as shameful).

In Ezekiel we meet the strongest, most abusive language. Ezekiel 16 presents Jerusalem as a foundling who grows up to become God's unfaithful wife.[15] Because she has given herself to her lovers, God will assemble all her former lovers and expose her naked body to their view (vv. 35-38), after which they will be given free rein to abuse her.

> [39]I will give you into their hand
> and they will throw down your mound
> and break down your high places.
> They will strip off your clothes
> and take the ornaments of your beauty
> and leave you stark naked.
> [40]They will summon a crowd against you,
> and they will stone you with stones
> and cut you to pieces[16] with their swords.

The prophet compares the treatment of the woman Jerusalem to the way women who commit adultery are judged (v. 38), and thus provides an implicit warning to women in general—a warning that will be made explicit in ch. 23. The punishment for adultery is death. Here the woman is raped (symbolized by the throwing down of the mound and breaking

14. Literally, 'I will strip off your skirts over your face.' Carroll (1986: 303) suggests that the use of euphemisms in the passage 'may conceal an obscene practice of exposing women by drawing their legs over their heads in order to uncover their vulvas completely'.

15. See the discussion of this chapter by Shields (forthcoming), who, in contrast to the usual interpretation, sees no signs of divine tenderness in this text. Shields argues convincingly that the text attributes only desire, not love, to God. Jerusalem is completely dependent on God, who provides everything for her ('but never forgot that it was his property', Ellwood 1988: 12) and who, in his anger, strips everything away.

16. Galambush (1992: 67, 71) suggests that the hapax *btq* might best be understood in terms of the violent phallic image of splitting the woman open by slicing her up the middle.

of high places)[17] and stripped naked before she is stoned to death. But this extreme abuse, apparently, is not enough, and so the woman is dismembered in order to satisfy the divine husband's wrath ('so I will satisfy my fury upon you', v. 42). Female sexuality, whose free expression is so offensive, is mutilated and its threat thereby diffused.[18] Having vented his anger on his victim, the abuser will feel better: 'I will be calm and will not be angry any more' (v. 42). The woman, of course, since she's metaphorical, won't be dead. She will live to be abused again.

And so we come to Ezekiel 23, the most pornographic example of divine violence, where the sisters Samaria and Jerusalem become God's wives (a violation of the law in Lev. 18.18). Before graphically describing the punishment that the jealous husband inflicts on his wives for voraciously chasing after other men, the male author seems to take pleasure in picturing the sexual attentions pressed upon them by 'desirable young men' (vv. 12, 23): the handling of their breasts and their defilement by their lovers' lust. He betrays a fascination with sexual prowess and an envy of other (foreign) men's endowment, fantasizing his rivals with penises the size of asses' penises and ejaculations like those of stallions.

The prophet takes advantage of two occasions to go into the sordid details of sexual abuse, for the same punishment befalls both sisters. One of God's wives, the Northern Kingdom, dies as a result of abuse. God threatens his other wife with the same treatment. Just as he gave Samaria over to men who violated her by exposing her naked body to view and then killed her (vv. 9-10), so he will rouse against Jerusalem the lovers she has spurned (vv. 22-35).

> [25]I will direct my jealousy against you
> that they may deal with you in fury.
> They will cut off your nose and your ears...
> [26]They will strip off your clothes and take the ornaments of your beauty...
> [28]I am delivering you into the hand of those you hate,
> into the hand of those from whom your desire has turned away.

17. In 16.24 and 31 the terms *gab* (mound) and *ramah* (high place) refer to the places the woman/city built for prostitution/illicit worship. I see double-entendre in v. 39, with the destruction of these places represented as rape. Vv. 24, 25, and 31 read singular, 'height' or 'high place', and LXX, Vulg., and some Hebrew manuscripts read the singular here in v. 39.

18. The classic biblical example of the dictum, 'If the female body scares you, cut it up!', is Judges 19; see Exum 1993: 170-201.

[29]They shall deal with you in hatred
and take all you have acquired,
and leave you stark naked,
so that your unfaithful genitalia[19] may be exposed.

God's anger at the woman will fuel the anger of her former lovers. She will suffer mutilation at their hands and her naked body will be exposed. In her misery and humiliation, she will be mocked and laughed at (v. 32). Finally God calls for a crowd to be summoned against the adulterous sisters to stone them, and hack them to pieces with their swords (vv. 46-47), so that, again, we have both the stoning and the mutilation we witnessed in Ezekiel 16. To bring home the lesson, the fate of the personified cities has a moral for all women, 'that all women may take warning and not commit lewdness as you have done' (v. 48). By detailing the sexual abuse of an 'unfaithful' wife, the text appeals to female fear of male violence in order to keep female sexuality in check.

In this sampling of texts we can discover some disturbing common and repeated features. One is scapegoating women. It is the woman's fault that she is sexually abused because she asked for it by deliberately flaunting her husband's will (control) and thereby antagonizing him. Sexual sin is punished sexually in the most degrading way. Related to this is the portrayal of the woman as solely responsible for the success of the relationship. The husband shares none of the blame and deserves our sympathy as the wronged party. 'God suffers under Israel's deceitful love affair', says Hans Walter Wolff (1974: 44). But what about the woman's suffering? Even if God does suffer (and his suffering is not physical, like the woman's), that two wrongs do not make a right is a simple ethical principle. But this is what we have in these texts.

Hosea, Jeremiah, and Ezekiel present us with the abusive husband's version of events. The woman's version, her point of view, is not represented; she is called upon to accept her abuser's accusations as valid and acknowledge her guilt. Lamentations goes a step further by coopting the woman's voice to have her blame herself. In Lamentations, as elsewhere, the woman is violated because of her sexual 'infidelity':

19. Following a suggestion of Galambush (1992: 76); the Hebrew reads literally, 'the nakedness of your prostitutions'.

> [8]Jerusalem sinned grievously,
> therefore she became impure.[20]
> All who honored her despise her,
> for they have seen her nakedness.
> Even she herself groans
> and turns away.
> [9]Her uncleanness was in her skirts;
> she took no thought of the consequences for her.
> She has come down extraordinarily,
> she has no comforter...
> [10]The enemy has stretched out his hand[21]
> over all her precious things;
> for she has seen the nations
> enter her sanctuary...(Lam. 1.8-10).

The rape imagery builds upon the correspondence between body and temple and between genitals and inner sanctuary.[22] Though the woman's voice breaks through momentarily in the suggestion that God has gone too far in his abuse ('you slaughtered without mercy', 2.21), she shows no anger, only remorse, and thus she remains powerless. She accepts the blame: 'the Lord is in the right, for I rebelled against his word' (1.18; cf. 1.20, 22). Is this not the dilemma of many women in abusive relationships (Ellwood 1988: 8-12)? Where else can she turn except to the abuser in the hope things will improve?

In these examples of biblical violence, physical abuse is God's way of reasserting his control over the woman. The prophets enjoin the sinful woman to seek forgiveness from her abusive husband. The picture they offer suggests that abuse can be instructional and that it leads to

---

20. The term *niddah* refers to a menstruous woman (for the difference in pointing, see GKC § 20 n R 1), a reading reflected in Aquila, Symmachus, and the Syriac. Hillars (1972: 9-10) prefers the translation, 'people shake their heads at her', but recognizes a word play on *niddah*. The association with 'menstruous woman' is hard to miss, especially in view of the reference to ritual uncleanness in v. 9.

21. The word *yad*, 'hand', in v. 10 is also a euphemism for penis.

22. Mintz 1982: 4. Mintz discusses the shift of speaker from female in Lam. 1-2 to male in ch. 3, suggesting that because 'a woman's voice, according to the cultural code of Lamentations, can achieve expressivity but not reflection', the male figure is introduced in order to make meaning out of the disaster. 'This is a figure whose maleness is unambiguously declared by the use of the strong word *gever* for 'man' and whose preference for theologizing rather than weeping is demonstrated throughout' (p. 9).

reconciliation.[23] In Isa. 54.4-10, for example, the divine husband shows compassion on the wife he had forsaken. In Hos. 2.14-15 [Heb. 16-17], God promises to speak tenderly to his wife and restore her to favor so that she will 'respond as in the days of her youth'.[24] Her life will clearly be better, but how much better? Because the marriage relationship is one of inequality, she will always be subservient and dependent on his good will. Ezek. 16.59-63 paints a more depressing picture: God will forgive all that his unfaithful wife has done, with the result that she will never open her mouth again because of her shame. In this vision of reconciliation, the woman's lot is to be submissive and silent, which keeps her in the role of victim within the marriage relationship.

The problem we face in interpreting these passages is not just the punishment/rape imagery; the problem is the ideology that informs this imagery.[25] The concept of harlotry has meaning only within an ideology that views women's bodies as the property of men. Only women can be harlots or whores; in Hebrew, as in English, if the terms are applied to men it is only in an extended or figurative sense.[26] This ideology gives

---

23. Ellwood (1988: 9-10) likens God's change of disposition in Jer. 30.17; Isa. 42.14-16; 43.1-4, 25; 49.8-26; 51.17-23; and 54.8-11 to the behavior of a battering husband who follows abuse with repentance and sincere promises to reform.

24. Gordon and Washington (1995) translate 'submit as in the days of her youth'; cf. LXX, which reads, 'she will be humbled'. See also the discussion in Andersen and Freedman 1980: 276-77. If this is the meaning (and I think obedience, faithfulness, and compliance to the husband's will is fundamentally at issue), then the bleak picture corresponds closely to that of Ezek. 16.59-63.

25. The fear of women's sexuality and the perceived need to control it motivates these and other biblical portrayals of women. By this I mean not just the negative portrayals but also the seemingly positive ones. They all serve androcentric interests; see Exum 1993. In ancient Israel, women's sexual activity was severely circumscribed. Before marriage women were under the control of their fathers or brothers, and after marriage, of their husbands. A woman who was found not to be a virgin at marriage was to be stoned (Deut. 22.20-21). The husband had exclusive rights to his wife's sexuality (the converse was not true) and any breach of fidelity or even suspected breach of fidelity on her part was a threat to his honor that called for severe punishment (Num. 5.11-31; whether or not this trial by ordeal was ever conducted is beside the point, since in principle the law gives the husband the *right* to demand it; for discussion, see Bach 1993). Though our modern social context is very different, this ideology remains influential, both in Western culture in general and especially for people who look to the Bible for ethical principles and moral guidance.

26. For discussion of the Hebrew root *znh* and its metaphorical use by Hosea, see Bird 1989.

rise to the prophetic marriage metaphor in which the unquestioned superior male position is further privileged by placing God in the husband's position. The divine husband's superiority over his nation-wife, in turn, lends legitimacy to the human husband's superiority over his wife, who, following this model, is subservient to him and totally dependent on him.[27] Through messages about gender relations encoded in these texts, men are taught to exert their authority and women are taught to submit.[28] As Drorah Setel points out in her study of Hosean pornography, the prophetic marriage metaphor creates a contrast between God's positive (male) fidelity and Israel's negative (female) harlotry (1985: 93). God (the male) by definition cannot be unfaithful; at most he can be, as Lamentations sometimes suggests, excessive (2.2, 17, 21; 3.43). And because most readers are likely to read with the text's ideology and privilege God, the abusive husband's behavior is not open to question. 'To involve God in an image of sexual violence', observes Judith Sanderson, 'is, in a profound way, somehow to justify it and thereby to sanction it for human males who are for any reason angry with a woman' (1992: 221).

In our prophetic examples, sin is identified with female sexuality, and specifically, with uncontrolled or unrestrained female sexuality. 'Bad' women are promiscuous and rapacious, and female desire is consuming and dangerous. And the one who suffers from it most is the woman herself. Male control, then, is seen as necessary and desirable, and sexual abuse becomes justified as a means of correction. To make matters worse, physical assault paves the way to the abused woman's reconciliation with her abusive spouse. Abuse is thus complexly and confusingly linked with love in a pattern that consistently challenges women's sense of worth and self-esteem. A depressing body of evidence demonstrates how such texts oppress women by encouraging scapegoating and

27. A feature of these texts I have not developed here is the picture of the woman's utter dependence upon male support; for development of this point, see Setel 1985: esp. p. 92; Ellwood 1988: 11-12. Ezek. 23 treats this dependence theme in a perverse way; see Shields, forthcoming.

28. While writing this paper, I happened to watch a BBC television program called 'The Hamar Trilogy' about the Hamar women of southwest Ethiopia. In this community women are ritually beaten at a young man's coming of age ceremony, and a woman interviewed explains that it shows you love him enough to suffer for him. Wife beating is also common; a man explains that it makes him feel like a man to beat his wife.

reinforcing the idea that physical abuse can be an appropriate measure for men to use against women.[29]

Gender Bias in Interpretation

In describing God's treatment of his wayward wife, the prophets rely upon a rhetorical strategy that encourages the audience to identify and sympathize with a male-identified deity. This is the privileged point of view, the 'I' that condemns the 'you', the other, whose view is not represented (Lamentations is no exception, since it uses the woman's voice to express the male point of view). When readers privilege the deity, which most readers of the Bible still do, they are forced into accepting this position, for to resist would be tantamount to challenging divine authority. This is the position taken almost without exception by biblical commentators, who, until recently, have been almost without exception male. Typically these commentators either ignore the difficulties posed by this divine sexual abuse or reinscribe the gender ideology of the biblical texts; usually they do both in their ceaseless efforts to justify God. Often they not only pick up on latent gender bias in the text but also read their own biases and stereotypes back into it. Hans Walter Wolff, for example, sympathizes with the suffering divine husband who 'would rather not' take abusive action against his unfaithful wife but 'finds it necessary', and who strips her naked to indicate his 'freedom from the obligation to clothe her',[30] as if freedom from obligation excuses cruelty. In their Anchor Bible commentary on Hosea, Francis Andersen and Noel Freedman accept the husband's 'demand for retribution' as 'legitimate' and describe the public humiliation of the woman as a 'subtle' application of the lex talionis (and not, for example, as an unreasonable punitive measure or as vicious and unethical behavior).[31]

---

29. For a compelling application of the biblical marriage metaphor to the situation of battered women, see Ellwood 1988. Ellwood also shows how child battering is part of the picture. See also Thistlethwaite 1985.

30. Wolff 1974: 34, 38. When Wolff explains that God 'refuses to accept as final the divorce his wife both *desired* and *initiated*' (p. 44; italics mine), he reinscribes the textual strategy of blaming the woman (divorce was not a woman's right in Israelite society). Anderson (1978: 89) similarly invites us to sympathize with God's suffering and to view the people's suffering as cathartic.

31. Commenting upon Hos. 2.12, they note the 'poignancy' (p. 248) of the

We saw above how Otto Kaiser, in his discussion of Isa. 3.16-24, reinscribes with a vengeance the ideology of the text. John Bright's Anchor Bible commentary on Jeremiah, and, more recently, William Holladay's (Hermeneia) are typical of the commentaries in these series in ignoring the problems posed by the imagery of divine sexual abuse in favor of discussion of philological and historical-critical issues. Bright, for example, in his comment on Jeremiah 13, deals only with the waistcloth incident in vv. 1-11, and has nothing to say about the salacious verses 20-27, except that they are poetry.[32] About the same passage Holladay speaks only of the references 'to the shocking harlotry which that city commits, harlotry which merits her public stripping and ravishment'.[33] Moshe Greenberg's 'holistic' approach to Ezekiel, because it seeks to encounter the prophet on his terms, also has the effect of suppressing the woman's point of view. Walther Eichrodt, in contrast, is not content to let the prophet speak for himself. He is concerned with God's image

display of the woman's naked body, but they never abandon the text's male point of view.

> Why the husband should now deliberately share this privilege [viewing his wife naked] with his rivals is not clear, although in view of the context of the former's outrage and legitimate demand for retribution (cf. v. 5), it is to be seen as a form of punishment appropriate to the crime. Just as in the past the errant wife has sought out her lovers and eagerly disrobed in their presence for the purposes of sexual gratification, so now she will be forcibly exposed in the same situation, and publicly humiliated. The subtlety of the talion here is essentially that what she did secretly and for pleasure will now be done to her openly and for her disgrace (p. 249).

32. Bright 1965: 95-96. I refer to the 'Comment' section; in his textual notes to v. 22, Bright observes that 'your skirts' is 'apparently a euphemism' and 'your heels' 'is also a euphemism', but he leaves it to the reader to decide what the terms are euphemisms for. Of v. 27 he writes, '"Your rutting" is literally "your neighings", i.e., animal passion, as in v. 8', and he continues, 'The verse refers to practice of the cults of pagan gods, and the immoral rites associated with them' (p. 95).

33. Holladay 1986: 417. Cf. the evasive treatment of this passage in a commentary designed as a resource for preaching:

> Pictured in the guise of a young woman who has abandoned all moral restraints (v. 27), Jerusalem is now to be faced with the inevitable fate of violence and rape that awaited a young woman captured as a prisoner of war (v. 26). The language is stark and the imagery has become rather conventional in the wake of the earlier prophecies of Hosea. There is therefore a certain lack of originality about it (Clements 1988: 87).

In another series designed to keep the 'Old Testament alive in the Church' (p. vii), Brueggemann (1988: 127) describes the picture of 'a humiliated slave girl' in 13.26 [!] as one of 'a rich variety of suggestive images' that convey a 'simple message'.

in ch. 23 (though apparently more with God's image as a husband than as an *abusive* husband): 'In view of the way in which sex-life is elsewhere completely excluded from the divine realm, it is monstrous to find it here stated bluntly how God contracted a marriage with a pair of harlots' (1970: 320). He assures us, moreover, that the abuse imagery is not to be taken seriously.

> One can see from the very beginning that the narrative in which this is clothed has no importance whatsoever; this is no parable story full of charm and poetic beauty, like ch. 16, 17 and 19. It is an allegory, which gives no more than the bare essentials, and applies only a few stereotyped pictorial images to bring out the point as clearly and unmistakably as possible. *The images which it employs have no life of their own*; their only purpose is to reproduce in quite coarse terms the unspeakable event they convey (1970: 320-21, italics mine).

From the scandalous imagery in Ezekiel 16, he draws a moral lesson that, like the prophetic marriage metaphor, places full responsibility for the success of the relationship upon the subordinate partner.

> The way in which expressions for God's wrath and jealousy are heaped up is to denote the inexorable, yet wholly personal, manner in which he reacts against every attempt to deny or ridicule his giving of himself in fellowship. Unless this is impressed with all possible seriousness upon the conscience of the creature, its value would become doubtful, and the absolute will behind it ambiguous. What is finally at stake is whether or not we realize the existence of that divine majesty, apart from which the dignity of man is empty or non-existent.[34]

Unfortunately, the female figure in the text has no dignity left to her.

I could easily multiply examples of biblical commentators who reinscribe the text's harmful gender ideology. What worries me most about them is the influence they have on those readers who rely on their commentaries for explication of the Bible and who often grant them the kind of authority to say 'what the text means' that they do not deserve.

The contributors to *The Women's Bible Commentary* show the difference reading as a woman makes. The authors of the entries on the prophetic books all wrestle with the implications of biblical violence

---

34. Eichrodt 1970: 209-210. The English translation 'man' does not capture the inclusiveness of German *Mensch*: 'Es geht letztlich um die Anerkennung einer göttlichen Majestät, ohne die auch der Adel des Menschen hohl und nichtig werden müßte' (1965: 126).

against women and struggle to find ways of dealing with it. Susan Ackerman looks behind the prophetic polemic for evidence of women's real religious experience (1992: 162). Gale Yee looks to other prophetic metaphors for the divine-human relationship as alternatives to the harmful marriage metaphor (1992: 200, 202). Similarly, Kathleen O'Connor finds alternative, positive models for women in certain prophetic themes (such as those that express opposition to oppression and hope for a new order of social relations based on mutuality) and in scattered instances of non-patriarchal divine imagery (1992:173-177). Katheryn Darr advocates keeping harmful texts in the canon not as an affirmation of their assertions but because they force readers to confront difficult questions (1992a: 190; see also 1992b). Judith Sanderson, perhaps the *Commentary*'s most resistant reader, relentlessly exposes the ideological prejudices that produce such negative female imagery (1992a, 1992b, and 1992c). One looks in vain in the standard commentaries for responses like these to the violence against women in the prophetic corpus.[35]

Regardless of how we decide to respond to it, sexual violence of which God is the perpetrator and the nation personified as a woman is the object, along with its destructive implications for gender relations, is there. It cannot be dismissed by claiming that it is only 'metaphorical', as if metaphor were some kind of container from which meaning can be extracted, or as if gender relations inscribed on a metaphorical level are somehow less problematic than on a literal level. When, for example, Bernhard Anderson assures us the point of Hosea 2 'is not to absolutize a particular understanding of masculine-feminine relations but to lift the

---

35. While I do not claim to have made an exhaustive study, Carroll's is the only major commentary I know of that faces this problem squarely and that consistently reveals the power of ideology to suppress competing discourses. Although the approach taken by the contributors to the *Women's Bible Commentary* is commendable, like their male counterparts they still seem to have a stake either in defending the 'real god' or defending the text, either because of their own commitment to the biblical text or for the sake of the commentary's stated audience of 'laywomen, clergywomen, and students' (p. xvii). This is also and especially true of Weems 1989 and Frymer-Kensky 1992, whose critique is greatly tempered by the privileged position they grant the deity. What distinguishes the work of these scholars from their male counterparts is their honesty about the problem.

whole discussion up to a metaphorical level',[36] he ignores what for Yee is the crucial question: 'To whose experience does the metaphor speak, and whose experience does the metaphor exclude?' Raising this question enables Yee to conclude that 'this metaphor makes its theological point at the expense of real women and children who were and still are victims of sexual violence'.[37] Nor is the prospect of reconciliation following punishment a solution to the problem posed by the imagery of sexual abuse because it is part of the pattern: it reinforces the harmful ideology of abuse as something for the victim's own good and makes acceptance of blame and submission the price of forgiveness. It leaves the woman powerless. Imaging the people as God's *faithful* wife does not exalt women either; it merely reinscribes patriarchal hierarchy.

Claiming that there is a suffering and loving god behind this imagery will not make it go away. For some readers of the Bible creating a canon within the canon, in which texts that are injurious are excluded, is one way of dealing with this offensive material. I prefer doing away with the notions of canon and biblical authority altogether. Because the Bible is an important part of our cultural heritage, it would be presumptuous to suggest that we can casually dispense with it. But I see no reason to privilege it. And, I would add, I think it important to recognize that God is a character in the biblical narrative (as much a male construct as the women in biblical literature) and thus not to be confused with any one's notion of a 'real' god. Increasingly, as investigation into the gender-determined nature of biblical discourse becomes more sophisticated, biblical interpreters will have to come to terms with this fact.

In conclusion, I would like to describe briefly a threefold interpretive

---

36. Anderson 1978: 87. The discussion of Hosea 2 appears on pp. 86-89. Blenkinsopp (1990: 99) similarly counsels us to 'concentrate on the point of the allegory' in Ezek. 23; he does, however, in contrast to many commentators who simply gloss over the problem, acknowledge that

> We cannot, and should not, ignore the current of antifeminism in the prophetic literature and indeed in much of the literature of antiquity...The ambiguity, suspicion, and fear aroused by female allure, and even more by the biological processes connected with birth and menstruation (one thinks of Baudelaire's *la femme est naturelle, donc abominable*), may help to explain but do nothing to render these attitudes less distasteful to the enlightened modern reader.

With regard to ch. 16, he mentions its pornographic nature but chooses the unfortunate title, 'the Nymphomaniac Bride' for the section 16.1-63 (p. 76).

37. Yee 1992: 200; on the problem of this metaphorical divine violence, see also Weems 1989.

strategy that seems to me especially promising as a response to the prophetic rhetoric of sexual abuse.

1. *Attention to the differing claims these texts make upon their male and female readers.* Readers of these texts are asked to make a dual identification—with God and with Israel—and for both sexes this involves taking the subject position of the other sex. But pressures to identify with a particular subject position pull male and female readers in different directions. Personified Israel, whose covenant infidelity is described as harlotry, is composed of women and men (indeed, male citizens would have been the primary audience of this material). Male readers are thus placed in the subject position of women and, worse, of harlotrous, defiled, and sexually humiliated women. They are required to see themselves in the wrong and to repent and change their behavior, and because a female identification is not 'natural' for them and identification with a debased woman is shocking and repulsive, they will be anxious to cast it off. The metaphor offers them another role with which they can more readily identify, that of the faithful husband, whose point of view they are already encouraged to identify with by the prophetic rhetoric. Female readers are also called upon to adopt the divine point of view, but in our case the identification is not 'natural' because God is identified metaphorically with the male. Our 'natural' identification lies with the sinful, humiliated woman. This situation, as I said at the beginning of this essay, forces women readers to read against our own interests and to accept the indictment of our sex encoded in these texts. Male readers, in contrast, are not reading against their interests when they adopt God's point of view toward the sinful woman. On the contrary, it is against their interests to stay in the humiliating female subject position.[38]

38. Galambush (1992: 161) describes an important effect of this rhetorical strategy on the male audience of Ezekiel:

> The depiction of Yahweh expunging his own shame by punishing (including shaming) the unfaithful Jerusalem thus serves to reinterpret the destruction of the city as a *positive* event, one that reestablishes the honor and potency of Yahweh. This metaphoric refurbishment of Yahweh's honor not only would have allowed Ezekiel's readers to avoid the shame of acknowledging their god's humiliation and defeat, but also would have allowed male Judeans to expunge their own shame by transferring it to the personified woman, Jerusalem. As men in solidarity with a divine, punishing husband, male Judeans could, at least momentarily, have seen Jerusalem (and her shame) as 'other,' a woman justly shamed. The humiliation of personified Jerusalem would thus paradoxically serve to recapture a sense of power and control for the militarily humiliated male residents of the city.

Recognizing how shifting subject positions function rhetorically to manipulate readers' responses along gender lines and how such rhetorical strategies affect what is at stake for female and male readers may help us all to become resisting readers. I wonder, for example, how often it is the case that the imagery of female harlotry is used to describe sin but a shift occurs to male imagery (e.g., faithful sons) when reconciliation is envisioned.[39]

2. *Exposing prophetic pornography for what it is.* The prophetic texts I have cited as examples of God's sexual abuse of a nation personified as a woman contain violent representations that involve, among other atrocities, exposing the woman's genitals to view—to the view of a hostile audience posited in the text and to our, the readers', view. We are asked to adopt, and approve, the pornographic gaze at the naked and physically abused female body—pornographic because it involves objectification, domination, pain, and degradation. Doubtlessly female violation is described in such brutal detail for its shock value, but is there also some righteous satisfaction or perverse pleasure in writing about it? In reading about it, we are complicit. What do we think we are doing when we read this prophetic pornography? Can we allow ourselves the moral high ground because the violence is metaphoric and presented with a theological justification; in other words, because we are reading the Bible? Can we afford to ignore the implications this imagery has for readers of the Bible, or to minimize its significance in the Bible? As Susan Griffin has shown in her subtle and compelling study, *Pornography and Silence*, it would be naive to think that pornography can be contained in such a way that it does not affect all of us. We cannot, she argues, overestimate the effect of images on our lives.

> For social science itself tells us that images shape human behavior. And thus, if the social scientist makes the argument that pornography has no effect on human behavior, we are faced with a strange and mysterious phenomenon. For in order to argue that pornography does not reach into the lives of the audience and change their behavior, we would have to say

39. As Shields (1995) shows, this is the case in Jer. 3.1-4.4. See also Shields (forthcoming) on Ezek. 16. Galambush (1992) documents a similar shift in imagery in Ezekiel, from the city as God's unfaithful wife to the faithful city no longer personified as a wife; threatening female elements are excluded from the vision of restoration.

that pornographic images are different from all other images, both actual and cultural, and that the mind, when confronted with the pornographic image, suddenly acts differently than it does when confronted with any other image.[40]

Would not the ethical response to these prophetic texts be to acknowledge what it is we're reading and take responsibility for doing something about it?[41]

3. *Looking for competing discourse(s)*. It is fair to say that female experience is denied or misnamed[42] in these examples of prophetic pornography. By asking what is the 'other' discourse with which the vituperative prophetic discourse is competing we may be able to uncover evidence of the woman's suppressed point of view in these texts. This involves looking for places where attempts to silence or suppress the woman's rival discourse—a discourse that threatens to subvert the dominant prophetic patriarchal discourse—are not completely successful.[43] For example, we can read Jer. 2.31 ('We are free; we will come no more

---

40. Griffin 1981: 105. Further, p. 119:

> It is not in the nature of a being, a thought, or an image to be confined...The pornographic image has a life like the life of a sound wave. Set in motion in one place in a city, it affects a man walking through this part of the city. He begins to resonate with its frequency. He carries the ugliness of pornography outside this neighborhood. Let us say an image of a man beating a woman makes him more ready to strike a woman he knows. Or if this is not the case, let us say simply that he carries this image of a man striking a woman with him in his mind. Unless he repudiates this image, argues with it, decides definitely that it is not part of his nature, and rejects it, it becomes part of him. And inside his soul a man beats a woman. But this is not all. The images we carry in our minds make us into who we are...Thus, in some way, this man comes to be like the image of a man beating a woman. Perhaps he becomes more callous. Perhaps he becomes cruel to his own softness. And now we, who have not walked in the neighborhood where pornography lives, see this man, we sense his brutality, his violence... Finally, pornography has succeeded in reaching us; it has even penetrated our notion of reality.

41. I am sure there are readers who will resist the designation 'pornographic' for this literature, and it is not my intention here to enter into a discussion of the complicated question, exactly what constitutes pornography? For a discussion of prophetic pornography and its damaging effects, see Brenner and van Dijk-Hemmes 1993: 167-195; Gordon and Washington 1995. On Ezek. 16 and 23 as pornographic, see Galambush 1992: 124-125, 161-163 *et passim*.

42. On this phenomenon, see Setel 1985 and van Dijk-Hemmes 1993.

43. For further discussion and demonstration of this approach, applied to Proverbs, see Newsom 1992; for applications to prophetic texts, see Shields 1995 and forthcoming.

to you') as the woman's claim to autonomy in the face of overweening possessiveness supported by patriarchal constraints; or Jer. 13.22 ('Why have these things come upon me?') as her unwillingness to accept blame. The recent studies of Fokkelien van Dijk-Hemmes and of Pete Diamond and Kathleen O'Connor profitably employ this reading strategy to challenge the dominant male discourse of Ezekiel 23 and Jeremiah 2-3 respectively. Van Dijk-Hemmes notes that the harlotrous activities of the sisters in Ezekiel 23 are described not with active verbs but in the passive: 'There their breasts were squeezed/There the teats of their maidenhood were pressed.' 'It would have been more adequate', she observes,

> to describe the events during the sisters' youth in the following manner: 'They were sexually molested in Egypt, in their youth they were sexually abused.' This way, justice would have been done to the fate of these metaphorical women, and the audience would not have been seduced into viewing women or girls as responsible for and even guilty of their own violation (1993: 172-73 [173]).

Diamond and O'Connor conclude their study of Jeremiah 2-3 with similar observations:

> What would happen if female Israel told the story? Would she tell of her husband's verbal abuse, his foolish jealousy, his despicable exaggerations, his claims to have 'planted her as a choice vine' (2.21), his continual distrust of her and her sexuality? Would she recount how loving he had been and tell how he had become more and more controlling and demanding? We cannot know, of course, because in this case the husband is God, and not such a nice god, even if broken-hearted. What we do know about this metaphorical woman, though, is that she makes a moral and religious choice. She does not return to him despite the safety and social status a return might provide. She refuses to speak the words he demands of her: 'Only acknowledge your guilt...' (3.13). She will not accept blame for the failure of the marriage, and she will not reject the gods and goddesses whom she loves. She accepts the price of her autonomy (Diamond and O'Connor, forthcoming).

Though I listed them separately for the purposes of discussion, these ways of dealing with gender-biased prophetic rhetoric overlap, and the important work currently being done on this topic draws on all of them.[44] Taken together they constitute not a solution to the ethical

---

44. Especially the studies mentioned above by Shields 1995 and forthcoming, Brenner and van Dijk-Hemmes 1993, Gordon and Washington 1995, and Diamond and O'Connor forthcoming.

problem of biblical violence against women but an important rhetorical counter-strategy for dealing with it.

BIBLIOGRAPHY

Ackerman, S.
1992   'Isaiah', in Newsom and Ringe (eds.) 1992: 161-68.
Andersen, F.I., and D. N. Freedman
1980   *Hosea* (AB, 24; Garden City, NY: Doubleday).
Anderson, B.W.
1978   *The Eighth Century Prophets* (Proclamation Commentaries; Philadelphia: Fortress Press).
Bach, A.
1993   'Good to the Last Drop: Viewing the Sotah (Numbers 5.11-31) as the Glass Half Empty and Wondering How to View It Half Full', in J.C. Exum and D.J.A. Clines (eds.), *The New Literary Criticism and the Hebrew Bible* (JSOTSup, 143; Sheffield: JSOT Press): 26-54.
Bird, P.
1989   ' "To Play the Harlot": An Inquiry into an Old Testament Metaphor', in P. Day (ed.), *Gender and Difference in Ancient Israel* (Minneapolis: Fortress Press): 75-94.
Blenkinsopp, J.
1990   *Ezekiel* (Interpretation, A Bible Commentary for Teaching and Preaching; Louisville: John Knox).
Brueggemann, W.
1988   *To Pluck Up, to Tear Down: A Commentary on the Book of Jeremiah 1–25* (Grand Rapids: Eerdmans).
Brenner, A.
1993   'On "Jeremiah" and the Poetics of (Prophetic?) Pornography', in Brenner and van Dijk-Hemmes 1993: 177-93.
Brenner, A., and F. van Dijk-Hemmes
1993   *On Gendering Texts: Female and Male Voices in the Hebrew Bible* (Biblical Interpretation Series, 1; Leiden: Brill).
Bright, J.
1965   *Jeremiah* (AB, 21; Garden City, NY: Doubleday).
Carroll, R.P.
1986   *Jeremiah* (OTL; Philadelphia: Westminster Press).
Clements, R.E.
1980   *Isaiah 1–39* (NCB; Grand Rapids: Eerdmans).
1988   *Jeremiah* (Interpretation, A Bible Commentary for Teaching and Preaching; Louisville: John Knox).
Darr, K.P.
1992a   'Ezekiel', in Newsom and Ringe (eds.) 1992: 183-90.
1992b   'Ezekiel's Justifications of God: Teaching Troubling Texts', *JSOT* 55: 97-117.

Diamond, A.R.P., and K.M. O' Connor
forthcoming   'Unfaithful Passions: Coding Women Coding Men in Jeremiah 2–3
              (4.2)', *Biblical Interpretation*.
Dijk-Hemmes, F. van
1993   'The Metaphorization of Woman in Prophetic Speech: An Analysis of
              Ezekiel 23', in Brenner and van Dijk-Hemmes 1993: 167-76.
Eichrodt, W.
1965   *Der Prophet Hesekiel. Kapitel 1–18* (ATD, 22/1; Göttingen:
              Vandenhoeck & Ruprecht).
1970   *Ezekiel* (trans. C. Quin; OTL; Philadelphia: Westminster Press).
Ellwood, G.F.
1988   *Batter My Heart* (Pendle Hill Pamphlet, 282; Wallingford, PA: Pendle
              Hill).
Exum, J.C.
1993   *Fragmented Women: Feminist (Sub)versions of Biblical Narratives*
              (JSOTSup, 163; Sheffield: JSOT Press; Valley Forge, PA: Trinity Press
              International).
Fetterley, J.
1991   'Palpable Designs: An American Dream: "Rip Van Winkle"', from
              The Resisting Reader (1977), in R.R. Warhol and D. Price Herndl
              (eds.), *Feminisms: An Anthology of Literary Theory and Criticism*
              (New Brunswick, NJ: Rutgers University Press): 502-508.
Frymer-Kensky, T.
1992   *In the Wake of the Goddesses: Women, Culture, and the Biblical
              Transformation of Pagan Myth* (New York: Free Press).
Galambush, J.
1992   *Jerusalem in the Book of Ezekiel: The City as Yahweh's Wife* (SBLDS,
              130; Atlanta: Scholars Press).
Gordon, P., and H.C. Washington
1995   'Rape as a Military Metaphor in the Hebrew Bible', in A. Brenner
              (ed.), *A Feminist Companion to the Latter Prophets* (Sheffield:
              Sheffield Academic Press): 308-25.
Greenberg, M.
1983   *Ezekiel, 1–20* (AB, 22; Garden City, NY: Doubleday).
Griffin, S.
1981   *Pornography and Silence: Culture's Revenge against Nature* (New
              York: Harper & Row).
Hillers, D.R.
1972   *Lamentations* (AB, 7A; Garden City, NY: Doubleday).
Holladay, W.L.
1986   *Jeremiah 1* (Hermeneia; Philadelphia: Fortress Press).
Kaiser, O.
1972   *Isaiah 1–12* (trans. R.A. Wilson; OTL; Philadelphia: Westminster
              Press).
Mintz, A.
1982   'The Rhetoric of Lamentations and the Representation of Catastrophe',
              Prooftexts 2: 1-17.

Newsom, C.A.
1989   'Woman and the Discourse of Patriarchal Wisdom: A Study of
            Proverbs 1–9', in P. Day (ed.), *Gender and Difference in Ancient
            Israel* (Minneapolis: Fortress Press): 142-60.
Newsom, C.A., and S.H. Ringe (eds.)
1992   *The Women's Bible Commentary* (Louisville: Westminster/John Knox
            Press).
O' Connor, K.M.
1992   'Jeremiah', in Newsom and Ringe (eds.) 1992: 169-77.
Sanderson, J.E.
1992a   'Amos', in Newsom and Ringe (eds.) 1992: 205-209.
1992b   'Micah', in Newsom and Ringe (eds.) 1992: 215-16.
1992c   'Nahum' in Newsom and Ringe (eds.) 1992: 217-21.
Setel, T.D.
1985   'Prophets and Pornography: Female Sexual Imagery in Hosea', in
            L.M. Russell (ed.), *Feminist Interpretation of the Bible* (Philadelphia:
            Westminster Press): 86-95.
Shields, M.E.
1995   'Circumcision of the Prostitute: Gender, Sexuality and the Call to
            Repentance in Jer. 3.1–4.4', *Biblical Interpretation* 3: 61-74.
forthcoming 'Ezekiel 16: Body Rhetoric and Gender', *Journal of Feminist Studies
            in Religion*.
Thistlethwaite, S.B.
1985   'Every Two Minutes: Battered Women and Feminist Interpretation', in
            L.M. Russell (ed.), *Feminist Interpretation of the Bible* (Philadelphia:
            Westminster Press): 96-107.
1993   ' "You May Enjoy the Spoil of Your Enemies": Rape as a Biblical
            Metaphor for War', *Semeia* 61: 59-75.
Watts, J.D.W.
1985   *Isaiah 1–33* (WBC, 24; Waco, TX: Word Books).
Weems, R.
1989   'Gomer: Victim of Violence or Victim of Metaphor?', *Semeia* 47: 87-
            104.
Yee, G.A.
1992   'Hosea', in Newsom and Ringe (eds.) 1992: 195-202.
Zimmerli, W.,
1979   *Ezekiel 1* (trans. R.E. Clements; Hermeneia; Philadelphia: Fortress
            Press).

SEX AND GENDER ETHICS AS NEW TESTAMENT SOCIAL ETHICS

Lisa Sowle Cahill

Introductory Overview

Flying, perhaps, against prevailing winds in biblical scholarship, I will adopt a forthrightly normative and theological approach to the relevance of the Bible to ethics. I also will assume—no less controversially—that there is a meaningful and theologically relevant connection between the life, teaching and deeds of Jesus and the interpretations of his religious significance as preserved in New Testament writings, and that those writings project a moral vision with some coherence.[1] I want to know how the New Testament recollections of Jesus, interpreted from a critical, feminist perspective, may shape moral values, principles, affections, and attitudes that guide actions and practices, including those of sex and gender.[2]

Although there is certainly pluralism in the New Testament memories of Jesus, there is considerable consistency in the moral ethos which emerges from Jesus' preaching of the kingdom or reign of God; and from his inclusive behavior, especially table fellowship and healing. This ethos is constituted by *compassion* for others, *active solidarity* in transcending social boundaries, and, especially by a bias toward *inclusion of*

---

1. Dale C. Allison, Jr, notes that 'we are almost instantly cynical of almost all significant continuity between Jesus and the early churches', but suggests that 'the Easter gulf is probably a modern mirage. Jesus made early Christianity into what it was just as much as, or more than, early Christianity made Jesus into what he was not' ('A Plea for Thoroughgoing Eschatology', *JBL* 113 [1994], p. 664).

2. The New Testament authors do not see ethics as an autonomous enterprise, but place it in the context of 'that style of relationship with God which Jesus initiated', a relationship both present in its qualitative newness and anticipatory in its expectation of a final divine realization and completion. The fundamental faith of the first Christians demands ever to be applied in a 'fresh setting' (J.L. Houlden, *Ethics and the New Testament* [New York: Oxford University Press, 1977], pp. 116-17).

the most marginal, *the 'outcasts'*.[3] Negative moral criticism in light of this ethos is directed primarily at those whose behavior (sexual, gender or race related, economic, or political) creates or underwrites exclusive status hierarchies.

I have found an important resource for Christian ethics in recent research into the social history of Palestine in Jesus' day, and of early Christianity. In interpreting the Bible for ethics, texts as literary units, the social settings assumed or projected by those texts, the layered construction and revision of biblical accounts in response to social factors, and the needs of the church today are all important pieces of the hermeneutical process.[4] In my view, no one is the supreme arbiter of biblical 'meaning'—each is a part of a cooperative process, and any one may rise to the surface in a move to criticize or enlarge some view currently afloat. Social history research is of special interest to ethics today, because it can help us move forward from the necessary acknowledgment that concrete behavioral models and prescriptions in the Bible may be morally repugnant today, toward a deeper, fuller and more positive appropriation of the moral aspects of New Testament discipleship.

Specifically, such research highlights the ways in which Jesus and the Gospels are responding to and challenging highly stratified social relationships. These relationships were governed by *economic relations* in which the poor were both dependent on the wealthy and often deprived of the basic necessities of subsistence; by a religious ideology which organized economic and social status around *purity laws*; and by a *patriarchal gender hierarchy* which intersected with these other two systems, making women subordinate at the top and the bottom of the economic, religious and social ladders. Of special relevance to developing Christian views of sex and gender was the centrality of the Greco-Roman family in defining one's economic, social and religious status.

Against the backgrounds of first-century Jewish Palestine and of first and second-century Greco-Roman culture, both the teaching of Jesus in

3. Obedience and Cross are biblical themes that are affirmed by some as central to Christian ethics, even more central than compassionate love of neighbor and enemy, as grounded in love of God. In my view, the way of the cross may be integrally related to and even required by compassionate action, but it is secondary rather than primary in defining the heart and inspiration of the Christian moral life.

4. For instance, Sandra M. Schneiders, IHM, sees the Bible as both the locus and mediator of revelatory encounters with God. These functions depend on the world behind the text, the world of the text, and the world before the text (appropriation) (*The Revelatory Text* [San Francisco: Harper Collins, 1992]).

his lifetime, and the subsequent formation of communities in the name of Jesus as the risen and exalted Christ, present a profound challenge to, if not an absolute reversal of, cultural boundaries of inclusion and exclusion, whether religious, social, economic, ethnic, sexual or gendered. The New Testament gauges all moral relations by their success in dislodging power elites and including 'the poor'. Specific New Testament instructions about sex and gender are, *generally speaking*, aimed to enhance compassionate and inclusive community over against entrenched definitions of status. Neither gender nor sexual status, especially one's place within or outside the patriarchal family, can be an axis for defining discipleship. Moreover, Christian community should make special efforts to include those excluded along these or other axes. While the New Testament certainly contains specific sexual and gender norms, these work, on the whole, to subvert social hierarchies.

Not all New Testament injunctions about sex and gender are equally successful in this aim, of course. Some specific instructions would not only have the opposite effect in other cultural contexts, but, at least to some extent, had such an effect in their own. Thus it is inappropriate to see the Bible as a source of distinct moral rules with simple authority for our own time or all times. It is probably more important to heed the fact that most or even all of the New Testament's negative criticism of sexual behavior is aimed at the 'righteous' power elites, rather than at the vulnerable and excluded 'sinners'. It is this function of New Testament moral teaching in context to which Christian ethics today should be analogous.

Building on the work of Mary Douglas and Peter Brown, I will argue that the New Testament proposes a discipline of the body that serves inclusive community. I see the New Testament as assuming human experiences of sex, gender, marriage, and family, and as presupposing that certain values in those realms are generally recognized (especially, permanent, monogamous, heterosexual marriage), rather than as addressing directly their content in any comprehensive, global or original manner. Rather, the 'message' of the New Testament on sex and gender is to place the relevant experiences and values within a transformed worldview and way of life, a life in which Christian community is continually being reconformed toward compassionate and practical identification with the other, and solidarity with those persons and classes of persons who have been pushed to the margins of human identity and relationship.

The argument of my paper will begin with the problem of unity and diversity in the New Testament. It will claim that a relatively unified foundation for Christian ethics can be located in Jesus' preaching of the kingdom or reign of God, as remembered by early Christians. Further, it will display the social effects of this preaching, in light of ancient economic assumptions, Jewish purity concerns and the Greco-Roman family, and propose that Christian ethics today should replicate the radical social challenge of early Christianity, if not necessarily its concrete moral practices.

Pluralism and Unity

One of the salutary results of historical criticism and literary analysis of the Bible has been the abolition of any simple notion that the New Testament—far less the New Testament and the Hebrew Scriptures together—exhibit a unity of religious symbolism and content which can easily ground systematic and coherent theological proposals with great specificity of content. Claiming that *'there was no single normative form of Christianity in the first century'*, James D.G. Dunn has asserted, not only that the lines between early Christianity and the Judaism out of which it arose were for some time blurred, but that 'the same faith in Jesus man and exalted one had to come to expression in words in a variety of different individuals and circumstances', provoking 'disagreement, dispute, and even some conflict'.[5] Nevertheless, even Dunn allows that the New Testament does have a unifying center in faith in 'Jesus-the-man-now exalted'. Jesus provides a paradigmatic relation to God, for in 'Jesus' life, death and life out of death we see the clearest and fullest embodiment of divine grace, of creative wisdom and power...'[6] In a more recent work, Dunn develops that paradigm in terms of a 'picture of discipleship' refracted through traditions probably

5. James D.G. Dunn, *Unity and Diversity in the New Testament: An Inquiry into the Character of Earliest Christianity* (Philadelphia: Westminster Press, 1977), pp. 372-73. To affirm the canon means to affirm diversity, according to Dunn, even to the extent of affirming '*whatever* form of Christianity can justifiably claim to be rooted in one of the strands that make up the New Testament' (p. 377). On Judaism and Christianity, see, more recently, Anthony J. Saldarini, *Matthew's Christian–Jewish Community* (Chicago: University of Chicago Press, 1994), pp. 18-26. 'False notions of a unitary and cohesive Christian development in the first two centuries and a strong concern to establish Christian identity have often lead to the assumption that a decisive break was made with Judaism in the 80s, or at least by the early second century (p. 20).'

6. Dunn, *Unity and Diversity*, p. 376.

going back to 'the earliest memories of what Jesus said and did'.[7] These traditions preserve a vigorous symbolism of the kingdom, or rule or reign of God; a dynamic exercise of power and authority that changes the reality in which human beings presently live.[8]

Kingdom or Reign of God

Certainly, the kingdom of God is presented as a central theme of the teaching of Jesus by New Testament authors, especially in the synoptic Gospels. As the earliest Gospel has it, '...Jesus came into Galilee, preaching the gospel of God, and saying, "The time is fulfilled, and the kingdom of God is at hand; repent, and believe in the gospel"' (Mk 1.14; cf. Lk. 8.1, 16.16; Mt. 5.23). The meaning and role of kingdom imagery for the historical Jesus is hardly non-controversial. It may receive a prominence in Mark's redaction of Jesus' teaching that it did not have in the original; and the eschatological and even apocalyptic expectations of Jesus have been a matter of debate since the rise of historical criticism in the eighteenth-century.[9] However, if the Gospels have any relation at all to the life of the historical Jesus, kingdom imagery was certainly one of the vehicles by which he advanced his experience of God and his vision of human relationships. The parables, so characteristic of his teaching, are primarily provocative communications of what the presence and reign of God are like (Lk. 8.9-15). The Lord's Prayer (Mt. 6.9-15; Lk. 11.2-4) is a prayer for the coming of the kingdom; and the Sermon on the Mount contains further explicit indications that the way of life it presents is to be associated with the kingdom of God (Mt. 5.3, 10, 19, 20; cf. Lk. 6.20).

Jesus was notorious in his own day for sharing table with tax collectors and other sinners (Lk. 7.34); his inclusive approach to women was also revolutionary for his time. The experience of God revealed in Jesus has as its social side an active and practical solidarity that breaks through stratifications and boundaries. It evokes an inclusive recognition of the 'other' in his or her humanity, across social lines. It also entails a willingness to forgive wrongs. The disciple thus acts as the Samaritan

---

7. James D.G. Dunn, *Jesus' Call to Discipleship* (Cambridge: Cambridge University Press, 1992), p. 3. The Easter faith centers precisely on the historical particularity of Jesus. 'In other words, the link between Jesus the proclaimer and Jesus the proclaimed, is Jesus proclaimed as the proclaimer' (*Unity and Diversity*, p. 208).

8. Dunn, *Unity and Diversity*, p. 10.

9. See Marcus J. Borg, *Jesus in Contemporary Scholarship* (Valley Forge, PA: Trinity Press International, 1994), especially chs. 3 and 4.

who rescues his traditional enemy from an abandoned death (Lk. 10.29-37). In the parable of the last judgment, giving food and drink to 'one of the least of these my brethren' is the criterion for inheritance of the kingdom (Mt. 25.31-46). The same point is illustrated by the parable of Lazarus and the rich man (Lk. 16.19-21), and by Jesus' instruction to hosts to prefer as banquet guests 'the poor, the maimed, the lame, the blind' over friends, kinsmen and rich neighbors (Luke 14.13).[10]

In *In Memory of Her*, Elisabeth Schüssler Fiorenza states that the Jesus movement 'had experienced in the praxis of Jesus' a God who called not Israel's righteous, but its 'social underdogs'. In Jesus' ministry, God is experienced as 'all-inclusive love', a God who especially accepts 'the impoverished, the crippled, the outcast, the sinners and prostitutes, as long as they are prepared to engage in the perspective and power of the *basileia*'.[11] Schüssler Fiorenza associates this experience of God with the image of *Sophia* in Jewish wisdom theology, as developed in Egypt, permeating apocalyptic literature and appearing in Qumran texts. 'Wisdom' is a feminine noun in both Hebrew and Greek. The tradition which personifies Wisdom as *Sophia* places God's goodness in a feminine *'Gestalt'*.[12] It appears in a saying of Luke which Schüssler Fiorenza identifies as 'very old'—'"Sophia is justified [or vindicated] by all her children" (Lk. 7.35[Q])'—and which Schüssler Fiorenza speculates may have had its setting in Jesus' table fellowship with tax collectors, prostitutes and sinners. According to her, Matthew identifies *Sophia* with Jesus, so that it becomes Jesus as *Sophia* who is justified by 'her' deeds.[13] In summary, the 'Sophia-God of Jesus' calls disciples to

10. Dunn remarks that 'it is not so much the *demanding* character of servant-love which Jesus emphasizes, as its *readiness for unconventional expression*, its willingness to reach across social boundaries...' (*Jesus' Call*, p. 89).

11. Elisabeth Schüssler Fiorenza, *In Memory of Her: A Feminist Theological Reconstruction of Christian Origins* (New York: Crossroad, 1983), p. 130. 'This inclusive graciousness and goodness of God is spelled out again and again in the parables' (p. 131).

12. *In Memory of Her*, p. 132. For a full development of the line of interpretation proposed in the 1983 book, see also, Elisabeth Schüssler Fiorenza, *Jesus: Miriam's Child, Sophia's Prophet* (New York: Crossroad, 1994).

13. *In Memory of Her*, p. 132. On Matthew, Schüssler Fiorenza cites M.J. Suggs, *Wisdom, Christology and Law in Matthew's Gospel* (Cambridge, MA: Harvard University Press, 1970), pp. 31-62. Ses Mt. 11.18-19 for the parallel to Lk. 7.33-35. Ses also Lk. 11.49-50 // Mt. 23.34-35, and Borg's comparison of these texts in *Meeting Jesus Again for the First Time: The Historical Jesus and the Heart of*

inclusive community, to a 'discipleship of equals' based in an 'alternative ethos' in which the despised are included equally with the righteous.[14]

As confirmed by other scholars, Jesus may be portrayed as wisdom teacher in view of the fact that he subverted conventional expectations. Cultural wisdoms invariably confirm the centrality of rewards and punishments for one's way of life, the social importance of hierarchies and boundaries, and the role of God as lawgiver, judge and enforcer.[15] Jesus, however, undermined conventions about religious righteousness, purity, honor, wealth and the patriarchal family, and made possible an alternative mode of transformed life in relation to God and to other persons.[16]

Jesus' words and actions, and especially the presence of the Spirit of the risen and exalted Lord in the community of faith, make present and accessible an existence in relation to God which consists of a reversal of conventional values, hierarchies and expectations. Disciples are those who can and do imitate the mercy, forgiveness and compassion of God, and whose actions have social consequences.[17] In Borg's words, 'the

Contemporary Faith (San Francisco: Harper & Row, 1994), p. 114, nn. 24, 25. Borg agrees that Matthew identifies *Sophia* with Jesus, as does Anthony Saldarini (*Matthew's Christian–Jewish Community*, pp. 183-84). However, as Saldarini points out, Matthew himself does not emphasize the identification of Jesus and wisdom; Matthew's point may be more to reject 'wisdom' as it was conventionally understood in the context of his community.

14. Schüssler Fiorenza, *In Memory of Her*, pp. 135-36.

15. Borg, *Jesus in Contemporary Scholarship*, pp. 149-50. Borg explicitly credits Schüssler Fiorenza, as well as Elizabeth Johnson, *She Who Is: The Mystery of God in Feminist Discourse* (New York: Crossroad, 1992), pp. 86-93, pp. 156-58. See, for instance, Borg's *Jesus Again*, p. 113, n. 23, and p. 114, n. 26.

16. 'He subverted conventional wisdom's image of God as a lawgiver and judge and regularly spoke of God as gracious and generous, as the intimate *Abba* and as womb-like compassion'. Both his message and behavior proclaimed that God does not observe the standards and boundaries of conventional wisdom' (Borg, *Jesus Again*, p. 151). See, as well, *Jesus Again*, chs. 4 and 5. On compassion in Hebrew tradition as 'womb-like', see *Jesus Again*, pp. 47-49. Borg's interpretation of the transformed life indicated by Jesus' alternative wisdom tends to reflect a Lutheran concern with freedom from God as lawgiver and from the requirements of the law, contrasted with a transformed life in which rewards and punishments are set aside. (Borg, now a member of the United Church of Christ, tells of his youth in a Scandinavian Lutheran family in North Dakota, and his years at a midwestern Lutheran college [*Jesus Again*, pp. 3-8].) See, for example, *Jesus Again*, p. 85.

17. According to Wolfgang Schrage, discipleship is 'adherence to Jesus based on the presence of the kingdom of God', and 'it takes precedence over all other earthly ties, traditions, and authorities' (Schrage, *The Ethics of the New Testament* [trans.

Jesus movement was a community of compassion, and to take Jesus seriously means to become part of such a community', in which compassion shatters all boundaries.[18] The Cross may be the inevitable consequence of such a life, but the Cross is in itself neither the primary content nor the objective of Christian discipleship.

The Jewish background[19] of Jesus' kingdom preaching makes it likely that he expected its future, eschatological, and even its apocalyptic completion.[20] Moreover, into the middle of the first century, most of those who believed in Jesus were still Jews. Matthew's gospel emerged from a reform movement in Judaism, and even in the fourth century, there were still law-observing Jews who affirmed a high Christology.[21] Thus, it is more than reasonable to conclude that Jewish apocalyptic expectation influenced not only the mentality of Jesus and the way his own preaching was heard, but also the interpretation of his teaching by communities after his death.

But the likelihood that the symbol kingdom of God had eschatological and even apocalyptic overtones in its first-century usages need not diminish the fact that it was also and simultaneously seen to have a present impact 'in the midst' of Jesus' hearers (Lk. 17.21). Jesus did not simply speak of the future kingdom, 'he also acted—indeed, acted out', and on at least some occasions explained, striking actions such as exorcisms 'in terms of the Kingdom of God having already come to his audience' (Lk. 11.20: 'If by the finger of God I cast out demons, the kingdom of God has come upon you)'.[22] In contrast to much Jewish apocalyptic thinking, Jesus 'does not envisage a "gap" between his ministry and the manifestation of God's rule (e.g. Mk 9.1; Lk. 10.18)'.[23]

David E. Green; Philadelphia: Fortress Press, 1988], p. 48).

18. Borg, *Jesus in Contemporary Scholarship*, p. 154. On the centrality of compassion for an ethics based on the New Testament, see also John Donahue, *The Gospel in Parable* (Philadelphia: Fortress Press, 1988), p. 134; and Charles M. Shelton, *Morality of the Heart: A Psychology for the Christian Moral Life* (New York: Crossroad, 1990).

19. On this see E.P. Sanders, *Jesus and Judaism* (Philadelphia: Fortress Press, 1985).

20. John P. Meier, *A Marginal Jew: Rethinking the Historical Jesus*. II. *Mentor, Message, and Miracle* (New York: Doubleday, 1994), pp. 350, 452.

21. Saldarini, *Matthew's Christian–Jewish Community*, pp. 194, 25, 21.

22. Meier, *Mentor, Message*, p. 452.

23. Pheme Perkins, 'Ethics, New Testament', in the *Anchor Bible Dictionary* (New York: Doubleday, 1992).

The kingdom is a present reality, made concrete in the ministry of Jesus himself. The disciples are expected to live as ones who experience God's reign, characterized by mercy and forgiveness, extended in the ministry of Jesus and their own to the oppressed and excluded. In his disruption of moral and social 'business as usual', Jesus does not so much emphasize a future act of God or the end of the world, but the present power of God, which also empowers disciples. Life in the kingdom is 'a way of being created by the kingship of God', which extends from the beginning of time into the present and expects completion in the end of time.[24]

Borg, Schüssler Fiorenza, and Dunn, like most other theological interpreters of the New Testament, see the early Christian portraits of Jesus and his significance (as 'the Christ') as being at some important level continuous with what Borg calls 'the pre-Easter Jesus'; that is, with the historical Jesus and his first followers (Schüssler Fiorenza's 'discipleship of equals').[25] The New Testament writings are the cumulative faith statements of early Christian communities that recall a memory of the historical person, life and impact of Jesus, now reinterpreted through those communities' experience of Jesus' exaltation by God, and as now present to them in Spirit. Hence, greater awareness of the social setting in which Jesus taught, and in which the first Christian communities formed, can highlight these themes, deepen our appreciation of their significance and direct us to forms of communal formation which would, in fact, be analogous today.[26]

24. Borg, *Jesus in Contemporary Scholarship*, p. 57.

25. Borg even goes so far as to say that the New Testament's portrayal of a compassionate God is rooted not only in the historical Jesus' speech about God as compassionate, but in 'Jesus' own experience of God' and of 'the Spirit' (Borg, *Jesus in Contemporary Scholarship*, p. 61).

26. The original nineteenth-century 'quest for the historical Jesus' was motivated by the same confidence in the modern scientific model of knowledge which pervaded many other disciplines, including philosophy and the social sciences. According to this model, 'real' knowledge is backed either by empirical investigation and 'data' or strictly logical deduction from self-evident or empirically established first principles. The historical critical method aimed to set out clear and definite criteria for knowledge, and to arrive at certain, demonstrable results, however minimal they might be. Whatever could not be affirmed by such methods was not reliable 'knowledge'. In the US, the recent efforts of the Jesus Seminar (founded in 1985 by Robert Funk, a past director of the Society of Biblical Literature) to categorize all New Testament sayings of Jesus as authentic or not—in color-coding from red through pink and gray to black—provides a current confirmation of the lasting hold of this 'scientific' model of certainty. For some theologians and believers, the scientific paradigm of

Economy

Many social historians of early Christianity draw on the proposal of Moses I. Finley[27] that ancient Palestine was like other ancient cultures in exhibiting an 'embedded economy'—that is, one in which the economy was not a separate sector or institution (as in modern cultures). Economic relationships were dependent upon and intertwined with religious, political and cultural ones. Social goods, whether material or

epistemological certainty has demanded the conclusion that Christian faith has rested historically on practically no 'evidence', and should be abandoned. But others, following Rudolph Bultmann, have rested Christianity on unabashedly 'unscientific' grounds, completely detaching the 'Christ of faith' from any empirically verifiable reality of Jesus and even from any necessity to suppose his historical existence two millenia ago. (Philosophical counterparts may be found in Kantian rationalism, intuitionism, emotivism and existentialism.)

Critics who employ 'scientific' historical criteria, some of whom are even motivated by deconstructionist aims similar to those of postmodern philosophy, can cling paradoxically to the idea that their tools can be employed objectively and can guarantee results uninfluenced by their own expectations. John Meier, for instance, introducing his otherwise very balanced investigation of Jesus' historically conditioned use of the symbol, kingdom of God, warns that modern concerns about consistency and non-contradiction 'must not be allowed to interfere with our weighing of the evidence' (*Mentor, Message*, p. 399).

The use of social history to expand our understanding of Jesus and the early Christians represents a new development out of historical criticism, insofar as the former is a 'softer' and more inferential approach to claims about the experiences of Jesus and the New Testament communities. Social history approaches New Testament writings as 'persuasive communications' which reflect new ideals and experiences of community. They are 'specifically designed to move targeted audiences to concerted social action'; action in an environment 'determined by an interlocking network of ecological, economic, social and cultural conditions' (John H. Elliott, *What Is Social Scientific Criticism?* [Minneapolis: Fortress Press, 1993], p. 101). Interpreters using social history are neither so absolutist nor so iconoclastic in their claims as were the first 'questers'. Approaches to early Christianity through the tools of social science and social history can admit the future revisability of present hypotheses, and need not claim to have discovered any 'unique' knowledge of Jesus not available through the New Testament texts themselves. Social history loosens the grip modern scientific rationality gained on the New Testament via the implementation of the methods of earlier historical critics; it also permits us to discern better some of the revolutionary effects of early Christianity on sex, gender and other social practices, but does not require us to deny that some specific New Testament prescriptions ratified, rather than challenged, hierarchies.

27. Moses I. Finley, *The Ancient Economy* (Berkeley: University of California Press, 1973).

non-material, were perceived to be limited, so that one person could gain only at another's loss. Access, even to the basic necessities of life, was determined for most people by their relation to the power elites whose clients they were or hoped to become. Patron–client relations were characterized by high degrees of hierarchy and asymmetry of power, which resulted in proportionately high levels of anxiety, envy, subservience and competition. Both purity and family become relevant here, insofar as purity was a way of defining status relationships—that is, of distinguishing the elite from the non-elite—and family identity and loyalty became a way of pooling resources, both material and political, and of enhancing access to scarce resources.

Several New Testament scholars employ this understanding of the social world of Jesus to highlight and expand upon the meaning of inclusiveness and compassion in his preaching of the kingdom of God.[28] For instance, Richard Horsley claims that 'kingdom of God' functioned as a symbol for communities of the Jesus movement which renewed the social order by forming new 'families' that were non-patriarchal, yet 'tight-knit and disciplined'. These communities fostered concrete cooperation and care among households by means of reciprocal generosity.

Similarly to Borg, Ched Myers uses the Gospel of Mark to suggest that Jesus sponsors alternative and subversive revolutionary communities that oppose the dominant ideologies maintained by violence, and establish a new political and economic order. Halvor Moxnes works with Luke to argue that Jesus conflicted with Jewish community leaders, exemplified by the Pharisees, on matters of community boundaries, status relationships and control over resources. 'Luke's Gospel represents a

---

28. In addition to Borg's *Jesus in Contemporary Scholarship* and *Jesus Again*, and Dunn's *Jesus' Call*, see, for instance, Halvor Moxnes, *The Economy of the Kingdom: Social Conflict and Economic Relations in Luke's Gospel* (Philadelphia: Fortress Press Press, 1988), pp. 28-30. On this theme, as well as those of reciprocity and redistribution, also note Richard A. Horsley, *Jesus and the Spiral of Violence: Popular Resistance in Roman Palestine* (San Francisco: Harper & Row, 1987), pp. 152-53; *idem*, *The Liberation of Christmas: The Infancy Narratives in Social Context* (New York: Crossroad, 1989), pp. 68-70; *idem*, *Sociology and the Jesus Movement* (New York: Crossroad, 1989), pp. 88-92; Ched Myers, *Binding the Strong Man: A Political Reading of Mark's Story of Jesus* (Maryknoll, NY: Orbis Books, 1988), pp. 47-53; Michael H. Crosby, *House of Disciples: Church, Economics, and Justice in Matthew* (Maryknoll, NY: Orbis Books, 1988), pp. 102-104; and John Dominic Crossan, *Jesus: A Revolutionary Biography* (San Francisco: Harper & Row, 1994), pp. 95-101.

protest against the abuse of the needy by the rich.'[29] A redistribution of goods to the needy (from the elite to the non-elite, whether urban or rural) is the practical implication of the 'reversal' the kingdom represents, expressed as giving without expectation of return.[30] Although it is doubtful that full communism of property ever completely abolished the existence of wealth among the early Christians, or even among Jesus' own disciples, it is certainly true that his teaching was profoundly subversive of customs and expectations that favored the traditional beneficiaries of the economic order.

Purity

Purity systems are related to economic ones, insofar as purity laws can reinforce distinctions between elite and non-elite; between those who do and do not have control of all kinds of social resources. Purity societies are organized around polarized categories of pure and impure, clean and unclean, applied both to persons and to social groups. The categories are the central way of structuring the social world. Purity and impurity may result from birth (caste), behavior, social position (including occupation) and physical condition (wholeness and health or disfigurement and disease, as well as sexual and reproductive functions). Gradations of purity establish sharp social boundaries, from the most pure, to those who are temporarily impure, to the socially marginal, to the outcast.[31] Purity laws typically tend to identify women more closely with impure states than men, stigmatizing as impure both sexual contact with women (for men), and, for women, menstruation and childbirth.

Purity laws found in ancient Judaism were developed and systematized during the exile, a time in which a displaced people needed to reestablish its distinctive identity before God, and over against the foreign cultures and cults with whom Israel was forced to dwell geographically.[32] Purity thus took momentum as a form of communal resistance to domination, although it eventually could be manipulated by the elites within the community to maintain their own position. First-century Jewish Palestine was a purity society centered around the temple and a

29. Horsely, *Liberation of Christmas*, pp. 92, 122-23, 125.

30. Moxnes, *Economy of the Kingdom*, p. 94.

31. Moxnes, *Economy of the Kingdom*, p. 156.

32. Borg, *Jesus in Contemporary Scholarship*, p. 108. See also Marcus J. Borg, *Conflict, Holiness and Politics in the Teachings of Jesus* (Lewiston, NY: Edwin Mellen, 1984).

particular interpretation of the Torah elaborated by the scribes—a 'retainer class' attached to the priesthood. According to their interpretation, holiness in God's eyes meant separation from everything that was unclean, as spelled out on the basis of Leviticus.[33] As in other cultures, Jewish purity has to do with controlling the body, especially what passes in and out of its orifices. These represent the 'entrances and exits of society'. Anthropologist Mary Douglas summarizes the 'purity rule' as prescribing that 'the more the social situation exerts pressure on persons involved in it, the more the social demand for conformity tends to be expressed by a demand for physical control'.[34] The intake of food and the emission of bodily fluids, especially those relating to waste products and sex, are key axes of purity status.

In Judaism, both ancient and modern, purity laws may be understood as a way of sanctifying ordinary life, of reminding the observant that every moment of the day is dedicated to God. Humanity may be sanctified through the most quotidian activities—those which are continuously renewed and repeated, and those most fundamental to the life process: nourishment, cleanliness, dressing, sex, giving birth and encountering death.[35] In addition, each of these activities, as ritualized, sustains a symbolic connection of everyday life with the sovereignty and providence of God, and places humanity against the entire creation and its divine source. 'Hence, when Israelites seek out and eat proper meat, they reinforce, emphasize and perhaps consciously recall the supremacy

33. Daniel L. Smith-Christopher, *Religion of the Landless: The Social Context of the Babylonian Exile* (New York: Meyer Stone Books, 1989).

34. Borg, *Jesus in Contemporary Scholarship*, p. 109. See also Jerome Neyrey, 'The Symbolic Universe of Luke–Acts: "They Turn the World Upside Down"', in *idem* (ed.), *The Social World of Luke–Acts* (Peabody, MA: Hendrickson, 1991), pp. 271-304; and L.W. Countryman, *Dirt, Greed, and Sex: Sexual Ethics in the New Testament and their Implications for Today* (Philadelphia: Fortress Press, 1988), pp. 45-65.

35. Mary Douglas, *Natural Symbols: Explorations in Cosmology* (London: Barrie and Jenkins, rev. edn, 1973 [1971]), p. 12. This is essentially Douglas's correlation between 'high group' and 'high grid'. However, even if it is not the case that groups with a strong sense of communal identity always express that strength through a highly demarcated and stratified social system, Douglas's point is well-taken—that is, that physical control always expresses a sense of group identity. Conversely, group identity will be expressed by means of physical behavior, even if that behavior is not necessarily symbolic of hierarchies within the group.

of God as well as their distinction from other nations.'[36]

Yet, at the same time, purity laws tend to serve as sustaining ideology for elites who get to define who and what counts as impure, who is thereby of lesser status, and who consequently lacks control over material and political goods. In ancient Palestine, the purity system not only upheld a positive ideal of holiness in community, but also in practice augmented the status of the high priestly families, even if the majority of priests were not rich.[37] The agricultural products of the peasants were taxed in order to support the temple and the temple elites. Pharisees, scribes and lawyers would have been invested in the social effects of the purity system by virtue of their dependency on the higher aristocracy.[38] Not all Jewish priests belonged to the wealthy, landowning classes; and purity laws did not affect all other Jews equally, since observance was tied primarily to Jerusalem and to participation in the temple cult. The ordinary Jew, peasant or urban dweller, was not expected to observe all rituals daily, and the importance of purity diminished outside of Jerusalem (e.g. in Galilee). Thus, it would be wrong to see Jewish peasants as universally oppressed by purity expectations or members of the priestly class as universally their economic beneficiaries. However, to the extent that economic and social differences did exist between priests and peasants, purity laws could reinforce them.

John Dominic Crossan spotlights Jesus' practices of table fellowship ('open commensality') and free healing as repudiations of the class-oriented aspects of the purity system of his culture. This does not, of course, mean that, as a Jew, Jesus rejected all observance of purity laws as a form of traditional holiness. Moreover, later controversies over Pharisaic attempts to extend purity observance into daily life are no doubt projected back by Gospel authors into their accounts of Jesus' own lifetime. Nevertheless, it seems clear that Jesus did engage in practices which upset some of the social expectations that had in his own day been

---

36. Jacob Neusner, *Purity in Rabbinic Judaism: A Systematic Account, The Sources, Media, Effects, and Removal of Uncleanness* (Atlanta: Scholars Press, 1994), pp. 48-49; Saldarini, *Matthew's Christian–Jewish Community*, p. 135; Judith Plaskow, 'Embodiment and Ambivalence: A Jewish Feminist Perspective', in Lisa Sowle Cahill and Margaret Farley (eds.), *Embodiment, Medicine, and Morality* (New York: Kluwer Publishers, 1995).

37. David P. Wright, 'Unclean and Clean', *ABD*, VI, p. 740.

38. Martin Goodman, *The Ruling Class of Judaea: The Origins of the Jewish Revolt against Rome AD 66–70* (Cambridge: Cambridge University Press, 1987), p. 119.

created by purity, and did so through iconoclastic behavior in precisely those areas of life that fell most firmly under purity laws (eating, disease, men's association with women and sabbath observance). Anthropologically, according to Crossan, meals and eating represent the rules of association and socialization. Table fellowship is 'a map of economic discrimination, social hierarchy, and political differentiation'.[39] Jesus ate with social outcasts, and through the parable of the wedding guests (Lk. 14.15-24; Mt. 22.1-13), commends to his listeners the inclusion at table of the good and the bad, the 'poor and maimed and blind and lame' (Lk. 14.21). This parable is dangerous because it replaces the social map of the purity system with a radical eclecticism and abandons the 'appropriate' social distinctions. The practice the parable reflects is coherent with Jesus' reputation for sharing meals not only with tax collectors, but also with sinners and whores (women outside the male control system)—the latter being standard terms of derogation for groups with whom the elites found open and free association intolerable.[40]

Similarly, Crossan portrays Jesus' healing miracles as changes that are clearly in the social world as well as the physical one of health and disease. Insofar as the individual's body, like commensality, represents the organization of the body politic, disease means ritual uncleanness and social ostracism. In his healings and exorcisms, Jesus restores the outcasts of society to social place. He challenges both the boundaries of the community and the authority of the priestly gate-keepers.[41] A striking example is Jesus' healing of the woman who had had a 'flow of blood' for twelve years (Mk 5.25-34). If the hemorrhage involved blood from her womb, she would have been, on that account alone, ritually impure, thus compounding by gender the stigmatization of physical illness.

In *Dirt, Greed, and Sex*, William Countryman describes the immense impact that purity and property concerns had on the sexual practices of the world in which Christianity arose. Granting the function of purity laws in maintaining Jewish identity, he nonetheless interprets the effect of both physical purity and property concerns on sexual morality in negative terms, reads in the New Testament a break with Judaism (at least on the former issue) and sees movement away from purity and property as a Christian moral *desideratum*. Although Countryman believes that even in the New Testament (Paul), sexuality remains

39. Borg, *Jesus*, pp. 109-110.
40. Crossan, *Jesus*, p. 68.
41. Crossan, *Jesus*, p. 69.

governed by the assumption that some people are the sexual property of others,[42] he claims that the New Testament writers were 'ethically indifferent' to what both the Jewish holiness code and later Christians viewed as 'dirty' sexual behavior.[43] Countryman maintains that Christians today must give up both these systems in favor of full adherence to the 'purity of heart' espoused by Jesus and Paul. According to Countryman, the key to Jesus' sexual ethics is intention.[44]

The corollary of this claim seems to be that all sexual norms beyond consent and equality are the illegitimate residue of a purity mentality. For instance, 'Any claim that a given sexual act is wrong in and of itself will be found ultimately to represent either a lack of ethical analysis or a hidden purity claim'.[45] And,

> the gospel allows no rule against the following, in and of themselves: masturbation, nonvaginal heterosexual intercourse, bestiality, polygamy, homosexual acts, or erotic art and literature. The Christian is free to be repelled by any or all of these and may continue to practice her or his own purity code in relation to them. What we are not free to do is impose our codes on others.[46]

While Crossan, Borg, Countryman and others are undoubtedly right to argue that Jesus rejected control of the body, especially the sexually differentiated body, as a means of defining social in- and out-groups, I do not want to move too quickly to the conclusion that control of the sexual body, even a highly socialized and communitarian control of the

42. Crossan, *Jesus*, p. 82.

43. Countryman, *Dirt, Greed, and Sex*, pp. 167, 219.

44. Countryman, *Dirt, Greed, and Sex*, p. 142. As discussed above, not all Christian interpreters would endorse the idea of an abrupt rupture between Judaism and early Christianity, or see residual Jewish influence in wholly negative terms. Although Mark's community challenged the validity of purity laws (Mk 7.1-23), Matthew's sees Jesus as fulfilling them, though they remain in a subordinate relation to the commandments. See Saldarini, *Matthew's Christian–Jewish Community*, pp. 19, 134, 162. The function of purity laws in demarcating class is particularly emphasized by those interpreting Mark: J. Neyrey, 'The Idea of Purity in Mark's Gospel', *Semeia* 35 (1986), pp. 91-127; Myers, *Binding the Strong Man*, pp. 69-80, 152-54; Fernanco Belo, *A Materialist Reading of the Gospel of Mark* (Maryknoll, NY: Orbis Books, 1981).

45. Countryman, *Dirt, Greed, and Sex*, p. 177. Countryman retains the language of property, but sees each individual as owning her or his own sexual property. He describes Jesus as seeing 'sexual access' as a 'fundamental good', and 'an important possession', of which his followers are forbidden to 'rob others' (p. 189).

46. Countryman, *Dirt, Greed, and Sex*, p. 241.

body, is inimical to the spirit of New Testament ethics. I do not concur that high social expectation of bodily control necessarily belies a repressive society; that control need be equated with the constraint of the oppressed by the oppressors; that control of sex need represent a patriarchal order; nor that liberal, democratic and more gender-equal modern societies do not control bodies. The question is not how the New Testament ethos helps us overturn bodily control (vis-à-vis sex and gender), but how it 'resocializes'[47] Christians into practices of bodily control that are self-appropriated and represent solidarity rather than hierarchy in community. This question can be pursued, if not fully answered, with the help of Mary Douglas's *Natural Symbols* and Peter Brown's *Body and Society*.

Although Douglas tends to concentrate her discussions of bodily control in society on those systems that have both high levels of classification ('grid') and strong pressure to conform ('group'), she does not in principle limit the phenomenon of control to such societies. Indeed, control of the body as a representation of social relationships seems endemic to the human condition and to the sociality of all human persons as embodied. Every culture is shaped by the human 'drive to achieve consonance between social and physical and emotional experience', which is expressed through the body as a natural symbol of the social order.[48] As is evident in her description of the 'smooth' behavior of socially conformist stockbrokers, accountants and lawyers, in contrast to the 'shaggy' styles of artists and academics who fancy themselves social critics, even what Douglas refers to as 'bodily abandon' can be, in its own way, highly structured and pressured to great social conformity.[49] Certainly, controlled and formal behavior will be highly valued in societies highly structured around social roles; but freedom of physical movement and expression—the individual's 'control' over his or her own body—can be in an equally tight symbolic correspondence to a set of social expectations about individualism, autonomy and the contractual nature of personal relationships.[50]

---

47. Countryman, *Dirt, Greed, and Sex*, pp. 243-44.

48. Wayne A. Meeks, *The Moral World of the First Christians* (Philadelphia: Westminster Press, 1986), p. 126.

49. Douglas, *Natural Symbols*, p. 98; see also p. 93. See also Mary Douglas, *Purity and Danger: An Analysis of Concepts of Pollution and Taboo* (London: Routledge and Kegan Paul, 1966), p. 115.

50. *Natural Symbols*, p. 102.

A further important point suggested by Douglas's fundamental view of the body in relation to society is that bodily symbolization—finding an 'appropriate bodily style' for social experience—need not be seen in negative, restrictive terms. The moral and social challenge for the first Christians was to find a set of social strategies—which implies a corresponding set of bodily strategies—for challenging the regnant ethos and installing, indeed 'embodying', a new one. As Crossan illustrates, Jesus began to do just this with his practices of open commensality and healing. These affected all kinds of social boundaries, including gender. On sex and gender in particular, the fact that one system of bodily control is being overthrown does not entail that the social meaning of the sexual body becomes simply indeterminate, or to be determined only on the basis of individual choice or contracts between individuals. Peter Brown shows how the sexual practices of the early Christians, especially their elevation of permanent virginity, were socially cultivated and personally appropriated forms of bodily discipline which, in effect, resisted a hierarchical and patriarchal ethos, centered in Greco-Roman culture on the family rather than on religious authorities.

Family
As one historian of ancient Greece states it, 'Greek society was (and is) patriarchal: the master of the *oikos* was the head of the family, its *kyrios*, as its governor, governing the slaves as master, the children as a sort of king because of their affection for him and his greater age, his wife like a political leader...the husband is always the head of the family'.[51]

Greek culture was a culture of honor and shame, focused on women's sexuality, which was fiercely controlled by men. This led to a strict separation of men's and women's spheres, and the sequestration of women within the home.[52] Citizen women (in contrast to slaves and free foreigners) were married in their early teens to men who could be many years their senior. The primary duty of women was to bear children, especially sons.

51. On this point, see also Charles Taylor's *The Ethics of Authenticity* (Cambridge, MA: Harvard University Press, 1991), where he reveals the modern ideal of individuality and 'authenticity' to a freely chosen life-plan to be not so non-conformist. It is a reflection of a strong social ethos, bearing the effects of Romanticism, existentialism and the privatization of any rationality that is not 'scientific'.

52. W.K. Lacey, *The Family in Classical Greece* (Ithaca, NY: Cornell University Press, 1968), p. 21.

As to the celebrated homosexuality and bisexuality of ancient Greece, it can hardly be said to represent thorough release of social control. The stages of male sexuality were strictly prescribed, and not much dependent on individual proclivities. 'The Greek man had to go through his homosexual experiences at the right moment, with the right people and according to the right rules.'[53] Youths who were receptive to the advances of adult lovers were expected at maturity to assume the active sexual role in relationships with women and with younger boys.

Roman law, which influenced Greek culture during the period of early Christianity, had given citizen women increasing legal rights. But women were still married young to older men, women's education was limited and they were raised primarily to be intelligent companions for their husbands and managers of their households. By the middle of the second century CE, women remained in the legal power of their fathers at marriage, rather than passing to that of their husbands. This meant that women could inherit property. Either party could dissolve a marriage, though this meant in practice that women could be divorced under pressure from natal families (fathers, brothers, uncles) who wanted to use their women in the formation of more advantageous alliances through marriage.

Under the Roman Empire, the state took an immense interest in procreation within the patriarchal family, encouraging and even mandating it for the social good. The state regulated marriage, divorce and inheritance, and gave ultimate control to fathers and husbands, who, at least in theory, had almost unlimited legal power over children. Yet the ideal was a companionate marriage, despite the facts that men were more educated, women were subordinate, male sexual infidelity was socially tolerated and divorce was frequent, at least among the upper classes.

High rates of divorce and remarriage were, not surprisingly, linked to a lack of emotional investment in marriage and even in the relationship to one's children. Even moderately well-off families used wet nurses, and in the event of divorce fathers retained custody of children. Keith R. Bradley observes that

> any attempt to characterize the upper-class Roman family must proceed
> from the perception that marriage for the Roman elite was not a
> permanently binding institution, and that as a result the families brought
> into existence by the procreation of children after marriage were subject to

53. David Cohen, *Law, Sexuality, and Society: The Enforcement of Morals in Classical Athens* (Cambridge: Cambridge University Press, 1991), pp. 140-41, 149.

a high level of impermanence and flexibility as the parents of children sequentially, and in some instances cavalierly, changed spousal partners and established new households.[54]

In 18 BCE and 9 CE, the Emperor Augustus passed two pieces of legislation which enforced penalties against celibacy, childlessness and adultery, while promising rewards to Roman citizens who propagated children in marriage. Augustus feared that a decline in fertility among the ruling classes, who wanted to conserve property against distribution among excessive numbers of children, would threaten the very existence of the elite, and disrupt the empire's social, civic and political structures. The survival of the governing classes was to be ensured by firm norms controlling the selection of an appropriate wife, the order of the household, and even the conduct of sexual relations in marriage. These norms were focused precisely upon the bodies of the elite.

In this context, Christianity's aversion to divorce (Mk 10.11-12; Mt. 5.31-32; 19.9; Lk. 16.18; 1 Cor. 7.10-11), lack of emphasis on procreation, warnings against family loyalties (Mk 3.31; Lk. 19.29; cf. 8.21), even qualified advocacy of equality in marriage (1 Cor. 7.2-5; and even Eph. 5.28-33), identification of female worth in roles outside household duties (Mary and Martha in Lk. 10.38-42), and above all its idealization of celibacy (1 Cor. 7.8 and 25-40), were dangerously countercultural. Both Schüssler Fiorenza and Borg suggest that Jesus' command to call no one 'father' but God (Mt. 23.9) displaces the lordship of any earthly father.[55] In the sexual as well as other areas, it is the powerful and prosperous who are most often (or even exclusively) the targets of moral criticism or condemnation. In fact, given the relatively low frequency with which sexual concerns emerge at all in the New Testament, one might even surmise that they arise virtually *only* when an issue of social exclusion or equality is at stake.

The divorce sayings are directed more against the actions of men than of women; and Jesus does not elaborate on the inviolability of marital fidelity when face to face with the Samaritan woman who had had five husbands (John 4.18). Paul's qualification of Jesus' divorce prohibition is designed to achieve 'peace' in the faith community (1 Cor. 7.15), and the woman caught in adultery is rescued and forgiven by Jesus (John 8).

54. Eva Cantarella, *Bisexuality in the Ancient World* (New Haven: Yale University Press, 1992), p. 213.

55. Keith R. Bradley, *Discovering the Roman Family: Studies in Roman Social History* (Oxford: Oxford University Press, 1991), pp. 190-91.

The homosexuality condemned (1 Cor. 6.9; 1 Tim. 1.10; Rom. 1.26-27) represented in its cultural setting an exploitative relationship, and particularly the contemptible habits of the dominant pagan culture.[56] It also flowed from misogynist attitudes as they had been institutionalized in the Greek family. Paul is shocked that Christian men would join prostitutes sexually to the body of Christ, but does not elaborate on the sinfulness of the women themselves (1 Cor. 6.15-16). And the incestuous man of 1 Corinthians 5 is excluded in the interests of community welfare, especially solidarity in Christ. It is conceivable here that Paul is reacting against status differences in the community, by which some were willing to tolerate behavior from an upper-class or prestigious convert that would have been unacceptable for the ordinary member. The fact that some had 'pride' (1 Cor. 5.2) and were 'boasting' (v. 6) about this man, who was living with his stepmother, may indicate that some believed that he deserved special treatment. Since Augustan laws required the widowed to remarry and decimated the inheritance of a childless widow, it is not incredible by cultural standards to think that a woman might be remarried to her husband's son in order to keep property in the family.

Brown's thesis is that it was virginity in particular that was a distinctive contribution of Christianity, the one which had the most radical effects on the social environment of sex, gender and family. Virginity in the first centuries could arise from a variety of motives; from personal and spiritual, to social and political. But the Christian commendation of permanent virginity was in effect (if not always in explicit intention) a form of bodily resistance to the control of the state. Virginity was for Christians a rebellion against the pervading tentacles of control with which the state reached every individual by means of the sexual body and its procreative and familial role. 'Sexual renunciation might lead the Christian to transform the body and, in transforming the body, to break with the discreet discipline of the ancient city.'[57] Permanent, vocational celibacy was a strike against the civic-minded procreation of social hierarchies through one's heirs. Sexual renunciation was also a democratization of access to religious status, since all—men or women, high or

---

56. Schüssler Fiorenza, *In Memory of Her*, pp.149-51; Borg, *Jesus in Contemporary Scholarship*, p. 107.

57. Robin Scroggs, *The New Testament and Homosexuality*, p.126. 'What the New Testament was against was the image of homosexuality as pederasty and primarily here its more sordid and dehumanizing dimensions' (p. 126).

low—were urged to consider giving up marriage in favor of a 'singlehearted' commitment to the Lord. Both in its potential accessibility to all believers, and in its association of bodily discipline with life-affirming holiness, Christian virginity built on some aspects of the Jewish commitment to purity. But, in context, it worked against the social hierarchization which purity laws, along with systems of economic distribution and the Greco-Roman family, had come to represent.

The sexual discipline of the body within Christian vision and early practice furthers compassion, active solidarity and inclusion of the outcast. Negatively, it undermines hierarchy and domination, whether in the family or society. The sexual behaviors which come under attack are those which function as markers of status or vehicles of exploitation. The sins of the powerless (even if against generally unquestioned values) rarely if ever come in for critique because such criticism and marking would only work toward their greater exclusion and otherness (as sexual teaching has so often done in Christian history).

The sexual paradigm assumed by New Testament authors and Jesus' teaching is faithful, heterosexual, procreative, monogamous marriage. But the primary concern of the New Testament is neither to justify religiously the validity of this paradigm, nor to enforce it, nor, on the other hand, to criticize or revise it as such. Specific sexual teaching in the New Testament, and for the most part, its treatment of gender (including the ambivalent and dangerous *Haustafeln*), are directed against abuses of power and disregard of the full humanity of those with whom one interacts *within* the accepted paradigm. Solidarity in Christ and disruption of power is the communal and social agenda motivating the Christian approach to both virginity and marriage, each of which can represent a gift to the community (1 Cor. 7.7). The New Testament reflects an ongoing practical process of transformation toward greater compassion and relationships of solidarity, a process whose gaps and backsliding (e.g. the restrictions on women's activity in 1 Corinthians 11 and 14, or 1 Timothy) should not scandalize but rather encourage the Christian community's potential to reform despite failures. It is also important not to overlook such failures in the New Testament itself. In addition to the *Haustafeln*, we must note the misogynism and violence embodied in the female metaphors of the Book of Revelation. Positive images include 'a bride adorned for her husband' (21.2) and a pregnant and birthing mother (12.1-6). On the other hand, 'Babylon the great, mother of harlots' (17.5) is hated, stripped, devoured and burned up with fire (v. 16). The

Gospel of Luke includes several affirmative representations of women disciples (as in the story of Mary and Martha; Lk. 10.38-42), but portrays them in primarily passive roles.[58]

The issue for Christian ethics is whether these counter-examples completely undermine the moral authority of the New Testament for Christian ethics. My conclusion is that the centrality of Jesus' kingdom preaching in early Christian memories of Jesus permit them and us to interpret his life, death, and resurrection as revelatory of the compassion of God for those who suffer. Compassionate, active solidarity is normative for Christian ethics today. To see the New Testament as a historical 'prototype'[59] of faith in action, rather than as a set of moral rules, frees us from the need to justify all its specific moral stances—as well as from the need to reject its moral authority entirely because of undeniable errors. What remains authoritative is a process of social transformation grounded in plural and dynamic memories of the 'exalted' Jesus, the one who mediates an experience of God as present, as powerful, as merciful and as all-inclusive. The ethical question today is what action, practices, and communities can mediate the same experience.[60]

Sally Purvis[61] rightly asks why Christians spend so much time debating issues like homosexuality, which is numerically a relatively small phenomenon, than abuses that occur within the supposedly normative heterosexual paradigm. Among many possible examples are domestic violence, sexual abuse, spouses' manipulative or callous behavior toward one another, emotional and physical neglect of children by narcissistic parents, irresponsible divorce and the indifference of Christian families themselves to suffering that occurs outside their homes, their church or their culture. The dominant sexual culture, whether hetero- or homosexual, needs to ask which behaviors and relationships best unite the human values of sex (such as pleasure, intimacy, commitment and family) with a Christian reorientation of social roles.

Norms that seem acceptable in light of the values respected in modern

58. Peter Brown, *The Body and Society: Men, Women and Sexual Renunciation in Early Christianity* (New York: Columbia University Press, 1988), p.31.

59. Loveday Alexander, 'Sisters in Adversity: Retelling Martha's Story', in George J. Brooke (ed.), *Women and the Biblical Tradition* (Lewiston, NY: Edwin Mellen, 1992), pp. 167-86.

60. Schüssler Fiorenza, *In Memory of Her*, p. 33. A prototype is an original model that 'is critically open to the possibility of its own transformation'.

61. Sally B. Purvis, 'Doing Violence: Homosexuals, Heterosexuals, and Contemporary Christian Ethics', *Prism* 7/1 (1992), p. 54.

North Atlantic cultures (freedom, privacy, autonomy, consent, the right to sexual pleasure and the centrality of sex to personal identity and fulfillment) must always be weighed in the light of active social inclusion of those whom *we* (the cultural elites) consider 'worth-less'. Negative condemnations of moral behavior should not so much serve the culturally influential as those whose voices are shrouded in disrespect. If Christian norms seem to verify the moral assumptions with which the classes in power begin (and with which they try to trump further discussion), then they deserve review in light of Jesus' kingdom reversals.

The shape of New Testament ethics is social, and that social ethics is also exactly the shape of New Testament sex and gender ethics: compassion, active solidarity and an inclusive bias toward 'the poor'. This does not mean that the only norms that need function in the sexual ethics of Christians are compassion, solidarity and inclusivity (though if we took these seriously, I think they would take us a long way toward an adequate sexual ethic). Sexual ethics is not only a matter of love and intention, or even mutuality and respect: in what is really a prelude to another paper, I would insist on the importance of the *embodiedness* of the experience of human sexuality, including parenthood and intergenerational family as well as mutual pleasure, as important to a full moral picture. However, a full vision of what embodied personhood means for ethics or sexual ethics is not the concern of the New Testament, and we cannot expect to retrieve such a vision from that source. Rather, the New Testament demands that *whatever* can be rightly discerned as the meaning of human sexuality and of woman–man relationships must be consistently challenged in its practical realization toward greater compassion, solidarity and inclusion of those who suffer most.

'YOU SHALL OPEN YOUR HAND TO YOUR NEEDY BROTHER': IDEOLOGY AND MORAL FORMATION IN DEUT. 15.1-18

Walter Houston

The Problem of Ideology

Among those who have reflected on the significance of the Bible for the struggle for justice for the poor in our world, varied positions may be identified. What one might call the classical liberation theology approach treats the Bible as a witness to a God who is on the side of the poor (e.g. Miranda 1977). Others, like Itumeleng Mosala (1989), see it as a document of social struggles with analogies in the modern world, and in large part the work of elites who benefited from the exploitation of the poor, and whose work can be seen as the ideological defence of their own position. Middle-class black theologians, Mosala contends, have been betrayed by their uncritical acceptance of the dominant theological ideology into proclaiming this document of conflicting interests as 'the Word of God' and taking the words of oppressors for the voice of liberation.

Mosala is surely correct in this: that the Bible is a social product reflecting the views and interests of groups within society and their views of reality. And the mere fact that it is a written product perpetuated by institutional means suggests that these groups must have been in ruling and influential positions in society. If the voice of God does indeed address the Bible's reader—and I for one believe that it does—it is not from above or outside of the social struggle, but from within it, and it must be sought for and discerned among the conflicting human voices to be heard within the Bible's pages.

However, if the Bible is the work of social elites, and if such elites profited by the exploitation of the poor, how comes it that there is such strong sympathy for the poor in the Bible, denunciations of oppression and legal measures in their favour—sufficient even for Mosala to detect sympathetic voices there, and for Miranda, who does not use the 'Word of God' language, to see it as a book that is essentially on the side of the poor?

It is, of course, true that individuals may speak and act in ways that are contrary to their class or individual interests. This is particularly true of people who are not closely involved in the economic activities of their class, and can stand back from them to criticize them. Academics are more likely than bankers to criticize the way the economy is organized. In the Hebrew Bible, the prophetic collections may have originated fairly close to the governmental and temple elites; but to a large extent they functioned as their conscience. However, this does not explain why such material, originating perhaps in the conscience of an individual, should be preserved and disseminated by social groups whose interests were threatened by them, even when framed, as Mosala shows Micah is, by material more acceptable to them (Mosala 1989: 101-153).

There are a number of possible answers. One, which applies to much of the prophetic material, is that the denunciation of the oppressive practices of long-dead elites was perfectly safe for their descendants. 'The word of the LORD which came to Micah of Moresheth in the days of Jotham, Ahaz and Hezekiah' was no threat to the leaders of the Second Temple community and could indeed sustain their reputation if they were seen to be interested in disseminating it.

Another answer is given by Marvin Chaney (1991). It is that the elite was riven into factions, as usually happens throughout history in societies of a similar type. Three of the nineteen kings of Judah after Solomon died by assassination, and the throne of Israel was constantly in contention. It was always open to these factions to bolster their power by appealing to the peasants against the outrageous exploitation being practised—by the other side! Nehemiah 5 is a vivid example of this. In a similar way, it would frequently have been to the advantage of the kings to get the better of their rivals by appearing before the public as the defenders of the poor, whatever exploitative activities they themselves may have been guilty of. This was particularly so as there was an immensely ancient tradition that one of the king's prime functions was as protector of the poor against the oppressor.

Although these answers are partly true, they do not go deep enough. The historian and political philosopher Michael Walzer (1987: 40ff.) discusses a related question: from where do social critics get the moral standards that they use to criticize their own society?[1] The answer is,

---

1.   I am grateful to Raymond Plant for drawing my attention to this work.

they get them from the traditions of their own culture, largely disseminated by intellectuals in the service of its ruling elites. And if it seems strange that such people should provide the ammunition for their own critics, it is very easily explained. Walzer turns to Marxist writers, particularly to Gramsci with his theory of hegemony; that is, the informal leadership of one class over others. The class that claims to direct society must, in order to make good their claim, present themselves as guardians of the common interest. They have to set standards for themselves

> ...they have to make a case for the ideas they are defending among men and women who have ideas of their own. 'The fact of hegemony', Gramsci argues, 'presupposes that one takes into account the interests and tendencies of the groups over which hegemony will be exercised, and it also presupposes a certain equilibrium, that is to say that the hegemonic groups will make some sacrifices of a corporate nature' (Walzer 1987: 41; quoting from Mouffe 1979: 181).

In other words, any enduring ideological expression of the leadership of a class in society will always carry with it concessions to the subordinate classes and in particular will contain moral ideas that are acceptable to them. It is essential to any ideology that it should claim to be universally and unquestionably true, a claim that cannot be made good if it contradicts fundamental moral ideas of the people. But this carries the consequence that the leadership of the dominant group may be criticized and contested in the light of its own ideology if it fails to act in accordance with such ideas.

In the case of the Bible and ancient Israel, these ideas are theological as well as moral. Psalm 72 is a simple example. The aim of the psalm is to support the monarchy by presenting it as divinely legitimated, but in order to do so effectively it must present the king as the defender of the poor. Once such ideas are in the public domain they become a standard by which the ruler is to be judged, and a mirror in which the ugliness of the sheer pursuit of self-interest can be revealed to the perpetrator.

Thus I would accept the contention that the Bible's ideas and language of social theology and morality originate in social contexts and serve social ends; but I would contend that knowing this enables us to discriminate among them, not to reject them wholesale, and to recognize those whose roots are deeper than the needs of the moment and the hegemonic class. These cannot be falsified by the uses to which they are put. As readers we may take a critical attitude to such uses, but we may allow the ideas to criticize our society to the extent to which they are applicable.

I should like to apply this double approach to the texts concerned with social welfare and reform in the Torah. Within this corpus there can be no doubt that the Deuteronomic code is the most consistently concerned with the poor and with marginal groups in society, and as an expression of that concern ch. 15, vv. 1-18, takes a central place. The chapter has been the subject recently of a detailed study focused on its ideas of social justice (Hamilton 1992), but this does not address the questions I have been raising.

The task is both important and difficult. It is important because there are relatively few passages in the Hebrew Bible that express an ideal for society, as distinct from giving moral instruction or condemning injustice. It is difficult because it is probably impossible to discover the historical background of any part of the Torah with any assurance, and because there is no consensus even about the original function or purpose of the codes. I make no assumptions here about the historical background of Deuteronomy (though towards the end of the essay I make some suggestions).[2] It is less important, as well as more difficult, to establish this than to establish the social world of the text—the relations of classes (and other groups, e.g. genders) that it *assumes*, the conception of ideal relations that it inculcates—and this is primarily what I shall be aiming at.

As for the function of the law-codes, the wise confess themselves at a loss. It would seem sensible to read them as expressing at least moral teaching and instruction in the principles of justice. There would then be no difficulty in reading casuistic and apodictic material alongside each other—as they tend to stand—or in understanding a mixture of decree, casuistic law, and moral appeal such as we have in Deuteronomy 15.

---

2. The view closely associating at least the kernel of the book with Josiah's reform measures described in 1 Kings 23 is still the most popular, and supports the reconstruction, from a politically critical and liberationist standpoint, of Nakanose (1993: 87-91, 104-111), who sees Josiah's measures as aimed at concentrating as many as possible of the rural surpluses in the hands of the Jerusalem elites. Nakanose, however, overlooks those elements of the constitutional sketch of Deut. 12–18 that restrict royal power and the centralization of surpluses, and strangely interprets the *consumption* of the passover and the first- and second-year tithes by the producer and his household at the chosen place as a *redistribution* of these surpluses to the elites. Crüsemann (1983: 86-92) sees the book as proposing to restrict the royal demands on the rural economy and to appeal to the free peasantry; this would make the book much less closely linked with the royal leadership. The analysis of ch. 15 that I go on to propose would fit better with Crüsemann's view.

Whether the chapter was intended as practical reform, to express an ideal or to encourage good conduct in society, is far from clear in the first instance. I hope that my analysis will shed some light on it. But what is beyond dispute is the fact that material of this kind is governed by, and serves to express, an ideal of social justice.

A peaceful and well-ordered society is, of course, to the advantage of any ruling power, whether native, as in the time of Josiah, or foreign, as in the Persian period. And that means a society in which economic and social relationships are acceptable to most of its members. Hence the emphasis on the welfare of the poor in all the codes. What matters, however, in this regard, is not the objective degree of exploitation—that is, the quantity of surplus transferred from the producer to the lord or creditor—but the degree of *perceived* justice or injustice; and that depends on the moral traditions of the people, built up over centuries, in part by intellectuals who may be seen as in the service of the ruling class—prophets, priests and psalmists—and in part coming from older tribal traditions of village communities.

The difference is illustrated by Kippenberg (1983) with the example of the land-reform decree of the former Communist government of Afghanistan. It was not dissimilar from those laws freeing the peasant from the power of the landlord which were welcomed by French, Russian and Chinese peasants with open arms, and which played a very important part in the early success of the respective revolutions in those countries. In Afghanistan, the decree raised great resentment, and played a significant part in the failure of the revolution there. Why? Because in the tribal society of Afghanistan, peasants do not perceive their landlords as exploiters but as protectors: their rent is reckoned to be fair exchange for a guarantee of protection from bandits, the tribe over the hill or, nowadays, rival guerrilla armies, and for help in bad times.

Kippenberg comments that the Marxist definition of exploitation as an objective fact ignores what the patron contributes to the relationship between himself and his client, which is unquantifiable, but may make all the difference between the perception of a relationship as legitimate and as illegitimate. 'Legitimacy is called into question if the conditions of exchange deteriorate for the dependents' (1983: 75), and this occurs particularly when they are threatened with proletarianisation (that is, with ceasing to be independent producers), or with enslavement. It is important to bear this in mind when we contemplate the apparently very limited degree of social justice offered by Deuteronomy 15: no equality, no abolition of slavery and the poor commended to the voluntary charity of the well-to-do.

But, it may be asked, does the opinion of the poor matter in relation to Deuteronomy 15? Surely its audience, its implied or ideal reader, is the well-to-do: those who use slaves, can give loans and have the money for hand-outs. Such a person is the 'you' who is addressed throughout. This has frequently been observed, most recently by Hamilton (1992: 137).

However, it is not quite as simple as that. At various points on the campus of Sheffield University a notice has been placed that says: 'For your safety this area is subject to closed-circuit television surveillance'. Now, to whom is this notice addressed? It is couched in the second person, so there should be no difficulty: it is you and me, the respectable citizen who is in need of protection. 'For your safety' a benevolent university administration has installed this protection. But this can hardly be the whole truth. It is no doubt useful for you and me to have this assurance: but it must be far more important for others to have the warning that it implies. Are not the true addressees of this text the enemies of society who lurk in the shadows to carry out their nefarious plans against us and who may be deterred by being warned that they are under observation?

Just as a warning to the evildoer is implied by that overt assurance to the potential victim, so inversely Deuteronomy 15, by its overt warnings and exhortations of the potential oppressor, may imply an assurance to the poor and the potential victim: 'Don't worry, God is on your side and things are being ordered in your favour'. Thus, as the text nevertheless leaves the well-to-do in earthly control, it fulfils the conditions of hegemonic ideology: it has something for everyone.

Background

Deuteronomy's attack on Judaean social problems in this chapter is aimed at their roots: it is targeted at the problems of secured credit (vv. 1-11) and debt-slavery (vv. 12-18). As Kippenberg (1977) has shown, the formation of ancient class-societies was achieved mainly through the use of surplus wealth to offer credit to peasants in difficulty on the security of their land and of persons; that is, generally the security of their own children. The forfeiture of the pledges led to the steady drift of peasants into landlessness and their families into bondage. This process can be illustrated from Neh. 5.1-5 (cf. Kippenberg 1982: 54-62) and is indirectly attested in the prophetic literature in such a text as Amos 2.6, which may suggest that creditors in Israel, like those in early Greece and Rome, were entitled to seize the debtor's own person if he or she defaulted. (2 Kgs 4.1 may be compared.) We have here a process which, if left unchecked, would certainly lead to the breakdown of anything recognizable as legitimate, just relationships between poor and rich.

Against this process, Deuteronomy is able to appeal in the first place to local agrarian institutions. The 'Year of Release' or sabbath year (Exod. 23.10-11) is referred to in v. 1: the same verb, שמט 'let go', is used as in Exodus, though with a different object. Deuteronomy does not mention the fallow; but if it was observed in the way attested in the Second Temple period, the fallow would be a time of stringency when relief might be needed. Another, in all probability old, custom that is taken up is the golden handshake for the released bondservant (vv. 13-14): David Daube (1963: 55-61) notes the allusion to it in Exod. 3.21-22: 'you shall not go out empty'—the Israelites are to trick the Egyptians into giving them what should be theirs by right. And, in general, the reliance on the generosity of the better-off members of the community must have been characteristic of a healthily functioning local community in ancient Judah. The main difficulty with which this writer is faced is that the old customs depended on community solidarity, which the new situation had corroded.

Secondly, there are two older laws, one at the basis of each of the two sections. It is easily seen that vv. 12, 16-17, repeat Exod. 21.2, 5-6, with modification. Verse 2, though not found elsewhere, is also an older law, as is shown by its formulation in the third person in distinction from the uniform second person around it (Seitz 1971: 167-68; followed by Mayes 1979: 248).

What does Deuteronomy do with these laws?

The Year of Release, vv. 1-11

Verse 2, the basic law taken up by the Deuteronomic author, requires a remission of debts every seven years, in the fallow year. It assumes loans are normally for relief of poverty, and without regular relief are likely to lead to distress. This verse has occasioned much difficulty, and the text has been brought into question.[3] However, in my view the traditional

3.   The most detailed recent discussion is in Chirichigno (1993: 263-75). It may make the text easier to insert משה את after בעל (see BHS and Merendino 1969: 108-

translation of v. 2aβ, 'every creditor [lit. lord of a loan of his hand] shall remit what he has lent to his neighbour', is correct.

But what is meant by 'remission'? Is it a one year suspension of the creditor's right to repayment or the cancellation of the debt?[4] The arguments are rather finely balanced. The presumption of v. 9, that lenders might be put off by the approach of the year of release, may be thought 'evidently more forcible' (Driver 1902: 179) if a cancellation is meant. However, the weight of this consideration depends on the usual term of loans of this kind. If, as seems likely, repayment would normally be expected within the year (i.e. by the next harvest), then even a year's suspension would be a serious deterrent to lending, though not as serious as a cancellation. A further argument for assuming a cancellation is that we have plenty of comparative material requiring the cancellation of debts—among them the *mīšarum* edicts of the kings of the Old Babylonian dynasty (Kraus 1958, 1965; Finkelstein 1969; cf. Epsztein 1986: 12-14; Hamilton 1992: 48-53) and revolutionary measures in the

109). But a more significant question is whether נשה ב (hiph.) here means 'lend to' or 'hold on pledge against' and whether משה (ידו) means 'debt' or 'pledge' (this is the only place where the noun appears). Does the sentence mean 'every creditor must give up what he has lent his neighbour' (Driver 1902: 175; RSV; Craigie 1976: 234) or '...return the pledge he holds against his neighbour' (North 1954; NEB; REB; Mayes 1979: 248; Hamilton 1992: 17; NRSV is ambiguous)? (For further interpretations, see Chirichigno 1993: 265-68.) This is partly tied up with the question whether cancellation or suspension is meant. To return the pledge would amount to cancelling the debt (probably: contra North); the issue is less clear if the sense is 'remit the debt'. The case was argued by North in relation to the widespread practice of handing over a pledge (e.g. a child of the debtor) at the time the loan was made. However, that is not a conclusive argument (and Chirichigno [270] denies that Deuteronomy envisages the taking of persons or land on pledge). The phrase in v. 3, אשר יהיה לך את־אחיך, on the other hand, is difficult to reconcile with North's view: 'that which is yours (which is) with your brother' must mean the loan, not a pledge (so Chirichigno, 271), and North's view can only be supported by the forced interpretation *'from* your brother'. The question of cancellation or suspension, therefore, seems to be left open so far as this factor is concerned.

4. Jewish tradition as far back as we can go has taken it in the sense of cancellation (Philo, *De Septenario* 8; *M. Sheb.* 10.1; cf. Driver 1902: 179; Neh. 10.32 uses the perhaps stronger verb נטש [from Exod. 23.11], which points in the same direction), and critical opinion has shifted towards this view in the twentieth century (for the nineteenth see Driver, who hesitantly marks the beginning of the switch); of recent commentators only Craigie (1976: 236) maintains the older view. For a detailed discussion see Chirichigno (1992: 272-75).

Greek states[5]—but none ordaining a temporary suspension. Against this it has to be said that all the examples of debt-cancellation we know of are irregular events, and the idea of a regular, periodic cancellation is as unexampled as that of a moratorium. While a one-off measure, which would have taken creditors by surprise, could be a very effective measure of relief—perhaps retarding, if not reversing progress towards a class-divided society—a periodic measure could be prepared for and neutralized in advance by the owners of capital. If observed in the spirit intended by Deuteronomy, such a measure would have a strong egalitarian effect; but how could that be achieved?

We must therefore choose between an interpretation that reads the law as a modest measure of relief consequent on the observance of the fallow year (Craigie 1976: 236) and one which takes it as a profoundly egalitarian measure verging on the utopian in its impracticality. The decisive argument is that of Jewish tradition, which is unanimous for cancellation from an early period (see n. 4); and this is also consonant with the tone of the Deuteronomic passage, which expounds the necessary conditions of a just society and not simply what can be practically achieved. In Judah around the turn of the eras, though the law was technically in force, it was deprived of effect by a legal device, the prozbul (*M. Sheb.* 10.3). The problem of creditors' unwillingness to let the law have full effect is dealt with in vv. 7-11.

The first modification of this law that comes to our attention is the use of the word אחיו in v. 2: literally, 'he shall not press his neighbour *and his brother*'.[6] It is clear that the second word explicates the first, and 'your brother', as the term for the person for whom the subject of the text must have concern, is typical of the Deuteronomic code: from this point on, it is used repeatedly, especially in social justice contexts. In ch. 15 it appears six times: vv. 2, 3, 7, 9, 11, 12. It is normally in the second person, '*your* brother'; the use of the third person in v. 2 shows that the author is deliberately adding to an older formulation. 'Neighbour' (רע) seems to be the older term, used in the Decalogue and the Covenant Code, and only here do the two appear alongside each other in this sense (Hamilton 1992: 37). Lothar Perlitt (1980) has devoted an article to the usage of 'your brother' in Deuteronomy, and much of what I have to say about it is indebted to this.

What does this usage imply? First, a summary of its occurrences in

5.   Solon's σεισαχθεία (Aristotle, 'Αθηναίων Πολιτεία 6.1) for example.
6.   Sam. omits 'and'.

this chapter. It occurs once in v. 3, where it is contrasted with 'a foreigner (וּנְכרִי)' (cf. 17.15; 23.20). In the passage vv. 7-11 it appears thrice, invariably referring to the poor community member towards whom generosity is required. In v. 12 we have 'when your brother, a Hebrew or a Hebrew woman [this is the literal translation!], sells himself [or 'is sold'] to you'. Compare this with Exod. 21.2: 'When you buy a Hebrew slave'. The awkwardness of the expression in Deuteronomy arises from the concern to bring in two special points: to designate the slave as a 'brother' and to make it clear that the law extends to women.

Despite this, the first thing obviously implied is that the object of concern is, ideally, a man; even though the text in v. 12 emphasizes that the law applies equally to men and women, and even though widows are likely to have been prominent among the recipients of charitable loans. The patriarchal character of Israelite society is, as ever, reflected in the use of language.[7]

Next, does v. 3 imply that only the true-born Israelite is worthy of just treatment, as opposed to the foreigner? There is a contrast with the foreigner, but not a chauvinistic one: the contrast is with נכרי not גר, and it has often been thought that the exception is intended to exclude commercial loans from the operation of the law. The *gēr* has the same claim on Israel's concern as the Israelite, as 24.14 shows. Perlitt argues (1980: 42) that the three passages that contrast the 'brother' with the foreigner belong to a later stratum, and (1980: 50-51) that the usage does not have a background in the idea of the blood relationship of all the members of the people, which has no interest for Deuteronomy. To this we shall return.

Perlitt lays stress above all on the word's emotional colouring, which emerges very strongly in its concentration in vv. 7-11. The colouring is so much stronger than that of 'neighbour', and this makes it appropriate to use where a strong ethical appeal is to be made to help and protect the needy. 'The (national) community of brothers arises out of the claim on the individual Israelite to see and treat his neighbour as a brother' (1980: 37). It is a more emotional and indeed a more religious way of saying 'your neighbour', a way which appeals more deeply to the heart; a way of expressing 'the common humanity of those who together live

---

7. Hamilton manages to obscure this by a stubborn political correctness which translates אח consistently as 'kin'. This also loses the emotional colouring of 'brother'. The NRSV's 'member of the community' is equally unsatisfactory in both respects, but has the advantage over 'kin' of not misleading the reader over its referent.

out of the liberating love of God' (1980: 42). The appeal to brotherhood is not the result of the natural relationship of all Israelites: the relation of all Israelites as brothers (and sisters) is the result of the law's appeal to treat each other as such.

But is Perlitt right in arguing (1980: 50-51) that it is not an extension of the older cultural ideal of responsibility within the extended family or clan? It is true that Deuteronomy hardly ever refers to this (the law of Levirate marriage might be an exception [25.5-10], and implicitly the reference to blood-vengeance in 19.6), and 13.7-12 (Heb.). makes it uncompromisingly plain that the Israelite has a higher loyalty even than that to his immediate family and his literal brothers. Perlitt may be exaggerating in saying (1980: 51) that Deuteronomy does not know of any division of the people into families and lineages; but it is an illuminating exaggeration. Whereas in the Holiness Code's 'welfare' provisions in Leviticus 25, the particular responsibility of the lineage or clan is provided for in the institution of the גאלה or 'redemption' (v. 25), this is, strikingly, not true of Deuteronomy 15, where responsibility is defined solely in terms of the 'brother', meaning the fellow-citizen in general. It is certainly one of the major objects of the book to promote national loyalty above local and family feeling, and in a passage like ch. 13 this works in a decidedly totalitarian way.

But all of this does not disprove that Deuteronomy is intending to depict the relationship between members of the national community as if it were an extended family or clan; indeed, it rather tends to confirm it. The text uses language which recalls the requirements of clan redemption. It also recalls the pragmatic fact that inequalities arose within the lineage because of the way in which this institution worked, tending to concentrate wealth within the senior branches and render the junior ones dependent on them (Kippenberg 1982: 33-41; cf. Crüsemann 1983: 93). But it extends and deepens the import of the language of 'brotherhood' in two ways: by extending its range to the nation as a whole, and by implicitly pleading that 'brothers', whatever their degree of blood relationship, should genuinely act as brothers; that is, with generosity, not with hard-heartedness.

It cannot therefore be sufficient to define the stress of אחיך in purely emotional and ethical terms. It does have emotional weight, and it is used to argue for an ethical stance, but it does that in part because it defines the nation in the image of the kin-group and redefines responsibility to kin as responsibility for fellow-nationals. Thus the idea of brotherhood, ethically central to this chapter, can be seen as the expression in a new context of a very old idea of community in which it defines the responsibility of people to those who, in the typical tribal village inhabited by members of one or a few clans (מִשְׁפָּחוֹת), would be both neighbours and relatives. Its practical expression would in most situations be very similar, even in the new situation.

Verses 4-6 are a theological reflection that if Israel were truly obedient, measures like this would not be required, because there would be no poor (so Driver 1902: 175-76). Many scholars (e.g. Seitz 1971: 169; Mayes 1979: 248) have attributed vv. 4-6 to a redactional layer on stylistic grounds. There is a consensus that the 'commandment' here referred to (v. 5) means the Deuteronomic code as a whole.[8] This consensus is ignored (not rebutted!) by Hamilton; this enables him to integrate this passage into the rhetoric of the chapter (1992: 15-16). But the contradiction with v. 11: 'the poor will never cease out of the land' has frequently been noted. There have been various attempts to overcome it. Thus Craigie (1976: 237) interprets this passage as a possibility 'contingent on the completeness of Israel's obedience', while v. 11 is 'a more realistic appraisal'. For Hamilton, vv. 4-6 represent the consequence of obedience, like v. 10b, while v. 11a expresses the situation that makes the law necessary.

But it is Lohfink's view (1991: 47) that is of particular interest for us. According to him, the whole passage partakes of the 'utopian' character often attributed to vv. 4-6. It sees poverty as a very temporary state arising quite naturally from, say, a bad harvest, which is instantly eliminated by the generosity of those who have not been affected to the same extent: so v. 11 means 'people will always be falling into poverty', and v. 4 means 'but there will be no *class* of poor people', provided that the command of generosity is heeded. It is an attractive view, but in the end I do not find it convincing. The consistent use throughout vv. 7-11 of the term אֶבְיוֹן 'poor', usually substantivized, suggests a person with this constant characteristic, and its use elsewhere points in that direction also. To express the idea in Hebrew of someone temporarily falling into financial straits one would expect a verb, as we find in Lev. 25.35:

וכי ימוך אחיך ומטה ידו עמך

if your brother *falls into difficulty* and becomes dependent on you (NRSV adapted).

---

8. E.g. REB: 'these commandments'; NRSV: 'this entire commandment'; Craigie 1976 (234): 'the whole of this code of law'.

Moreover, as we shall shortly see, v. 12 assumes that poor people are going to continue to have to go as far as selling their children into slavery to get out of difficulties.

Therefore, despite all these considerations we must say that there is a contradiction, and it is more than formal: the utopianism of vv. 4-6 contrasts with the realism of vv. 7-11, and is undermined by it.

The realism of vv. 7-11 is seen in its highlighting in v. 9 of the potential ineffectiveness of the base law. It would choke off credit in the year or two leading up to the year of release. The way the text deals with the problem is not to introduce a refinement in the law but to call for a generosity going beyond the demands of the law, and to appeal to concern and compassion. Give loans anyway, whether you expect them back or not! It is not your advantage you should be concerned with, but your brother's need.

There are several points to note here. First, the repeated use of 'your brother', more concentrated in this passage than anywhere else in Deuteronomy. Secondly, Hamilton (1992: 31-4) notes the repeated strategic use of 'somatic' vocabulary—'hand' and 'heart' and 'eye': open your hand, let there not be a villainous thought in your heart, let your eye not be evil. This concentration of terms for parts of the body, closest of all things to us, as our brother is closest of all people, intensifies the emotional power of the rhetoric.

Thirdly, there is a religious appeal. It is of two kinds: the stick and the carrot, the threat and the promise. In v. 9 we have the threat of the poor man's appeal to God, as in the Covenant Code (Exod. 22.23, 27-28). Verse 10 is more characteristic of Deuteronomy: the promise of blessing if the command of generosity is heeded; this refers to this specific commandment, not like vv. 4-6 which refers to all in general. There is no question here of a rule that can be enforced. This is an appeal straight to the heart. As Perlitt says of it (1980: 33), 'macht man der Liebe Beine'—'it gets love moving'. The text presents this as the only way of counteracting the deterrent effect of the base law, quite correctly if one grants the basic, and indeed quite realistic, premise in v. 11: there will always be poor in the land. However, one finds oneself asking, if the well-to-do could be counted on to respond to such an appeal, what need would there have been for the debt-remission law in the first place, and if not, what use would it have been?

In other words, the text, by its premise in v. 11, presumes the

There is fundamentally a strategic relationship

continued existence of inequalities and of the patron-client relationship.[9] There will be poor, and there will be others who will be in a position to help them. The fundamental relation of dependence is not abolished by the law or by the circumstances that it presumes. If we had temporarily to reckon with such a revolution through vv. 4-6, we are rapidly disabused. Yet it is precisely this part of the text, vv. 7-11, that most urgently insists on the transformation of relationships between the dependent and those on whom they depend. As Hamilton puts it, the text places dependents 'at the center of society, not at the margins', indeed, with the power to call down the wrath of God upon the hard-hearted and close-fisted. Above all, it makes them members of one family. No social revolution is assumed, but there is a call for a moral revolution to transform the relationships within society, and make perceived exploitation impossible.

A further point may be made. Deuteronomy may accept that the poor will not cease from the land, but it does not accept the continued existence of the rich as an exploiting class, and as Crüsemann argues (1983: 86-92; and above, n. 2), many of the social provisions would undermine the power of the capital-city elite. The class appealed to appear to be well-to-do farmers. They could be seen as the 'people of the land' of 2 Kings, or in a later period as the 'citizens' of the *'Bürgertempel-gemeinde'* of Weinberg's thesis (1992). This could be a simple (too simple?) ideological deception: the ruling classes to whom the intellectual elite who composed the book are responsible appear in the guise of benevolent fellow-citizens. But, on Crüsemann's showing, it would seem more likely that the free peasantry are, in Gramscian terms, the class aiming at hegemony under the leadership of the Deuteronomists.[10]

These conclusions are confirmed when we turn to the second section on the release of debt-slaves.

9. Although the relationship in Judaean society may not have the same customary and legal character as the *clientela* at Rome, it seems reasonable, following Kippenberg (1982: 22), to use the same terms for a relationship that is functionally analogous. (Kippenberg refers to Gellner & Waterbury 1977.)

10. Nakanose (1993: 110-11) maintains that Josiah's reform offered advantages to the proletarianized poor while exploiting the free peasants. If so, it can hardly have had much to do with Deuteronomy, which plainly appeals to the voluntary support of the free peasants as a leading class.

Slave-Release

those who Are In debt

The text here accepts that (debtors) are going to continue to sell family members into bondage to pay off debts (Chirichigno 1993: 221-23). In view of the use of the verb מכר 'sell', this seems more likely to be the situation than the offering of persons on pledge (though it could also be creditors who are envisaged as selling forfeit debtors). If the text envisages the taking of persons as surety, this has already been covered in v. 2 (cf. Kippenberg 1983: 80). The old law requiring the release of bondservants after six years' service is modified in three directions.

First, it is to apply equally to women (vv. 12, 17b; against Exod. 21.7-11).[11] This is achieved by simple and rather awkward additions to the older text. The addition of העבריה in v. 12 implies that women are members of the community in the same 'brotherly' sense.

Secondly, all implications are dropped that the master can control the bondsman's personal life (e.g. by giving him a wife who remains the master's property).

Thirdly, on release, the freed man should receive a generous share of the master's own agricultural wealth (vv. 13-14).

This law is also brought home to the hearer by personal appeal to feeling for the 'brother' (or sister!). Even at the expense of stylistic smoothness, 'your brother' is added in v. 12. The 'slave' is actually a brother! Where all are brothers, there can be no masters and slaves. The contract is not one of slavery, but of the sale of one's labour for a fixed term.

Verses 13-15 may have put an old custom into words, but it could be enforced only by the pressure of public opinion, and where that failed, by appeal to 'brotherly' feeling. It is not an enforceable rule, but again relies on generosity that goes beyond the law. And like vv. 7-11, this responds to an inadequacy in the law. It was not sufficient to provide for a fixed term of service: for released bondservants would have no recourse but to return to their families, which, with an extra mouth to feed, would be left in no better position than before. If they brought with them a substantial addition to their resources that might make all the difference.

11. Jackson (1989: 198) may be correct in maintaining that for literary reasons the case of a female sold for non-sexual services is passed over in Exod. 21.2-11; but the fact remains that the text fails to make it clear that she is entitled to be released after six years like a male slave.

Here the prime religious appeal is very pertinent: the master is reminded that his own current prosperity is due solely to the divine blessing (v. 14), and further to 'remember that you were a slave in Egypt and YHWH your God redeemed you' (v. 15). This underlines that all are in the same boat: there can be no class divisions where everyone is a freed slave and all owe their liberty and prosperity to God. The point is essentially the same as with the language of 'brotherhood'. Also implied here may be an appeal to the imitation of God. The God whom the master serves is one who releases slaves! How can the servant of this God do less with his own servants?

Thus in this section, in an even more marked way than with the year of release, the institutional structure of dependency is retained, but the expectation is that it will be transformed by a new understanding of social relationships.

Conclusion

It is painfully easy to deconstruct this chapter. The social and moral assumptions pull in opposite directions. Hillel with his prozbul is able to thwart the fundamental intention of the law of Deut 15.2 because nothing had been done between Deuteronomy's time and his to conform society in practical terms to Deuteronomy's moral rhetoric, and Deuteronomy itself did not require it. To rely on personal generosity and goodwill was, surely, to rely on precisely that quality in social life whose absence had caused the social grievances in the first place. Yet Deuteronomy's appeals are not simply appeals to individual generosity. When they are read in context we see that they are attempts to re-create a sense of community.

The appeal to brotherly generosity is bound up with the inadequacy of the law in the narrower sense to achieve a real change in social relationships. Was this just a failure in the specific measures offered? Does it not rather reflect a general problem in achieving and preserving social justice? The problem is this: that legal and institutional changes, even revolutionary ones, are not enough by themselves. They must be accompanied by the personal and communal commitment to their intention that Deuteronomy calls for. And that can only be achieved by moral education, by the influence of a recognized moral tradition.

In the search for social justice, no people can do without such a moral tradition—and that is part of the point Walzer is making in the book I referred to earlier. Whatever the inadequacies of Deuteronomy's institutional contribution, its renewal of the sense of community of Israelite tribal society in a national context is a profound contribution to the kind of moral tradition that any society aiming to be just requires; and it is there waiting to be picked up by anyone—social critic, reformer, revolutionary—bold enough to take it seriously, even against the social implications of the Deuteronomic context. The evidence is that it was picked up very quickly by the compilers of the Holiness Code, who use the 'your brother' language five times in Leviticus 25.

And it is surely not irrelevant to modern society. The French revolution proclaimed as its goal 'liberty, equality and fraternity'. The history of the last two hundred years has been largely one of the promotion by rival political forces of liberty and equality. Fraternity has been forgotten, yet one might argue that it is the glue without which the other two must inevitably fall apart and appear, as they do, to be rivals. Mark Chapman reminds me that fraternity was a significant ideal of the Christian Socialists of the nineteenth century in England. Others object that in an age when we are conscious of the frequent oppressiveness and dysfunction of the family, an image drawn from the family is not attractive. This may well be true for modern Western societies: members of the Colloquium whose sphere of work lay largely in the Third World had no objection. In Western societies, words such as 'solidarity' or 'community' may well need to be substituted.

The point, however, remains. To achieve equality, or something approaching equality, must mean the restriction of my liberty; that is, I must be coerced, *unless* I recognize my poorer fellow-citizen as a brother or sister or fellow community member. Conversely, as we in this country have learned with brutal clarity over the past 16 years, the cry of liberty must result in increasing inequality, unless, once more, we deepen the sense of community which we have instead seen eroded. We need to learn that we belong together. We could do worse than learn it from Deuteronomy.

I would argue that in the long run a people's moral tradition must be supported by a religious tradition. What vitiated the socialist experiment in Russia and led to the horrors of the Gulag Archipelago was not only the distortion of morality but the contemptuous rejection of religion. At a minimum, we need to accept that the world is structured in such a way that justice is possible and will result in happiness for the society that truly lives by it. And that, of course, is Deuteronomy's ground-bass:

'because of this YHWH your God will bless you in all your works and all you undertake'. Beyond that, Deuteronomy maintains that the God who guarantees blessing is a just God who is concerned for the poor, and will hear their cry and deliver them as he delivered Israel from oppression. To act justly is to imitate YHWH.

BIBLIOGRAPHY

Chaney, M.
1992 'Debt Easement in Israelite History and Tradition', in D. Jobling, Peggy L. Day, Gerald T. Sheppard (eds.), *The Bible and the Politics of Exegesis* (Cleveland: The Pilgrim Press): 127-40.

Chirichigno, G.C.
1993 *Debt-Slavery in Israel and the Ancient Near East* (JSOTSup, 141; Sheffield: JSOT Press).

Craigie, P.C.
1976 *The Book of Deuteronomy* (NICOT; Grand Rapids: Eerdmans).

Crüsemann, F.
1983 ' "damit er dich segne in allem Tun deiner Hand..." (Dtn 14,29)', in Luise and Willy Schottroff (eds.), *Mitarbeiter der Schöpfüng: Bibel und Arbeitswelt* (Munich: Chr. Kaiser Verlag): 72-103.

Daube, D.
1963 *The Exodus Pattern in the Bible* (Oxford: Oxford University Press).

Driver, S.R.
1902 *A Critical and Exegetical Commentary on Deuteronomy* (ICC; Edinburgh: T. & T. Clark, 3rd edn).

Epsztein, L.
1986 *Social Justice in the Ancient Near East and the People of the Bible* (London: SCM Press; ET of *La Justice sociale dans le Proche-Orient ancien et le Peuple de la Bible* [Paris: Editions du Cerf, 1983]).

Finkelstein, J.J.
1969 'The Edict of Ammiṣaduqa: A New Text', *RA* 63: 45-64.

Gellner, E., and J. Waterbury
1977 *Patrons and Clients in Mediterranean Society* (London: Duckworth).

Hamilton, J.M.
1992 *Social Justice and Deuteronomy: The Case of Deuteronomy 15* (SBLDS, 136; Atlanta: Scholars Press).

Jackson, B.S.
1989 'Ideas of Law and Legal Administration', in R.E. Clements (ed.), *The World of Ancient Israel* (Cambridge: Cambridge University Press): 185-202.

Kippenberg, H.G.
1977 'Die Typik antiker Entwicklung', in Kippenberg (ed.), *Seminar: Die Entstehung der antiken Klassengesellschaft* (Frankfurt): 9-61.

1982   *Religion und Klassenbildung im antiken Judäa: Eine religionssoziolo-gische Studie zum Verhältnis von Tradition und gesellschaftlicher Entwicklung* (Göttingen: Vandenhoeck & Ruprecht, 2nd edn).

1983   'Die Entlassung aus Schuldknechtschaft in antiken Judäa: Eine Legitimitätsvorstellung von Verwandtschaftsgruppen', in G. Kehrer (ed.), *Vor Gott sind alle gleich: soziale Gleichheit, soziale Ungleichheit und die Religionen* (Düsseldorf: Patmos): 94-104.

Kraus, F.R.

1958   *Ein Edikt des Königs Ammiṣaduqa von Baylon* (Leiden: Brill).

1965   'Ein Edikt des Königs Samsu-iluna von Babylon', *AS* 16: 225-31.

Lohfink, N.

1991   'Poverty in the Laws of the Ancient Near East and of the Bible', *Theological Studies* 52: 34-50.

Mayes, A.D.H.

1979   *Deuteronomy* (NCB; London: Marshall, Morgan & Scott).

Merendino, R.P.

1969   *Das deuteronomische Gesetz: Ein literarkritische, gattungs- und über-lieferungsgeschichtliche Untersuchung zu Dt 12–26* (BBB, 31; Bonn: Peter Hanstein).

Miranda, J.P.

1977   *Marx and the Bible* (London: SCM Press; ET of *Marx y la Biblia* [Salamanca: Ediciones sígueme, 1971]).

Mosala, I.J.

1989   *Biblical Hermeneutics and Black Theology in South Africa* (Grand Rapids: Eerdmans).

Mouffe, C.

1979   'Hegemony and Ideology in Gramsci', in Mouffe (ed.), *Gramsci and Marxist Theory* (London: Routledge & Kegan Paul).

Nakanose, S.

1993   *Josiah's Passover: Sociology and the Liberating Bible* (Maryknoll: Orbis Books).

North, R.

1954   '*Yād* in the Shemitta-Law', *VT* 4, pp. 196-99.

Perlitt, L.

1980   'Ein einzig Volk von Brüdern', in D. Lührmann and G. Strecker (eds.), *Kirche: Festschrift für Günther Bornkamm zum 75 Geburtstag* (Tübingen: J.C.B. Mohr): 27-52.

Seitz, G.

1971   *Redaktionsgeschichtliche Studien zum Deuteronomium* (BWANT, 5.13; Stuttgart: W. Kohlhammer).

Walzer, M.

1987   *Interpretation and Social Criticism* (Cambridge, MA: Harvard University Press).

Weinberg, J.

1992   *The Citizen-Temple Community* (Sheffield: JSOT Press).

Weinfeld, M.

1972   *Deuteronomy and the Deuteronomic School* (Oxford: Clarendon Press).

WORK AND SLAVERY IN THE NEW TESTAMENT:
IMPOVERISHMENTS OF TRADITIONS

Margaret Davies

In Raymond Williams' study of social and cultural relations in England
from the sixteenth century, *The Country and the City*,[1] the following
definition of a 'charity of consumption' is advanced:

> The providence of nature is linked to a human sharing: all are welcome,
> even the poor, to be fed at this board. And it is this stress, more than any
> other, which has supported the view of a responsible civilisation, in which
> men care for each other directly and personally, rather than through the
> abstractions of a more complicated and more commercial society. This, we
> are told, is the natural order of responsibility and neighbourliness and
> charity, words we do not now clearly understand, since Old England fell.

> Of course, one sees what is meant, and as a first approximation, a simple
> impulse, it is kindly. But the Christian tradition of charity is at just this
> point weak. For it is a charity of consumption only…And then, as Adrian
> Cunningham has argued, this version of charity—as loving relations
> between men expressed as a community of consumption, with the
> Christian board and breaking of bread as its natural images, and the feast
> as its social consummation—was prolonged into periods and societies in
> which it became peripheral and even damaging. A charity of production—
> of loving relations between men actually working and producing what is
> ultimately, in whatever proportions, to be shared—was neglected, not seen,
> and at times suppressed, by this habitual reference to a charity of
> consumption, which when applied to ordinary working societies was
> inevitably a mystification. All uncharity at work, it was readily assumed,
> could be redeemed by the charity of the consequent feast. In the complex
> of feeling and reference derived from this tradition, it matters very much,
> moreover, that the name of the god and the name of the master are
> significantly single—our Lord.

The purpose of this paper is to determine how far New Testament
texts encourage a 'charity of consumption' to the exclusion of a 'charity

1.   London: Chatto and Windus, 1973 (Hogarth Press, 1993), pp. 30-31.

of production'. By a 'charity of production' I mean concerns for the types of work and the social relations in working situations appropriate to people who are attempting to live out the exhortations to love one another and to avoid greed and extortion. It would be anachronistic to expect from New Testament texts the social and economic analyses to which we have become accustomed since the nineteenth century. Rather, I shall be looking for the kinds of concerns about social relations in the working world that are expressed in the exhortations and laws of the Jewish Scriptures. New Testament texts became the Holy Scripture of Christianity and were read out of their original contexts to enlighten or to justify and support different social structures. How far are the texts themselves open to the kind of interpretations that Williams discerns? The study is arranged in three main sections. The first part is concerned with an analysis of the Gospels and the Acts of the Apostles. The second is concerned with the Pauline epistles' statements that Paul worked to support himself and with their admonitions to Christians that they should work. The third part focuses on teaching about slavery because slaves were the most exploited and dispossessed people in the first-century world. Before embarking on these matters, however, the introduction will, first, briefly outline relevant teachings from the Jewish Scriptures, Scriptures Christianity took over as its Old Testament, and, second, highlight differences between the circumstances of Jewish and Christian communities in the first-century Roman Empire.

Introduction

1. *The Jewish Scriptures*

New Testament texts assume the authority of the Jewish Scriptures, and often appeal to them through allusions and quotations. But to just which parts of these Scriptures appeal is made depends on the interests of New Testament texts.

The Jewish Scriptures, taken together, could not be read as privileging a charity of consumption over a charity of production. They contain a wealth of theological reflection on social justice. The denunciations of the unjust treatment of the poor by the rich in the prophetic books, especially those of Amos and Isaiah, injustice which God is understood to have punished through the Assyrian conquest of North Israel, the Babylonian conquest of Judah and the Babylonian exile, seem to have borne fruit in the attempts to develop not only exhortations but also laws for more just societies (should Israel ever regain autonomy or relative independence), especially in the books of Deuteronomy and Leviticus.[2] These writings encourage a 'charity of consumption' in their exhortations to generosity, but they also recognise that the structures of society could be tyrannical, and there are attempts legally to restrict power, especially the power that came from the ownership of land in an agricultural society.

The book of Deuteronomy is concerned to advocate the social ethos of a community that lives in devotion to a just and merciful God, who had rescued Israel from slavery in Egypt as an expression of his love (7.6-11), given a beneficent land (8.11-20), entered into a covenant relationship with Israel (like a father with sons and daughters; 14.1; 32.19), and who expects, as an obedient response, love towards God (6.4-9) and the creation of a community of brothers (29.1-29). Since this God takes no bribes but executes justice for the vulnerable, the fatherless and the widow, and gives food and clothing to the sojourner, Israel should act as sons (and daughters) who follow their father's example (10.17-20; 16.18-20; 27.19; cf. Exod. 22.21-27; 23.1-9). Since this God had saved Israelite slaves, Israel should be generous towards servants and slaves: they are to share the sabbath rest (5.15; cf. Exod. 20.15), they are to rejoice with their masters at festivals (12.1-14; 16.9-12) and male and female debt-slaves are to be released in the seventh year, in memory of Israel's release from Egypt (15.12-18; cf. Exod. 21.1-11; 22.3). Moreover, an escaped slave, perhaps from a foreign master, is neither to be returned to his master nor to be oppressed (23.15-16). Stealing a man to enslave him or to sell him into slavery is punishable by death (24.7; cf. 5.19; Exod. 21.15). Hired servants are not to be oppressed, but are to be paid each day (24.14-15). Pledges should be accepted when offered, but should not be taken by entering the debtor's house (24.10-11); pledges should not be of a kind to deprive the debtor of his livelihood (24.6), and, if a cloak were pledged, it should be returned at night (24.12-13; Exod. 22.26-27). Moreover, only weights and measures that are just are to be used (25.13-16). The provisions for release from debt in the seventh year, coupled with the exhortation to generosity towards those in need (15.1-11; see the essay in this collection by Walter Houston), and the prohibition of usury in relation to 'brothers' (23.19; Exod. 22.23), would help to prevent the accumulation

2. See the collection of essays by R. Westbrook, *Property and Family in Biblical Law* (JSOTSup, 113; Sheffield: JSOT Press, 1991).

of land by the rich and the permanent enslavement of the poor.

In particular, legislation relating to the king would prevent tyranny (17.14-20; cf. 1 Sam. 8.11-18). He is to have no autonomous power base through riches, a standing army or foreign marriage alliances. Again, legislation in relation to the hereditary Levites, who are to minister at the sanctuary (33.8-10), and who are to make the law known to all members of the covenant community, including men, women, children, servants and sojourners, every seventh year at the Feast of Booths (29.10-15; 31.10-13), are to own no land (11.9; 18.1-8), but are to be dependent on the community's tithes and sacrifices. This would mean that they would share the community's bounty in good years, but also its poverty in bad years. Their vulnerable position is acknowledged by commands to remember them (e.g. 14.29). To them, difficult legal decisions are to be referred, and they are to judge impartially (17.8-13). Another group of community leaders, elders, are to be chosen for their wisdom, understanding and experience (1.13), and are also to judge impartially (1.16-17; 16.18-20; cf. 24.17-18; 27.19). Moreover, no one is to be convicted on the evidence of a single witness (19.15); punishment is to fit the crime (19.21), and false accusers are to be punished with the punishment they try to have inflicted on their victims (19.16-20). The only other group of leaders to whom reference is made is prophets, whose status rests solely on their insight, which can be tested, and presumptuous prophets are to suffer death by stoning (18.15-22).

Similarly, in Leviticus, the response to God's holiness is to be the creation of a just and generous society. Leviticus 19 requires that gleanings be left for the poor and the sojourner (9-10; cf. Deut. 24.19-22), and that just weights and measures be used (35-37). It excludes stealing, dealing falsely, lying, swearing falsely by profaning God's name, oppression of and robbery from a neighbour, withholding the wages of a hired labourer all night, cursing the deaf or putting a stumbling block before the blind (11-14; cf. Deut. 27.18), partiality to the poor or deference to the great, injustice, slander, standing forth against the blood of a neighbour (15-16), hatred of a 'brother', taking vengeance or bearing a grudge (17-18) and wronging a sojourner (33). The legislation is summed up in two positive commands: to love your neighbour as yourself (19), and to love the stranger as yourself (34).

According to Leviticus 25, during the seventh year, when the land was to lie fallow, what grows of itself is to provide food for all, including male and female slaves, hired servants and sojourners (1-7). Every fiftieth year, a Jubilee year is to be kept, in which land that had been sold is to be returned to its former owner (13-28). The agricultural interests of the community are clear from the distinction drawn between the return of agricultural land and village houses (28, 31; cf. Deut. 27.17), and the sale of houses within a walled city, which are not to be returned at the Jubilee (29-30). Like Deuteronomy, Leviticus goes on to advocate the support of the poor, who are not to be lent money at interest nor given food for profit, so that debt does not force them into slavery (35-38). Leviticus 25 even tries to outlaw the enslavement of Israelites altogether by insisting that they should fall no lower than hired servants, who would be released at the Jubilee, together with their families (39-43). Only foreigners are to be slaves (44-46). Israelites enslaved by foreigners within the land should be redeemed by relatives or by themselves, should be treated as hired servants rather than as slaves, and should also be freed at the Jubilee (47-55). This would ensure that no group of Israelite hereditary slaves could exist.

These attempts at legislating and exhorting for the creation of a more just Israelite society, responsive to God's generosity and holiness, encompass the whole of the social order, and promise prosperity in the land as God's reward. Of course, such attempts are concerned with the establishment of justice within Israel and among Israelites and sojourners. Foreigners outside the land, and Canaanites within it, are to be treated differently (Deut. 23.19; 20.10-18; but cf. 21.10-14; 28.10-14; Lev. 25.44; 26.7-8).[3]

3. See G.C. Chirichigno, *Debt-Slavery in Israel and the Ancient Near East* (JSOTSup, 141; Sheffield: JSOT Press, 1993). The requirements of Deuteronomy and Leviticus may often have been ignored, but, as part of the Scriptures, appeal could always be made to them (e.g. Jer. 34.8-20; Philo *Spec. Leg.* 2.71-123; 3.137-43, 184, 195-203; 4.1-4; *Virt.* 122-24; and note Philo's justification of owning non-Jewish slaves: *Spec. Leg.* 2.123; Jos. *Ant.* 4.273). See also E.E. Urbach, 'The Laws Regarding Slavery as a Source for Social History of the Period of the Second Temple, the Mishnah and Talmud', in J.G. Weiss (ed.), *Papers of the Institute of Jewish Studies*, I (Jerusalem: Magnes, 1964), pp. 1-94. The same problems, of debt and land-loss, faced the poor citizens of Greek and Roman societies, but these were mainly resolved by foreign conquest and colonization; see M.I. Finley, *Politics in the Ancient World* (Cambridge: Cambridge University Press, 1983). Of course, other Jewish literature also influenced the New Testament. In the second century BCE, when those Jews who were considered faithful to their traditions suffered persecution at the hands of Syrian governors under Antiochus Epiphanes (1 and 2 Macc.), the promises of Deut. 28, Lev. 26 and some other prophetic literature underwent development and

2. *Differences between Jewish and Christian Communities in the First-Century Roman Empire*

The books of the New Testament were written, mostly in the first-century CE, by Christians and for Christian communities, which arose as a messianic movement within Judaism, but which expanded through the establishment of small groups of Jewish and Gentile believers in the cities of the Roman empire—primarily in the eastern, Greek-speaking region, but also in Rome. The writings reflect the concerns of some members of these communities in their relations with Jews, Greeks and Romans, and with the Roman imperial system. In Graeco-Roman culture, there was no concern to invest wealth in order to increase production, and giving wealth was assumed to impoverish the giver. Wealth, considered as finite, could be hoarded by the rich, or be used by them in luxurious consumption, or could be given to help others (either friends among their own elite group or less wealthy clients, and through gifts to cities and associations). Helping others brought honour and influence to the giver. There was, however, no tradition of caring for the destitute.[4]

The scattered first-century Christian communities, for all their consciousness of their own importance in God's plan of salvation for the whole world, did not form a united ethnic group with roots in a particular land, as Israel did, and did not produce writings like Deuteronomy or

reinterpretation. Those promises could only be fulfilled for martyrs in a life after death. Beliefs in future resurrection (e.g. 2 Macc. 6–7; Dan. 12.1-3) and in other forms of postmortem survival (e.g. 1 En. 22; Wis. 1–8) led to the reinterpretation of passages like Ezek. 37 and Isa. 53 in individualistic terms, and to the development of wisdom stories about the persecution and vindication of just people in this life (e.g. Joseph in Gen. 37–50) into assurances about the postmortem vindication of martyrs. Moreover, some Jewish writings looked forward to a final, eschatological triumph of faithful Israel over its enemies, brought about miraculously by God through human agents (e.g. Dan. 2; 7; *1 En.* 37–72). These writings seem not to have inspired quietism among Jews who lived under foreign empires, however, but rather to have inspired them to fight against enemies when God seemed to be providing them with opportunities for freedom (e.g. 2 Macc.; and the revolts in 66–74 CE and 132–135 CE).

4.   See Aristotle, *Nichomachean Ethics* 1163a.29, on the distinction between reciprocity and friendship between rich and poor, and its corruption into charity; but 'the poor' in this discussion are citizens, not the destitute. See A.R. Hands, *Charities and Social Aid in Greece and Rome* (London: Thames & Hudson, 1968). The New Testament takes up the teachings of its Scriptures in its strong condemnations of the accumulation of wealth and in its encouragement to help those in need, including the destitute. See below and Jas 2.1-7; 5.1-6; 1 Tim. 6.3-19.

Leviticus for the just ordering of social life in a semi-autonomous part of the Roman Empire. Even the Gospels provide nothing like the breadth of vision in social affairs to be found in the Jewish Scriptures. Rather, they developed an already existing ethos in the light of belief that Jesus of Nazareth was the messiah, who was crucified by his enemies, whom God raised from the dead and who would return in judgment at the end of the age in the near or not quite so near future. Most of the epistles were written to meet the particular and immediate needs of small Christian communities as their lives developed in the Graeco-Roman world. In doing so, however, they helped to create and define the ethos of these various groups within the larger society.

We should not overlook the political vulnerability of these groups within the Roman imperial system. That system did not regard religion as a matter of personal conscience but as a means of upholding Roman hegemony. Judaism and the Christianity which grew from it, however, regarded Roman and Greek religious practice as idolatrous. In the first century BCE, Judaism was able to gain religious concessions from Rome, which were renewed in the first century CE, in spite of Gaius Caligula's attempt to overturn them in 39 CE.[5] These gave Jews the right to sacrifice to the Jewish God in the Jerusalem temple, provided that sacrifices were offered for the Emperor and the Roman people. Jews were also allowed to pay the temple tax and to make other gifts, and Jews in Palestine could pay priestly and levitical tithes, and could keep the sabbatical year. All Jews could keep the weekly sabbath and their food laws. After the destruction of the temple in 70 CE, Vespasian converted the temple tax into the fiscus Judaicus, and gave the money to support the temple to Jupiter Capitolinus in Rome.[6] In paying the tax, Jews both gained exemption from practices they regarded as idolatrous, and acknowledged Roman rule.

Once Christians formed groups that were separate from Judaism, and that were identifiable social entities—as the Pauline churches were from the beginning—their religious practice, which separated them from worship at local pagan temples,[7] brought them under Roman suspicion as an illegal superstition, dangerous to Roman security.[8] In the first

---

5. Jos. *Ant.* 14.213-267; 18.261-275; 19.280, 287-292.
6. Jos. *War* 7.218.
7. E.g. 1 Cor. 8 and 10.
8. See the accounts of Nero's persecution of Christians at Rome, 64 CE, in Tacitus *Annals* 15.44.4 and in Suetonius, *The Twelve Caesars*, Nero 16.2, and the

century, numbers in Christian communities seem to have been so small that they could usually escape the attention of local Roman governors, provided they did not incur the wrath of Jewish or pagan neighbours. Most of the references to Jewish or pagan persecution in the New Testament concern leaders and missionaries, who would draw public notice.[9] But there are some references to more general persecution of whole communities,[10] and every local community must have been aware of its precarious position in relation to Roman officials. Moreover, these writings recount or refer to Jesus' life, his crucifixion and his resurrection, as paradigmatic for the lives of his followers. That Jesus had been crucified by the Romans, but had, by implication and even through explicit teaching, eschewed meeting violence with violence, meant that the eschatological hopes of Christians did not lead to their violent resistance of Jewish or Roman authorities in the first few centuries CE.[11]

New Testament writings define their communities in ways that distinguish them from Jewish, Hellenistic and Roman groups, yet, in ways that ensure that Christians did not completely withdraw from the societies in which they lived. On the contrary, they continued to interact with them in order to engage in missionary activity. Inevitably, therefore, these writings reflect a variety of attempted balances between separation from and involvement in the larger social complexes.

The Gospels and the Acts of the Apostles

1. The Focus on Jesus and his Disciple-Missionaries
The Gospels are short works which relate Jesus' life, death and resurrection for the instruction, inspiration, encouragement and, perhaps, criticism of the communities to which they were directed. They focus on Jesus and, to a lesser extent, on his disciples. They present Jesus' ministry of miracles and teaching; teaching that included references to an

persecutions of Christians in Bithynia when Pliny was governor at the beginning of the second century (Epistle 10.96).

9. E.g. Acts 4–5; 7.54–8.1; 9.23-25, 29-30; 16.16-40; 17.5-9; 18.5-8, 12-17; 19.23-41; 20.3, 25, 38; 21.27–28.31; 2 Cor. 11.23-26; Mt. 10.17-25; Mk 13.9-13; Lk. 21.12-19; Jn 15.18–16.21; 2 Tim. 1.8–2.13; 3.10-17; Jos. *Ant.* 20.200-202.

10. E.g. Mt. 24.9-22; Mk 13.14-20; 1 Pet. 3.9-22; 4.12-19; the book of Revelation.

11. E.g. Mt. 5.38-48; 26.36-56; Lk. 6.27-36; 22.35-53; Jn 15.18–16.11; 1 Thess. 1.6-7; 2.14-16; 1 Cor. 1.18-25; 2 Cor. 11.16–12.10; Rom. 12.14-21; Col. 1.24; Heb. 11–12; 1 Pet. 3.9-22; 4.12-19; Revelation.

eschatological judgment and transformation of the world in the near or relatively near future (e.g. Mk 1.15 and par.; Mt. 5.3-12 and par.), and they present what happened to him. They invite others to follow his way of life through God's inspiration. But Jesus' itinerant ministry, as it is described, required participants to leave their ordinary occupations[12] and the narratives suggest and depict their living by accepting the hospitality they were offered, which was not considered to be wages,[13] or by accepting gifts from others.[14] Although Jesus is sometimes represented as accepting hospitality from people whose wealth is reckoned to come from extortion,[15] the stories seem to imply that Jesus was attempting to teach generosity and a new commitment to God and his kingdom.

Similarly, Acts focuses attention on the apostles and other missionaries, most of whom are described as eschewing ordinary work, and as relying on the hospitality and charity of other believers.[16] Stephen and Philip, first introduced among those appointed to organise a daily distribution to widows, are the only members of that group to be mentioned again, and their stories are of their preaching or miracle-working.[17]

This focus means that little consideration is given to those who supported Jesus and his missionaries, or to the work or the ownership of property that gave them the wealth for such support. Moreover, even the miracle stories focus on the healed person's relationship with God, and show no concern about his or her ability to work and escape from poverty. The endings of these stories often refer to praise of God and assurance of salvation, not to the cured person's finding work. Also, the emphasis on miraculous healings obscures the need to care for the sick. The parable of the good Samaritan, found only in Luke (10.29-37), the Lukan version of the parable of the banquet (14.12-13) and the Matthaean vision of the last judgment (25.36, 43) are the only passages in which such care is encouraged. Again, in Acts, only in Paul's speech to the Ephesian elders, in which they are instructed to work in order to

12. E.g. Jesus' carpentry or building (Mk 6.3); disciples' fishing (Mk 1.16-20 and par.); or toll-collecting (Mk 2.14 and par.).

13. Mark 1.31; 2.15-17; 6.7-13; 7.24; 9.41; 14.3-9, 12-16 and par.; Lk. 7.36; 10.38-42; 11.37; 14.1; 19.5.

14. Mk 11.1-3 and par.; Lk. 8.2; Jn 12.6; 13.29.

15. A tax-collector (Mk 2.15-17 and par.; Lk. 19.5); Pharisees as 'lovers of money' (Lk. 16.14 cf. Mk 12.40; Lk. 20.47; 7.36; 14.1).

16. E.g. Acts 3.6; 4.36-37; 8.9-24; 9.9, 11, 19, 43; 12.12; 21.16. The case of Paul will be considered below.

17. Acts 6.1-6; 6.8–7.60; 8.14-23, 26-30; 21.8.

care for the weak, which could include the sick (20.35), is such care countenanced. These few passages seem to assume that among second generation Christians there would be sick people who had not been miraculously healed, and who would need support from people who were not members of their own family, but members of their surrogate Christian family. The demonising of some forms of illness, however, especially madness (though not in the Fourth Gospel), seems to recognise that illness is part of a wider reality than that brought about by individual actions; but the form of the recognition obscures the need for social and political reforms, outside as well as within Christian communities.

2. *Trust in God rather than Wealth*

Schmidt's study[18] is correct in pointing out that much of Jesus' teaching in the synoptic Gospels takes up wisdom traditions, which emphasise the need to trust God rather than wealth, traditions which are interested in people's relationships with God rather than with the poor. For example, Mk 10.17-31 (and par.) teaches that those who have possessions should divest themselves of them, follow Jesus, and gain 'treasure in heaven', which is eternal life. The rich are not quite viewed as beyond hope, since 'all things are possible with God', but the difficulties of the rich's entry into God's kingdom are stressed. The disciples serve as examples of those who had left everything to follow Jesus, and who could look forward to having a surrogate family, with persecutions in this world, and, in the age to come, eternal life. The teaching is addressed, not to the destitute, but to those who had possessions. Of course, this story includes Jesus' command to the man to sell his possessions and give to the poor, but that element is not emphasised, and the disciples are not depicted giving their possessions away.[19] The focus is on people's dependence on God rather than wealth.

The Gospels according to Matthew and Luke include other related teaching about 'treasure in heaven'.[20] In Luke, it is introduced by a request from a member of the crowd that Jesus bid his brother to divide an inheritance with him. Jesus' reply includes both a warning against covetousness and a declaration that a person's life does not consist in the

---

18. T.E. Schmidt, *Hostility to Wealth in the Synoptic Gospels* (JSNTSup, 15; Sheffield: JSOT Press, 1987).

19. Mark 1.16-20; 2.14 and par.

20. Luke 12.13-34 and par.

abundance of his possessions (teaching illustrated by the Lukan parable of the rich fool, who 'laid up treasure for himself and was not rich toward God'). This fool is not criticised for his failure to share his surplus with the poor, but for depending on his riches rather than on God. What is involved in being rich toward God is explained in the following section. People are encouraged to trust God wholeheartedly, even for their basic necessities, food and clothing. God's feeding birds and clothing lilies are brought forward to encourage trust, and a person's inability to add to his or her span of life (or stature) points the contrast with God's power. Human life is to be devoted to seeking God's kingdom in dependence on God's bounty. There is, however, no denial that people need food and clothing, and reflection would soon suggest that birds sometimes die of starvation and that lilies wilt in drought. Perhaps Lk. 12.33 implies that God's support would be provided through people's alms, but again the focus is on people's relationship with God: 'where your treasure is, there is your heart also'.

The same emphasis is found in the prayer that Jesus is said to have taught his disciples (Lk. 11.2-4 and par.). Sanctification of God's name and a petition that his kingdom come precede the request for bread. Again, the metaphor of the servant of two masters illustrates the maxim: 'you cannot serve God and mammon' (Lk. 16.13 and par.). Here in Luke, the 'Pharisees', Jesus' opponents, are presented as scoffing at the teaching because they were 'lovers of money' (16.14), and, according to Matthew, Judas betrayed Jesus for money (26.14-16). The same point is illustrated in Mark and Luke by Jesus' drawing his disciples' attention to the poor widow who gave her whole living to the temple treasury (Mk 12.41-44 and par.). The widow's selfless generosity forms a contrast with the behaviour of the 'scribes' whose religion is a mask for extortion (Mk 12.38-40 and par.). Similarly, the 'delight in riches' or 'riches' themselves are seen as a distraction that prevents believers from 'bearing fruit' (Mk 4.19 and par.).

3. *Generosity to the Destitute: A Charity of Consumption*[21]

In addition to this teaching, however, in both the Gospels and Acts, there is teaching that encourages generosity towards the poor and destitute. The gifts and hospitality enjoyed by Jesus and his disciples,

21. Luke–Acts has particularly attracted scholars who are interested in social justice. See, for example, L.T. Johnson, *The Literary Function of Possessions in Luke–Acts* (Missoula: Scholars Press, 1977) and *Sharing Possessions: Mandate and*

who had divested themselves of their livelihood, have already been mentioned. They are the only subjects within the narratives who are in receipt of charity. Otherwise, the destitute are represented as the objects of charity, through teaching addressed to those with possessions. Luke–Acts provides an abundance of examples: the parable of the rich man and Lazarus illustrates the reversal that God would bring about, and encourages generosity in the present;[22] the parable of the banquet requires the rich not to invite their relatives and rich neighbours to meals, which would be repaid in kind, but to invite 'the destitute, the maimed, the lame, and the blind',[23] and any rich person who put the teaching into practice in the Graeco-Roman world would soon have been ostracised by his or her peers; the parable of the good Samaritan shows how people should care for vulnerable neighbours, even across social and cultural boundaries.[24] There is a certain lack of realism, however, in the way in which the story is told. The Samaritan is described, not only as binding the man's wounds and taking him to an inn where he paid for his immediate care, but also as promising to pay whatever further costs might be incurred. Nothing is said about the Samaritan's means, nor about the effects on himself and his family, which such unlimited generosity might bring. Similarly, in the story of Zacchaeus, which includes his declaration that he would give half his goods to the poor and restore fourfold anything he had defrauded (19.1-10, cf. 3.13), the financial implications for himself and his family are not mentioned. The teaching is summed up in 6.30 and 35: 'give to everyone who begs from you, and of him who takes away goods do not ask for them again', and 'lend, despairing of no one, and your reward will be great and you will be sons of the Most High; for he is kind to the ungrateful and selfish' (see the Matthaean parallels). The practice of this teaching would relieve the destitute of the burden of debt, and would

Symbol of Faith (Philadelphia: Fortress Press, 1981); W.E. Pilgrim, *Good News to the Poor; Wealth and Poverty in Luke–Acts* (Minneapolis: Augsburg, 1981); P.F. Esler, *Community and Gospel in Luke–Acts. The Social and Political Motivation of Lucan Theology* (SNTSMS, 57; Cambridge: Cambridge University Press, 1987), ch. 7; H. Moxnes, *The Economy of the Kingdom, Social Conflict and Economic Relations in Luke's Gospel* (Overtures to Biblical Theology; Philadelphia: Fortress Press, 1988); J.H. Neyrey (ed.), *The Social World of Luke–Acts: Models for Interpretation* (Peabody, MA: Hendrickson, 1991).

22. Luke 16.19-31; cf. 6.20-21, 24-25.
23. Luke 14.16-24; contrast Mt. 22.1-14.
24. Luke 10.29-37.

prevent them from becoming debt-slaves (see also Lk. 11.4 and par.). Moreover, this teaching does not suggest that generosity should be restricted to members of any particular community, but urges generosity to all in need.

In Acts, however, generosity is to benefit members of the Christian community. The idealised picture of the Jerusalem church in 2.44-47 and 4.32-37 exemplifies a charity of consumption internal to the community and centred on the meal. Haenchen[25] draws attention to the mixture of classical Greek and Septuagint vocabulary in the depictions. Two types of charity are involved. The first type, which pictures the community as having all things in common, conforms to the classical Greek ideal of friendship. The second type involves the sale of property to meet the immediate needs of destitute members. Barnabas provides an example of the second type: he sold a piece of land that belonged to him and laid the proceeds at the apostles' feet (4.36-37). Three matters need to be noted. First, Barnabas, like others, sold the land and gave the proceeds. He did not give the land to poor members of the community so that they could support themselves. Second, in giving the proceeds to the apostles, he relinquished the honour and loyalty with which acts of charity were generally rewarded in the Graeco-Roman world. Honour and loyalty were transferred to Christian leaders. Third, these gifts were voluntary; they were not required on joining the community as seems to have happened among some Essenes.[26] This is made clear by the following story about Ananias and Sapphira (5.1-11), who were condemned, not for keeping back some of the proceeds from their sale, but for pretending otherwise.

Acts 6.1-6 describes a further development in church administration when numbers of Christians in Jerusalem had increased. It creates the impression that there were many dependent widows without families, from both the native and Hellenistic Jewish population. The story pre-supposes that the Christian community was completely separate from the Jewish community, and that Jewish-Christian widows received no support from the active charity of non-Christian Jews in Jerusalem. It explains that murmurings about unfairness in the Christian distribution led to the choice of seven men to take over this responsibility, in order to leave the apostles free for prayer and preaching. In this section,

25. E. Haenchen, *The Acts of the Apostles* (ET; Oxford: Basil Blackwell, 1971), pp. 330-35.

26. 1 QS 1.11-12; Jos. *War* 2.122.

nothing is said about the source of the wealth distributed, so it has to be assumed that 'having all things in common' involved redistribution from the richer to the poorer, and that, when this proved insufficient, the sale of property by members would make up the deficit. Moreover, the story views the widows as mere dependent consumers, and mentions no positive contributions they may have made to community life, through their labour or in other ways.

Later, in Acts 9.36-43, set at Joppa, the story of Dorcas' resuscitation creates the same impression. Widows are particularly mentioned as mourning her death, showing the garments and other things she had made, and, apparently, given to them. Dorcas is praised for her good works and charity, but the widows are mentioned only as consumers of that charity. The story also seems to assume that Dorcas' property would not have been inherited by the local community. All these stories represent a charity of consumption. Nowhere is a redistribution of property described that would have enabled the destitute to support themselves. Rather, the poor are made dependent on the Christian community for further support. Individual patronage is replaced by church patronage.

The story of Agabus' prophecy of famine during the reign of Claudias, and of the relief sent to the elders of the Judaean Christians through Barnabas and Saul from Christians in Antioch, illustrates intercommunal support.[27] Again, the contributions are represented as voluntary and as delivered to church leaders, here for the first time called elders. Later, Paul is described as declaring to Felix that the purpose of his visit to Jerusalem was to bring alms and offerings to his people.[28] Acts does not explain the source of these gifts, nor is Paul represented delivering them. Rather, he is advised to pay the expenses of four Jewish Christians under a vow, and to join them in their purificatory rite in the temple, in order to conciliate Jewish Christians who had doubts about the efficacy of his mission.[29]

---

27. Acts 11.27-30; 12.25; cf. Suetonius, *The Twelve Caesars* Claudius 18; Jos. *Ant.* 20.101.

28. Acts 24.17. It is unclear whether 'his people' refers to Jews or only Jewish Christians.

29. Acts 21.17-26; 24.18; cf. the earlier reference to Paul's vow in 18.18. References in the genuine Pauline epistles to the contributions Paul organised among Gentile churches he had founded, and which he planned to take to Jerusalem for the relief of poor Jewish Christians there, seem to express Paul's concern not only to help the poor but also to show that his churches acknowledged their debt to the

In the Gospels and Acts, then, there are expressions of concern for the destitute, whose needs are to be met by those with possessions through a charity of consumption. The teaching includes no encouragement to provide the destitute with the kinds of means that would allow them to support themselves. Patronage, not empowerment, is advocated.

4. *Dangerous Teaching*

The Gospels and Acts present Jesus as king and son of David.[30] The title 'Christ' is acknowledged by Jesus, whether privately (Mk 8.29-30 and par.) or publicly (Mk 11.1-10; 14.61-62 and par.; cf. Acts 2.31; 3.18, 20). The story of Jesus is, of course, nothing like that of David, which describes his establishing an empire through military manouevering. The Gospels' understanding of Jesus' kingship is more like that of Deut. 17.14-20, or like that of a persecuted prophet after the pattern of Moses and Elijah (e.g. Mk 8.27–9.8 and par.). This kingship does not require service but offers service (e.g. Mk 10.42-45 and par.), which is what makes it superior to David's (Mk 12.35-37 and par.). Nevertheless, it is presented as a lordship, with power to exercise judgment on God's behalf at the eschaton.[31] The retention of the language of king and kingdom could be used, and was used, to endorse monarchical power from the fourth century onwards, with its hierarchical power structure and patronage. That is why Gerald Winstanley and the Diggers of seventeenth-century England replaced it with discourse about the commonwealth of God. In particular, the Lukan reference to God's kingdom as an earthly reality (17.20), which allowed the church to

---

founding Jewish church in concrete evidence of love. He also seems to have wanted the Jerusalem church to acknowledge the full membership of uncircumcised Gentiles by its acceptance of the gift (Rom. 15.25-28, 31; 1 Cor. 16.1-4; 2 Cor. 8–9; Gal. 2.10). The contributions were to be voluntary and according to means, and were understood to bring about a kind of material equality (2 Cor. 8.13). They were to be expressions of generosity engendered by God's grace (2 Cor. 8.7) in conformity to Christ's example (2 Cor. 8.9). See A.J. Malherbe, 'The Corinthian Contribution', *Restoration Quarterly* 3 (1959), pp. 221-33; K. Nickel, *The Collection: A Study in Pauline Strategy* (London: SCM Press, 1966); B. Holmberg, *Paul and Power* (Coniectanea Biblica, New Testament Series, 11; Lund: Gleerup, 1978), pp. 35-43; D. Georgi, *Remembering the Poor: The History of Paul's Collection for Jerusalem* (NY: Abingdon, 1992).

30. The Fourth Gospel does not call Jesus the son of David.

31. Mark 9.1; 13.26-27 and par. Mt. 19.28 and par. includes the 12 disciples as judges along with the son of man.

identify itself as the kingdom, also allowed the churches to develop their own monarchical structures.

Moreover, the parables, which reflect the injustices of the first-century world in order to teach religious messages, could be read as endorsements of the social distinctions they reflect. As Raymond Williams remarks (above): 'the name of the god and the name of the master are significantly single—our Lord'. For example, the parable of the vineyard let out to tenants who were required to give some of the harvest to an absent landlord (Mk 12.1-9) condemns the tenants for their refusal to pay and for their violence towards the master's servants and son; and the parable of the master who left his servants in charge of his home when he was away (Mk 13.34-37) encourages the servants to serve their master's interests. The version in Lk. 12.35-38 does suggest that the master, when he returned, would serve faithful servants at table, but this is recognised as an extraordinary reversal of the master's normal behaviour (cf. Lk. 17.7-10), appropriate as a metaphor for the Lord's return at the eschaton. It was concretised only at Christian harvest suppers once a year, a custom which itself seems to have been a continuation of pagan practice. Similarly, the parable of the talents or pounds (Mt. 25.14-30 and par.) could be read as endorsing the practice it reflects. Many of the Lukan parables daringly refer to unjust and ungenerous characters.[32] Of course, these parables convey messages about the need to pray, to repent, or to make good use of opportunities. Set in the context of the Gospel's teaching about repentance, forgiveness and generosity, the behaviour of these characters is not encouraged on a social level. Yet, the Gospels do not directly criticise absentee landlords, unjust judges, lending at interest or the unfair acquisition of land and property, as Deuteronomy and Leviticus do, so the appearance of such characters in what became Christian Scriptures could be used to justify injustice.[33] Here I am highlighting the kinds of interpretation favoured by the right wing of Christian churches. In recent years, liberation theologians and New Testament interpreters like Luise Schotroff have also taken parables out of context and have argued that they encourage solidarity. Once parables are taken out of context and read in

32. For example, the friend at midnight (11.5-6); the rich fool (12.16-21); the prodigal son (15.11-32); the unjust steward (16.1-9); and the unjust judge (18.1-8).

33. See B. Barton, *The Man Nobody Knows* (London: Constable, 1925); G.E.M. de Ste. Croix, 'Early Christian Attitudes to Property and Slavery' in D. Baker (ed.), *Church, Society and Politics* (Oxford, 1975), pp. 1-38.

terms of social issues, they can be used to support different social structures. What is noticeable about the Gospels, however, is that their appeals are always made to individuals. Hence, social dimensions are often obscured. The synoptics attribute to Jesus a quotation of Lev. 19.19, but, significantly, without the illustrations of what 'love of neighbour' involves (Mt. 22.39 and par.).

Even the Beatitudes (Mt 5.3-12 and par.)—which promise the destitute, the humble and the persecuted rewards at the eschatological reversal—can be read, not as encouragement to help such people in the present (as they may be understood in their contexts), but as a reason for doing nothing about their present situation since God would reward them after death (see also Lk. 16.19-31).

5. *Glimpses of those who Supported Missionaries*

The Gospel according to Mark provides very few glimpses of those who supported missionaries: Levi, the ex-tax-collector who provided a meal (2.15 and par.) and Simon the leper who provided his house at Bethany (14.3-9 and par.); although this story is more concerned with the woman who anointed Jesus. This woman, so the story relates, was criticised by the disciples on the grounds that the ointment could have been sold and the proceeds given to the poor. Jesus' recognition of the woman's action as worthy of remembrance and as an anointing for his burial does not deny that helping the poor is appropriate, but the form of the expression, 'the poor you have always with you', provides an excuse for complacency towards the poor which Deuteronomy and Leviticus sought to overturn (see the essay in this collection by Christopher Rowland).

The Gospel according to Matthew includes more glimpses of supporters and of ordinary community life than do the other Gospels. Mt. 10.40-41 (cf. Mk 9.41) and 18.5-6 assure those who receive or reject missionaries that God will reward or punish them at the eschaton. Moreover, the disciples addressed in Matthew 18 seem to represent, not the missionaries of Matthew 10, but humble leaders of local communities who had to deal with problems arising after the first missionary efforts had met with success (18.10-20). Another reference to this community is found in Mt. 23.8-12, where Jesus is presented as the one teacher and one master, and the whole community of followers is conceived as a brotherhood, as in Deuteronomy, for whom God is the only father.[34]

---

34. Women as 'sisters' are rarely included explicitly, but see Mt. 12.46-50 and par.

Humility and service are emphasised, and warnings about an eschatological reversal intensify the message. The leadership that is mentioned
here and elsewhere—wandering missionaries (10.5-23), leaders of settled
communities (18.1-35), scribes trained for the kingdom of heaven
(13.51-52; 23.34), wise men (10.16; 23.34) and prophets (23.34)—distinguishes roles but denies a social hierarchy.[35] Finally, in 25.31-46, the
verdicts at the eschatological judgment are presented as for and against
people who had lived in settled communities and who had or had not
ministered to the hungry and thirsty, the sick, strangers, and those in
prison, amongst whom were the missionaries. In spite of these glimpses,
however, nothing is indicated about ways in which these people should
work or give from their wealth in order to avoid contravening other
teachings in the Gospel against greed or prostitution (e.g. Mt. 15.19 and
par.).

Only Luke names women who supported Jesus financially (8.2-3), but
of those named, only 'Joanna the wife of Chuza, Herod's steward' is
given a socio-economic status. Two other women, Martha and Mary, are
also represented as providing hospitality (10.38-42). In spite of Jesus'
acceptance of financial support from women, however, in this Gospel,
women are actually denigrated as untrustworthy witnesses (24.11). In
other words, they are presented as useful providers of material means for
the male missionaries whose activity is reckoned more important. This
attitude helps to explain why so little attention is paid to the providers.[36]

35. See also Lk. 14.11; 18.14; 22.26-27.
36. The Gospel according to Luke opens its account of Jesus' ministry by setting
him in a synagogue at Nazareth, where he is presented as reading from the prophet
Isaiah and pronouncing: 'Today, this Scripture has been fulfilled in your hearing'
(4.21). The allusion to Isa. 61.1-2 (with echoes of 58.6; 29.18-19; 35.5-6) serves as
an introduction to the whole narrative. It includes references to preaching good news
to the poor, release of captives, recovery of sight to the blind, setting at liberty the
oppressed and proclaiming the acceptable year of the Lord—a reference to the Jubilee
year in Leviticus 25. The passage could be understood in socio-economic terms, but
the rest of the narrative reinterprets it in religious and eschatological, not political
terms. The poor are assured of an eschatological reversal (6.20) and of sustenance
within the community of Jesus' followers through church patronage (e.g. 19.8; Acts
2.44-45; 4.32-37; 6.1-6; 11.27-30; 12.25). Release of captives refers to God's
forgiveness of sinners who repented (e.g. 5.18-26). Recovery of sight to the blind
refers to miraculous healings (7.21-22; 18.35-45; cf. 14.13, 21). Moreover, the blindness of those who are understood to oppose God's purpose is emphasised in the
story of Saul (Acts 9.8, 10-19; 22.11-13), and of Elymas (Acts 13.8-11), and is
applied metaphorically to Jews who do not respond to preaching (8.10; Acts 26.18).

Nevertheless, Acts occasionally mentions the occupations of some of the characters who offered hospitality. Peter is said to have stayed at Joppa with Simon, a tanner (9.43). Tanners normally lived on the outskirts of towns because of the unsavoury aspects of their work. By picturing Peter as a guest of Simon, Acts gives some dignity to a craft that was generally despised. According to chs. 10 and 11, Peter stayed at Caesarea with Cornelius, 'a centurion of what was known as the Italian cohort, a devout man who feared God with his whole household, gave alms liberally to people, and prayed constantly to God' (10.1-2). The narrative is concerned with the admission of Gentiles to the church, and presents this Roman soldier as pious and generous, a worthy, ideal type. But there is no suggestion that his conversion to Christianity involved his changing his profession. The Gospel according to Luke, like the other Gospels, includes teaching that forbids people from meeting violence with violence,[37] but this story suggests that Roman soldiers could become Christians while remaining as soldiers in the service of an oppressive empire. Apparently, they had only to be content with their wages and to rob no individual by violence or false accusation (Lk. 3.14) for the rest of their work to be ignored. Cornelius' personal qualities are allowed to mask the violence of his occupation, which provided the wages from which he gave alms. A distinction between private piety and public work is endorsed.

According to Acts 16.14-15, at Philippi, Paul stayed with Lydia, a seller of purple goods who came from Thyatira. She was baptised together with her household. Purple goods were luxury items, and the implication of the story is that Lydia was quite wealthy, since her house, like Mary's in Jerusalem (12.12), was apparently big enough to serve as a meeting place for local Christians (16.40). No comment is made about

---

Setting at liberty the oppressed refers to exorcisms and to the release of Gentiles from Satan's bonds (e.g. 4.31-41; 8.26-39; 10.17-20; 13.10-17; Acts 16.16-18; 26.18; 28.3-6). In parallel to Mark, the reference to the demoniac as 'legion' (8.26-39) may intimate that Roman rule is demonic, but Lukan references to centurions and other Roman soldiers present them as just and effective administrators, protective of Christians (7.1-10; 23.47; Acts 10–11; 21.31-40; 22.22-29; 23.16-35; cf. Lk. 3.14). According to Luke, Jesus' ministry demonstrated God's forgiveness of penitent sinners and created a new, quietist life for his followers; a life which should continue, without conflict with Roman power, until the eschaton. The statements in the canticle attributed to Mary (1.52-53; cf. 1 Sam. 2.4-5) would be fulfilled only at the eschaton.

37. 6.27-29, 32-33, 35-36; 22.50-51 and par.

the suitability or otherwise of gaining a livelihood by providing luxuries for the rich.[38]

These references to people who supported the Christian mission, therefore, exhibit Lukan complacency with regard to work. They implicitly support Graeco-Roman society, and there is little attempt at developing guidance about what kinds of work people should undertake in order to avoid the greed and violence condemned in the teaching.[39]

Alongside these references, however, are references to Paul. According to Acts 18.3, at Corinth he stayed with a Jewish couple, Aquila and Priscilla, because he shared with them the craft of leather-work. Unfortunately, the specification of leather-work is absent from western manuscripts, and the Pauline letters only state that Paul 'worked with his hands', without indicating in what way. If the reference to leather-work is secondary, Acts presents Paul as practising a craft. Hock's study[40] accepts leather-work as Paul's occupation, and suggests ways in which the practice could have provided opportunities for missionary work, but Acts makes nothing of this (18.4, 11). It does, however, endorse the work of craftsmen as appropriate for missionaries. Moreover, Acts relates Paul's speech to the Ephesian elders (in which he refers to his own practice of working to provide necessities for himself and others) as a model for them to follow. In this way, they are encouraged to work in order to support the weak. In support of the teaching, a saying of the Lord Jesus is recounted: 'it is more blessed to give than to receive' (Acts 20.33-35; cf. Lk. 6.38). The saying, however, includes a denigration of those whose poverty necessitated their receipt of alms. Nevertheless, in contrast to all the other missionaries whose stories are told in Luke–Acts, Paul is presented as someone who worked at a craft to support himself and others, and it is his example which second generation leaders are encouraged to follow. Here we have a recognition of the need for production, but that makes it all the more surprising that so little guidance is given about the kinds of work to be practised or avoided.

---

38. Contrast *Dio Chrysostom, Discourse* 7.110-11, 117-18.

39. Cicero's list of occupations suitable for free men, *De Officiis*, of course, is written from the perspective of the elite, but the form was available for adaptation in different religious and cultural contexts of *M. Kidd.* 4.14 and *Sanh.* 3.3.

40. R. Hock, *The Social Context of Paul's Mission* (Philadelphia: Fortress Press, 1980).

Conclusion

The Gospels and Acts[41] teach that Christian missionaries and the destitute (in Acts only the Christian destitute) should be supported by a charity of consumption. In this way, the teachings of the Jewish Scriptures about support for the poor and destitute were taken over into the Graeco-Roman world as something quite new. The narratives assume that those who gave such support would have to work or draw on inherited wealth to put the teaching into practice. Disinvestment of property as an expression of trust in God is also advocated, but not for all followers of Jesus. Moreover, the emphasis on a charity of consumption encourages a patronage that makes the destitute dependent on church alms, and that does nothing to empower them to support themselves. This emphasis also obscures (to the point of mystification in Luke–Acts) questions about the kinds of ordinary work that Christians should undertake in a social world engendered by violence and exploitation. Little guidance is given even about the types of work to be avoided. Since Luke–Acts allows both tax-collecting and the work of a Roman soldier, hardly anything is excluded except prostitution (Lk. 7.36-50; see also Mt. 15.19 and par.). These texts do not meet the obvious need for a charity of production.

References to Paul's 'Work With His Hands' and to the Ordinary Work of Other Christians in the Pauline Epistles

The Roman historian Tacitus, living at the end of the first and the beginning of the second century CE, accused Jews of idleness because they kept the sabbath day and the sabbath year.[42] Josephus' apologetic work, *Against Apion*, rebuffs such a charge by emphasising Jewish love of self-sufficiency and labour (2.174, 291). Both the accusation and the defence suggest that people who were seen not to work, whether at the level of the elite who were engaged in diplomacy, administration and war, or at the level of artisans and peasants, were regarded as potentially dangerous to Roman rule. Moreover, many philosophers did not regard the teaching of philosophy as work for which it was appropriate to

41. I have made very few references to the Fourth Gospel because that Gospel, even more than the synoptics, focuses on Jesus, and summarises his ethical teaching as service like his (13.13-17) and love like his (13.34; 15.12-17). Such general commands are open to a multiplicity of interpretations.

42. *Histories* 5.4.

accept a wage, and philosophers who charged fees or who were paid as tutors or who begged came under criticism as behaving like merchants.[43] This is part of the cultural context in which the Pauline epistles were written.

Paul's letters often refer to his working while he was a missionary, at Thessalonica, Corinth and Ephesus.[44] Since his missionary endeavour required extended periods of residence in one place, so that he could build up communities, in contrast to philosophers who appealed to individuals, his working seems to acknowledge a common assumption that hospitality should be accepted for only short periods.[45] Hence his explanation of his hard work, 'day and night', in terms of his desire not to burden his coverts.[46] His relation to them is likened to that of a parent to children.[47] Moreover, 1 Cor. 9.12 mentions that reliance on community support could have been an obstacle to the good news of Christ, implying either that Paul would have been perceived as a mercenary philosopher or that the community was too small and impoverished to provide support at the beginning of his mission.

None of these references provides details about the kind of work Paul practised in order to support himself. The 'working with our hands'[48] of 1 Cor. 4.12 has been interpreted by most commentators in the light of Acts 18.3's reference to craft or leather work, but we have no way of knowing whether that reference is accurate or not. If we were to take 'work with one's hands' literally, it could refer to either craft or unskilled manual labour. That his working at all could open him to criticism is clear,[49] but the criticism does not imply that the actual work was particularly despised in itself. And Paul was able to argue in ways that not only deprived the gibes of their sting but also gave him grounds for boasting.[50] But should the expression 'work with one's hands' be

43. E.g. Plato, *Protagoras* 349A; *Meno* 91D; *Apology* 20B; *Cratylus* 384B; Xenophon, *Memorabilia* 1 2.5-6, 14; 6.5.

44. 1 Thess. 2.9; 1 Cor. 4.12; 16.8; 2 Cor. 12.14.

45. E.g. *Didache* 11.5; Philostratus, *Life of Apollonius of Tyana* 2.23; 5.10. See Hock, *The Social Context*.

46. 1 Thess. 2.9; 1 Cor. 9.5-15; 2 Cor. 11.9, 27; 12.3.

47. 1 Cor. 4.14-15; 2 Cor. 12.14.

48. It is not clear from this reference who, besides Paul, is included, but 1 Cor. 9.6 includes Barnabas.

49. 1 Cor. 4.10-13; 9; 2 Cor. 11.7.

50. 1 Cor. 9; 2 Cor. 11–12; see D.B. Martin, *Slavery as Salvation. The Metaphor of Slavery in Pauline Christianity* (New Haven: Yale University Press, 1990), which

taken literally? In the Jewish Scriptures, the expression is frequently used of God's work of creation, of his love and fidelity, and of his deliverance.[51] It is used of human work in agriculture or in fashioning idols, but also of Levi's work of teaching and offering sacrifices.[52] Psalm 90.17 refers to all human work as 'work with their hands'. In the New Testament, Acts 14.3 calls the signs and wonders performed by Paul and Barnabas 'work done by their hands.' All this suggests that 'work with one's hands' is a colloquial expression for all kinds of work, manual and non-manual, so that nothing about the kind of work Paul undertook can be gathered from his own references in the epistles.

Nor was Paul's work sufficient to sustain his mission, in spite of his living at a level of relative poverty.[53] There are references to his accepting hospitality from Gaius at Corinth and from Philemon at Colossae.[54] Moreover, there are acknowledgements of gifts from churches in Macedonia while he was at Corinth, and from the church at Philippi while he was at Thessalonica, and again while he was in prison.[55] Malherbe has also argued that the expression 'send on his way', addressed to the Corinthians in relation to Paul and Timothy, meant 'equip with all things necessary for the journey'.[56]

In 1 Thessalonians, the Pauline reference to his own work is used to provide an example for Christians there to follow. The Thessalonians are reminded to 'work with their hands', both to express their love and to command the respect of outsiders. Idlers are to be admonished.[57] 2 Thessalonians, probably written by a Pauline disciple, develops the tradition. 2 Thess. 3.6-13 goes further in that it requires that those who live in a disorderly manner, doing no work, should be shunned, and that believers should imitate Paul and his companions by working. The principle, 'if anyone will not work, let him not eat' (cf. Gen. 3.19), is to

demonstrates the subtlety of the argument in 1 Cor. 9 in undermining a patriarchal ideology.

51. E.g. Job 14.15; Pss. 92.4; 143.5; Isa. 45.11.

52. E.g. Deut. 33.11; 2 Kgs 22.17; Isa. 65.22; Jer. 1.16; and it is also used of the work of the rich man Job in Job 1.10.

53. 2 Cor. 6.10; 11.27; Phil. 4.11-13.

54. Rom. 16.23; 1 Cor. 1.14; Phlm. 22.

55. 2 Cor. 11.8-9; Phil. 4.14-20.

56. 1 Cor. 16.6-11; 2 Cor. 1.16; A.J. Malherbe, 'The Inhospitality of Diotrephes', in J. Jervell and W.A. Meeks (eds.), *God's Christ and his People. Essays in Honour of N.A. Dahl* (Oslo: Universtetsforlaget, 1976), p. 230 n. 11.

57. 1 Thess. 4.9-12; cf. 2.9-12; 5.14; compare *Dio Chrysostom, Discourse* 7.4, 7.

be put into practice. Believers are to work in quietness and to eat their own bread. Idlers are caricatured as busybodies.[58]

Since 'work with one's hands' seems to be a colloquial expression, nothing can be gathered from this expression about the kinds of work to be undertaken, nor about the social level of the Thessalonians addressed. Since the expression could be taken literally, however, and could include manual work, it at least does not exclude such work as inappropriate. Nevertheless, work is considered solely from the perspective of the sustenance it could provide, either for the worker or for others. It is not considered from the perspective of its general contribution to society. It is never considered as a charismatic gift. Hence, one kind of work seems to be as good as any other (except prostitution). The Paulines, therefore, provide next to no guidance about the kinds of work to be undertaken or avoided. They express a charity of production, but without developing its implications.

Conclusion

None of these writings provides a sufficiently developed charity of production to encourage justice, much less loving relations, at work. Even the half-hearted attempt to exclude extortion and violence in Lk. 3.12-13 is more mystifying than effective, as Acts 10–11 demonstrates. There is no serious concern for the implications of the criticisms of extortion in relation to ordinary work. This blindness allowed an even greater lack of discernment in relation to the evils of slavery in the Graeco-Roman world.

The New Testament Epistles' Teaching about Slavery, Including the Admonitions to Slave-Owners and Slaves

Roman wars always led to the enslavement of those who were allowed to survive.[59] In the first century CE, however, Rome fought relatively few wars, and most of the slaves in the Roman Empire were the children of people enslaved in earlier wars, or were enslaved through piracy, brigandage, sale or the exposure of infants.[60] Slaves were regarded as 'living property' or 'living tools', subject to their master's absolute

---

58. Compare Plato, *Apology* 3.19B.

59. E.g. *Jos. War* 4.414-34; 7.24-39, 153-55.

60. Roman citizens were apparently exempt from both debt bondage and being sold abroad as slaves (Livy, *History of Rome* 8.281).

power. They had no right to marry and no rights in relation to their children, who belonged to their master.[61]

They were made to work in a whole variety of circumstances. One of the worst fates for male slaves was to be sent to the mines, where the work was so hard and hazardous that life was short.[62] One of the worst fates for female and boy slaves was to be sent to the brothels. At the other extreme, imperial slaves did the work of civil servants. They might accumulate wealth, rule over households, and exercise great power as agents of the wealthy and powerful. In between, there were slaves employed by cities and temples as public servants, there were slaves who worked in commerce, or who were skilled or unskilled manual labourers, or who worked in chain gangs or as bailiffs on large estates, or who worked in households as general servants, cooks, hairdressers, spinners, weavers, dressmakers, launderers, child-minders, teachers, doctors, midwives and the like. Some slaves were entertainers. When there were no wars to provide a glut of slaves, buying slaves was more expensive, and this, together with any skills they might have, offered the only real protection against brutal treatment.[63] Moreover, a badly treated slave would have an incentive to run away, although that involved risks.[64] Some slaves, engaged in household, commercial or administrative work, could sometimes save enough from money allocated for their use to buy their freedom, although their children would be left with their masters (if they had been brought up and had not already been sold elsewhere). Masters sometimes promised future manumission as an incentive for good service, but the most common time for such manumission was on the death of the master, in a stipulation of his will.[65] Moreover, most freed slaves continued to work for their masters' families, at least for some days each year, and all continued to owe the family loyalty. In this way, they were integrated into the system of patron–client relations.

M.I. Finley is right to emphasise the distinction between slave labour

61. Aristotle, *Politics* 1.4-5; Zenophon, *The Householder* 9.5.

62. Diodorus Siculus, *The Library of History* III 12.1–13.3; V 35.4; 38.1.

63. See M.I. Finley, *Ancient Slavery and Modern Ideology* (NY: Viking Press, 1980); K.R. Bradley, *Slaves and Masters in the Roman Empire: A Study in Social Control* (NY: Oxford University Press, 1987); Seneca, *Moral Essays* III; *On Anger* 40.1-5; Varro, *On Agriculture* 1.17.5; Pliny, *Natural History* 18.7.

64. Seneca, *Moral Essays* III, 5.4.

65. See the collection of texts on Greek and Roman slavery translated by T. Wiedemann, *Greek and Roman Slavery* (London: Croom Helm, 1981).

and other types of compulsory labour. Slaves were property. They were bought and sold. Many were overworked, beaten and tortured, and sometimes put to death. That some slave-owners did not exercise their full rights over their slaves was a matter in the masters' control, not the slaves', and special privileges granted by slave-owners could be revoked at any time. Slaves had no control over either their labour or their persons.[66]

In the genuine Pauline epistles, there are only four occasions when slaves are mentioned. 1 Corinthians 7.21-24 forms part of a general admonition that people should remain in the social position they occupied when they were called, but 7.21 is ambiguous. It could mean either that slaves were to remain as slaves even if they had the chance to gain their freedom, or it could mean that they should avail themselves of an opportunity to gain their freedom. The second interpretation is more likely because the verb is aorist, not present. But no exhortation follows, to encourage others to redeem Christian slaves. Verses 22-24 provide some dignity for slaves in suggesting that a slave is to be understood as a 'freedperson of the Lord', while a free person is to be understood as a 'slave of Christ'.[67] The rhetoric implies that, within the community, both slave and free would be treated with the same honour, but it does not suggest that the slave would become a freedperson in society at large. In this context, therefore, 'do not become slaves of people' must be a continuation of the teaching about free people who are to see themselves metaphorically as 'slaves of Christ'. Later, in 7.31, the instructions are justified by the perspective: 'for the form of this world is passing away'. The expectation of an imminent eschaton is offered as a reason for failing to make social changes.

The epistle to Philemon is addressed to a Christian slave-owner on behalf of his slave, Onesimus, whom Paul had met and apparently converted to Christianity (if that is the correct understanding of v. 10) during Paul's imprisonment, and whom he was intending to send back to Philemon. Whether Onesimus is to be understood as a runaway slave, as most commentators suggest, or as a slave whom Philemon had sent to Paul, is a contentious issue, since the letter does not specifically

---

66. *Ancient Slavery and Modern Ideology*, pp. 69-77, 95-96.

67. See D.B. Martin, *Slavery as Salvation*; S.S. Bartchy, *Mallon Chrestai: First Century Slavery and the Interpretation of 1 Cor. 7.21* (Missoula, MT: Scholars Press, 1973).

mention that Onesimus had run away.[68] Nevertheless, the reference to the possibility that Onesimus had wronged Philemon or owed him something (18) can be read to imply that he had run away.[69] In the letter, Philemon is called 'our beloved fellow worker' (1), and he is praised for his love and faith (4-7). Onesimus is called Paul's 'child' (10), who had become 'more than a slave, a beloved brother' (16), and Philemon is urged to receive him as such, and as Paul himself (16-17). The rhetoric of the letter both emphasises Philemon's freedom (9-10, 14), and implies that his obedience to Paul's demands is required; that is, he should receive Onesimus amiably and return him to Paul, free of charge, so that Paul can make use of his service during his imprisonment (8, 11, 13, 18-20). But the letter does not require Philemon to free Onesimus, since he was to send him back to Paul as a gift from himself (20). That is, in 20, Onesimus is still regarded as Philemon's property to be given to Paul as a useful tool. Moreover, that the church at Colossae is said to be meeting in Philemon's house shows that slave-owners were not required to free their slaves when they became Christians. Deuteronomy 23.15-16 forbids the return of a runaway slave. If Paul was returning Onesimus as a runaway, this would mean that the Christian churches he founded ignored or treated as inapplicable this command from Scripture. It is also noticeable that the letter makes not a single reference to Onesimus' wishes. As a mere 'living tool', he remains voiceless.

Even if we try to explain this apparent callousness by noticing Paul's vulnerable status in prison, or by highlighting the value of slaves to their owners so that using someone else's would count as theft, there is nothing explicit in the letter that would give hope to slaves.[70] As it

68. See J. Knox, *Philemon among the Letters of Paul* (London: Collins, 1960). S.S. Bartchy argues that v. 18 could refer to something other than running away as the wrong that Onesimus did to Philemon, but the epistle nowhere suggests that Philemon had sent Onesimus to Paul, so Onesimus' implied absence without permission would, in any case, be regarded as wrongdoing ('Philemon, Epistle to', *ABD*, V, pp. 305-310.

69. J.M.G. Barclay, 'Paul, Philemon and the Dilemma of Christian Slave-Ownership', *NTS* 37 (1991), pp. 161-86. The suggestion by B.M. Rapske, 'The Prisoner Paul in the Eyes of Onesimus', *NTS* 37 (1991), pp. 187-203, that Onesimus had fled to Paul as a friend of Philemon who could intercede against harsh treatment he had received, goes beyond the very limited evidence that the letter provides.

70. Barclay's suggestion, 'Paul', pp. 176-77, that local churches needed to meet in the houses of rich Christians and that, since such houses could not function (sic)

stands, the letter endorses the social institution of slavery and accepts the slave-owner's absolute power over his slave. There is nothing in the New Testament to compare with Philo's description of Essene belief and practice: 'They denounce the owners of slaves, not merely for outraging the law of equality, but also for their impiety in annulling the statute of nature, who like a mother has borne and reared all alike as genuine brothers, not in name only but in reality.'[71]

The other two places in the genuine Paulines where slavery is mentioned are in the visionary statements of 1 Cor. 12.13 and Gal. 3.27-28. The Pauline epistles provide evidence that in the cases of relations between Jews and Greeks, and between men and women, the visions bore fruit 'not in name only, but in reality'. In the case of slaves, however, there is no clear statement that Christian slave-owners should give freedom to their slaves, and the epistle to Philemon suggests the contrary. There is also no suggestion that Christian communities should redeem their slaves, not even out of a concern for the slave's ability to practice his or her religion and avoid idolatry (contrast *Jos. Ant.* 16.1-2). The belief in an imminent eschatological transformation hardly justifies the lack of interest. It might explain why no reference is made to the Jubilee of Leviticus 25, but the absence of any allusion to Deuteronomy 15 is more puzzling. It could be argued that the passage refers only to debt-slaves, and that, therefore, it did not apply to slaves in the Graeco-Roman world since they became slaves through captivity or birth. This would then be a case of following the letter rather than the spirit of the Deuteronomic passage. But no argument is advanced; the passage is simply ignored. Moreover, Jesus could be called 'our Paschal lamb' without any promise of the freeing of slaves (1 Cor. 5.7).

The Deutero-Pauline epistles, Colossians and Ephesians, contain

without slaves, no objections could be voiced about Christian ownership of slaves, is merely cynical. Even the most effete aristocrat, incapable of manual labour, could hire paid servants, and, had Christians stood out against slave-owning, they would not have met in the houses of slave-owners, but somewhere else, even in the open if necessary. And would there have been no rich people who would have been prepared to free their slaves when they became Christians?

71. *Quod omnis probus liber sit* 79; cf. *Jos. Ant.* 18.21. R.M. Grant, *Early Christianity and Society. Seven Studies* (London: Collins, 1978), ch. 4, contrasts New Testament teaching with Jewish, and highlights the contradictions in the teaching of John Chrysostom, who, in a homily on 1 Cor. criticises Christian ownership of slaves, but, in comments on Philemon, justifies Christian ownership of slaves.

household codes.[72] These adaptations from Graeco-Roman literature of advice to wealthy young men about their management of household affairs contain admonitions to household (not other) slaves and to owners of household slaves. Each addresses the subordinate partners, wives, children and slaves, before the dominant partners, husbands, fathers, masters. In Col. 3.22-25, slaves are told:

> Obey *in everything* those who are your earthly masters, not with eye-service, as people-pleasers, but with singleness of heart, fearing the Lord. Whatever you do, work with liveliness, as serving the Lord and not people, knowing that from the Lord you will receive the inheritance as your reward; you are serving the Lord Christ. For the wrong-doer will be paid back for the wrong he did, and there is no partiality.

We do not know whether this is addressed to the slave of a Christian or non-Christian master, since no distinction is made. In any case, the admonition lacks any sense of the real situation of slaves. Slaves in households had to obey their masters, whatever their demands. How could young male and female slaves who might be required to provide their masters with sexual services 'work with liveliness, serving the Lord'?[73] How could they do so if they were required to lie or cheat? These slaves are addressed as if they were free, able to make their own moral decisions about what kinds of service they would perform. Moreover, one of the few ways in which slaves could resist their masters was in working slowly and grudgingly. This command forbids them even that kind of resistance. And threatening God's punishment for wrongdoing pushes them into a double bind: they should obey their masters in everything, but God would punish any wrongdoing. Slaves controlled neither their work nor their persons.

In Col. 4.1, Christian masters are told: 'Grant to slaves what is just and equitable, knowing that you also have a master in heaven'. Taken with full force, this admonition could require masters to free their slaves, yet the fact that it is addressed to Christian slave-owners, who had obviously not freed their slaves when they became Christians, suggests that its full force is hardly intended. Something more like 'brothers in

---

72. Col. 3.18–4.1; Eph. 5.21–6.9; see J.E. Crouch, *The Origin and Intention of the Colossian Haustafel* (Göttingen: Vandenhoeck and Reuprecht, 1972); D.L. Balch, *Let Wives be Submissive: The Domestic Code of 1 Peter* (SBLMS, 26; Missoula: Scholars Press, 1981); D.C. Verner, *The Household of God: The Social World of the Pastoral Epistles* (SBLDS, 71; Chico, CA: Scholars Press, 1983).

73. See Petronius, *Sayricon* 75.11; Horace, *Satires* 1.2.116-19.

name but not in reality' seems to be implied. A requirement to free slaves would have to be expressed in unambiguous terms if it were to have that effect. A justice and equality determined by a slave-owner, not by a slave, would be likely to result in something less than the slave's freedom. No reference is even made to Exod. 21.26-27, which gives instruction to set free male and female slaves who suffer physical abuse. The teaching might save a slave from semi-starvation and cruel beatings, but little more.

In Ephesians, slaves are told:

> Be obedient to those who are your earthly masters, with fear and trembling, in singleness of heart, as to Christ; not in the way of eye-service, as people-pleasers, but as slaves of Christ, doing the will of God with liveliness, rendering service with benevolence as to the Lord and not to people, knowing that whatever good anyone does, he will receive the same again from the Lord, whether he is slave or free.

There is some improvement over the Colossian parallel. Slaves are not told to obey in everything, fear and trembling are recognised as a reasonable response to masters, and slaves are not warned of God's punishment for bad deeds but of Christ's reward for any good deeds they might be able to do. They are not specifically told to resist any commands to do wrong, whatever the punishment, unless the earlier teaching of 4.25–5.20 (especially 5.1-2) is addressed to slaves as well as free people. If so, it would be a fortunate slave who could escape cruel punishment at the hands of an unjust earthly master.

The Ephesian command to Christian masters reads: 'Do the same (good) to them (slaves), eschew the threat, knowing that your Lord and theirs is in heaven and that there is no partiality with him'. Once more, this command does not encompass freeing slaves since 'doing good' is too general a command to have such an effect. At best, eschewing the threat could imply that punishments threatened, like whipping, scourging, starvation and even death, might also be eschewed. The warning about the Lord's impartial judgment might also discourage cruelty.

In 1 Tim. 6.1-2 Timothy is given instruction about the appropriate behaviour of Christian slaves, but there is no corresponding admonition about the behaviour of Christian masters. Verse 1 concerns all slaves, whether their masters were Christian or not, and verse two concerns the slaves of Christian masters:

> Let slaves under the yoke regard their own masters as worthy of all honour, so that the name of God and the teaching may not be defamed. Let not those who have believing masters despise them because they are

brothers; rather they must serve them as slaves, since those whom they help with a good deed are believers and beloved (or, those who devote themselves to a good deed are believers and beloved).

It is again certain that Christians in this community who were slave-owners were not required to free their slaves when they joined the community. Moreover, slaves are encouraged to honour all their masters, whether Christian or pagan. It would have been difficult, however, for any slave who suffered violent punishments, abuses and humiliations from a bad master to distinguish between hating the violence and hating the violator. Furthermore, that is not quite what 'regard their own masters as worthy of all honour' means. Slaves are actually being told to regard their masters, whether their behaviour were good or bad, as *worthy* of all honour. In other words, slaves are being told, unreasonably, to abandon any moral insight they might have. The command to slaves of believing masters also makes clear that they are brothers in theory but not in practice. Perhaps some slaves in the community had noticed or even voiced the contradiction. If so, they got no support from the letter, which is more concerned with the supposed views of outsiders than with effecting the Pauline vision of a brotherhood. Moreover, the letter encourages financial community support for some widows and for elders (5.3, 17), but never suggests that Christian slaves should be redeemed.

Titus 2.9-10 gives advice to Titus about the behaviour of slaves, without any corresponding advice about masters: 'Slaves are to be submissive to their own masters in everything, to be pleasing, neither answering back, nor pilfering, but demonstrating complete and faithful goodness, so that they may adorn the teaching of our Saviour God in every way.' A caricature of a slave's bad behaviour is used to endorse complete submission. These slaves are not even allowed to protest about any bad actions they might be required to perform. By forbidding 'pilfering', the possibility that slaves might alleviate semi-starvation by eating food not specifically allocated to them is also excluded. 'Goodness' seems to be understood as 'whatever a master commands', without any expression given as to what that might be. Elsewhere in the New Testament, 'to be pleasing' refers only to people's relations with God. Moreover, this Saviour God is not understood to save people from slavery.

Finally, 1 Pet. 2.13–3.7 encourages Christians to maintain good conduct among Gentiles (2.12; 3.9-17), from whom they can expect persecution as Christians (3.14-18; 4.1-6, 12-19). The advice includes commands about behaviour towards the Emperor and governors, as well as admonitions to slaves (2.18-25), and to wives and husbands. Again, then, there are no admonitions to slave-owners. Those to slaves are the longest in the New Testament, and here a slave's difficulties under a crooked master are recognised. It is assumed that crooked masters would beat slaves who did good deeds as well as those who did bad deeds. Slaves are encouraged to do good deeds and to endure any violent repayment after the pattern of Jesus, who did not retaliate when violently abused. Moreover, not only slaves are so encouraged, but all Christians who might suffer persecution. Nevertheless, slaves would have suffered worse tortures than others during times of persecution.[74]

Why did the people who wrote these epistles, who were Christian leaders of communities that had accepted the Jewish Scriptures as authoritative—including Exodus, Deuteronomy and Leviticus—exhibit such callous indifference to the evils of slavery? Why did Paul not require slave-owners who became Christians to free their slaves, if only in the seventh year? In Graeco-Roman society, freeing slaves was neither illegal nor was it regarded as reprehensible. Pagans did it. Pagans may have despised slave-owners who did not control their slaves as slaves, but there was nothing to prevent slave-owners from changing relations by freeing their slaves. Moreover, Christian slave-owners were in such a small minority in the Graeco-Roman world that their freeing their own slaves would have required no major social revolution, as freeing all slaves would have done. Again, there is nothing in the New Testament which encourages Christian communities to buy the freedom of Christian slaves, not even to ensure that they could practise their religion. There are commands to Christians with possessions to give to the poor and destitute, but none are applied to freeing slaves. The Pauline vision of 1 Cor. 12.13 and Gal. 3.27-28 could have been actualised in relation to slaves, as in Philo's portrait of the Essenes. Moreover, in spite of the New Testament's indifference, some second-century Christians may have bought the freedom of Christian slaves, as may be inferred from Ignatius's denigration of the practice (*Pol.* 4.3). These possibilities were neither unthinkable nor impracticable. Concern with reputation among pagans or belief in an imminent parousia cannot explain the callousness. But had Christians tried to develop a charity of production that avoided extortion and violence, they would have been alerted to the

74. Pliny, *Epistle* 10.96.

unacceptable nature of slavery, and might even have left more traces in the literature of opposition to the institution. In this matter, a comparison with Deuteronomy and Leviticus shows that the New Testament represents an impoverishment of traditions, an impoverishment which allowed gross injustice to flourish in Christian countries through the centuries.[75]

75. Christians arguing for the abolition of slavery in the nineteenth century had to appeal to Old Testament texts like Exod., Lev., Deut., or to Rev. 18.13, or to general principles, like Jesus' love command, or to the fact that first-century Christians did not actually introduce slavery into the Graeco-Roman world as Christians in the eighteenth century introduced it into the new world. They also tried to argue that passages addressed to slaves and masters in New Testament epistles, if taken seriously, encouraged the freeing of slaves. See W.M. Swartley, *Slavery, Sabbath, War and Women* (Scottsdale, PA: Herald, 1983); P. Kolchin, *American Slavery* (Toronto: Harper Collins, 1993; Harmondsworth: Penguin, 1995).

HOW THE SPIRIT READS AND HOW TO READ THE SPIRIT

Stephen Fowl

'For it seemed good to the Holy Spirit and to us...' This is the way that the substantive decisions of the so-called Jerusalem Council are introduced in Acts 15.26-29. The narrative leading up to these decisions runs from Acts 10 through ch. 15. In these chapters we read how the earliest followers of Jesus addressed one of the most significant theological, moral and ecclesial issues ever to confront the church: how and under what conditions should Gentiles be admitted to this Jewish body?

In the course of the narrative the characters in these chapters make numerous explicit judgments about the work of the Spirit. In addition, there is a presumption that the Spirit generates their scriptural interpretation. Throughout this narrative the central characters show a remarkable facility for recognizing, interpreting and acting upon the work of the Holy Spirit.

As Christians have struggled both to interpret and embody Scripture in the various contexts in which they find themselves, they have traditionally made reference to the role of the Holy Spirit in these struggles. Christians hope and expect that the Spirit will guide, direct and confirm their readings of Scripture, as well as the practices generated and underwritten by such readings. In short, Christians presume that proper interpretation and embodiment of Scripture must be guided by the Spirit.[1] At this formal level, I expect that all Christians would agree with these claims about the Spirit's role in interpretation.

It is more difficult, however, to account for the practical force of claims about the Spirit's role in scriptural interpretation. How, especially in the absence of miraculous signs, can an individual or a community

---

1. See, for example, the Westminster Confession (1646) which claims that 'The Supreme Judge by which all controversies of religion are to be determined...can be no other but the Holy Spirit speaking in the Scripture' (ch. 1 art. x). In the Vatican II document *Dei Verbum* (par. 23) the Church reading Scripture is referred to as the 'Pupil of the Holy Spirit'.

discern Spirit-inspired interpretation and practice from more mundane varieties? Are there particular exegetical methods that will generate Spirit-inspired interpretation? How might we know this? Are there ways of talking about the hermeneutical significance of the Spirit that do more, in practice, than pay lip-service to the role of the Spirit?

One can, of course, take a long-range view. This view would note that over time one can distinguish Spirit-inspired interpretation and practice by its effects. Readings which lead to faithful worship, practice and belief are retrospectively seen to have been Spirit-directed. Such a position would tend to remain agnostic about the role of the Spirit in certain contemporary interpretive and practical disputes. There is much to be said for this view. In fact, it is narratively represented in Acts 5 by the advice Gamaliel gives to the Sanhedrin about how to deal with the first followers of the resurrected Christ and their teachings about Christ. This form of patient discernment must be part of any attempt to account for the hermeneutical significance of the Spirit. I am, however, more concerned with what might be said about the more immediate role of the Spirit in interpretation and practice. While specific decisions and resolutions of disputes within the church should be open to revision, Christian communities, like everyone else, must also make decisions and resolve disputes without the benefit of hindsight. Can Christians in the midst of interpretive and practical disputes, like those Christians in Acts 10–15, recognize, account for, and interpret the Spirit's work in more immediate ways.

I will argue that there are habits, practices and dispositions narratively displayed in Acts 10–15 that are crucial for contemporary Christian communities as they struggle to read and enact the Scriptures in the Spirit. I will begin by addressing some particular objections to drawing implications and analogies from Acts to contemporary Christian communities. Then I will move to discuss Acts 10–15, articulating some of the communal structures, habits and practices which seem to facilitate the recognition and interpretation of the Spirit's work. I will then try to show how an absence of these structures, habits and practices works to undermine the abilities of contemporary American Christian communities to address a whole range of critical, moral and theological issues.

Objections to Acting according to Acts

There are several objections one might raise to the notion of finding guidance about the hermeneutical significance of the Spirit by looking to

Acts. First, historical critics have raised numerous questions regarding the historicity of the events portrayed in Acts generally, and chs. 10–15 in particular. Without question, if one is interested in reconstructing a narrow historical record of the first generation of the Christian movement, then these chapters will have a relatively circumscribed value. The narrative related here, however, has much to say about the role of the Spirit in the formation of theological, moral and scriptural judgments. For my reflections, the prescriptive (and to some degree, idealistic) picture found in these chapters is more important than its historical accuracy.[2]

Secondly, one might object that Acts makes it clear that one discerns the work of the Spirit through the presence of 'signs and wonders'. These 'signs and wonders' are the only reliable markers of the Spirit's activity. In the absence of such miraculous occurrences, we cannot do much more than carry on our present struggles over scriptural interpretation and practice, hoping in some general way that the Spirit will hover over our debates and discussions.

Without question, one's interpretive position is made more persuasive if one can call down fire from heaven in the manner of Elijah. This, however, is a relatively rare event. Can we expect the Spirit to play a role in struggles over how to interpret Scripture so as to live faithfully before God in the absence of such devisive divine interventions? Relative to the rest of Acts, such miraculous verification of one's position is not a central element in the narrative of Gentile inclusion in Acts 10–15. Further, an examination of these chapters will indicate that the central characters are not credulous bumpkins, easily swayed by magic posing as miracle. Even when miraculous events play crucial roles in the story, however, these events are not self-interpreting. Rather, there are several very practical social structures, practices and habits at work here that enable the characters to recognize, interpret and enact the work of the Spirit. My suggestion is that in the absence of these elements, no amount of miracles will be able to account for the transformations in people's views related in these chapters.

Acting according to Acts 10–15

Much of the early chapters in Acts focuses on the eschatological reconstitution of Israel. This is displayed in chs. 1–7 by the transformations

---

2.   This is similar to the strategy Luke T. Johnson adopts in *Decision Making in the Church* (Philadelphia: Fortress Press, 1983).

and restorations that occur in and around Jerusalem. Under persecution in Jerusalem, the gospel begins to spread to those on the margins of Israel, Samaritans (8.4-25) and an Ethiopian eunuch (8.26-40).[3] It seems only a matter of time before the gospel reaches Gentiles. Indeed, there have been numerous foreshadowings of this in Luke/Acts. What comes as no real surprise to readers of Luke/Acts, however, is cloaked in mystery to the central characters of the narrative, particularly Peter.

In ch. 10 we are introduced to Cornelius, a Roman centurion. Cornelius does much to tie himself to the people of Israel: he 'fears God' and prays constantly. 'Cornelius is clearly an uncircumcised Gentile (cf. 11.3), yet his piety parallels that of a devout Jew.'[4] In a series of parallel episodes he and Peter are brought into contact.

Cornelius is given a vision as the result of his devotion (10.4). He is told to bring Peter from Joppa to his home in Caesarea. While Cornelius is responding to his vision, Peter is receiving another vision. Peter is clearly perplexed by the vision he receives (10.17). In part he seems to take the vision as a test of his fidelity to food laws. When the voice from heaven replies 'What God has made clean you must not call unclean', however, it becomes clear that the issue here is not Peter's faithfulness. Rather, the problem lies with his overly rigid use of the terms 'common' (κοίνον) and 'unclean' (ἀκάθαρτον).[5]

---

3.   There is some ambiguity regarding the status of this eunuch. Is he a Jew or a Gentile? This question is of some importance given the clear indication in chs. 10–11, 15 that Cornelius is the first Gentile convert. The text notes that he was worshipping in Jerusalem (8.27) and that he possessed a scroll with at least part of Isaiah on it (8.28). This would indicate that he was Jewish. According to Deut. 23.1 a eunuch could not be a member of the assembly of the Lord. Alternatively, Isa. 56.3-6 includes eunuchs who keep the sabbath and keep the covenant among those on the margins of Israel whom God will in no way cut off. Further, Isa. 11.11 mentions Ethiopia as one of the places from which God will gather the 'remnant of his people'. In the light of these prophetic allusions, and given the pattern in Acts of moving out from Jerusalem to those on the margins of Israel, I agree with Johnson in saying, 'Whoever the "historical Ethiopian" might have been, therefore, Luke clearly wants his readers to see him as part of the "ingathering of the scattered people of Israel"' (Johnson, *Decision Making*, p. 159).

4.   See Robert Tannehill, *The Narrative Unity of Luke–Acts* (2 vols.; Minneapolis: Fortress Press, 1990), II, p. 133.

5.   B.R. Gaventa, *From Darkness to Light: Aspects of Conversion in the New Testament* (Philadelphia: Fortress Press, 1986), p. 114, notes, 'What is at issue between Peter and the voice is not whether Peter eats some particular item for lunch but how he applies the terms "common" and "unclean". His practice is not the

Even if Peter understood this much, it is by no means clear what he is to make of this vision. While he is pondering these things, the men from Cornelius arrive looking for him. Peter does not put this event together with his vision. Instead he has to be prodded by the Spirit not to make any dismissive or overhasty judgment regarding these men.[6] In line with the Spirit's prompting, Peter welcomes them, shows them hospitality and agrees to go with them. This welcome is paralleled by the one Cornelius extends to Peter and his companions. In v. 28 Peter makes it clear that by the hospitality he extended in Joppa and the hospitality he accepted at Cornelius' house he has managed at least partially to understand the thrust of the vision.[7]

Following Cornelius' account of what God has told him (vv. 30-33), Peter begins his own account of the gospel. Peter 'truly understands' now that the boundaries of God's people are not constrained by racial or ethnic considerations, by human barriers of 'clean' and 'unclean'. Peter concludes his message by proclaiming that forgiveness of sins is granted to those who believe. No promises are made regarding the Spirit.[8]

While he is speaking, however, the Spirit descends upon all those listening. They speak in tongues just as those early Jewish followers did in 2.1-4. The fact that even the Gentiles received the gift of the Spirit astonishes Peter's circumcised companions (v. 45). Luke seems to emphasize here that the amazement of those believers of the circumcision (οἱ ἐκ περιτομῆς πιστοὶ)[9] is not focused on the event of glossolalia but on the fact that 'the gift of the Holy Spirit has been poured out even on the Gentiles'.

It is not yet clear what the full implications of this will be. It is clear both that God accepts Gentile believers and that God confirms Peter's practice in going to Cornelius. Not only does Peter baptize Cornelius and his household, he accepts their hospitality when they ask him to remain for several days. 'Consistent with the entire narrative, this request suggests that the inclusion of Gentiles does not have to do

subject here, but his assumption that he knows what is clean and what is unclean!'

6.   See my further comments below regarding the significance of the use of μηδὲν διαδρινόμενος in v. 20.

7.   Indeed, I think Gaventa is right to indicate that the real conversion here is Peter's not Cornelius' (see Gaventa, *From Darkness to Light*, pp. 107-108).

8.   It is also curious that no mention is made of any explicit response to Peter's message by Cornelius and his household.

9.   Given the role of these witnesses in 11.2-18, it is more important that we know they are circumcised believers than we know their names.

merely with a grudging admission to the circle of the baptized. Including Gentiles means receiving them, entering their homes, and accepting hospitality in those homes.'[10]

Indeed, as the story moves into ch. 11, the point at issue seems to be the fact that Peter accepted (and offered) hospitality to 'uncircumcised men' (11.3). What is crucial for my purposes, however, is the way this dispute is addressed and resolved in vv. 2-18. The scene is set when Peter goes up to Jerusalem and is confronted by 'those of the circumcision' (οἱ ἐκ περιτομης).[11] (Notice the absence of the adjective πιστοί that is used in 10.45 to characterize 'those of the circumcision' who go with Peter to Cornelius' house.) These characters 'criticized him' (διεκρίνοντο πρὸς αὐτὸν) for eating with uncircumcised men. 'Διακρινόμαι' is the very thing the Spirit commanded Peter *not* to do in 10.20.[12] That is, these Jerusalemites are engaging in the very type of hasty and dismissive judgment that Peter was told to avoid.[13]

In response to this judgment, Peter testifies to the things he has seen, both earthly and heavenly (11.4-17). He relates the vision of the sheet lowered down from heaven and the arrival of the men from Caesarea. He includes the Spirit's injunction not to dismiss this matter too quickly (μηδὲν διακρίναντα).[14] He notes that he had six witnesses with him as well. We already know that they are circumcised; their presence counters possible claims that Peter's account is idiosyncratic. Peter continues by relating Cornelius' vision. Without recounting the content of his preaching, Peter cuts straight to what is the decisive point for him: 'And as I began to speak, the Holy Spirit fell upon them just as it had

10. See Gaventa, *From Darkness to Light*, p. 120.

11. Just as Peter and John went out from Jerusalem to confirm what was happening with the Gospel in Samaria (8.14-15), here, too, Luke wants to see these events validated by the Jerusalem church (cf. also 11.22; see, too, Johnson, *Decision Making*, p. 199).

12. 'Luke exploits the polyvalence of *diakrinomai* in a fascinating way. What the Spirit forbade Peter to do toward the Gentiles, namely, "debate/make distinctions/ doubt", (10.20), these fellow Jews are now doing toward him' (Johnson, *Decision Making*, p. 197).

13. See the similar comments of Luke T. Johnson, *The Acts of the Apostles*, Sacra Pagina (Collegeville, MN: Liturgical Press, 1992), p. 197.

14. The NRSV translates this occurrence of the phrase as 'not to make a distinction between them and us'. This reads 11.12 in the light of the more explicit 15.9 which seems unjustified given the explicit use of 'between us and them' in 15.9. Hence, it would be better to follow 10.20 and translate the phrase 'without hesitation'.

upon us at the beginning' (v. 16).[15] Peter interprets this in the light of
Jesus' words foretelling the coming of the Spirit. He then concludes that
if God has given the Gentiles the 'same gift he gave us when we
believed in the Lord Jesus Christ, who was I to hinder God?' (v. 17) For
Peter, the pouring out of the Spirit upon the Gentiles takes this matter
out of his hands. It is the decisive point which convinces him that this is
God's doing. To disagree or criticize (διακρινόμαι?) would be to
hinder God. For Peter's audience, testimony to the pouring out of the
Spirit upon the Gentiles is convincing.

While this seems to settle the issue of whether Gentiles can be included
in this body, an issue whose outcome was widely foreshadowed, the
question of how and under what conditions Gentiles should be admitted
to this Jewish group is left unaddressed.

It is not until ch. 15 that this issue is directly confronted. Following the
rather intensive examination of one incident, running from 10.1–11.18,
the narrative speeds up. The tribulation that began in ch. 8 and was set
in Jerusalem is rejoined. Likewise, this tribulation leads to a further
spreading of the gospel and the establishment of a primarily Gentile
church in Antioch. There is a type of symbiotic relationship between
Jerusalem and Antioch. Jerusalem sends Barnabas to Antioch (from
whence he is subsequently passed on to other churches) to supervise and
confirm what is going on there. Agabus (also from Jerusalem) predicts a
famine which leads those in Antioch (and elsewhere) to send food to
Judea (including Jerusalem). While Jerusalem becomes the locus for
persecution, Antioch becomes the locus of a spreading mission to Jews
and Gentiles. Finally, having returned to Antioch from what becomes
known as the first missionary journey, Paul and Barnabas encounter
'certain individuals from Judea'—later identified as from Jerusalem
(15.24)—arguing that Gentiles must be circumcised in order to be saved.
Paul and Barnabas disagree so sharply with these unnamed characters
that it is agreed that they should go up to Jerusalem to discuss the
matter with the 'apostles and elders' (15.2).

As they proceed up to Jerusalem they tell stories about the conversion
of the Gentiles (15.3). These stories are greeted with great joy, and they
remind us that the issue here is not whether Gentiles can turn to God,
but whether or not they should be circumcised. As Peter welcomed the
men from Cornelius, and was, in turn, welcomed by Cornelius, we read

15. This does not quite agree with ch. 10 which has the Spirit falling on the crowd
in the midst of Peter's address.

that those from Antioch are welcomed by the Church in Jerusalem. Serious disagreement does not rule out hospitality.

At this point in the narrative the issue of whether or not Gentile believers need to be circumcised and keep the law is directly joined. The demand for circumcision of Gentile converts in v. 5 starts off a long debate. Those who proposed circumcision and Torah observance for Gentile believers had a strong case. Like Luke, I will regard this side of the argument as so self-evident that it does not need treatment here. This debate reaches its climax in three distinct speeches. Peter begins by giving an account of his encounter with Cornelius which focuses primarily on the synthetic and systematic judgments rather than on the specific details of his visit to Cornelius.[16] Peter's testimony is, in fact, transformed into God's testimony in v. 8. God has borne witness to the acceptability of the Gentiles by sending the Spirit on them. God has not 'discriminated' (οὐθὲν διέκρινεν) between 'us and them'. Finally, God has cleansed their hearts.[17] That is, as 10.15 indicated, God has made the Gentiles 'clean'. By its third telling, it is clear that Peter has caught the importance of the vision he first saw in Joppa.[18] Without requiring circumcision and Torah observance, God has poured out the Spirit on the Gentiles. The Spirit is the decisive marker of God's acceptance. Hence, the fact that the Gentiles have received the same Spirit as the Jewish believers apart from circumcision indicates that circumcision should not now be required of them. Indeed, he goes so far as to imply that those who do not see things this way are hindering God (v. 10).

We are then briefly told about Paul and Barnabas' account of the 'signs and wonders' God had done among the Gentiles. This testimony confirms that Peter's observations, based on a single encounter with Cornelius, are repeated among the Gentiles more generally.

James then renders his judgment (κρίνω) in 15.19. This judgment contrasts both with the hasty and unformed judgment Peter is urged by the Spirit to avoid (μηδὲν διακρινόμενος) in 10.20, and with the

---

16. Tannehill, *Narrative Unity*, II, p. 184, calls this a 'distinctly theological' rather than a personal account.

17. In relation to the issue of circumcision, this comment may well echo texts such as Deut. 10.16; Jer. 4.4; Ezek. 44.7 where 'circumcision of the heart' is more important than physical circumcision (cf. Col. 2.11).

18. This pattern might have some interesting implications for understanding and interpreting visionary material.

negative judgment (διεκρίνοντο) rendered on Peter's actions by 'those of the circumcision' in 11.2. In Peter's summary of this event in 15.7-11, he urges his audience to recognize that God does not discriminate (οὐθὲν διέκρινεν) between 'us and them'. Thus, the only times that διακρίνω appears in Acts are in relation to Peter's visit to Cornelius and subsequent discussions of its significance. The appearance of διακρίνω in Acts ceases with James' use of κρίνω in 15.19, rendering the judgment the Spirit has been pointing to at least from ch. 10.

James begins by making reference to how Simeon 'has related how God first looked favorably upon the Gentiles, to take from them a people for his name'. I have argued elsewhere that this reference to Simeon should be taken as polyvalent.[19] That is, it should be read as a reference to Simon Peter's comments in vv. 7-11. It also, however, alludes to the words of the prophet Simeon in Lk. 2.32, that through Jesus God was causing a light to shine among the Gentiles. Further, the words written in the prophets agree with these testimonies.[20] This leads to a citation of Amos 9.11-12. This collocation of individual testimony and scriptural agreement, leads James to issue his judgment that the Gentiles need not be circumcised. James does, however, advocate sending an epistle to the Gentile congregations urging them to avoid certain things.

Without necessarily pinning down the exact wording of the council's decision, there are several elements to be noted that are relevant to my present discussion. First, while it is James who articulates a judgment here, it becomes the basis for a communal consensus. Unlike the abortive moments of διακρίνω which appear earlier in the narrative, James' κρίνω 'seems good to the Holy Spirit and all of us'. While James' judgment becomes authoritative, it does so because it articulates for the community the sense of the Spirit's work. It is not authoritative simply because James, the leader of the church in Jerusalem, says so.[21]

19. See my 'The Simeons of Acts 15:14' paper read to the Biblical Criticism and Literary Criticism section of the SBL, Nov. 1995, which argues this point (initially made by Chrysostom) more fully.

20. Johnson, *Decision Making*, p. 84 and *Acts*, p. 265, stresses the fact that the Greek clearly has the prophets agreeing with the testimony (τούτῳ συμφωνοῦσιν).

21. 'James makes judgment (*krino*, 15.19), but does not decide alone. The apostles and the elders must agree *with the whole Church* for that decision to be carried (15.22). In fact, it is not enough for the Mother Church to decide the issue unanimously; the local churches who are addressed must also "rejoice at the consolation" and send the emissaries back "in peace" for the decision truly to have been reached (15.31, 33). Not only the communication of a decision from on high, but the steady

Further, the constraints imposed on the Gentiles seem to have two functions. First, it enables Jewish and Gentile believers to enjoy a minimal degree of table fellowship without insisting that the Jewish believers fundamentally compromise their Jewish identity. This is also significant given the importance Paul places on a certain type of 'agape' meal for Christian identity (cf. 1 Cor. 11.17-34).

Secondly, James bases the conditions to be imposed on the Gentiles, which seem (in whatever form one examines) to draw on Leviticus 17–18 on the claim that 'Moses has those who proclaim him in every city'. The point seems to be that 'Luke regards these conditions as rooted in Torah, and that Torah's own norms for proselytes and sojourners (Lev. 17.8, 10, 13, 15) would be known already to Gentiles close to the Synagogue such as had converted'.[22] Although they are not required to be circumcised, Gentile converts are not free simply to live as they please. The work of the Spirit, which sustains the decision not to require circumcision, does not indicate that one can ignore Scripture. In fact, James' entire speech reflects a complex series of interactions between interpretations of the Spirit's work and Spirit-inspired interpretation and application of Scripture. Understanding these interactions will be essential for any Christian community if the Spirit is to play a significant role in the interpretation and embodiment of Scripture.

Acting according to Acts:
Reading the Spirit as Essential for Reading with the Spirit

As Luke Johnson has repeatedly stressed in regard to James' judgment, the interpretation of Scripture is guided by the testimony about the Spirit's work, rather than the other way around.

> What is remarkable, however, is that the text is confirmed by the narrative, not the narrative by the Scripture. As Peter had come to a new understanding of Jesus' words because of the gift of the Spirit, so here the Old Testament is illuminated and interpreted by the narrative of God's activity in the present.[23]

---

presence in the affected community of prophets who can console and strengthen, teach and preach the word of God, finish off this process of decision-making in Luke's idealized rendition' (15.32, 35a; Johnson, *Acts*, p. 279).

22. Johnson, *Acts*, p. 267.

23. Johnson, *Decision Making*, p. 84.

Experience of the Spirit provides the lenses through which Scripture is read rather than *vice-versa*. This is perhaps the most significant point the New Testament has to make about the hermeneutical significance of the Spirit; and it runs against the grain of modern interpretive presumptions.[24] Nevertheless, we should not treat this as an abstract hermeneutical rule. The pattern of reading Scripture found in Acts and elsewhere in the New Testament cannot be easily or profitably separated from the very specific types of ecclesial contexts in which that reading takes place. As my overview of Acts 10–15 has indicated, the Spirit's activity is no more self-interpreting than Scripture is. Understanding and interpreting the Spirit's movement is a matter of communal debate and discernment over time. This debate and discernment is itself often shaped both by prior interpretations of Scripture and traditions of practice and belief. This means that in practice it is probably difficult, if not impossible, to separate clearly whether one's Scriptural interpretation is prior to or dependent upon a community's experience of the Spirit.

The difficulty, if not impossibility, of distinguishing moments of scriptural interpretation from moments of interpretation of the Spirit is not a reason simply to dissolve or subsume reflection and debate about the Spirit into reflection and debate over Scripture. Such a reduction will leave Christians merely paying lip-service to the hermeneutical significance of the Spirit. Instead, if believers are to follow the examples found in Acts 10–15 and read with the Spirit or as the Spirit reads, then it will be essential to learn to read the Spirit, that is, to discern what the Spirit is doing. In this section I would like to point out several practices, habits and structures related to the specific contexts of Acts 10–15 that appear to be crucial for the characters' abilities both to discern what the

24. See, for example, Richard Hays' comment regarding the question of whether the Spirit illumines the text of Scripture or whether Scripture measures and constrains one's experience of the Spirit:

> Paul's unflinching answer, to the dismay of his more cautious kinsmen then and now, is to opt for the hermeneutical priority of Spirit-experience. This choice leads him, to be sure, not to a rejection of Scripture but to a charismatic rereading, whose persuasive power will rest precariously on his ability to demonstrate a congruence between the scriptural text and the community summoned and shaped by his proclamation.

See *Echoes of Scripture in the Letters of Paul* (New Haven: Yale University Press, 1989), p. 108. I have commented more fully on this way of formulating the matter in 'Who Can Read Abraham's Story? Allegory and Interpretive Power in Galatians', *JSNT* 55 (1994), pp. 77-95.

Spirit is doing and to act upon this discernment.

It is clear that in both Acts 11 and 15 Peter's testimony (among that of others), that Gentiles had received the Spirit upon hearing the gospel, is the primary component in persuading those in favor of Gentile circumcision that this was not necessary. It is perhaps not surprising to claim that both the practice of testifying or bearing witness and the practice of listening wisely to such testimony are essential to a community's ability to 'read the Spirit'.[25]

In an American context, it is certainly the case that our society and our churches are overrun with testimony of one sort or another. There are, however, several distinguishing features about the practice of testifying in Acts 10–15 that separate this type of speaking from both the adversarial nature of a law court and the self-promotional context of a television talk-show.

First, it is testimony about the Spirit by those who are already recognized as people of the Spirit. Peter stresses that God has poured out the same Spirit on the Gentiles as he and his fellow Jews had received. It is the Gentiles' reception of this same gift, apart from circumcision, that is ultimately decisive here. The basis for Peter's claim is his, and his fellow Jews', prior reception of the same Spirit. Peter's status as one who already knows the Spirit lends weight to his testimony about the Spirit's work in the lives of others. It may well be the case, then, that giving testimony about the Spirit normally cannot be done well by just anybody. Testimony about the Spirit's work in others tends to be done best by those who have experienced the Spirit's work themselves.

While noting that those who are recognized people of the Spirit are likely to be the best ones to testify about the Spirit's work, it is also crucial to note that Peter's testimony is, in two crucial respects, not his testimony. That is, there are two respects in which Peter is displaced as the subject of his testimony. First, Peter's testimony is not so much about what he has done as what he has seen God doing. In the various accounts he offers, Peter makes it plain that the inclusion of the Gentiles is not his pet project, rather it is the work of God. This is made most clear in 15.8 when he claims that God has testified (ἐμαρτύρησεν) to the 'cleansed hearts' of the Gentiles by 'giving them the Holy Spirit'.

---

25. Tannehill's comment (*Narrative Unity*, II, p. 130) in regard to 10.1–11.18 is applicable to the entirety of this section: 'Study of the composition of the narrative also reveals another important factor in discernment of the will of God: the sharing of divine promptings with other persons'.

Here God not only becomes the subject of Peter's testimony, but the primary witness to it, as well.[26]

The second respect in which Peter's testimony is not strictly his testimony concerns the fact that his account is not so much about what God has done to him (although that figures in passages such as 10.34) as about what God had done to others. Peter's testimony is not about himself and his experience of the Spirit. Rather, the subject of Peter's testimony is the work of the Spirit in the lives of others.

To be able to read the Spirit well, one must not only become and learn from people of the Spirit, one must also become practiced at testifying about what the Spirit is doing in the lives of others. In our present age, which favors self-authentication above all else, believers may find it hard to recognize this as a crucial element in testimony about the Spirit's work.

Both ecclesially and socially we Christians are becoming so isolated from each other that when we must make judgments about Scripture, our common life or about others, we have little recourse but to rely on the self-authenticating testimony of virtual strangers or merely to repeat the practices, demands and strictures we have used before. This is not to say that believers should always innovate, ignoring or actively transgressing past convictions and commitments. At the Jerusalem Council, past commitments and convictions are articulated and applied in what seems to be an obvious way—Gentiles joining this Jewish body must be circumcised and obey Torah. The burden of proof seems to lie with those who would innovate. In response, Peter (along with Paul and Barnabas) testifies to the work of the Spirit in the lives of Gentile converts, interpreting this work in such a way that indicates that God does not demand circumcision. James articulates a judgment that both accounts for the Spirit's creative movement and, by means of his scriptural citation and reliance on the Torah-based, practical 'burdens' to be placed on the Gentiles, aims to retain both long-range continuity with God's work among the people of Israel and practical continuity exhibited in a unified table fellowship.

Of course, such continuities are always contestable matters of interpretation. There are no guarantees that Christians' attempts to follow the Spirit will always result in belief, practice and worship that faithfully continue the life of the people of God. Alternatively, simply repeating

---

26. See also Peter's claim in 5.32: 'And we are witnesses of these things, and so is the Holy Spirit whom God has given to those who obey him'.

what has been done before will not insure fidelity. Changing historical circumstances will change the significance, meaning and effects of traditional words and practices whether we like it or not. Believers have no choice but to struggle, argue and debate with one another over how best to extend their faith, worship and practice in the present and into the future while remaining true to their past. In this struggle, testimony about the Spirit's work in the lives of others must become as central to contemporary believers as it was to the characters in Acts.

The only way to counter the privatizing tendencies of contemporary church life—which make it unlikely or impossible that we Christians would be in a position to testify about the work of the Spirit in the lives of our sisters and brothers—is to enter into friendships with them (largely through extending hospitality to them). There are at least two respects in which the practice of testifying depends upon our abilities both to overcome our tendencies toward isolation and to nurture and sustain certain types of friendships. First, no matter how acute one's spiritual insight, one will not be able to detect the Spirit's work in the lives of others unless one knows them in more than superficial ways. While the narrative of Acts 10–15 is quite compressed, there still is a hint of the importance of forming particular sorts of friendships through the brief but significant announcements of hospitality and welcome being extended. When they finally meet, Cornelius is not exactly a stranger to Peter. Those sent to Joppa to find Peter informed him about Cornelius. They stayed with Peter and traveled from Joppa to Caesarea together. Cornelius, too, extends hospitality to Peter. Initially, we must assume that Peter would have called Cornelius 'unclean'. In the course of directly encountering him and speaking the good news to Cornelius in his home, Peter is able to recognize the Spirit being poured out on Cornelius and his household and to come to see the practical significance of this in regard to all Gentile converts. We do not know if Peter would have called Cornelius a friend. We do know that Peter did not consider him some alien element who can only be labeled 'unclean'.

Secondly, the formation of friendships is also crucial to a community's abilities to be wise hearers of testimony. It seems likely that Peter's relationships with the various parties whom he confronts in Jerusalem affects the ways in which his testimony is received. That is, one is more likely to respond wisely to the testimony of a friend. Unlike the adversarial nature of a law court where we look for jurors who do not have connections to either the defendant or to witnesses, wise listening in the church is usually founded on friendships between witnesses and listeners.

Even within the context of specific friendships that can sustain and act upon testimony about the Spirit's work, we should not forget that discerning the work of the Spirit takes time.[27] It is only on the third time of reflecting on the events surrounding his visit to Cornelius that Peter comes to the conclusion that the upshot of God pouring out the Spirit on Gentiles, apart from their circumcision, indicates that the church should not require that Gentile converts become Jews, as well. Even for the most insightful testifiers and for the wisest listeners, interpreting the Spirit so that one can interpret with the Spirit demands patience or what Luke Johnson calls 'the asceticism of attentiveness'.[28] More basically, simply forming the friendships needed to be able to detect, much less interpret, the Spirit's work in the life of another is time consuming. Rushing into judgments risks lapsing into the patterns of discrimination characterized in Acts by the use of διακρίνω as opposed to the κρίνω offered by James which 'seems good to the Holy Spirit and to us'. It is only within communities who both sustain and nurture certain types of friendship and exhibit patience in discernment that we will find the sort of consensus emerging that is narrated in Acts.[29]

Conclusion

Thus far, I have argued that close study of Acts 10–15 provides crucial insights into the hermeneutical significance of the Spirit. This narrative (among other passages) indicates that if Christians are to interpret with the Spirit, they will also need to learn how to interpret the Spirit. Further, our prospects for interpreting the Spirit are closely linked to a community's proficiency at testifying to the Spirit's work, particularly the Spirit's work in the lives of others. Such testimony depends on the forming and sustaining of friendships in which believers' lives are

27. L. Gregory Jones has provided an important homiletical meditation on this point in 'Taking Time for the Spirit', *The Christian Century* (29 April, 1992), p. 451.

28. L. Johnson, 'Debate and Discernment, Scripture and Spirit', *Commonweal* (28 Jan. 1994), p. 11.

29. I am not saying that such consensus is always a prerequisite. In fact, without the communal friendships and patience needed to testify to the work of the Spirit we should not really expect such consensus to emerge. In such cases, however, the remedy is not further reflection on the processes needed to achieve consensus, but more fundamental revisioning of a common life that is not yet adequate to consensus forming.

opened to others in ways that display the Spirit's working. Welcoming strangers and the extension of hospitality become building blocks for such friendships. Finally, building such friendships, becoming people of the Spirit, and recognizing and interpreting the work of the Spirit all take time and demand patience.

Experience of the Spirit, in both the NT and the present, is not self-interpreting. It is often quite difficult to read the Spirit. As related in Acts, the very manner in which the Gentiles were included as full members of the people of God, presupposes a whole set of communal practices that are largely absent from North American Christianity. Most churches do not train and nurture people in forming the sorts of friend-ships out of which testimony about the Spirit's work might arise. We Christians are generally suspicious about claims about the Spirit; we are not generally a people who either testify well or listen wisely to the testimony of others. We largely favor self-authentication and despise common patterns of discernment. We abhor the notion that our lives ought to be disciplined by a concern for one another. In short, most Christian communities lack the skills and resources to debate what a life marked by the Spirit might look like in the present. Without these communal practices and structures in place, one cannot be hopeful that most Christian churches will be able to do more than pay lip-service to the hermeneutical significance of the Spirit.

INDEXES

INDEX OF REFERENCES

OLD TESTAMENT

OTHER ANCIENT REFERENCES

INDEX OF AUTHORS

JOURNAL FOR THE STUDY OF THE OLD TESTAMENT

Supplement Series